Bodies of Evidence

Bodies of Evidence

Evidence

The Practice of Queer Oral History

Edited by Nan Alamilla Boyd and
Horacio N. Roque Ramírez

OXFORD
UNIVERSITY PRESS

Oxford University Press, Inc., publishes works that further
Oxford University's objective of excellence
in research, scholarship, and education.

Oxford   New York
Auckland   Cape Town   Dar es Salaam   Hong Kong   Karachi
Kuala Lumpur   Madrid   Melbourne   Mexico City   Nairobi
New Delhi   Shanghai   Taipei   Toronto

With offices in
Argentina   Austria   Brazil   Chile   Czech Republic   France   Greece
Guatemala   Hungary   Italy   Japan   Poland   Portugal   Singapore
South Korea   Switzerland   Thailand   Turkey   Ukraine   Vietnam

Copyright © 2012 by Oxford University Press, Inc.

Published by Oxford University Press, Inc.
198 Madison Avenue, New York, New York 10016

www.oup.com

Oxford is a registered trademark of Oxford University Press

Library of Congress Cataloging-in-Publication Data
Bodies of evidence : the practice of queer oral history / edited by Nan Alamilla Boyd and
Horacio N. Roque Ramírez.
   p.   cm. — (Oxford oral history series)
Includes index.
ISBN 978-0-19-974273-8 (pbk. : alk. paper) — ISBN 978-0-19-989066-8 (hardcover : alk. paper)
1. Gays—United States—History. 2. Oral history—United States. 3. Gays—Interviews. I. Boyd,
Nan Alamilla, 1963- II. Roque Ramírez, Horacio N.
HQ76.3.U5B63   2012
306.76′60973—dc23   2011031590

1 3 5 7 9 8 6 4 2

Printed in the United States of America
on acid-free paper

We dedicate this book to Elizabeth Lapovsky Kennedy.

Contents

PART II: SEX

PART III: FRIENDSHIP

Acknowledgments

The idea behind this project began many years ago, while I was working with the GLBT Historical Society's oral history project. Everyone collecting oral histories seemed to have a favorite story about a particular narrator—a lesson learned that subsequently informed their style and method. These stories were sometimes funny but just as often poignant or sad. Then, in 2005, two things happened to bring this book into focus. I joined a panel on oral history methods at the Berkshire Conference of Women Historians, where Liz Kennedy and Ron Grele pushed me to expand my analysis of queer oral history methods. A few months later I attended a conference in Oregon, where I happened to be staying at the same middle-of-nowhere hotel as Horacio Roque Ramírez. We had dinner together and talked for hours about our mutual and overlapping projects. Later, we excitedly discussed co-editing a book on queer oral history that would include both oral histories and the sad, funny, poignant stories that oral historians swap with each other. I couldn't have found a better person to share this experience. Thank you Horacio!

Because this book has been years in the making there are too many people to thank, but I want to quickly mention a few: my wonderfully smart colleagues in the Women and Gender Studies Department at San Francisco State University, Deborah Cohler, Julietta Hua, "AJ" Jaimes-Guerrero, Kasturi Ray, and Jillian Sandell; my extraordinary friends at the GLBT Historical Society in San Francisco, Daniel Bao, Marjorie Bryer, Rebekah Kim, Terence Kissack, Martin Meeker, Don Romesburg, and Amy Sueyoshi; the dean of the College of Humanities at SFSU, Paul Sherwin, whose consistent support has made all the difference; and the folks at Oxford who believed in this project and ushered it through, Kathryn Nasstrom, Nancy Toff, and Sonia Tycko. I also want to thank the contributors to this volume whose remarkable patience is matched only by their genuine commitment to oral history. Finally, a big thank you to Max, who brings an irrepressible enthusiasm to all things, including his mom's many projects.

—Nan Alamilla Boyd

Over the course of nearly five years, this project has truly been a collective effort, and I want to thank all the contributors to the volume, and also those who submitted proposals for chapters that unfortunately we could not include. Queer oral history research has really taken off in the last decade or so, as this volume proves. I also want to express deep appreciation to my amazing co-editing colleague Nan Alamilla Boyd, whose leadership, camaraderie, and all-around wise and caring partnership made all the difference. Thanks, Nan!

A 2006–2007 Postdoctoral Visiting Scholar Fellowship at UCLA through the Institute of American Cultures, the Center for Oral History Research, and the Chicano Studies Research Center allowed me to concentrate for a year on oral history pedagogy, theory, and practice, which strengthened some of my ideas leading to this volume's Introduction and my own contribution. I want to thank my UCSB Department of Chicana and Chicano Studies' former Chair Chela Sandoval and my Social Sciences Dean Melvin L. Oliver for allowing me to be away from my home campus for one year. A University of California Office of the President Postdoctoral Research Fund helped me hire undergraduate and graduate students to support the extensive procedure of processing dozens of oral history interviews.

Over the years Elizabeth Lapovsky Kennedy, Sherna Berger Gluck, Teresa Barnett, Alva Moore Stevenson, Ricardo A. Bracho, Luis Alberto Campos de la Garza, Karla E. Rosales, Evelyn Nakano Glenn, Julia E. Curry Rodríguez, Linda Shopes, Kathryn Nasstrom, Rina Benmayor, and Waldo E. Martin have been caring allies and friends who have nurtured my oral history work, some of which culminated in this project. I thank them all for being there for me. Finally, my family has remained steadfast with me—in all our Latino immigrant queerness—with love and care, making all the difference for me to survive and thrive in what are too often treacherous academic moments. ¡Gracias!

—Horacio N. Roque Ramírez

INTRODUCTION: CLOSE ENCOUNTERS

The Body and Knowledge in Queer Oral History

Horacio N. Roque Ramírez and Nan Alamilla Boyd

Queer oral histories begin with an agreement between a narrator and a researcher to record memories of queer genders, sexualities, and desires. If there is not a narrator to claim that sexual space of queer historical being and its retelling, and a queer researcher to hear, record, and draw out yet more details, desire, and meaning from it, no queer oral history is possible. It is in the spirit of recognizing more than three decades of queer oral history collaborations that we offer this volume.

Bodies of Evidence: The Practice of Queer Oral History asks questions about researchers' methods. How has queer oral history evolved? Are queer methods different than other oral history methods? What has it meant for narrators to talk openly with researchers about queer life, especially when queer genders, sexualities, and desires have been protectively hidden or vowed to secrecy? What has it meant for researchers to focus their work on queer history? The title of our book, *Bodies of Evidence*, refers to the body of knowledge created by decades of queer oral history projects, but it also hints at untold stories and invisible lives. Recognizing that queer histories often go unmentioned in mainstream historical texts, activists and scholars have used a variety of methods to gather data and, thus, evidence of the existence of queer lives. Like the criminal justice stories that dominate popular television—and from which we draw our title—this book recognizes that an injustice has occurred and that those seeking justice sometimes have to create new methods. As such, queer oral histories have an overtly political function and a liberating quality, which the essays in this collection repeatedly underscore.

Bodies of Evidence also draws its meaning from the concept of body-based knowing.[1] This concept asserts that the sexuality of the body (or bodily desires) is an important, indeed material, aspect of the practice of doing oral history work. It argues that the physical presence of sexual or gendered bodies affects the oral history collaboration. In other words, in addition to documenting the political quality of the oral history work done by generations of queer narrators and historians, this volume seeks to better understand the role the body itself has played in the way queer oral histories have been conducted. Because queer oral histories are intense interactions, as the oral history collaboration proceeds the contract between narrator and researcher often evolves into something more: a bond, friendship, or political commitment. As the following chapters explain, in the social space of the queer oral history, something transformative seems to occur as new knowledge is produced.

The editors of *Bodies of Evidence* conceived of this book as a place where researchers could reflect on their experiences in conducting queer oral histories. We hoped the collection would reveal methodological patterns, but we also wanted to include the voices of narrators that together would tell the story of their collective experiences, so we asked contributors to pair an oral history excerpt with an original essay that reflected on the practice of oral history. What emerged, as we began culling through the manuscripts, were four broad themes that often overlapped: silence, sex, friendship, and politics. Through the paired interviews and critical essays collected here, these four themes demonstrate what is queer about queer oral history methods. Bringing together scholars, community-based researchers, and a host of narrators, *Bodies of Evidence* creates a critical dialogue between narrators and researchers. It also bridges two seemingly minor subfields in history: oral history and LGBT/queer historiography.[2] It is surprising that these two subfields have not come into more open conversation, given the latter's heavy dependence on the former and queer history's ability to inform larger theoretical and methodological debates in oral history practice. We hope this book begins to fill this obvious gap and produces yet more productive questions and conversations about what it means to employ oral history methods to explore queer genders, sexualities, and desires.

QUEER ORAL HISTORY'S FEMINIST BEGINNINGS

Although there were certainly many stories being told prior to the 1970s, it was in that decade that queer oral history methods sprang from a combination of impulses, including methods deployed by the new social history—a people's history from below—and the related political, historiographic, and academic movements of second-wave feminism. This feminism, including lesbian feminism, placed women's bodies and perspectives at the center of historical renditions of family life, labor and leisure, cultural production, health and disease, and social change broadly defined. As part of these movements, Elizabeth Lapovsky Kennedy and Madeline Davis's *Boots of Leather, Slippers of Gold: The History of a Lesbian Community* can be seen as a pivotal bridge between historicizing women's bodies and genders and the subsequent rise of queer oral history methods. In their preface to this groundbreaking oral history–based study of working-class lesbian cultures in Buffalo, New York, Kennedy recalls the following:

> I resolved to use my skills to do useful, woman-centered research for a local group. At this time my interest in the history of working-class lesbian community was piqued by the wonderful tales graduate students told about older lesbians in the bars. After coming out in the context of the feminist movement in 1976, I felt optimistic that I could design a research project with older, working-class lesbians that would focus on their culture of survival and resistance in the context of twentieth-century U.S. history, and would meet my new standards for ethical and useful research.[3]

Coauthor Davis echoes these concerns from a slightly different perspective:

> As a result of the influence of a burgeoning women's movement that gave me a new understanding of the confluence of economics, sexuality, oppression, and consciousness in the lives of women with whom I had been associating since the late 1950s, I became interested in lesbian history. I also wanted to write an accurate and compassionate chronicle of the lives of these brave women who had cared for me so generously when I came out in the mid-1960s.[4]

A conscious 1970s woman-centered, feminist standpoint fueled Kennedy's and Davis's commitment to "ethical and useful research." But even more central than these academic anchor points is the lesbian bar, which figures prominently in both of their respective stories about the making of their community-based study. It is in that erotic space that stories were first made and lived, told, and then retold to a new generation of lesbians, eventually making their way into a collaborative project coming together at the right time and with the right researchers, fueled by the passion, commitments, and sense of liberation of the 1960s and 1970s. As Davis points out, just as an older generation of lesbians had given of themselves to a younger generation coming out into a community as a form of relative safety away from a hostile society, so, too, did Kennedy and Davis reciprocate that generosity by turning their and their students' audio recorders on to engage in the mutually giving commitment that is telling and receiving a story.

Around the same time that Kennedy and Davis were beginning to record working-class lesbian oral histories, another queer community historian, similarly fueled by the political fervor of the day, began an oral history project of his own. The late historian Allan Bérubé (1946–2007), an independent scholar, explains his inspiration to write the history of gay women and men during World War II as follows:

> One day in the fall of 1979, I was sitting on my living room floor in the Haight-Ashbury District of San Francisco sorting hundreds of World War II letters into piles by author, date, and place. A neighbor's friend had salvaged these papers and photographs from a dumpster when he noticed that they included letters written by gay GIs. Having stashed them in the closet for five years, he gave them to me when my neighbor told him how interested I was in gay history.

> As I carefully opened each envelope and read the letter inside, I found myself entering the secret world of gay soldiers who served in the [U.S.] army during World War II. . . .
>
> Reading those letters . . .changed my life. It made me want to know more about lesbian and gay GIs in World War II, so I set out to uncover and make public their hidden histories. Sponsored by the San Francisco Lesbian and Gay History Project, I put together a slide presentation—"Marching to a Different Drummer"—that was based on my preliminary research. Using it to spread the word about what I was learning, raise funds for my research, and find veterans to interview, I presented the slide show more than one hundred times throughout the United States and Canada, sponsored by local community groups, churches, veterans' organizations, universities, and informal networks of friends. . . .[5]

There are several critical facets in Bérubé's story about how his pioneering work came to being. First, the initial historical artifacts needed to be rescued literally from the trash by an interested party. These rescues have been crucial for documenting gay male and male-to-female (MTF) transgender histories, especially in the early 1980s, when the advent of AIDS added yet another stigmatizing layer of either denial or conscious disavowal by blood relatives of those dying from AIDS. Second, an informal personal network among gay men facilitated transferring the rescued documents to yet another interested party, Bérubé, who began to consider the historical potential of what he then held in his hands. Third, as a grassroots community historian not beholden to an academic history department—but also without access to its financial resources—Bérubé was able to conceive and carry forth a multidimensional and engaging public history and oral history project that itself generated yet more original documents. Finally, a diversity of groups, institutions, and networks—including those bridging the academy with the larger public, such as the Gay and Lesbian History Project of San Francisco, established in 1978—supported his initial endeavors. That his project began outside the academy and not from within its disciplinary regulations speaks to the challenges he and others interested in researching and writing queer history then faced. But this outsider research position also afforded him the opportunity to venture into an innovative historical project without the formal policing of overly rigid historiographical standards that privilege the papers and collections of the literate and the archived.

Kennedy, Davis, and Bérubé were not the only feminist oral historians articulating a new history—herstory, rather, to be semantically accurate about the period. In the summer of 1977, barely two years into its existence, the feminist journal *Frontiers: A Journal of Women Studies*, based at the women's studies program at the University of Colorado, Boulder, devoted its first ever special issue to "Women's Oral History."[6] Initiated by Sherna Berger Gluck and Joan Jensen in the form of a letter to the Frontiers collective in August 1976, the 1977 special issue (edited by Gluck and Jensen) featured twenty-six women who individually and jointly

contributed oral history–based articles on topics ranging from trade union organizing to southern women, suffragists, and Chinese women.[7] But it was Gluck's
own gutsy contribution that set the methodological and conceptual stage for years
to come. Her provocatively titled essay, "What's So Special about Women? Wom-
en's Oral History," spoke to the political moment of the 1970s and the multiple
exclusionary practices inside and outside the academy. Gluck's pithy methodological dictum on behalf of women's oral histories retains its edge even today:

> Women's oral history, then, is a feminist encounter, even if the interviewee is not
> herself a feminist. It is the creation of a new type of material on women; it is the
> validation of women's experiences; it is the communication among women of dif-
> ferent generations; it is the discovery of our own roots and the development of a
> continuity which has been denied us in traditional historical accounts.[8]

What remains useful to this day, more than three decades after her original
analysis, are the multiple levels of methodological and conceptual intervention
Gluck names in her essay.

Gluck's claim that oral history among women is a "feminist encounter," even
if the narrator has no personal or political investment in feminism per se, speaks
to the researcher's commitment to challenge structures of power. Also, while
early narrators often deemed themselves unworthy of an audio recording, those
who worked to identify and contact narrators, often setting up and transcribing
recordings without any institutional support, have been quite articulate about
the liberationist urge that drove their early work in the field. Indeed, queer and
feminist oral history methods commit to the creation of new material, new
sources, and new records. Unlike researchers who choose to work with special
collections of well-preserved documents, those who study women, queers,
and—we might add—other subaltern groups such as communities of color and
migrant workers by and large have had to start from scratch: where no documents or acid-free folders existed, researchers set out to create them.

Creating a new vision (and version) of history requires a leap of faith. It
means taking narrators' voices and oral history methods seriously. While the
self-understood and often unspoken validation of narrators' subjective perspectives does not entail taking every recorded declaration as factual truth, it does
require that researchers commit to listening carefully for what narrators' recollections reveal about their time and place in history. Gluck invokes the different
generations that become involved in the living method of oral history. Indeed,
there is a tacit mutual responsibility for elders to sit, reflect, and recall while
younger generations commit to recording, processing, and analyzing the previous generations' historical knowledge. Finally, and related to the last feature,
oral history with subaltern or historically undervalued communities entails
making historical and generational discontinuities explicit. It necessarily dis-
rupts historical paradigms that do not or will not acknowledge the existence of
bodies, genders, and desires invisible to previous historical traditions.

Only six years after that first influential volume, *Frontiers* went at it again with its 1983 special issue, "Women's Oral History, The Second Decade."[9] Straddling oral history's then still precarious methodological position in the academy and its more accepted and appreciated intervention into recording women's every-day historical lives, the journal sought to move the method forward, to go beyond what Susan H. Armitage referred to as the surprise and euphoria of discovery. Armitage explains:

> There will always be a place for personal discovery, especially in the classroom. Oral history is a wonderful teaching tool. Students are usually excited and frequently amazed by the women they interview. When women "speak for themselves" about the activities and concerns of their own lives, they usually talk freely and fully, revealing lives of purpose and significance. . . . That is a natural place to start. It *is* important to celebrate the compelling stories that women tell about their lives. But the truth is that those lives are not unusual; we just thought they were! Furthermore, we can do much more than simply illuminate neglected lives. We can push ahead to the harder job of analysis and connection. To move from the single story to the whole picture requires that we be systematic and critical—while remaining caring and appreciative. We need to move ahead without losing touch with the personal and meaningful discoveries of women's oral history.[10]

Armitage's call to "be systematic and critical—while remaining caring and appreciative" speaks well to the efforts behind and goals for *Bodies of Evidence*. Recognizing that since the late 1970s oral histories with queer women and men have in many ways created the field of queer history, we now take a break from recording and transcribing and, with the many contributions that comprise this book, shift our analytical lens to an engaged and critical analysis of the narrative structures, living exchanges, ways of remembering, detailed contents, and interactions across differences in our work with queer oral histories.

Finally, a pivotal 1991 publication serves as an important precursor to this book, bringing to light the importance of racial and national difference as critical categories of analysis across a wide range of gendered subjects, geographies, and cultures. Sherna Berger Gluck and Daphne Patai's *Women's Words: The Feminist Practice of Oral History* heeds Armitage's earlier call to move beyond the pleasant methodological "surprise" of discovering new narratives in oral history.[11] Along with their contributors, Gluck and Patai take up the more challenging space of critical social analysis by acknowledging the field's internal contradictions and some of its essentialist assumptions. "Most striking, in retrospect," wrote Gluck and Patai,

> were the innocent assumptions that gender united women more powerfully than race and class divided them, and that the mere study of women fulfilled a commitment to do research "about" women. Although we had questioned the value of traditional androcentric methodology, not all of us had yet learned to be skeptical of the claims for a single feminist methodology. Our assumptions had the effect of

foregrounding gender while obscuring the possible centrality of other factors—race and class, in particular—in the identity of our narrators. To define feminist scholarship as work done by, about, and for women had seemed simple. Experience, however, demonstrates that these three little words positioned the scholar within a complex web of relationships, loyalties, and demands.[12]

Exploring language, authority, research dilemmas, and community advocacy, *Women's Words* moved the field further as it reflected on the internal structures of the research experience, without doing away with the centrality of women's words themselves. Indeed, *Women's Words* was a welcomed and necessary intervention into a still undeveloped oral historiography not yet explicitly conscious of gender, sexuality, and the body.[13]

THE BODY AND KNOWLEDGE

The body, and how and what it remembers, should be central to all oral history work, and *Bodies of Evidence* critically examines the role the sexual body plays in the production of queer oral histories. For instance, the body's memories are particularly significant for narrators drawn to discussions of sexual consciousness, erotic desire, and gender expression. Not at all the same, these fields of the body can be sites for productive memory and dialogue about pivotal queer moments of the lifespan: the first childhood memories of feeling "different"; the first encounter with a mirror of the self, that is, another "different" body in public that communicates back an unspoken yet felt affiliation; or the first instance when a queer body makes explicit its desires to a listening or viewing public. Indeed, queer oral history as a genre works in many ways to generate a series of intelligible (or predictable) sexual signposts that mark the queer body's passage through time. Interestingly, and as several contributions to this book reveal, these signposts can become contested spaces during the oral history where narrator and researcher engage in a dance between generating explicit speech about sex, sexuality, and pleasure, and the no less valuable but more highly coded articulations about how sex and desire have shaped individuals and communities in history.

In Karen Krahulik's chapter, for instance, narrator Beata Cook eludes Krahulik's questions about Cook's unidentified sexual identity. Similarly, narrator Rikki Streicher in Nan Alamilla Boyd's chapter resists direct conversation about sex. Perhaps because queer oral histories have the added burden of documenting what we can argue have been until recently undocumented (or undocumentable) bodies, there is no guarantee that all aspects of queer experiences will emerge through the oral history exchange. Indeed, it would be foolish to expect anything more than partial or fractured histories to emerge—and this is a limitation but also the promise of queer oral history work. The gulf between tropological scripts that engage narrators in a predictable articulation of queer desire or identity, for instance, and the near absence of scripts that code experience outside or beyond culturally intelligible meanings (non-gay-identified same-sex sexual expressions, for instance) makes knowledge production a rich but difficult project.

Storytelling, the most basic performative ingredient to oral history, is an embodied practice. As such, it is a collaboration between at least two bodies seeking expression through voice and gesture to create and document public meanings. Despite the almost unquestioned assumption that oral history must involve what we can refer to as an "auditorily legible" exchange between a narrator and an interviewer, other types of recordings with differently abled people, including those unable to speak, see, or hear, challenge this assumption. A useful example of what new technologies (such as instant messaging) can accomplish to broaden the meaning and possibilities for "oral history" is the University of California, Berkeley's Regional Oral History Office's Artists with Disabilities Oral History Project. Of particular note are the interviews Esther Ehrlich conducted with the playwright and performance artist Neil Marcus, who has dystonia, by using a method that mixed instant messaging at two side-by-side computers with interspersed spoken questions and answers.[14]

Jeff Friedman explores another such methodology in this book by expanding the concept of "verbal data" to include embodied performances through movement and dance. In the process of producing formal oral history documents, Friedman argues that nonverbal data provide alternative storytelling modes and, thus, alternative representations of reality that allow nonnormative narrative structures to emerge. In this way, queer storytelling can be an ideal conduit for expanding living expressions of erotic desires because it permissively allows the narrator's body to "speak" in different ways. At the same time, queer storytelling engages researchers in new modes of methodological and historical interpretation. The desire for new queer voices, both those of narrators and researchers, is pivotal for generating projects, theses, conferences, and publications, such as this one, where readers can examine yet more closely the relationship between queer embodiments, narratives, and desires.

In addition to generating new modes of communication, the bodies of knowledge that queer narrators and researchers often contend with during their collaborations can be painful or uncomfortable in unpredictable ways. More so than is the case for nonqueer narrators, women and men who experience same-sex desires or transgender identities risk opening up themselves to vulnerability or trauma during an oral history exchange. Even after discussing in detail what it is that researchers and narrators seek from an oral history interview, there is no way of predicting what will emerge in the dialogue and what kind of feelings may be attached to a particular memory. Along these lines, Ann Cvetkovich's oral history work on public feelings and lesbian AIDS activism offers insight into how queer oral history can be an especially apt tool to document the relationship between trauma, activism, and public memory:

Queer community histories share something with testimony, the genre that brings
together trauma studies and oral history. Testimony has been viewed by some as an
impossible genre, an attempt to represent the unrepresentable. Trauma poses limits
and challenges for oral history, forcing consideration of how the interview process
itself may be traumatically invasive or marked by forms of self-censorship and the
work of the unconscious. Gay and lesbian oral histories, as forms of insider ethnog-
raphy, have much to contribute to this project, including a sense of the complexity
of gathering information about sexual intimacy that can be applied to the study of
trauma's emotional intimacies.[15]

Forms of collective knowledge that build on memories of disease, trauma,
and death have the potential to compound the narrator's trauma in remembering and also traumatize the researcher in listening, especially as researchers
are officially left with the evidence of the affective methodological exchange. As
Horacio N. Roque Ramírez has explored among queer Latina and Latino narrators in San Francisco, recording queer life and death in the context of the 1980s
and 1990s AIDS epidemics has a double-edged quality; it allows a grieving community to address its current state of mourning, but it also risks the reenactment
of traumatic and painful feelings of loss.[16] Just as memory work can offer the
opportunity for queer narrators to connect with previous generations, it can also
bring back to emotional life the feelings associated with unjust loss and death.

Sexual embodiment, as an aspect of body-based knowing, is crucial to understanding queer oral history methods because it flags important sociosexual signposts in time, it generates new modes of sometimes nonverbal communication,
and it invites conversation about sexual trauma, vulnerability, or pain. But
sexual embodiment also invites pleasure and the possibility that sexual feelings
will emerge during the queer oral history exchange. There are at least two levels
of sexual intimacy in queer oral history collaborations: the intimacy created in
the physical encounter between narrator and researcher and the less predictable
intimacy of the sexual feelings that emerge between narrators and researchers as
their conversations broach the subject of sex. As such, queer oral histories are
especially productive but potentially risky methodological encounters.[17] Anthropologist Esther Newton offers a candid assessment of how she as a queer
scholar maneuvered her self-identity in relation to her research subject. "My
research experience has been fraught with sexual dangers and attractions that
were much more like leitmotifs than light distractions."[18] The sexual, Newton
continues, cannot simply be "done way with," as if it is not part of the methodological exchange; instead, she argues that it adds a level of intimacy-as-trust,
with both narrator and researcher being *more* to one another than is the case
during an exchange between two oral history collaborators who simply do not
understand what it means to occupy similar positions of sexual objectification:

> By the "erotic dimension," I mean, first, that my gay informants and I shared a very
> important background assumption that our social arrangements reflected: that

women are attracted to women and men to men. Second, the very fact that I *have* worked with other gays means that some of the people who are objects of my research were also potential sexual partners. Partly because of this, my key informants and sponsors have usually been more to me than an expedient way of getting information, and something different from "just" friends. Information has always flowed to me in a medium of emotion, ranging from passionate—although never consummated—erotic attachment through profound affection to lively interest, that empowers me in my projects and, when it is reciprocated, helps motivate informants to put up with my questions and intrusions.[19]

Particularly important in Newton's description of the "erotic dimension" she experienced with one narrator, Kay, are the cross-generational linkages that bridge a mutual lesbian/queer identification. When a twenty- or thirty-year-old researcher goes into a community to record memories with significantly elder narrators (forty years her senior, in Newton's case), the research equation is even trickier as it positions the researcher—much more so than the narrator, though this is often not acknowledged—as less capable and less experienced in handling what may be the uncomfortable and unsettling space of negotiating erotic attractions in an ethical, responsible way.

Generationally and erotically structured oral history collaborations are even more accentuated when narrators and researchers belong to historically distinct queer periods: before/after liberation movements, before/after AIDS, before/after the availability of effective antiretroviral medications, and so on. Jason Ruiz, in this book, analyzes the complexities of charting one man's sexual history as he moved between vastly different and generationally informed attitudes toward public sex during the course of the oral history. "There were stark contrasts between what he did with his body for sexual pleasure, what he thought about sex, and how he talked about sex as a pastor and public figure. In other words, he quite literally did not practice what he preached."[20] In his comments, Ruiz notes the intimate nature of cross-generational oral history work but also the sexual politics at play in determining permissible modes of speech. Similarly, Daniel Marshall develops a theory of intergenerational queer kinship via the oral histories he conducted with activists Gary Jaynes and Graham Carbery, key figures in the 1970s Australian Gay Teachers and Students Group and contributors to the 1978 collection *Young, Gay, and Proud.*[21] Marshall argues that cross-generational activism, particularly actions that involved students, were "made impossible by profound and generalized fear about any contact between homosexual adults and children."[22] In other words, the overtly politicized social fear that teachers would seduce students thwarted cross-generational activism, and the specter of sexual impropriety diffused the liberationist promise of cross-generational mentoring and sexual freedom. Similarly, the intimate nature of cross-generational oral history work and explicit talk about queer sex invites a certain amount of sexual energy into the oral history exchange that, for some researchers and narrators, produces intimacy and trust. As several contributors acknowledge, these methodologically useful feelings are risky and difficult to maneuver during the oral history exchange, but they are also difficult to discuss as a methodological practice. The specter of sexual impropriety makes sexual feelings (and the intimacies that accompany them) a vital but virtually unspeakable aspect of queer oral history work.

ETHICAL, POLITICAL, AND ACADEMIC CHALLENGES

Conducting queer oral histories requires researchers to navigate a particular set of ethical, political, and academic challenges—and this dramatically affects the methods that researchers develop and deploy. It is still a relatively recent opportunity for scholars to be to able to research, write, and produce a history of queer sex and genders without the risk of academic sanction or public reprisal. Women's and gender studies programs; the few existing queer studies academic majors, minors, and emphases; interdisciplinary fields such as racial/ethnic studies and American studies; and the case-by-case opportunities in disciplines such as sociology, history, and anthropology—these interventions still struggle to seek and maintain institutional grounding and support that goes beyond the volunteer efforts of researchers and scholars committed to these subjects.

In the United States, the Committee on Lesbian and Gay History (CLGH) has been an officially recognized affiliate of the American Historical Association (AHA) since 1982, and it has grown to become a critical network for researchers in the field of LGBT/queer history, many employing oral history methods.[23] The U.S.-based Oral History Association (OHA) has served as yet another annual vehicle for bringing together scholars of LGBT/queer history more explicitly engaged with oral history methods. For its 2007 conference in Oakland, California, for example, the OHA had ten presentations, panels, exhibits, and a reception on the uses of oral history in queer history—a record number. Still, neither the useful CLGH panels and professional activities over the several decades nor the more queer-inclusive OHA conferences in recent years have generally been forums to engage in close and critical reflection on how queer historical inquiry and oral history methods inform one another. As a result, many researchers have the feeling of going it alone or reinventing the wheel. Without scholarly attention (or, in an ideal world, tenure lines) dedicated to queer history and its methods, researchers attracted to the field face isolation and burnout, and methodological approaches can be individualistic, idiosyncratic, or scattersho

The challenges faced by researchers wanting to do queer oral history a rored by the challenges faced by many queer narrators: the heavy social stig... tization of queer desires, the active state policing of queer behaviors and public expressions, the medicalization and psychiatric classification of bodies feeling and expressing queer meanings, and the religious intolerance of queer and non-nuclear family units and forms of spiritual kinship. As more and more grounded historical scholarship continues to elucidate, these active forms of exclusion, repression, and censorship do not manifest equally across time, regions, communities, racial groups, and nations. These historical, political, and social forces occur unevenly, often in contradictory ways, but also in conjunction with active and subtle forms of counteraction by queer people, individually and collectively, challenging repressive systems in their blood families, churches, schools, and institutions of employment.

In this book, many such stories are told. Vera Martin, in Daniel Rivers's chapter, defends the custody of her children against accusations that lesbians are unfit parents; Laura, in Carrie Hamilton's chapter, recounts how she negotiated same-sex love affairs during the Cuban Revolution; and Brian Hughes, in Steve Estes's chapter, uses his position as a war hero to publicly decry the U.S. military's "don't ask, don't tell" policy. Again, the liberating quality of many queer narrators' stories reveals the intensity and drama of the oral history exchange—and the bond often formed between narrator and researcher.

To go public—through a recording—with the memory of one's and others' erotic bodies continues to be a challenging position to take. Beginning with the activist-researchers and community-based historians who were energized by the liberationist zeal of the 1960s and 1970s, there continue to be individual young scholars both in and out of the academy eager to carry out queer community history work. But this enthusiasm to seek out and connect with potential narrators and begin to record oral histories often comes crashing against distinctly queer roadblocks. Many of the recorded interviews John D'Emilio carried out for his influential 1983 book, *Sexual Politics, Sexual Communities*, were those of pre-Stonewall era activists, women and men quite willing to go on the record and narrate their struggles.[24] For them, the historical record itself was part of their ongoing struggle against queer criminalization and pathologizing. Less visible queer women and men, however, are not as easily reached by even the most ambitious oral historian. For Bérubé's work on World War II, while the majority of interviewees (his term) recorded in the 1980s chose to use their given names, a third opted for a pseudonym.[25] For their 1993 community history, *Boots of Leather, Slippers of Gold*, Kennedy and Davis go to great lengths to protect the given-name identity of their forty-five narrators, even when some of them desired not to hide. Writing from the historical moment of late-1980s and early-1990s United States, the authors explain that

> Research in the lesbian community—finding narrators, archiving oral histories, or writing a book—raises immediately the problem of protecting the narrators' identities. We had to be extremely careful in order for people to feel comfortable about introducing us to others and supporting our work. But also for our own peace of mind. Although the lesbian and gay movements of the past fifteen years have achieved a less repressive social climate, the recent rise of right-wing social movements and their homophobic positions, in the context of knowledge about the

persecution of gays and lesbians during the 1950s, convinced us that we did not want a file with the names of our narrators.[26]

For Kennedy and Davis, recording the stories of women who occupied a small and insular community required that they be extra careful about not betraying confidences. However, Kennedy and Davis also raise the specter of the unforeseen future, informed by the past, where assumptions of social and political progress cannot be taken for granted. In this regard, queer oral history cannot afford to ask questions solely about the past and its narration but also about how public memories in the present continue to have a politically implicated life in the future.[27]

The fact that we do not all occupy the same historical time period and its attendant politics of identity in relation to sexual consciousness makes queer oral histories methodologically tricky. Just as repressive forces have not always been evenly distributed across time and place, neither are forms of acceptance or support equally present today (nor are they likely to be in the future) for queer women and men. Across all racial, national, religious, and economic groups, there are different degrees of both acceptance and rejection: within our blood families, at our employment sites, within our particular neighborhood, town, city, school, and so on. For individuals in communities already historically undervalued and stigmatized, taking on yet another stigmatized social identity can add quite an additional burden to their existence.

It should not be surprising, then, that there is comparatively little oral history research on U.S. queer communities of color and that white researchers have been consistently unsuccessful in reaching these community members.[28] The exceptions to this pattern have most often come from the efforts of queer community scholars of color themselves reaching out to "communities of their own." But even in these so-called insider research experiences, there are other vectors of social position, experience, and identity to negotiate. Even as insiders, queer scholars of color continue to have problems when interviewing across sex, gender, language, national origin, or immigrant status.[29]

Writing as a Bangladeshi American woman with political ties to multiple communities of color in the United States, Naheed Islam cautions that in researching everyday forms of racism experienced but also perpetuated in the Bangladeshi community of Los Angeles, she encountered the methodological paradox of how to acknowledge both forms of exclusion. "Scholars facing such dilemmas," she observes, "may choose to remain silent about how minority communities can participate in and reproduce racist ideologies. Ultimately such silences subvert an analysis and understanding of how racism operates and how racialized systems of domination and inequality are maintained."[30]

Queer oral histories still have quite a task ahead in terms of addressing the differential investment queer narrators have in being out in terms of their desire when compared with their working-class, butch/femme, national, or racial ethnic identifications. Necessarily privileging the erotic, the sexual, and the queerly gendered in terms of identifying potential narrators, queer oral history work can benefit from an earlier generation of women's/feminist oral history that often failed to appreciate how women (and men) were not "essentially" united along a sex/gender axis. We hope that the contributions in our collection bring to light how language, class, gender, nation, and racial/ethnic positions work alongside sexuality and desire to make queer oral history an intervention not solely along the lines of sexual identity or queer visibility. Queer oral historians should be especially cognizant of internal stratification, given that we engage with communities who have experienced and continue to experience multiple challenges around AIDS, racialized gentrification, drugs and alcohol, economic displacement, nationalist exclusions, and different gender phobias.

The queer oral history methods we explore here have taken place in a distinct historical moment. In the academy, some universities and disciplines, such as history, sociology, and anthropology, and especially interdisciplinary fields, such as women's and gender studies, comparative ethnic studies, and LGBT/ queer studies, have slowly opened up more intellectual and political space to allow students and faculty to engage living narrators about their stories. Still, the individual experiences of these scholars and the support they may or may not find for their projects depend on the particular culture of their departments and programs—the degree to which, for example, a thesis or dissertation committee member will allow oral histories to be a primary source of evidence. Every form of documentation or evidence is culturally constructed and open to interpretation within the context of its creation, whether a police report, a court transcript, a novel, or an oral history. Though none of these is any more or less valid than the others, many scholars still place more critical faith in police reports or court transcripts and render more seemingly subjective documents like oral histories to a secondary evidentiary status. By foregrounding a variety of nuanced and carefully crafted discussions of method in relation to the production of queer historical narrative, this book seeks to illustrate the rich and documented potential of oral history as a source for larger discussions about the relationship between fact and fiction, truth and memory, self and subjectivity.

ABOUT THIS COLLECTION

Collectively, the contributors to this book represent more than three decades of engaged oral history research with hundreds of women and men across varied sexualities, genders, regions, nations, and political economies. We offer a variety of approaches in our analyses, but as contributors, we each put oral history narratives at the center of our research agenda. Each contribution, as a result, begins with a selection of an edited oral history transcript collected by the researcher, followed by the researcher's critical analysis of method and meaning. The book is organized into four overlapping themes: silence, sex, friendship, and politics.

Silence, as a theme, surfaces in most of the book's fourteen essays. Karen Krahu-lik's essay, for instance, carefully analyzes how narrators assert their stories, in-cluding and omitting key aspects of the data put forward for the historical record. Krahulik mines a particularly potent interview in which she struggled to "get the narrator" to name her sexual identity, but the narrator refuses. Through silence, Krahulik analyzes what she calls "the arts of remembering," posing dif-ficult questions about the meaning of historical memory. Also in this section are chapters by Carrie Hamilton and Daniel Rivers that grapple with the silences imposed by political repression and homophobia. Hamilton's oral history work stems from a project that documents the Cuban Revolution, and Rivers's work is based in a larger project on the history of lesbian mothers and gay fathers. Both authors argue that silences imposed by political repression are accessible, to a certain extent, via oral history methodology. The final chapter in this section, by Jeff Friedman, questions the limits of oral history as a verbal genre, arguing that dancers' nonverbal communications suggest new ways of thinking about sexual embodiment.

The second thematic section, on sex, presents a paradox. Although sex is clearly an important aspect of queer social and political life, several researchers note narrators' reluctance to engage in candid discussions about sex and its meanings. Two chapters specifically address this phenomenon. Nan Alamilla Boyd analyzes the reluctance of lesbian narrators to engage with questions about sex and sexuality in the oral histories she conducted as part of a project on the history of pre-Stonewall San Francisco. Her close reading of two different oral histories reveals narrators' fears of addressing sex too directly, seeming sexually improper, or stretching the limits of acceptable speech. Boyd argues that narra-tors' reluctance can be read as a symptom of the neoliberal uses of LGBT oral history projects and their association with academic discourse. Jason Ruiz, writing about the contradictions between sexual and social worlds, analyzes a narrative that uses frank talk about sex to stage larger questions about social propriety, moral goodness, and sexual pleasure. Ruiz also turns to an analysis of neoliberal discourse to argue that epistemologies of sex construct queer subjec-tivity in contradictory ways. An essay by Kelly Anderson makes an important methodological intervention by inviting two prominent and outspoken lesbian feminists, Dorothy Allison and Carmen Vázquez (who is also the lover of the researcher), to talk with each other about the sexual politics of lesbian feminism in the 1980s. By staging the oral history as a conversation and directly addressing sexual politics, Anderson enables Allison and Vázquez to bounce their ideas off each other and, perhaps, speak more candidly about sex than they might have otherwise.

The third section of the book—on friendship—offers numerous insights about the interpersonal dynamics at play during oral history interviews. Interest-ingly, this section also underscores the community-based and activist impulses of many researchers. The first contribution, by Michael David Franklin, provides an analysis of how friendship between narrators and researchers can exceed the limits of institutional review board (IRB) control. In his essay, Franklin analyzes his relationship with Carol, a male-to-female (MTF) transvestite who, late in life, comes to identify as transgendered. Franklin's friendship with Carol mirrors Carol's vivid friendship experiences with other transvestites who met secretly as part of Virginia Prince's heteronormative Transvestia clubs in 1950s Minnesota and Wisconsin. Friendship, Franklin argues, is an important aspect of queer oral history because it functions as "excess," moving beyond the grip of institutional (in this case, IRB) control to a place where researchers can collaborate more effectively with narrators toward the goal of knowledge production. Two other chapters on friendship echo these concerns. Daniel Marshall's interviews with two early gay liberation movement activists from Sydney, Australia, poignantly describe the friendships, collaborations, and mentoring relationships that developed between queer kids and queer adults in the 1970s and 1980s. Marshall reasons that cross-generational relationships are crucial to any future-focused queer culture-building project, and the institutionalized fear of cross-generational relationships, especially between gay men, has worked historically as a repressive force. Horacio N. Roque Ramírez's chapter pushes these insights further by describing a years-long process of interviewing and collaborating with the late MTF transgender *mexicana* ranchera singer Teresita la Campesina. In his essay, Roque Ramírez discusses shared authority by highlighting the complex negotiations and intimacies that surfaced through an extended oral history process and also by exploring how transgender Latina and gay Latino histories compete for attention in the struggle for queer memory.

The fourth and final section includes a variety of approaches to the political. Two chapters use close readings of a single oral history to frame an analysis about the formation of early gay and/or lesbian political organizations. Marcia M. Gallo's essay on the formation of the Daughters of Bilitis, a post–World War II lesbian civil rights organization, argues that it was only through her five-year research-based relationship with a central narrator that she was able to understand the race and class dimensions of early lesbian organizing. A second chapter focuses on an oral history by historian Martin Meeker with Quentin Kopp, an important California state politician and a key player in early gay and lesbian civil rights legislation. Here, Meeker explores the ethics of being closeted while interviewing and argues for the value of cross-sexuality and cross-ideology interviewing. A chapter by Steve Estes on the U.S. military's "don't ask, don't tell" policy circles back to issues of silence and political repression by tracing the impact of this silencing military policy on the life of one gay Gulf War veteran, Brian Hughes, who famously helped rescue Jessica Lynch and then used his celebrity to criticize "Don't Ask, Don't Tell." Finally, Eric C. Wat's chapter on the motivations behind cross-racial relationships, specifically Asian gay men who sought, through the 1980s, sex with white men (also known as "rice queens"), centers on the politics of racial identity formation for Asian gay men who participated in Los Angeles's Asian/Pacific Lesbians and Gays (A/PLG). Wat's searing self-examination of his own discomfort with one narrator's desire for validation acknowledges the limits of shared authority in queer oral histories. Wat's insight into racial formation and the power dynamics of researcher-narrator collaborations also functions as an appropriate conclusion to the book in that it underscores the power relations that structure all oral history work. Power relations are a fundamental aspect of queer oral history collaborations, and each of the essays collected here grapples in some way with the inequities that play out during the oral history process.

Oral history narratives' multilayered textures and meanings make qualitative analyses of sexuality and gender in history that much more important to understand. Closely mined and diligently listened to, oral histories—including their many silences—can bring personal affect, individual significance, and personal memory to bear especially on sensitive themes and experiences such as sexual consciousness, gender identity, and sex acts. How these aspects of human existence come to bear on what are considered historical events has become increasingly important as social history and cultural theory cross paths.

As the work of current and future queer oral historians takes form, we need to recall Elizabeth Lapovsky Kennedy's wise words about the conceptual and theoretical possibilities for queer oral history, and how to move it forward: "In arguing . . . that there is a tremendous amount to be learned by fully exploring the subjective and oral nature of oral histories, I have also suggested that the 'empirical' and the 'subjective' should not be falsely polarized. They are fully complementary to one another. I am convinced that gay and lesbian oral history is at a point where, to grow, it needs to fully embrace the subjective and oral nature of its documents. By doing so its 'empirical' goals are not compromised but expanded."[31] Echoing these words, we hope this volume inspires a next generation of queer oral historians by providing concrete examples of what has been made possible by queer oral history collaborations—and what has not (yet).

Notes

1. On the concept of body-based knowing, especially as it is discussed in queer and trans theory, see Sara Ahmed, *Queer Phenomenology: Orientations, Objects, Others* (Durham, NC: Duke University Press, 2006); Jay Prosser, *Second Skins: The Body Narratives of Transsexuality* (New York: Columbia University Press, 1998); and Gayle Salamon, "Boys of the Lex: Transgenderism and the Rhetorics of Materiality," *GLQ: A Journal of Lesbian and Gay Studies* 12, no. 4 (2006): 575–97. See also Susan Stryker, "(De)Subjugated Knowledges: An Introduction to Transgender Studies," in Susan Stryker and Stephen Whittle, eds., *The Transgender Studies Reader* (New York: Routledge, 2006) 1–17.
2. The acronym LGBT (the most pervasive, as well as Anglo- and Euro-centric globally) is meant to describe nonheterosexually identified women and men: lesbian women, gay men, bisexual women and men, and transgender women and men who may be gay, bisexually, or lesbian identified but also heterosexual or straight. The acronym, emerging from conceptual, historical, and political assumptions that these individual identity-based categories are fixed and static, fails to capture a great deal of queer erotic life and gender expressions, especially when

we examine those that existed prior to the identity-based civil rights era and social movements dependent on a public politicized identity. It also fails to capture many of the identities and expressions emerging in nonwhite communities and non-European or European-descent nations and populations. "Queer" was meant to respond to some of these conceptual limitations by connoting sexual and gender transgression more broadly, but it carries its own Euro-centric historical formation. The term (still derogatory to some while liberating for others) was born out of the more in-your-face (rather than mainstream and assimilationist) grassroots political struggles in the late 1980s and early 1990s in large urban centers in the United States, among mostly white young adults generally affiliated with the multisited political group Queer Nation. "Queer" was then taken up by some (queer) academics mostly in the humanities (and in particular English, rhetoric, and the arts), eventually emerging into the intellectual corpus now typically recognized as "queer theory," which itself has numerous manifestations and origins. It is important to note that, historically, academic queer theory followed the grassroots innovations, not the other way around. We also note a serious limitation in this anthology—and more generally—that the *B* in the acronym LGBT is left unexplored, not because we do not believe in bisexual practices and identities but because few narrators or researchers take up an exploration of bisexual practices or politics in this work. Two useful discussions of some of the political and historical implications of LGBT and queer are Michael Warner, "Introduction," in Warner, ed., *Fear of a Queer Planet* (Minneapolis: University of Minnesota Press, 1993), vii–xxxi; and Nan Alamilla Boyd, "Who Is the Subject? Queer Theory Meets Oral History," *Journal of the History of Sexuality* 17, no. 2 (May 2008): 177, note 1.

3. Liz Lapovsky Kennedy, "Preface," in Elizabeth Lapovsky Kennedy and Madeline D. Davis, *Boots of Leather, Slippers of Gold: The History of a Lesbian Community* (New York: Routledge, 1993), xv.

4. Madeline Davis, "Preface," in ibid., xvi.

5. Allan Bérubé, *Coming Out under Fire: The History of Gay Women and Men in World War II* (New York: Free Press, 1990), ix–x. For the beginnings of the San Francisco Lesbian and Gay History Project (SFLGHP), see Members of the Gay and Lesbian Historical Society of Northern California, "MTF Transgender Activism in the Tenderloin and Beyond, 1966–1975," *GLQ: A Journal of Lesbian and Gay Studies* 4, no. 2 (1998): 367–68, note 2. According to Estelle Freedman, the SFLGHP began at Allan Bérubé's apartment in the late 1970s sometime between fall 1978 and winter 1979, with original members being Bérubé, Jeffrey Escoffier, Freedman, Lynn Fonfa, Amber Hollibaugh, Gayle Rubin, Bertie Yusba, Joanne Castillo, Eric Garber, Robert Epstein, Frances Reid, Elizabeth Stevens, and, when in the city conducting research, John D'Emilio. Freedman, personal communication, August 4, 2008. For more on the life and significance of Bérubé and the now-renamed GLBT Historical Society, see John D'Emilio, "Allan Bérubé's Gift to History," *Gay and Lesbian Review Worldwide* 15, no. 3 (May–June 2008): 10–13.

6. Sherna Berger Gluck and Joan Jensen, eds., *Frontiers: A Journal of Women Studies* 2, no. 2 (summer 1977). In England, the journal *Oral History* dedicated a "Women's History Issue" also in 1977.

7. Sherna Gluck, Joan Jensen, and the Frontiers Editorial Collective, "To Our Readers," *Frontiers: A Journal of Women Studies* 2, no. 2 (Summer 1977): iv–v.

8. Sherna Gluck, "What So Special about Women? Women's Oral History," in ibid., 5. An updated version of Gluck's original essay is "Women's Oral History: Is It So Special," in Thomas L. Charlton, Lois E. Myers, and Rebecca Sharpless, eds., *Handbook of Oral History* (Lanham, MD: AltaMira, 2006), 357–83.

9. "Women's Oral History Two," *Frontiers: A Journal of Women Studies* 7, no. 1 (1983).

10. Susan H. Armitage, "The Next Step," in ibid., 3. See also Susan H. Armitage, ed., with Patricia Hart and Karen Weatheron, *The Frontiers Reader: Women's Oral History* (Lincoln: University of Nebraska Press, 2002), which brought together several of the original contributions from the 1977 and 1983 special issues, including an updated and very useful exchange between Armitage and Gluck.

11. Sherna Berger Gluck and Daphne Patai, eds., *Women's Words: The Feminist Practice of Oral History* (New York: Routledge, 1991).

12. Ibid., 2. Two other anthologies, not emerging centrally from the academy, are worth noting, given their inclusion of autobiographical narratives and also oral history excerpts. Cherríe L. Moraga's and Gloria E. Anzaldúa's now classic third world feminist collection, *This Bridge Called My Back: Writings by Radical Women of Color* (Berkeley: Third Woman Press, 2002, 3rd ed. rev.; first edition by Persephone, 1981), intervened into much of the white essentialism and middle-class bias of the women's and (lesbian) feminist movements in the United States. The more lesbian-specific collection by Juanita Ramos, ed., *Compañeras: Latina Lesbians* (New York: Latina Lesbian History Project, 1987; 2nd ed. by Routledge in 1992), similarly included oral histories, although not from the more critical perspective called for by the second generation of women's oral historians.

13. Alessandro Portelli's influential *The Death of Luigi Trastulli and Other Stories: Form and Meaning in Oral History* (Albany: State University of New York Press, 1991) addressed "women" sporadically in its various essays, but neither gender or sexuality surfaced in either of the other two influential and useful oral history collections by the early 1990s: Ronald Grele, ed., with Studs Terkel, Jan Vansina, Denis Tedlock, Saul Benison, and Alice Kessler Harris, *Envelopes of Sound: The Art of Oral History* (New York: Praeger, 1991, 2nd ed. rev.; originally published in 1975 by Precedent); and Michael Frisch, *A Shared Authority: Essays on the Craft and Meaning of Oral and Public History* (Albany: State University of New York Press, 1990). Portelli furthered his gender analysis more explicitly in his second collection of essays. See especially "Luigi's Socks and Rita's Makeup: Youth Culture, The Politics of Private Life, and the Culture of the Working Classes" in his *The Battle of Valle Giulia: Oral History and the Art of Dialogue* (Madison: University of Wisconsin Press, 1997), 232–48. In a similar vein, the fourth volume of the *International Yearbook of Oral History and Life Stories*, dedicated to "Gender and Memory," brought together a group of essays exploring femininities and masculinities in relation to memory and silence. Because this volume was never available in paperback, unfortunately also bringing to an end this brief Oxford University Press series, it did not have a large circulation. Still, its wide-ranging and critical contributions are useful here. See Selma Leydesdorff, Luisa Passerini, and Paul Thompson, eds., *International Yearbook of Oral History and Life Stories: Gender and Memory*, vol. 4 (Oxford: Oxford University Press, 1996).

14. See http://bancroft.berkeley.edu/ROHO/projects/artistsdis/ and www.storylineshistories.com/pdfs/OHA_Spring07_p3.pdf. See also "Telling Stories Reveals Power to Transform," *OHA Newsletter* 41, no. 3 (Winter 2007): 3.

15. Ann Cvetkovich, *An Archive of Feeling: Trauma, Sexuality, and Lesbian Public Cultures* (Durham, NC: Duke University Press, 2003), 167.

16. Horacio N. Roque Ramírez, "Memory and Mourning: Living Oral History with Queer Latinos and Latinas in San Francisco," in Paula Hamilton and Linda Shopes, eds., *Oral History and Public Memories* (Philadelphia: Temple University Press, 2008), 165–86.

17. See Don Kulick and Margaret Willson, eds., *Taboo: Sex, Identity, and Erotic Subjectivity in Anthropological Fieldwork* (New York: Routledge, 1995).

18. Esther Newton, "My Best Informant's Dress: The Erotic Equation in Fieldwork," in Newton, *Margaret Mead Made Me Gay: Personal Essays, Public Ideas* (Durham, NC: Duke University Press, 2000), 250, emphasis in original.

19. Ibid., 250–51, emphasis in original. It is worth considering to what degree Newton's useful analysis of the "erotic dimension" compares with the insider-insider (but also insider-outsider) status collaborators of color (queer or not) conducting oral history work share in white-/European-dominant societies. See Maxine Baca Zinn, "Field Research in Minority Communities: Ethical, Methodological, and Political Observations by an Insider," *Social Problems* 27, no.2 (December 1979): 209–19.

20. Jason Ruiz, chapter 6 in this book.

21. An Autonomous Collective of the Melbourne GTSG, *Young, Gay and Proud* (Melbourne: An Autonomous Collective of the Melbourne GTSG, 1978).

22. Daniel Marshall, chapter 9 in this book.

23. In December 2008, the CLGH voted to change its name to the Committee on Lesbian, Gay, Bisexual, and Transgender History (CLGBTH).

24. John D'Emilio, *Sexual Politics, Sexual Communities: The Making of a Homosexual Minority in the United States, 1940–1970* (Chicago: University of Chicago Press, 1983).

25. Bérubé, *Coming Out under Fire*, 286–87.

26. Kennedy and Davis, *Boots of Leather, Slippers of Gold*, 18–19, 396–97, notes 67–70.

27. Sherna Berger Gluck has made critical observations about the potential dangers of carrying out oral history research in the post-9/11 (U.S.) world, specifically about making available online interviews with particular narrators whose subjects in the present or at some point in the future may be deemed dangerous, subversive, and/or antipatriotic and have the potential of garnering the attention of the investigative and policing apparatuses of the state. Gluck, "Oral History on the Web: Promises and Perils," Oral History Association conference, Little Rock, Arkansas, October 26, 2006.

28. See Kennedy and Davis, *Boots of Leather, Slippers of Gold*, 24–25, and Bérubé, *Coming Out under Fire*, 285–86. Of the 55 interviewees' names listed in John Howard's "Southern queer history," there is no indication of how many of the interviewed men and women are of African American descent, although we know from the text that several of them are. See *Men Like That: A Southern Queer History* (Chicago: University of Chicago Press, 1999), 307–9. Similarly, Steve Estes does not specify a racial or ethnic breakdown for the fifty-eight U.S. military veteran women and men he interviewed for his *Ask & Tell: Gay & Lesbian Veterans Speak Out* (Chapel Hill: University of North Carolina Press, 2007), 255–61.

29. These include E. Patrick Johnson, *Sweet Tea: Black Gay Men of the South* (Chapel Hill: University of North Carolina Press, 2008); Eric C. Wat, *The Making of a Gay Asian Community: An Oral History of Pre-AIDS Los Angeles* (New York: Rowman & Littlefield, 2002); Horacio N. Roque Ramírez, *Memories of Desire: An Oral History from Queer Latino San Francisco, 1960s–1990s* (forthcoming); María Cora, "*Nuestras Auto-Definiciones*/Our Self-Definitions: Management of Stigma and Identity by Puerto Rican Lesbians" (unpublished M.A. field studies report, San Francisco State University, 2000); Trinity Ordona, "Coming Out Together: An Ethnohistory of the Asian and Pacific Islander Queer Women's and Transgendered People's Movement of San Francisco" (unpublished Ph.D. diss., University of California, Santa Cruz, 2000); and Karla E. Rosales, "Papis, Dykes, Daddies: A Study of Chicana and Latina Self-Identified Butch Lesbians" (unpublished M.A. thesis, San Francisco State University, 2001).

30. Naheed Islam, "Research as an Act of Betrayal: Researching Race in an Asian Community in Los Angeles," in France Winddance Twine and Jonathan W. Warren, eds., *Racing Research, Researching Race: Methodological Dilemmas in Critical Race Studies* (New York: New York University Press, 2000), 59.

31. Elizabeth Lapovsky Kennedy, "Telling Tales: Oral History and the Construction of Pre-Stonewall Lesbian History," in Robert Perks and Alistair Thomson, eds., *The Oral History Reader*, 2nd ed. (New York: Routledge, 2006), 281.

PART I

SILENCE

1

SEX, "SILENCE," AND AUDIOTAPE

Listening for Female Same-Sex Desire in Cuba

Carrie Hamilton

Oral history by Carrie Hamilton with "Laura," Havana, Cuba, 2005–2007

Between 2005 and 2007, I conducted three interviews with a Cuban woman named Laura.[1] The interviews were part of the "Cuban Voices" oral history project, under whose auspices a group of eight Cuban and three British researchers collected stories from some one hundred Cubans across the island about their lives since the revolution of 1959.[2] Our narrators were young and old, black, mestizo,[3] and white, female and male, urban and rural dwellers, religious people and nonbelievers, supporters and detractors of the revolution. There were also a number of narrators whose primary sexual relationships were with people of the same sex. As scholars with diverse backgrounds in the humanities and social sciences, the interviewers have followed their own research interests in analyzing the interviews. My work focuses on narratives of sexuality in the interviews,[4] and my analysis of Laura's interviews here forms part of this wider project.[5]

SEPTEMBER 2005

Interview with Laura by two interviewers, Nina and Carrie, at Laura's house.

NINA: Your skin is black, the same as my partner's; . . . have you had any difficulties because of your skin color?

LAURA: Not so far. At least it's never limited me from doing anything. . . . I was checked out by Counter Intelligence but no, there was never any problem because I've always led a quiet life, a normal life. I've participated in the CDR [Committees for Defense of the Revolution],[6] in normal activities, without drawing excessive attention to myself. But yes, my family has also been a quiet family, no conflicts or problems. . . .

NINA: And your partners [*compañeros*], have they always had your skin color?

LAURA: No.

NINA: They've been interracial relationships?

LAURA: No, no, no. I've never had a *compañero* the same color as me. Fairer, more or less *mulato*, but I've never been in love with a *compañero* of my skin color. [. . .]

NINA: How do you perceive . . . people who aren't your, who aren't heterosexual? For example, homosexual?

LAURA: No, no, no, no. I have always had that sensitivity. . . . I've never had prejudices. I've never been a person with prejudices. I've always, I say I treat everyone with their defects and their virtues. People who are homosexual and behave properly in society, I don't have any kind of taboo. And I have homosexual friends, women as well as men. . . . They're normal people, the same as anyone else. As long as they maintain respect. Because depraved people, that's something I don't like at all. [. . .]

CARRIE HAMILTON: And do you have a *compañero*? Can't you come home with . . .

LAURA: He comes here as a mate but not as a relationship.

CARRIE: You have to have the relationship outside your house?

LAURA: My mother. My mother is, she's selfish. . . .

NINA: Have you had stable, legalized relationships or only—

LAURA: No, I've had stable relationships.

NINA: Legally married?

LAURA: No, no. Not legally. No, not the signature, no. I haven't. I don't really agree with the paperwork. But well, yes, stable, for some years, of course. Nine years. Quite a bit for the times we live in. . . .

NINA: And have you never been pregnant or had a termination?

LAURA: No, no, no. I've never got pregnant. I've always protected myself. . . .

CARRIE: [. . .] if you speak to your female friends . . . about the topic of contraception. . . . Do women take responsibility for protecting themselves, or do the men also take some? . . .

LAURA: No. Look. The campaigns that have been around here for some time say that the couple should protect themselves. But it's always the woman who has most to lose. So the woman is the person who has to protect herself and demand that men use protection. . . . But well, there are lots of young girls, and when I talk to them they tell me no, in the case of condoms, no. "It's a problem for you young girls, because now we have AIDS."

DECEMBER 2006

Interview with Laura and one interviewer, Carrie, in a friend's house in Havana.

CARRIE: . . . you say you're a religious person. . . . Can you talk to me a bit about . . .

LAURA: Yes. Of course. I practice the Yoruba religion . . . what is popularly known here as santería. . . .

CARRIE: And you were raised in a Catholic family, or at least your mother was . . .

LAURA: She is. She is because, even though she doesn't go to church, she's Catholic.

CARRIE: And were there other people in your family interested in, your religion? Santería?

LAURA: At home we all practice Yoruba. All of us. . . .

CARRIE: And in your neighborhood are there many people who practice this religion?

LAURA: Yes, of course. . . . All over Cuba . . . What a shame you're leaving so soon, because [a friend] is celebrating her saint day on January third. . . . They're lovely ceremonies. I like them. And they don't interfere with my life at all.

CARRIE: I was going to ask you about that because we know that there was a time when religion was not well regarded by people committed to the revolution, right?

LAURA: That was a big mistake. But well. They say that to rectify is to be wise. . . . And that's been rectified.[7] And well, things are more or less getting better. But in this country, well. Cubans have been taught to have a *doble moral*.[8] I'd say even three morals. . . . Up to three and four or five, too. And I'm not going to talk to you about that now. I'm not going to make your life difficult.

CARRIE: No? But have you not experienced any kind of prejudice? Comments among your Party comrades, for example?

LAURA: The thing is my Party comrades, the vast majority of them also practice santería.

CARRIE: . . . Is this all over Cuba or specifically in your neighborhood or at your work? Or do you think many Party activists are religious?

LAURA: They practiced it before, but couldn't say it because you would be sanctioned. They adopted a *doble moral*. That happens with religion, and it happens with other things, too.

CARRIE: What kind of things do you mean by that? [Pause] This is all anonymous. Well, say what you want, there's no pressure, but remember what I told you the last time. . . .

LAURA: It happens like that as well with the problem of homosexuality. That's why I say that *dobles morales* exist and *triples morales*. You're not repudiated as such if you're a homosexual now, and nothing comes down on you, as long as you maintain a conduct that's in accordance with the [revolutionary] process. But it's always poorly regarded, people talk about it, point at you. In some things, I'm telling you, things have got better. But it's like everything. Because each person has their sexual conduct as they want to have it. I have a lot of respect for that. But well, it's something that hasn't been achieved. I don't think much has been achieved in that. But, well, as long as the person behaves well, I think they deserve respect.

[. . .]

CARRIE: And are you with someone right now? Do you have . . .

LAURA: Yes, I have my partner.

CARRIE: Yes? And how long have you been together?

LAURA: Almost eleven months.

CARRIE: Well, tell me something. How did you meet? What are they like?

LAURA: Ah! Now you want to know too much. Well, we'd known each other for some time already. What I didn't know was that there was an interest. Very frank. We Cubans are very open, and one fine day he challenged me. He said to me, "Girl, you don't drink, you don't dance, you don't do anything." I was left like that, thinking well so-and-so's a bit cheeky. But well, that's where it started and now we've been together a number of months; everything's really good. Not as we would like because he lives in his house and I in mine. But well, we're struggling along.

CARRIE: And where does he live?

LAURA: . . . Close by. So it's someone with a very happy character. That helps me because, I'm a bit more sedate, you know? . . . I like listening to music. But I'm not much of a dancer. And he loves dancing, parties, beer. And since we don't have anything in common, it seems that's what makes the thing work. . . .

CARRIE: I don't know whether we talked the last time about how you feel as a woman, if you've ever felt any kind of machismo in your life yourself, or if you've seen it or how you see the relationship of women's equality today.

LAURA: Look. Women have had a position in this society that they've never ever had. But machismo, we ourselves foment machismo inadvertently. I have three nephews, they're boys, the three boys, my sister's sons are all boys. What happens? "Leave the house and go play in the street." Women are the ones who stay at home. Without meaning to, we strengthen machismo. But this society has changed a lot. Now men take children to child care, pick them up from school, take them to the doctor. In that sense, society has advanced quite a bit. My father, never. He paid for the clinic, but that was my mother's problem. In my house, I never saw my father cook. Cook or help out. I see my brothers-in-law cooking, washing, cleaning, everything, washing the dishes, everything. Not my partner. My partner is lazy.

CARRIE: He's lazy.

LAURA: Lazy. [Laughter] He doesn't do anything. You have to . . .

CARRIE: Ah no?

LAURA: You have to do everything for him.

CARRIE: And who does it? His sister?

LAURA: Well, his sister. Because sometimes I take the clothes to my house, and I wash them for him at my house, and I iron and that, but he's lazy, lazy, lazy. Bad habits.

CARRIE: Bad habits. But you see changes, nonetheless?

LAURA: Yes, of course. When I tell him that I don't feel well, I have a pain some-where, he does it. But he always has a way of looking for the weak point so people do things for him or at least cooperate. My brother is the same. My brother is super *machista*, but since he doesn't have anyone to do things for him, he ends up doing them himself. Because I don't do anything for him. I don't cook for him or iron for him or wash for him or anything.

DECEMBER 2007

Interview with Laura and one interviewer, Carrie, at the house of a friend of Laura's.

LAURA: I feel good in my relationship. It helps me quite bit, emotionally. [Pause] And yes, I feel good. At work I've had some positive successes. In my work life, yes, I feel good. Everything's good. Everything's good, without problems.

CARRIE: Tell me a bit about, about the relationship you began, I believe, not much before the last interview. Just over a year ago. . . .

LAURA: Two years ago. . . . This relationship, up till now, is getting stronger and stronger. We've adapted to each other's ways of being. Things are moving along. There are always things. We're two people, aren't we? Each one with her things. But things are getting better. They've got better. There are always little things, aren't there? But well. That helps relationships too. [Pause] But there's a lot of exchange. And arguments; we've never argued. . . .

CARRIE: You told me last year, when we did the interview, that you were in a re-lationship, a new relationship. But nevertheless, you talked about your partner—now you're laughing [laughter] because you know where I'm going—You talked about your partner as if she were a man. And now it turns out that your partner is a woman.

LAURA: Uh-huh.

CARRIE: So, I'd like to ask you, first, if you've had other relationships with other women before that?

LAURA: Yes, I've had some other experiences. Not many, not many. But yes, there've been other relationships.

CARRIE: And with men as well.

LAURA: Yes.

[. . .]

CARRIE: Let's see. There's been a lot of talk about the history of repression against homosexuals in Cuba. . . . Did you have an awareness that that was hap-pening, that people talked about it, when you were young, or did you find out later?

LAURA: This has always been regarded as something ugly in society. It's never been well received.

CARRIE: Homosexuality?

LAURA: Yes, in the general sense. I don't have much experience with that. Since I never had relations with people with that, with that inclination. In the environment where I was raised, nobody talked about that. So there are a lot of things you don't know about. As you start to see things a bit, you start to learn a bit, you start to realize about all the situations that have happened. But there's always been a lot of denial. In that sense, they seem to accept you. At work. But there are comments behind your back. Unpleasant things. When they realize, of course. They never see you as an upright person. . . . They always say, "Hey, look at Florilla. Look. She likes women." "He likes men." They always say bad things. . . . If you say it, you're looking for trouble. You can't live like that. That's why there's a *doble moral*. I already talked to you about the *doble moral*, the triple moral, up to four morals. They force you to live with the *doble moral*. Because if you want to live, as I am. Because they renounce you. Your family. Your work. Everyone. . . . And you can't live like that. You feel bad. [Pause] You feel bad. Because Cubans. We're like that. There are even people who *appear* to accept homosexuals. Because they have family members or because they have that inclination themselves. But they still speak badly about them. You know? But how is that? Unfortunately, that's how it is.

CARRIE: And have you had some experiences like that? You, personally? Negative comments. . . .

LAURA: As a person? No, because I don't publicize myself, as they say.

CARRIE: So your workmates don't know?

LAURA: No, no. They may think it, but. . . . It's my personal life. . . . If they find out, they'll talk about me too. . . . You have to have a double life. . . .

CARRIE: Well, we've talked a bit about the difficult aspects, of having a certain sexual orientation, haven't we? But you obviously also enjoy your relationship with your partner. Have you also been able to enjoy a community of female friends who also have relationships with women?

LAURA: Yes. You always know someone. Not a lot. Because, I'm a bit serious, you know. I don't have tons of friends in this world. My partner, yes. She's also been longer than me. She's older. She's not bothered. She's not bothered if people know. She doesn't watch out a lot. . . . She's much more open. Her children know. Her mother knows. . . .

CARRIE: If you had to define your sexual identity, how would you define yourself?

LAURA: Normally. I feel good. Normal. For me it's something very normal. I don't reject men, no way. But, I prefer women.[9]

Commentary

This essay is located at the crossroads of oral history and the history of female same-sex desire.[10] Scholars in both fields are interested in silences. Oral historians, influenced in large part by psychoanalysis and literary theory, have argued that what remains unsaid in an interview is often as important as that which is spoken,[11] while scholars of female same-sex desire and lesbian history have sometimes used the tropes of "silence" and "invisibility" to explain the absence of women who love women from the historical record.[12]

In my title, therefore, *silence* sits in quotation marks between *sex* and *audiotape* to signal one aim of this essay: to explore the relationship between the supposed silence surrounding female same-sex desire in Cuban history, on one hand, and the usefulness of silence as an analytical concept for oral history and the history of female same-sex sexuality, on the other. Additionally, with its debt to Steven Soderburgh's 1989 film *Sex, Lies and Videotape*, my title replaces *lies* with *silence* to make the point that omissions in oral histories have a range of meanings beyond forgetfulness or deliberate falsification. I focus on themes of absence, representation, and revelation in relation to Laura's sexuality. In so doing, I aim to problematize the concept of silence and suggest ways that listening to tales of female same-sex desire in Cuba can contribute to the growing transnational scholarship on female same-sex sexualities.

The themes chosen as the focus of the "Cuban Voices" project—race, gender, class, religion, and sexuality—reflect both key social questions in the history of the revolution and the researchers' individual research interests. In this context, sexuality was largely associated in our project with the controversial history of male homosexuality and institutionalized homophobia since 1959. This meant that interviewers were conscious from the outset of the political nature of sexuality, but that sexuality was somewhat narrowly defined as something specifically relevant to interviews with homosexual men.[13] Thus in the early stages of the project a number of men in homosexual relationships were interviewed, whereas few women in same-sex relationships figured among the narrators.

To redress this imbalance, in 2006 and 2007, I interviewed ten women in Havana and Santiago de Cuba who either identified as lesbians or had had sexual relationships with other women. I met these women through contacts with the lesbian discussion group at the Cuban National Centre for Sexual Education (CENESEX) in Havana. Laura did not originally form part of this subset of narrators; she had been selected by one of the Cuban researchers who knew her through her local activism in the Communist Party in a poor neighborhood of Havana. On Laura's request, I subsequently arranged to interview her alone, and this led to a friendly relationship between us. During my final field trip to Cuba in December 2007, I met with her again, and this time Laura introduced me to her girlfriend. Since I was in the course of conducting interviews with women in same-sex relationships, I interviewed Laura a third time, this time introducing questions about her sexual relationships and identity.

I first interviewed Laura in September 2005, along with a white female Cuban colleague, Nina. The interview took place in the small front room of Laura's home in Havana. She was living with her eighty-seven-year-old mother, who was present but did not speak during the interview. The two women also share the house with Laura's older brother.

Born in 1958, just six months before the revolutionary victory of January 1, 1959, Laura opens the interview by describing herself as someone "born with the revolution." She comes from a provincial black middle-class family strongly committed to the revolution. Unlike many of the narrators, Laura does not emphasize the poverty or humility of her childhood. But she does attribute much that is positive in her life to the changes brought by the revolution, either directly or indirectly. For example, the opportunity to study in a boarding school (*beca*) gave her independence as an adolescent, and the people she met in this period of her life have remained friends. Laura returns to this period and these friendships time and again in this first interview. She has been an activist since her youth—first in the Communist Youth and later in the party. She takes this activism seriously and dedicates a lot of time to it, although she complains of long meetings and prefers to get down to concrete tasks. But her criticisms are reserved for individuals rather than the political system itself. Similarly, she denies that she has ever experienced racism, at work or elsewhere, even though Nina insists on this point more than once. When I ask her what the revolution means to her, Laura replies with a stock list of improvements in the areas of education, health, and economic equality. Laura works for a state firm and claims that, notwithstanding Cuba's economic crisis and the thriving underground economy, she survives on her small state salary.

In many ways, Laura's story sounds like a success story of the revolution. There is no reason to doubt the sincerity of her political commitment, yet her contemporary situation is also a reflection of some serious social problems, in particular, the ongoing housing crisis. The revolution gave Laura the opportunity to become independent and not have to rely on her family. But both her family's traditional values and the problems with housing have kept her tied to her family in middle age. At the end of the interview, Nina comments that Laura is reticent about her personal relationships. Laura attributes this to her conservative upbringing. I agreed that missing from the interview is an exploration of more personal relationships, as well as a sense of whether Laura sees contradictions in Cuban society and politics.

I decided to try to interview Laura again on my next trip to Cuba. When I called her, she agreed to a second interview but asked that I meet her without the Cuban researcher and that the interview not be held in her home. She indicated that there were things she had not said in the first interview because her mother and brother had been at home. I arranged for Laura to come to a friend's house on one of my last days in Havana. This second interview is remarkably different from the first. Whereas the year before Laura had spoken little about personal issues, this time she goes into much more detail about her life, in particular her religion. Once again, she speaks at length about the days in the boarding school. Laura refers often to the fact that she is the youngest child. This may have something to do with her identification with her generation (and would also explain the nostalgia for the boarding school days), but it also seems to represent freedom in contrast to the restrictions and frustrations she identifies with her family. Laura defines herself as someone who doesn't like to have taboos in her life, as someone liberal, especially in her respect for people with different sexual identities, and contrasts herself in this regard with the rest of her family and, indeed, Cuban society generally.

Following this interview in December 2006, Laura requested that the next time I came to Cuba I call her so that we could meet as friends. When I returned to Havana a year later, I arranged to go to the beach with her and a gay male friend. I met them at the train station and when another woman, Nachy, showed up, Laura told me this was her girlfriend. As we walked along, I laughed and asked Laura why she hadn't told me this before, but she didn't offer a clear answer. Later at the beach, when Laura and I were swimming together, I asked her if she'd always dated women. "Usually," she replied. Her family may know but doesn't say anything, and they are not supportive.

I interviewed Laura a third time at the house of Tania, another woman who had accompanied us to the beach. Tania has a small and cozy place not far from Laura's house. As of a few weeks before the interview, Laura had been sleeping in Tania's living room; she had had an argument with her mother, and though she was still going "home" every day to prepare food, by seven or eight o'clock each night she was at Tania's. Sometimes Nachy, who also lived nearby, came to stay. After dinner, Tania went to her room, and Laura and I chatted for a few minutes. I asked her about the second interview transcript, which I had given to her the previous day. She said she'd read it—twice—and didn't have anything to add. The third interview lasted almost an hour. Laura answered all the questions I had from the second interview but didn't expand a lot. I asked her about her partner and about her previous relationships with women. She spoke of her relationship but only briefly, never mentioning Nachy's name. She did speak at some length about discrimination and negative comments about homosexuals (she used this term frequently to refer to others, but never the word *lesbian*).

After the interview, we continued talking, and Laura spoke more directly now, referring specifically to the problem of discrimination. She mentioned the importance of the release of the film *Strawberry and Chocolate* in 1993 in helping to change attitudes toward homosexuality in Cuba. She talked about the younger generation, claiming that they are freer and take on a sexual identity more easily. Earlier I had mentioned the lesbian wedding I had attended at CENESEX,[14] and Laura said it wasn't the first—she had heard of others, but usually with one woman dressed in white and the other as *el novio* (the groom). After a while, Laura accompanied me to a main road, where we said farewell before I caught a communal taxi back to my Havana lodgings.

In the excerpts that accompany this essay, I have edited the translations to render them more easily readable, but I have left in the interviewers' questions to convey the sense of the interviews as intersubjective processes. I have also described the location of each interview. Although many histories based on oral history interviews leave this information out, in this case the location and the questions asked are fundamentally important to understanding how Laura presents herself and her past. For example, in the first interview Nina introduces interracial relationships using the masculine Spanish word *compañeros.* Until this point, Laura has made no mention of her intimate relationships, and Nina's question assumes that Laura is heterosexual. All further mentions of Laura's partners in this interview—by Laura, Nina, and myself—are in the masculine. Later in the first interview, Nina introduces the issue of homosexuality by assuming that this is something different from Laura's own sexual identity. In both cases, the narrator's sexual identity is constructed through the interviewer's question and the subsequent course of the discussion. In the second interview sensing a hesitation on Laura's part after I asked her to elaborate on the problem of the *doble moral*[15] in Cuban society, I remind her that the interview is anonymous. Laura replies that homosexuality, like religion, is subject to "two morals" in Cuba. It is impossible to know whether Laura would have given me more details without this coaxing. However, both Laura's hesitation and my intervention underscore the fact that naming the *doble moral* is a delicate and possibly dangerous act.

Furthermore, Laura's interviews and, most important, the differences among them in tone and content cannot be fully understood without reference to their location and the conversations that occurred between us outside them. In the first interview, the lack of details about Laura's personal life and the rather rosy picture of Cuban society and politics can be explained partly by her reluctance to speak in the presence of her mother and the Cuban interviewer. There is evidence in other interviews that the presence of Cuban interviewers could prove a hindrance to narrators who feared social or political repercussions of openly criticizing some aspects of Cuban society. But even in the second interview, held in a stranger's house and without Nina, Laura did not discuss her sexual relationships with women. A year later, she had decided to introduce me to her female partner, by which time I had also told Laura that I was dating a female-to-male (FTM) transgender person. However, in the third interview, Laura was still reticent about her personal relations. As with several interviews I did in Cuba, some of the most interesting discussions occurred when the recorder was turned off. But even if Laura and I discussed issues of sexuality, homophobia, and personal relationships in more detail during our later meetings, it would be naïve to assume that she had "revealed all."

Over the past twenty years, oral historians have become increasingly attuned to the importance of the interviewer-narrator relationship.[16] But incorporating the historian's role in the interview process into the analysis can prove a difficult balancing act. As Valerie Yow notes, while many scholars are sensitive to the relevance of our own subjectivity to our research, there is a risk "that every research article or book will deal with the researcher's personal experiences and the research topic itself will take second place in the presentation."[17] Indeed, other oral historians have expressed concerns about the confessional tone of some oral history studies.[18] But I concur with Yow that an awareness of our subjectivity has two aims, which follow one from the other: "1) understanding the subjective aspects of the research and interpretation so that 2) we can carry out the project with as much objectivity as possible and use subjectivity to advantage."[19]

My influence on the course of the interviews with Laura and other women who had same-sex relationships in Cuba went beyond my questions during the interviews to a range of other factors, including my sexual preferences, background and social position, and how these were negotiated and received in the Cuban context. These factors are far from straightforward and are open to changing interpretations. It might be tempting, for example, to suggest that the progressive openness of Laura's interviews was due to the combined factors of my outsider status, my coming out, and our developing friendship beyond the boundaries of the interviews. In addition, by presenting myself as what would be called queer in a Western, English-language context, as well as a leftist and feminist activist, I was no doubt able to make specific kinds of connections to some of the women I interviewed.

At the same time, however, and following writing on the ethics of feminist oral history,[20] my interpretation of the interviews bears in mind the things that distanced me from the narrators, specifically my position as a white, English-speaking, European professional with access to significantly more economic resources than my Cuban narrators. Thus, although on one level Laura's interviews could be interpreted as a progression from relative silence, omission, or cover-up to greater revelation (a version that would fit comfortably with the common metaphor of breaking the silence in some lesbian and oral history), such an analysis would fail to take into account the array of things that I do not, and perhaps cannot, know about Laura's life, even when she may seem to speak directly about them. What I will do here is offer analyses of three related themes in the interviews—sexuality, racial identity, and gender—and suggest how they might help us to expand our understanding of the history of sexuality and the Cuban Revolution.

Although in retrospect we know that in the first interview Laura's sexuality was misrepresented, or at least simplified, through the course of questioning, the interview nevertheless provides important material for consideration of the history and memory of sexuality in revolutionary Cuba.[21] Taking up the heterosexual position assigned to her by the interviewers' questions, Laura discusses what she perceives as generational changes and continuities in heterosexual relationships (see the first interview), perceptions that echo those presented in interviews with narrators in relationships with men. Laura positions herself as a mentor to young people, encouraging them to use safer sexual practices, a stance consistent with her revolutionary commitment. But absences in Laura's narrative are likewise consonant with gaps in other interviews, pointing to wider patterns of collective memory in revolutionary Cuba.[22] In both cases, Laura expresses nostalgia for her days at boarding school during the mid-1970s. This memory resonates with contemporary popular discourse inside Cuba, in which the 1970s and 1980s appear as a golden age of the Cuban Revolution, between the tumultuous first decade of the 1960s and the economic crisis of the 1990s. Laura remembers her school days as a time when she learned how to lend and share things and contrasts this with her overprotected and even egotistical childhood, which may in turn be interpreted as a hangover from prerevolutionary Cuba. But it is equally interesting to consider what this memory of coming of age in a period of socialist equality does not represent: the repression of those years, including institutionalized homophobia. Laura's boarding school years overlap with the "five gray years" between 1971 and 1976, a period now remembered openly among Cuban intellectuals as a period of intense repression, including state-sanctioned homophobia.

I do not suggest that Laura has no knowledge of the history of institutionalized homophobia in Cuba. When I ask her about this in the third interview, she replies that it is something she has learned as she has grown older but does not elaborate. This may reflect the lack of a public narrative within which to frame this knowledge. Nonetheless, suggestions of a historical consciousness about taboo topics in Cuban society can be garnered through associations in the three interviews with Laura, in particular the implicit link between sexual, religious, and racial discrimination (the word *taboo* is used by many narrators to refer to silences surrounding these three themes in contemporary Cuba). For example, two topics that were virtually absent from the first interview emerge in the second: the importance of Afro-Cuban religion in Laura's life and homophobia at work and in the party. In the second interview Laura makes a direct link between the persecution of religious practice and homophobia, citing both as examples of the *doble moral*. Although she does not refer to it, there is a wider historical link as well: homosexual men and religious practitioners were the main groups committed to forced labor camps (the notorious UMAP—Military Units for the Aid of Production) during the 1960s. Given this historical association between religious persecution and homophobia, we might speculate that for Laura, Afro-Cuban religion provides a space relatively free from homophobia. When I ask her, in the third interview, how the issue of sexuality is treated in the Yoruba tradition, Laura replies that some high-ranking figures are openly homosexual, although she also insists that she keeps her religious and private lives separate and that religion has nothing to do with sexuality. The importance of religion as

SEX, "SILENCE," AND AUDIOTAPE | 35

a refuge is also suggested by Laura's repeated assertion that she became involved in santería because of health problems, in particular, depression. While she does not discuss the origins of her depression, the fact that Laura identifies religion with both tolerance and healing, in contrast with the repressive atmosphere of work and political life, suggests that social and institutional discrimination have had a negative impact on Laura's mental health.

Religion relates as well to a third aspect of Laura's story: her Afro-Cuban heritage. In the early twenty-first century, Afro-Cuban religions are practiced by Cubans of all racial identities. Nonetheless, they have a strong historical and cultural association with Cubans of African descent, and the central place accorded to santería in Laura's life story may represent a way of claiming this history in the context of a society that discourages discussion of racial identity and, in particular, racism. Laura was part of the first generation in Cuba to experience the significant structural changes in race relations brought about by the revolution. After 1962, however, the government declared that racism had been eliminated in Cuba, thereby stifling public debate about ongoing discrimination. Thus, while Laura and her generation enjoyed the benefits of greater equality after 1959, they lacked a framework within which to discuss racial difference and racism.[23]

It should come as no surprise, then, that Laura denies having experienced racism, at work or elsewhere, even though Nina insists on this point more than once in the first interview. The fact that Laura was speaking to two white women, one of them a fellow party member, may have made Laura particularly wary. But there are indications in this first interview that racial identity and racism have shaped Laura's life. For example, her remark that she passed counterintelligence tests without a problem because she had led a "normal" life and came from a "quiet" family may be a reference to the stereotype of black families as rowdy or troublemaking. In the second interview, Laura tells us that her grandfather was a *mambí* (a soldier in the Cuban War of Independence, 1895–1898) who was buried with full honors, giving this as an example of her family's "revolutionary roots." By telling this story, Laura locates herself and her family firmly in a political tradition that has been dominated publicly by white men. Similarly, talking about santería allows Laura to affirm her African heritage.

Finally, I want to look at gender as a third theme that may be best approached in the interview via associations and anecdotes rather than direct references. By gender, I do not only mean Laura's perception of male-female relations in Cuba, although she does offer some interesting reflections on these. I refer as well to how Laura represents gender in relationships between women, including her relationship with her partner, Nachy. In the second interview, following the discussion about the repression of religion and homosexuality in Cuban society, I ask Laura whether she is "with someone." This question comes after a discussion about her difficult housing situation and the fact that she cannot invite people to her own house. When Laura answers in the affirmative and I ask to know more about her partner, she protests that I "want to know too much." But she then talks about how she met her partner, using the masculine pronoun in Spanish, *él*. This conversation continues for some time until I introduce the topic of Laura's experience as a woman, asking her whether she has seen examples of *machismo*. She replies in the affirmative and claims that women are partly responsible for *machismo*. However, she recognizes as well the advances in gender equality under the revolution and gives several examples, including men doing the housework. At this stage, she stops and says, "Not my partner. He's lazy," before giving a series of examples to illustrate this, even comparing her partner to her equally lazy brother.

Laura's coding of her partner as masculine, then, is not a mere substitution of the male for the female pronoun. She attributes to "him" a series of characteristics popularly associated with masculinity in Cuban society. I want to suggest that while Laura evidently chose to present her partner as male in response to my desire "to know too much" about her love life, her characterization of her partner as masculine may also reflect a gendered element to their relationship. I do not argue that Laura thinks of Nachy as "a man," as "male identified," or as an example of "female masculinity." Nor do I argue that we should interpret Laura and Nachy's relationship as butch-femme, with its clear Western heritage. Certainly, when Laura eventually introduced me to Nachy, it was as her *novia* (girlfriend). However, I do want to make some tentative suggestions for further consideration of gendered subjectivities in Cuban same-sex female relationships.

During my trip to Cuba at the end of 2007, I had several conversations with women about masculinity and femininity among lesbians and women in same-sex relationships. At a party for the Havana lesbian discussion group, I talked to Daisy, a middle-aged black woman from the same neighborhood as Laura. She told me she liked feminine women ("the more feminine the better") and that she didn't like *mujeres fuertes*—literally, "strong women," whom she described as dressing "with men's shirts and closed shoes." Daisy called them *mujeres de bajo mundo* ("low-life women") and said she often sees them on the Malecón[24] at night. I was reminded of the comments made by Nancy, a young lesbian-identified woman I interviewed in Santiago de Cuba, about "manly" (*varonil*) women in the Plaza Dolores, with their knives and very feminine girlfriends. Later, I interviewed Odalys, a woman of Laura's age who has been a lesbian all her life. Odalys defines herself as a *mujer fuerte* and talked about the homophobia she sees among many Cuban lesbians. When I asked if she meant by this that many defend femininity and reject masculine women, she said yes.[25] My friend Raquel also commented that many Cuban lesbians rejected *mujeres fuertes*, even if they adopted some characteristics associated with masculinity themselves or were attracted to such women. Although it wasn't easy to establish what exactly these women meant by terms like *masculine* or *feminine*, and Cuban women in same-sex relationships have a variety of styles, which also reflect their cultural differences and preferences, the *mujer fuerte* seemed to carry a certain stigma for many of them. Laura, although seemingly wary of "lesbians" in general, did not mention *mujeres fuertes*, nor did she express negative attitudes toward women she associated with masculine gender characteristics, including her own partner.

In the growing fields of lesbian studies and history, butch-femme and, more recently, transgender identities figure prominently. Although early studies focused primarily on English-speaking Western cultures, since the 1990s, this literature has paid increasing attention to gendered same-sex female relationships and communities in Asia, Africa, and Latin America. In these studies, scholars emphasize the importance of understanding the formation of female sexual subjectivities, relationships, and communities within the context of day-to-day struggles against traditionalist gender regimes, racism, poverty, and imperialism, as well as homophobia. In other words, although same-sex gendered subjectivities and relationships among women are found in numerous historical periods and geographical regions, they are neither universal nor independent of wider material and cultural contexts. In Cuba, where both female and male same-sex relationships have existed historically without necessarily being named, sexual desire and preference need not be accompanied by a spoken sexual "identity." While my interviews suggest that there is a generation difference and that some younger women may describe themselves as lesbians, the history of official and popular homophobia under the revolution makes public naming of sexual identity difficult and even dangerous. Furthermore, the public silence that surrounds female same-sex desire in Cuba affects women from different social groups on the island in different ways.

For this reason, listening for female same-sex desire in Laura's interview cannot be only about searching for signs of lesbian identity. It must also take into account the intersection of sexuality with class, race, religious practice, age, and other factors. In particular, I suggest that Laura's representation of her relationship with Nachy should be understood in relation to changing constructions of black masculinities and femininities in Cuba. Notwithstanding the growing literature on race and blackness in Cuba, in addition to the substantial work on gender and sexuality, this scholarship has not to date focused on the intersections between race, class, gender, and sexuality. If research on Cuban homosexuality should expand beyond its current focus on men to consider female same-sex desire, this must be accompanied by greater analysis of how changes in class relations, as well as racial identities and racism, inform women's and men's sexual identities and practices.

Laura's interviews, in which the themes of sexual and gender identity, religious practice, and racism emerge slowly, and often in the form of allusion or anecdote, may at first glance appear to be an exemplary case of silence in oral history. In lesbian history, silence as a conceptual tool has allowed scholars to pay particular attention to the ways female subjects who had intimate and/or sexual relationships with other women in the past expressed their desires and articulated their experiences without necessarily naming themselves lesbian. But in spite of its potential usefulness in allowing historians to listen or read for history between the lines, silence, like invisibility, is a problematic concept because it places the burden of representation on the historical subject, casting the historian in the heroic role of breaking the silence. I suggest that the task of the oral historian or historian of lesbian culture is not to break silences, but to act as a translator. Those of us who work across languages are particularly sensitive to problems of translation in relation to oral and written sources. But I am thinking as well of translation in the broader, cultural sense.[26] Whether we consider Laura's sexual relationship, her representation of her partner's gender identity, or her Afro-Cuban religion and heritage, what we encounter is not silence so much as language and representations that do not fit easily within existing public narratives in revolutionary Cuba or with dominant constructions of female same-sex sexuality in Western English-speaking contexts. What is perhaps most surprising in Laura's interview is that in spite of the lack of public representations of black and female same-sex experience in contemporary Cuba, whether in official discourses, popular culture, or scholarship on race, gender, and sexuality, Laura's interview speaks to a complexity of female same-sex desire, one that has comparisons with other contexts but is nonetheless grounded in the particulars of contemporary Cuban history.

Notes

1. Laura and all other names used in this chapter (except my own) are pseudonyms, and I have changed details that might identify the narrator, the Cuban interviewer, or other Cubans mentioned in the essay. Some details have been changed to protect the narrator's anonymity. The interviews with Laura are the property of the "Cuban Voices" oral history project.

2. Although in the early part of the project, the majority of the interviews were vetted through contacts with governmental organizations, the other British researchers and I later conducted a number of unvetted interviews. In most cases, narrators were interviewed by a pair of researchers using the broad "life story" format, with the interviewee encouraged to tell her life story according to her own memories. Nonetheless, in the early interviews especially, interviewers asked a set of questions preagreed among members of the team. The additional use of questionnaires reflected both the empirical training of many of the Cuban researchers and the desire to focus on categories of analysis central to the social and political history of the revolution: class, race, gender, religion, and sexuality.

3. In popular language, *mulato/a* is still widely used to refer to Cubans of mixed African and Spanish heritage. In choosing the term *mestizo/a*, commonly used in Latin America to refer to mixed Spanish/indigenous heritage, the interview team recognized both the inadequacy of *mulato/a* to describe people with Chinese and/or indigenous Cuban heritage and also its increased use on the island.

4. See Carrie Hamilton, *Sexual Revolutions In Cuba: Passion, Politics, and Memory* (Chapel Hill: University of North Carolina Press, forthcoming 2012).

5. I wish to express my thanks to the project's director, Professor Elizabeth Dore, funders (the Ford Foundation and the Swedish development agency SIDA), and host institutions (the University of Southampton and the Cuban National Centre for Sexual Education [CENESEX]).

Additional funding for this chapter was provided by the British Council, the Feminist Review Trust and the University of Roehampton.

6. Mass organization established in 1960 to protect the aims of the Cuban Revolution of 1959 against counterrevolutionary activity.

7. *Rectificar* is the official term given to past mistakes that have been recognized and corrected by the revolutionary regime. After banning religious people from party membership and other positions of responsibility for many years, during the 1990s, the regime adopted a more relaxed attitude toward religion.

8. *Doble moral* literally means "double moral." The term is used widely in Cuba to describe the ways people adopt different positions or views vis-à-vis delicate issues such as religion or politics, depending on the company they are in. It implies a division between the revolutionary stance that must be adopted in public and a more relaxed position in private.

9. Laura interviewed by author (Carrie Hamilton) in Havana, September 2005, December 2006, and December 2007. The audio version and transcript of this interview are the property of the "Cuban Voices" oral history project, directed by Professor Elizabeth Dore and held at the University of Southampton, United Kingdom.

10. Aware of the debates surrounding nomenclature, I have opted to use the term *same-sex* instead of other words, including *lesbian*, *bisexual*, or *queer*, for reasons I outline later in the essay. *Same-sex* is not without its limitations, but its use avoids imposing an identity on Laura and other narrators that they may not claim for themselves. For a discussions of terminology, see Leila J. Rupp, "Toward a Global History of Same-Sex Sexuality," *Journal of the History of Sexuality* 10, no. 2 (April 2001): 287–302.

11. Luisa Passerini, "Memories between Silence and Oblivion," in Katharine Hodgkin and Susannah Radstone, eds., *Contested Pasts: The Politics of Memory* (London: Routledge, 2003), 238–54; Paul Thompson, *The Voice of the Past: Oral History*, 2nd ed. (Oxford: Oxford University Press, 1988), 154–57.

12. Recent examples include Elena M. Martínez, *Lesbian Voices from Latin America* (New York: Garland, 1996), 12; and Rebecca Jennings, *Tomboys and Bachelor Girls: A Lesbian History of Post-War Britain 1945–71* (Manchester, England: Manchester University Press, 2007), 6–7.

13. Nonetheless, by including sexuality among our key themes, we were able to gather important information on sexual relationships from narrators of different sexualities. See Hamilton, *Sexual Revolutions in Cuba*.

14. In December 2007, two women celebrated a "wedding" at the National Centre for Sexual Education in Havana. Although not recognized legally, the event, held in an official location, was of symbolic importance at a time when the director of the center, Mariela Castro, was proposing a change to the law to recognize same-sex unions.

15. See above, note 8.

16. Valerie Yow, "'Do I Like Them Too Much?': Effects of the Oral History Interview on the Interviewer and Vice-Versa," in Robert Perks and Alistair Thomson, eds., *The Oral History Reader*, 2nd ed. (London: Routledge, 2006), 54–72.

17. Ibid., 63.

18. Susan H. Armitage and Sherna Berger Gluck, "Reflections on Women's Oral History: An Exchange," in Susan H. Armitage with Patricia Hart and Karen Weatherman, eds. *Women's Oral History: The Frontiers Reader* (Lincoln: University of Nebraska Press, 2002), 75–86.

19. Yow, "'Do I Like Them Too Much?'" 63.

20. For example, Ann Phoenix, "Practising Feminist Research: The Intersection of Gender and 'Race' in the Research Process," in Mary Maynard and June Purvis, eds., *Researching Women's Lives from a Feminist Perspective* (London: Taylor and Francis, 1994), 49–71.

21. For reasons of space, I do not include here references to the significant comparative literature on gender, race, and sexuality in Cuba and elsewhere. I develop these themes further with reference to this literature in *Sexual Revolutions in Cuba*.

22. See Maurice Halbwachs, *On Collective Memory*, ed. Lewis A. Coser (Chicago: University of Chicago Press, 1992).

23. See Alejandro de la Fuente, *A Nation for All: Race, Inequality and Politics in Twentieth-Century Cuba* (Chapel Hill: University of North Carolina Press, 2001), 259–316.

24. The Malecón is the seaside area in Havana, known as a gathering and cruising area for homosexual men in particular.
25. Nancy and Odalys both come from families of mixed heritage, but neither named a racial identity during the interview.
26. I am conscious of the limitations of cultural translation as a metaphor for wider processes of communication across meanings and borders. But I think it is a more promising metaphor than silence, even when the latter term is subject to the subtle theorizations of an oral historian such as Passerini (see above, note 11). As Mary Louise Pratt writes, "Translation is a deep but incomplete metaphor for the traffic in meaning. It is probably not in the long run an adequate basis for a theory of cross-cultural meaning making and certainly not a substitute for such a theory. But exploring the metaphor may be a productive way of clarifying what such a theory might look like." See Pratt, "The Traffic in Meaning: Translation, Contagion, Infiltration," *Profession* (2002): 35.

2

REMEMBERING PROVINCETOWN

Oral History and Narrativity at Land's End

Karen Krahulik

Oral history by Karen Krahulik with Marguerite Beata Cook, Provincetown, Massachusetts, January 22, 1997

From 1996 to 1999, I founded and directed the Provincetown Oral History Project in Provincetown, Massachusetts. Working with local archivists and librarians, I captured residents' experiences of Provincetown as it changed from a Yankee whaling seaport and Portuguese fishing village into one of the world's most renowned gay and lesbian resort destinations. While most gay and lesbian community histories published at this time focused on the evolution of a gay community, my history of Provincetown looked closely at the effects of this evolution on local populations. The interview with Marguerite Beata Cook, a Portuguese native of Provincetown, was one of more than fifty interviews that I conducted using both audio and video recorders. The interview was set up by a library volunteer and filmed with a video recorder in the home of Cook's aunt, Ruth O'Donnell. I had interviewed O'Donnell one hour earlier and met both women for the first time on the afternoon of the interview, January 22, 1997. I published a community history of Provincetown several years later, Provincetown: From Pilgrim Landing to Gay Resort *(New York: New York University Press, 2005). My book on the oral history project in Provincetown is forthcoming.*

KAREN KRAHULIK: What was it like growing up in Provincetown?

MARGUERITE COOK: It was wonderful, it was really wonderful. You don't appreciate how wonderful it is when you're a kid; it's when you look back that you know it was beautiful. We played games. You had very simple games, there was no television of course, you listened to the radio—*Jack Armstrong, the All-American Boy,* and then there was one, *Just Plain Bill.* And so you spent a lot of time with the radio, listening to Franklin Delano Roosevelt's fireside chats; those were interesting to listen to even as a kid. And you played outdoors. You had a lot of snow in the winter so you did a lot of sliding down hills, and those were the things that you did that were fun.

KRAHULIK: How about during the summer?

COOK: Summertime you went swimming. Because I lived up at the West End, we would go swimming down at [the] beach [near Sal's restaurant]. They talk about the environment [now], my God, we swam in more dirt and sewage. Sewage! Some of the houses [had] wooden sewers coming out into the harbor, and they came from the houses that were right there on the harbor. Absolutely, any older person would remember that. And the beaches, the local beaches, were always full of cut glass, rusty cans. I was always going home with a cut on my foot because I stepped on a piece of glass. But, I'm seventy-two. I made it. We thrived on it somehow or other. . . . I'm sure if now all of these sewers were emptying into the harbor, it would be one hell of a mess. [laughs] But we did it.

KRAHULIK: When you were growing up, were there a lot of tourists in town during the summer?

COOK: No, not a lot, you couldn't even compare it to what it is now. There were the artists, it was a bohemian period of time, lots of artists, lots of would-be writers.

KRAHULIK: What time period is this?

COOK: I was born in twenty-four, so up until the time I was six or seven or eight, I don't remember too much; I knew there were artists painting around. But it was when I got older, when I was in my teens that I knew that it was bohemian and that I got to know some of the writers, would-be writers, a lot of them never made it.

KRAHULIK: So the artists were not rich people coming here from the leisure class?

COOK: Oh no, no, they were very poor people, they were struggling, struggling to make the grade; it was not an easy time for them. But because it was a free town, you could even sleep on the beach then, there was no National Seashore that was going to stop you, so they could do that in the summer if they wanted to. A lot of them camped out on the dunes and lived very freely. And I am not an artist, but they say, our artists say, that the light here is perfect for painting. So it would attract artists and writers. In fact, my father PC, when he was in the Coast Guard, he was out at Peaked Hill bars [and] Eugene O'Neill used to have a little shack out there where he would do his writing. And Dad would say, "Boy, he came home rip-roaring drunk again the other night, hollering and hooting." Dad had some pretty good stories about Eugene O'Neill and his antics.

KRAHULIK: How did you meet the artists? On the street?

COOK: It was in my later years, after I was twenty-one, I was coming back home in the summer time and I was a cocktail waitress in the Old Colony, that I met some of those people that were into painting and into writing. And as I told you, Norman Mailer would come in and they would talk, and they would mingle with the Portuguese fishermen who used to come in there because they loved the fishermen. The fishermen would give them a lobster if they happen to pull it up in their nets, which they very often did, and they would say, "Hey, do you want a nice lobster?" Of course they did, they were hungry. So it was all very amicable, very democratic, and a wonderful period of time.

KRAHULIK: This was the forties?

COOK: Yes, this would be the forties.

KRAHULIK: What were some of the other clubs? Did you go to Weathering Heights?

COOK: Oh, Weathering Heights I went to a lot, yes. I was a big bar person in those days; I went to all of the places.

KRAHULIK: And were the crowds mixed or gay or straight?

COOK: Mostly they were mixed, yes, Weathering Heights was mixed, certainly the Moors was mixed. I would say the Moors was mostly gay, but it was certainly not strictly gay because people loved the sing-alongs. And the same thing was true of the Town House, the back room of the Town House, that was mixed. So most of these places were very much mixed. They were not as segregated as they are now. There was not a place where you would say this is for lesbians, or this is where the gay guys go, you did not have that so much. Even in the A-House, I spent a lot of time in the A-House when Reggie was getting show people down. But he did not have the macho room then, and it was a much more mixed crowd. He had Billie Holiday, he had Jeanne Cooper, he had Ella Fitzgerald. He had them all.

KRAHULIK: Back in that time, the forties, fifties—

COOK: It was more in the fifties when Reggie had those show people down.

KRAHULIK: How did people who grew up in the town identify? Did you call yourselves locals or now I hear the term *townies*, or native, or Portuguese?

COOK: You see with me I had left town. I went to college for one year, but I kept coming home summers, and then I would go to various places in the winter. I moved around, I was a nomad, I moved here, I moved there. So I consider myself a native. You never are not a native if you were born and brought up in Provincetown. Nobody can believe anyone was born and brought up here.

KRAHULIK: When you say that no one can believe that someone was born and brought up here, what is that about?

COOK: First of all, I think they fell in love with this town, most people do, and to believe that somebody was hanging out where they hang out, that was not put away in their own houses doing their own thing, was a native, was hard for them to believe.

KRAHULIK: So were you almost famous?

COOK: No, I don't think I was famous, but I was pretty well known in those days, but famous? Infamous, maybe.

KRAHULIK: But as a native?

COOK: Oh, yes, you became kind of a spokesperson for the town and what went on, you know, the feeling of the natives, the feeling of the locals, about the tourists. I feel also that it was very friendly for the most part. You are going to find a few that have animosities. And also it is true that when the season ended, when every tourist season ends, the feeling was "Oh, I will be so glad to see them go." But then come March or April and they are saying, "Boy, it gets lonely down here. Jeez, it will be nice when these people come back for the summer, won't it?" So you can't please them, but that is the way it goes. [laughs]

KRAHULIK: When did you notice that the tourist crowd started to become more gay?

COOK: Ah, there were always gay people here, there just weren't as many, and in those earlier days, they were not so flamboyant. And I think that trend, I wouldn't dare put a date on it, but maybe the eighties, maybe the late seventies. I think after the hippie era maybe came that openly gay kind of thing. Or with the lesbians [saying] "I can beat up any guy around this place." Although that trend has changed. The lesbians are more, much more intelligent, not butch and rugged and ready to beat anybody up. But the openness, of course, has gone with the times. Things are much more acceptable now, they are out in the open, probably as it should be.

KRAHULIK: During the forties and fifties, what sense did natives have of the tourist crowd?

COOK: I think that of acceptance. Acceptance. There were some, if you said to them, for instance, "Come on, join me." Somebody that probably wouldn't have gone into a club, normally, on their own, but they went and they found they had a good time. And they would say, "Gee, this wasn't so bad, I had a pretty good time here." And then they would tell someone else. And I believe that that was the feeling for most people. Again, you can't speak for all people, I think that this town is probably one of the most tolerant towns in the world. You know, that is what got me mad one time with that Act Up thing, when they had that parade was so disgusting—"I kiss butts" or "I fuck butts" or something like that—they had on a sign. It created a divisiveness that should not have been there and that never was there. Take this to the Midwest, take it to anywhere, take it down south to rebel country, but certainly not this town; it is not the place for it because it is a very tolerant town, and a very accepting town, and I think the coexistence is wonderful. Gay, straight, no matter what, it is who you are. If they like you, you are accepted. And if you are an ass, then you're not. It's just as simple as that.

KRAHULIK: When you were growing up in the thirties, as a young girl, a tomboy about town, did you notice gay couples even then?

COOK: Not particularly, no. If they were around, I didn't notice them, I was not aware of them. There was one woman in town, I think she is now dead, I would not even use her name, but it wouldn't matter anyway because I think she's gone, and they used to say she was gay. And the term then was queer. "She is queer, you know? She is a queer." "Oh, yeah?" It was said in passing, it wasn't thought much about, it was just something to mention, that is all. And then there were a couple of guys that I knew of growing up that they would say that [about]. But you are not really aware of it because you didn't really care about it. You led your life, nobody was bothering you, and that is the way it went.

KRAHULIK: So you mentioned that they used the term *queer*, was that a term for both men and women?

COOK: Yes, a queer. He is a queer, she is a queer.

KRAHULIK: Is that what they would call themselves?

COOK: No, I do not think they called themselves that. I think they preferred gay.

KRAHULIK: When did the term *queer* drop out or was replaced?

COOK: Probably the seventies, I suppose, around then. There was some gay bash-ing at one point in this town, nothing like it now, but there was a witch hunt on gay people and I can't pinpoint that particular period of time. But I remem-ber Cookies Tap, the boys were running it then, when I say the boys I mean my cousins, Wilbur and Joe, and this set of bylaws came out from the selectmen saying that you shall not knowingly, we used to call it the ten commandments, serve a homosexual. And it went on and on, it was ten rules. And the boys said, "This is insane. If a guy comes in here and he swishes a little and I say to him, 'I can't serve you, I'm sorry, you look gay to me,' and he is not, he is apt to draw up and nail me." Which was true, you just can't do that. So that did not last long, it lasted maybe a year before the businesspeople, they put a stop to it.

KRAHULIK: The selectmen just came out with this?

COOK: I guess, I do not know why they did that, I really can't tell you why. I just know it was so overwhelming, it was such a shock that they did it, and I know that the businesspeople didn't like it one bit. So it didn't last very long. So after that hate gay people era passed, and that was not shared by everyone, then the views became much more tolerant.

KRAHULIK: I have not seen the ten commandments that you speak of, but I did see a different list, I think it was later, 1960, that said that no club could employ any so-called female impersonators.

COOK: It could have been that time, that could have been one of the rules, it is possible because they were so outrageous and so ridiculous that—what are they crazy? You can't do this. Later, everybody and their brother was a drag queen doing a drag queen show. But I don't think there were that many [female impersonators] then, really. Phil Bayonne, though, he had his nice wide hat on and the skirt over his trousers, and I bet you would call that female impersonating.

KRAHULIK: Did you have a group of friends, you certainly were not the only na-tive about town, were you?

COOK: No, I had a group of friends. I was living in New York, and we would come down summers, stay at home. And those were the days of Billie Holiday and Ella Fitzgerald and all that sort of thing and Kaye Ballard. And so we got to know, not the weekend ones like Ella Fitzgerald and all that, but Kaye Bal-lard would be down for a week or two weeks at a time and so we got friendly with them. And then when we got back to New York, we would go wherever they might be performing . . . just to say hi and to see them. So it was a world that I loved, you know.

KRAHULIK: How about the minstrel shows? You mention just briefly that your father was in them, did he help to produce them?

COOK: He didn't help to produce them, I think the Catholic church put them on, St. Peter's I believe, I may be wrong about this, but I think that was it. I think they were produced by the interlocutor, whoever he might happen to be. He was the man that asked these dumb questions—how did the chicken cross the road or did the chicken cross the road, why did the chicken cross the road—to get on the other side, would be the answer from the black man. And then they all would laugh and holler and hoot and bang tambourines. But interspersed with all of this would be music. My father was one of the end men, they call them end men, the fellows in blackface, [and he] would get up and do his number. It was just a lot of fun . . . until they were no longer. It wasn't only that it wasn't politically correct, I don't think that was totally the reason why it ended. I think the old timers got tired of doing it, people moved out of town, some people retired, some people died, and it was just one of those things that unfortunately dies out.

KRAHULIK: We spoke earlier about the shows and you had said that there were black people in town but they, but the shows were not meant to—

COOK: No, they were not meant in any way to defame or disparage the black people. They were not in any way thought about as different. There was one black family, the Roaches, Nate Roache, long dead, very good friend of my father's, he would come to our house and my mother would fry fish, she would fry these little tinker mackerel, Nate loved those tinker mackerel, he would eat them bones and all. So he spent a lot of time at the house. So no, there was no problem with them.

KRAHULIK: Where do you think the tolerance comes from in this town?

COOK: I don't know because—I can tell you this brief story where there wasn't this tolerance. My father was Portuguese. My mother was Portuguese and Yankee. Here's the background: My mother's father, Manuel Patrick, was a Portuguese man. My mother's mother was on the Yankee side, her name was Newcomb. Now big Yankees never liked the Portuguese, from what I understand, and I saw it right there in my own family when [great] grandma Newcomb became senile and my grandmother, Sadie, had to take her into her home. Now here is my grandmother Sadie, who is her daughter, and my grandfather, Manuel, who is Portuguese, is also there—[great] Grandma Newcomb, not knowing that Sadie is her daughter, is saying, "Oh I would like to know where my Sadie is, she has gone off with that God damn black Portygee somewhere, I think she went to Gloucester with that black Portygee." My grandfather would yell, "Shut your mouth, Sarah!" and so it would go. There was that intolerance. So the town was not born with tolerance.[1]

Commentary

In a town where performers, mostly in the form of drag queens, accord unusually high status as showmen and showgirls, and where native Portuguese cultures are slipping with each passing moment into the margins of community life, Portuguese American resident Marguerite Beata Cook held her own in front of the oral history video camera. Beata began immediately by putting forth two interrelated identities, one conscious and the other subconscious. With pride, she identified as an "insider," a native of Provincetown, Massachusetts, and she also, perhaps subconsciously, identified as a "rebel," a transgressive entertainer in her own right. Throughout her interview, she maneuvered deftly between the dual narrative identities of the "insider" and the "rebel."

My analysis of Beata Cook's narrative is methodological in its insistence that the oral history interviews I conducted in Provincetown, Massachusetts, in the 1990s warrant further investigation. In my book, *Provincetown: From Pilgrim Landing to Gay Resort*, I emphasized content rather than form and used an array of sources including, but not limited to, oral histories. The result was a cohesive narrative based on empirical evidence, which produced an expansive view of Provincetown's past.[2] I focused on change over time in a Portuguese fishing village turned gay resort town, rather than on how people explained or made sense of these changes.

By contrast, in this chapter I am more interested in the literary and performative strategies narrators like Beata Cook used to interpret and discuss the past. How did residents reconstruct dignity, triumph, or defeat in their acts of remembering? How do their stories illuminate not simply events that took place in the past but relationships between the politics of the past and those of the present? And how was I, the oral history interviewer, complicit in furthering some narratives while hindering others?

To explore questions such as these, I've turned to a subset of historians who focus on the methodological nuances of oral history practices. Luisa Passerini, for instance, pays exquisite detail not simply to the content revealed by memories but to the form memories take. What do certain stories mean in a wider cultural or symbolic context?[3] Drawing on the work of anthropologists and literary critics such as Bronislaw Malinowski, Raymond Williams, Antonio Gramsci, Lucien Febvre, and Mikhail Bakhtin, Passerini calls oral histories "highly relevant to historical analysis" as "first and foremost, statements of cultural identity in which memory continuously adapts received traditions to present circumstances."[4] Passerini led the field in arguing that personal narratives are valuable not only for their ability to reconstruct the past but also, and more important, for their ability to suggest how past events are related to present thoughts and sensibilities. For example, oral history transcripts might allow historians to comprehend better how a person or group of people make sense today of successful or disappointing experiences that took place years ago.[5]

Alessandro Portelli's work also focuses on form as well as content. Parsing the differences between written and oral sources—the former he calls "documents" and the latter "acts"—Portelli insists that oral histories reveal less about the details of an event and more about the meaning of an event both in the past and the present.[6] Memory, in this sense, might yield content, but the process of remembering, the telling, illuminates the investments narrators have in specific versions of the past. Far from static entities, oral histories, according to Portelli, help narrators conceptualize past situations and rationalize past choices.[7]

Taking Passerini and Portelli's cue, Daniel James devoted an entire book to the oral history of one working-class woman, Doña María Roldán. James sees oral histories as "cultural constructs," products of both the interviewer and the interviewee that stem from "possible roles, self-representations and available narratives." Only by analyzing these narratives in detail can historians comprehend fully the structure and logic of the stories and the meaning these stories held for the person recounting them.[8] Through oral histories, James argues, historians carry the ability to understand how people today process and articulate difficult memories of the past.[9]

Despite a paucity of book-length projects on American history that utilize a literary approach to oral history narratives, a number of scholars have contributed significantly to this methodology. Julia Cruikshank, for instance, argues that historians must heed "the very real *work* that stories do." Turning to the theories of Pierre Bourdieu, Walter Benjamin, Bakhtin, and others, Cruikshank supports the "transformative potential" of oral histories and notes how "social capital accumulates with practical competence that eventually reinforces who has the capacity to be listened to, believed, and obeyed—the entitlement to speak and to be heard."[10] Carolyn Steedman contends that oral histories are, ultimately, "about how people use the past to tell stories about their life" so that they can at least begin to "explain how they got to the place they currently inhabit."[11] Each of these positions lends itself to the idea that people tell stories to negotiate present circumstances with past experiences.

This last statement rings especially true in considering my interview with Beata Cook. My conversation with Beata reveals three dynamics that often prevail in oral history interviews. First, oral history interviews, regardless of recorders, cameras, or microphones, often generate an "informal conversational narrative, framed as personal experience stories, anecdotes, gossip."[12] Second, the topics, sequence of events, and time periods discussed are the result of a "compromise" between the interviewer and interviewee, the latter of whom may, if necessary, resort to creative uses of time and linguistic closure.[13] Third, the interviews themselves are best described as, in Portelli's words, "*learning* situations."[14] Rather than the expert scholar leading the narrator down the road to illumination, in my interview with Beata I learned from her refusals both at the time of the interview and afterward.

Outlining theoretical approaches to oral history as a mode of knowledge production frames my project, but I also want to convey a sense of my analytical practice. What am I looking for in the text that Beata and I generated? Relying heavily on Passerini and James, I am interested in both "recurrent self-representations" and "recurrent narrative patterns."[15] In the interstices of Beata's articulations lives the "tension between forms of behaviour and mental representations expressed in particular narrative guises," as Passerini puts it.[16] My approach investigates competing visions of the past; it notes the function of backstories, anecdotes, and asides; and it pays attention to macro community myths, as well as micro identity tales.[17] By shedding light on these tangled webs of articulation, the parts that make up the sum, I aim to deliver a greater understanding of the ways in which people jockey for power over the interpretation of their lives and over the way things in Provincetown were, are, and ought to be.

I begin my analysis as I often did my interviews, with the narrator's "origin" story. In the following exchange, Beata's first foot forward authenticates her, without a doubt, as an insider to Provincetown's unique community of natives, residents, and tourists:

KRAHULIK: Welcome, Beata. Let's start at the beginning; please tell us a little about when and where you were born.

COOK: Born in Provincetown, July 13, 1924. So that makes me seventy-two. In a house on Franklin Street, and delivered by Dr. Daniel Hebert, the famed town doctor, who delivered all of my mother's kids. I grew up here. Born and brought up in this town.

Establishing herself as a native resident, indeed literally born at home with Provincetown's only doctor in attendance, Beata positioned herself at the apex of a local pecking order—with natives on top, "wash-ashore" residents next (visitors who washed ashore and decided to stay), part-time and seasonal residents in third place (with workers slightly higher than second home owners), and tourists occupying the lowest rungs.[18] With this opening statement, Beata assumed a kind of innate epistemological authority bestowed only on those who can claim knowledge and authenticity based on length and form of residency at Land's End. This authority had evolved into a precious gem in Provincetown. It signaled a form of residential status that could not be purchased or stolen, and it was one of the last vestiges of native privilege in a town increasingly populated and owned by middle- and upper-class gay and lesbian outsiders. Later in the interview, Beata confirmed her enduring status: "I consider myself a native. You never are not a native if you were born and brought up in Provincetown." This kind of "biological predestination," or "the formula of 'having been born something,'" as Passerini calls it, is common in personal narratives and "often appears in the guise of boasting that where one comes from is better than anywhere else in the world."[19]

After establishing native status, Beata unleashed the flip side of her identity: the rebel creating gender trouble long before drag queens and others monopolized Provincetown's streets and beaches. Elaborating on her childhood activities—a recuperative gesture as Provincetown's turn into a gay resort rendered children and children's activities nearly invisible—Beata set the stage for her complementary persona. "I was always a tomboy, so my games were marbles. You have these marbles and you have what they call iron bullets [and] you knocked these iron bullets out of the ring. I was good at it too. Very good, better than the boys."

Through the two fundamental registers of her life story, the native and the rebel, Beata constructed "an image of herself that was worthy of authority."[20] Her narrative emphasized her own cultural prowess, heightened by the fact that gender bending is an esteemed trait in this particular locale. Her story was also community oriented. With nostalgic aplomb, Beata positioned the local Portuguese community as one that valued respect, discretion, and fairness through hard work and simple fun. Again, although Beata's story seems unique and noteworthy, other oral historians, such as Passerini, have also found a preponderance of working-class women who cast themselves as "'always having been rebels.'" Symbolically, this is critical, as Passerini writes, "The rebel stereotype, recurrent in many women's autobiographies, does not primarily aim to describe facts and actual behavior, but serves a markedly allegorical purpose. . . . It is a means of expressing problems of identity in the context of a social order oppressive of women."[21] I agree with Passerini's assessment that the woman rebel conveys something of the tension regarding identity, but for Beata the tension revolves less around her status as a woman and more around her gender as a tomboy and her questionable sexuality.

Throughout the interview, Beata established herself as a unique bridge to Provincetown's other claim to fame—its status as uniquely artistic, risqué, and queer—and she did so by relying on the trope of comedic anecdote. For instance, to "prove" that she was one of the boys and to demonstrate that the vision of herself that she created was consistent with her actions in the past, she relied on humor with a punch line. When I asked her how she met or mingled with local artists, she replied: "You'd see them on the beaches, [but] you didn't really get to know them that well. You didn't want to disturb them when they were painting because they were so absorbed in their painting." But then she elaborated by putting forth a backstory:

> But what I used to do—we lived up near George Elmer Browne's studio, and I think I mentioned that I used to go blueberrying up there. So a neighbor kid and I, we were about the same age, Joe Burgess, we called him Joe Blockie. Joe Blockie and I used to go up the hill to George Elmer Browne's studio, and he would say to me, "Boy, they got a lot of naked women in there posing. That artist is painting naked women." And we would be peeking in the windows to see the naked women at George Elmer Browne's before we went on blueberrying. [laughs] But then I never stopped and had any conversation with George Elmer Browne, but I knew full well who he was. He was quite well known.

This particular anecdote held symbolic weight in two familiar arenas. First, it showcased Beata as the rebel and communicated that not only was she "better than the boys," as she mentioned earlier, but also she eroticized women, just as boys did. Indeed, the erotic import of her voyeuristic tendencies at first escaped me. During the first half of the interview, I was not concerned with Beata's sexuality. I had met her for the first time that day, and I was not told whether she was gay or straight. Because no one had applied the "gay" tag to her as a potential interviewee (I used the snowball method for interviewing), I had assumed she was straight. In other words, I had bought into the dichotomy of the straight native versus the gay tourist. As Beata communicated her childhood exploits to me, her gender-transgressive persona did not resonate with my—at the time, meaning in the late 1990s—less pliable notions of coming out and identifying. Indeed, despite Beata's cues, I continued to think of her as straight. Moreover, the anecdote about spying functioned to position Beata, despite being a native, as controlling the gaze rather than being the object of the artist's gaze, as native Portuguese residents often were. Just before this anecdote, Beata mentioned that her father "had some pretty good stories about Eugene O'Neill and his antics." Taking after her father, Beata, too, had stories to tell that positioned Portuguese residents as the authors rather than the subjects of humorous tales or, in this case, of history.

Beata's portrait of herself as the native rebel gained texture as she discussed both her and Provincetown's golden years—the 1950s. Despite the fact that Provincetown had launched its own local witch hunt, Beata romanticized this period as "just a great fun time." So, too, on the one hand, her narrative challenges one of the town's long-standing dichotomies that positions straight, Portuguese natives who work in Provincetown in opposition to gay tourists who play in Provincetown. On the other hand, Beata reproduced this distinction continually by asserting the innate authority of native status and her position as both outsider (to the gay community) and insider (to Provincetown and its glorious entertainment culture). If Beata relied on the structure of the comedic anecdote to suggest her transgressions before, in the following story she also used performance to enhance the vividness and, hence, authenticity of the present and past moments.

Providing the perfect stage for Beata's acts of remembering was Provincetown's post–World War II nightclub scene. Immediately, Beata established herself as an authority figure:

> I was a big bar person in those days, I went to all of the places. I went to the Moors, the shows up there, they had Roger Kent playing the piano, sing-alongs. It was a ritual, here is what you'd did if you were in the club circuit. You went to the beach, you went to Herring Cove, and then after the beach about four o'clock you came down and you went to the Moors for their cocktail hour and did the sing-alongs with Roger Kent. That ended at five o'clock, that went four to five. Five o'clock you hightailed it to Weathering Heights where Phil Bayonne was putting on a show, and he did a little review type thing. He used to have all his waiters and waitresses a part of it, he didn't pay them for the extra work, but he made them a part of it. And he did the trapeze thing. He would come down from the ceiling on a trapeze

with a great big wide hat on. He was quite, quite a showman actually. Then, when you were through with that, you went to the Town House where again there was a sing-along to a piano and everybody would sing. It was all the musicals, Broadway musicals and a lot of show tunes.

Beata provided closure with the following statement: "It was just a great fun time. Of course there was no disco. There was no loud rock, there was none of that in those days." Indeed, the 1950s, not today, brought out the best in show at Land's End.

The story did not end there, however. Beata also used humor to poke fun at the tourists attempting to marginalize her or make her feel somehow primitive. In this way, although they exposed her at the time as somewhat backward, she overturns this now, in an aptly carnivalesque way, by revealing their ignorance and her authority.[22] At the conclusion of the story, she chuckles, providing closure with a proverbial last laugh.

> People would introduce me to someone in the bar and say, "Hey, this is Beata, she's a native, you know?" like you feel like you ought to do a native dance or something. "She was born and brought up here." Nobody can believe anyone was born and brought up here . . . to believe that somebody was hanging out where they hang out, that was not put away in their own houses doing their own thing, was a native, was hard for them to believe . . . they would get all excited when they would find out that I was a native. "She's a real native, you know."[laughs]

Beata not only refused to be marginalized by gay tourists in the past but also refused to allow this gay interloper, meaning the intrusive academic, to pigeonhole her identity in the present. Indeed, despite my best efforts, Beata held on to the coherence of her authority in discussing the way Provincetown was, is, and ought to be. After hearing the now familiar butch coming of age story about being a tomboy, and listening to Beata regale me with stories about the glorious day of Broadway musical sing-alongs, I started to wonder if I was missing something about Beata's sexual preferences and community alignments.[23] My interviewing style at the time—I was in my late twenties and still a graduate student—was to ask nonthreatening questions that would open up rather than close down conversations. Some might say I was being elusive and not direct enough; I focused on being strategic yet amiable. Consistent with this demeanor, I tried to elicit Beata's sexual identity using a few subtle questions. My first pitch:

KRAHULIK: So, what did you like so much, you are a native Portuguese girl, growing up in town, what did you like so much about these shows and the nightclubs?

COOK: Well I loved it because I loved show business, I loved the minstrel shows, my father was in them. I loved, I just loved entertainment, I love anything that reeked of entertainment and singing and it's a damn shame I can't carry a tune because I knew all the words to all the songs and I would sing them. And Dad would say, Dad used to call me Tommy Tucker, and he used to say to my mother, "By the jingles, Ninsy," my mother's name was Nelly, he called her Ninsy, nickname for everybody. "By the jingles, Ninsy, my Tommy knows the words to all the songs, and they all sound like 'Turkey in the Straw.'"

My interest, Beata insisted, was in show business, not queer business. Thus, after denying a queer component, she returned immediately to a gender-transgressive theme, not only with her Tommy Tucker anecdote but also by following this anecdote with an aside wherein she mentions living with the same woman in New York City and in Provincetown. "And then by this time, the days of the Atlantic House, and Reggie getting these name people down and all, I was living with a girl who was a hostess at the A-House. I was living in New York and we would come down summers, stay at home."

   With the distance of twelve years since I conducted this interview, I can detect now that Beata and I were engaged in our own duel of sorts during this delicate negotiation. Having latched onto the idea that the tomboy narrative was the precursor to a coming-out story, I attempted get Beata to out herself as a lesbian. Meanwhile, Beata had distanced herself from the gay community—"No, I do not think *they* liked queer very much. I don't know because I was too young to ask *them* what they thought"—while also embracing many aspects of gay life in Provincetown. Toward the end of the interview, I tried one last time to see if Beata would come out as a lesbian. And she replied with a disciplining, but genial response. Note how many times she utters the word *no*:

KRAHULIK: And now you chose not to marry?

COOK: No, no, no, oh no, oh no.

KRAHULIK: That wasn't for you?

COOK: Not for me, no, no, no, no, no, no. In fact, many years later I saw a boy, then a man, that I had dated slightly in high school. And so I went my way, I went away and I went here and went there and he married. And I saw him at Cookies Tap one night. And he says, "Oh Jesus, Beata, you and I should have gotten married." And I said, "Oh yeah? You would be in the barroom drinking, and I would be home taking care of the house, no, no, no, thank you very much." [laughs] No, no, no, no, that was not my cup of tea at all. No, I want to move around and I wanted to wander, and I wanted to travel and I wanted to go wherever I wanted to go when I wanted to go there. And I was never crazy about kids, anyway, still am not. Not crazy about them at all.

In the end, Beata positioned herself as a tomboy and an "independent woman," a native rebel, not a native queer.[24] The latter would have torn the fabric of her oral narrative, while the former allowed her to retain the innate rights and privileges of residential status. Native rebels understood the town's priorities—frugality, modesty, diplomacy—even as they transgressed some of the town's neater dichotomies. To reinforce this understanding, Beata also externalized the contemporary gay community as inappropriately outlandish: "There were always gay people here, there just weren't as many, and in those earlier days, they were not so flamboyant. For instance, the queens would not run down the street with their little pocketbooks in their hands and their high heels, they just didn't do it, it was unheard of. They might do it in a private party, but they do not do it on Commercial Street. And they certainly weren't kissing and holding hands on the street."

Beata distanced herself from specifically queer entertainment by noting that she loved all entertainment, even the minstrel shows. Later in the interview, I brought us back to the topic of the minstrel shows—as much as Beata was interested in maintaining coherence, I was interested in learning how residents today reconciled a thorny cultural past. Beata began by saying that the Catholic church produced the shows, a move that might have been meant to legitimize their presence—how could the shows be anything but "Christian" if they stemmed from members of the cloth? She continued by explaining in detail the role of the interlocutor, the jokes that were told, the blackface characters who became the butt of the jokes, and the songs that were sung: "'When the Sun Goes Down in Dixie and the Moon Begins to Rise,' I can just see them doing it now, it was just a lot of fun," she reminisced. To explain why the minstrel shows ended, an explanation that was not solicited, Beata used an aside to neatly insert the backstory and to locate the seat of power with the Portuguese residents responsible for the shows. Like the decline of the Portuguese ritual of the Blessing of the Fleet, the decline of the Portuguese-led minstrel shows took place not because other political players exerted influence but because, in her words, "The old timers got tired of doing it. It was just one of the those things that unfortunately dies out."

Beata evaded the thorny issue of covert racism in Provincetown—a potential tear more than a wrinkle in her hometown's reputation as exceptionally democratic—by adding that the shows were "not meant in any way to defame or disparage the black people." In fact, she put forth, "There were very few black families that lived here, but there were black families nevertheless and they were an integral part of the community." To prove this she noted that Nate Roache, a black man who came from a well-known family, used to spend time at her house, fraternizing with her father and enjoying her mother's cooking. "To my knowledge, I can't speak to all the black people, but to my knowledge," she concluded, "they didn't object to it." Beata's story tells us a fair amount about the actual shows but even more about the tension that still exists regarding the symbolic violence that the shows enacted—at some level, Beata acknowledges that, in her words, "political correctness" became an issue, but she is able to retain Provincetown's coherence as "friendly, amicable, and democratic" by assuring her listeners that celebrating the minstrel shows was acceptable social practice because the town's black residents "didn't object to it." My empirical research would find that they did not approve of it, either. In fact, one of the Roaches wrote several letters to the editor protesting the minstrel shows. I included these letters—along with opposing letters that supported the minstrels—in my book to piece together a more complicated picture of Provincetown's postwar linguistic community.[25] In the context of my interview with Beata, the value of this empirical evidence resides in its ability to say something about racial tensions not only in the past but also as they are conceived in the present.

Ultimately, Beata's split narrative identity as the native rebel and the comic conventions she deployed as she regaled her audience with one anecdote after another allowed her to make several important gestures. Her native authority and participation in Provincetown's 1950s entertainment culture meant she could celebrate a gay past (in the clubs) *and*, at the same time, be critical of a "flamboyant" gay present. Interestingly, by showcasing the entertainment aspects of the clubs rather than the opportunities they afforded for sexual exploration, Beata was able to position herself as an authority figure of gay male culture even as she distanced herself from a fixed sexual identity. Her performative role in the interview also earned her no small measure of cultural capital and went recognized in an economy that relentlessly celebrates staged performances. I was entirely complicit in this not only in deciding to interview her but also because I put this interview on Cape Cod's local cable television channel. Beata stopped me on the street more than once to tell me that she was, indeed, famous now. In this way, she and I put a different vision of Provincetown into circulation. This vision reframed Provincetown's "golden era" as taking place in the 1950s, not today, and it interrupted the straight native versus queer tourist dichotomy. During a time when Portuguese residents felt increasingly disempowered in their own hometown, Beata and I—a pair of tomboys—restored them as representative of Provincetown, the landfall of the *Mayflower* Pilgrims and the home of America's peculiar form of democracy.

Notes

1. Marguerite Beata Cook, video recording with Karen Krahulik, Provincetown, January 22, 1997, Provincetown Public Library Oral History Collection, Provincetown, Massachusetts.
2. Karen Christel Krahulik, *Provincetown: From Pilgrim Landing to Gay Resort* (New York: New York University Press, 2005).
3. Luisa Passerini, *Fascism in Popular Memory: The Cultural Experience of the Turin Working Class* (Cambridge: Cambridge University Press, 1987), 4. See also Richard Bauman, *Story, Performance, and Event* (Cambridge: Cambridge University Press, 1986).
4. Passerini, *Fascism in Popular Memory*, 17.
5. Ibid., 5.
6. Alessandro Portelli, *The Order Has Been Carried Out: History, Memory, and the Meaning of a Nazi Massacre in Rome* (New York: Palgrave Macmillan, 2003), 9.
7. Alessandro Portelli, *The Death of Luigi Trastulli and Other Stories: Form and Meaning in Oral History* (Albany: State University of New York Press, 1991), 50. On remembering versus recollection, see Daniel James, *Dona Maria's Story* (Durham, NC: Duke University Press, 2000), 154, 219.
8. James, *Dona Maria's Story*, 124.
9. Ibid., 208.
10. Julia Cruikshank, "Oral History, Narrative Strategies, and Native American Historiography: Perspectives from the Yukon Territory, Canada," in Nancy Shoemaker, ed., *Clearing a Path: Theorizing the Past in Native American Studies* (New York: Routledge, 2002), 6, 12, 21.
11. Carolyn Steedman, *Landscape for a Good Woman: A Story of Two Lives* (London: Virago, 1986), 6.
12. James, *Dona Maria's Story*, 134.

13. Portelli, *The Death,* 64, 66.
14. Portelli, *The Death,* x.
15. See Passerini, *Fascism in Popular Memory,* 18–31; James, *Dona Maria's Story,* 160, 183.
16. Passerini, *Fascism in Popular Memory,* 31.
17. On the function of punch lines, see Bauman, *Story,* 59. Bauman's intellectual debt here is to Erving Goffman, *Forms of Talk* (Philadelphia: University of Pennsylvania Press, 1981).
18. On "wash-ashores," see Krahulik, *Provincetown,* 14.
19. Passerini, *Fascism in Popular Memory,* 24, 25.
20. Penelope Ekert in James, *Dona Maria's Story,* 182.
21. See Passerini, *Fascism in Popular Memory,* 17, 28.
22. Here I am referring to Bakhtin's analysis of the topsy-turvy world of the carnival, when hierarchical order is reversed, even if momentarily. Natalie Zemon Davis's "woman on top" theory also comes to mind. See M. M. Bakhtin, *Rabelais and His World* (Cambridge, MA: MIT Press, 1968); and Natalie Zemon Davis, "Women on Top: Symbolic Sexual Inversion and Political Disorder in Early Modern Europe," in Barbara A. Babcock, ed., *The Reversible World: Symbolic Inversion in Art and Society* (Ithaca, NY: Cornell University Press, 1978), 147–90.
23. On the prevalence and predictability of the tomboy as butch coming of age story, see Kath Weston, *Render Me, Gender Me: Lesbians Talk Sex, Class, Color, Nation, Studmuffins . . .* (New York: Columbia University Press, 1996).
24. Provincetown was host to many "independent women" during the first half of the twentieth century. See Krahulik, *Provincetown,* 13, 86–105, 162–68.
25. Krahulik, *Provincetown,* 64–67.

3

QUEER FAMILY STORIES

Learning from Oral Histories with Lesbian Mothers and Gay Fathers from the Pre-Stonewall Era

Daniel Rivers

Oral history by Daniel Rivers with Vera Clarice Martin, Apache Junction, Arizona, September 2, 2006

This is an excerpt from a three-day interview that I conducted in 2006 with Vera Martin, a longtime activist in the Los Angeles lesbian community. Martin raised her children in that city as an African American lesbian mother in the 1950s. Her recollections of growing up in Louisiana, marriage, lesbian spaces in postwar Los Angeles, and the struggles she faced as a lesbian mother in the pre-Stonewall era vividly illustrate historical intersections of race, sexuality, gender, and reproduction. Her story shows how people resisted heteronormativity, classism, sexism, and racism and created queer possibilities in the pre-Stonewall era.[1]

DANIEL RIVERS: Vera, if you would give me your full name for the record.

VERA MARTIN: Vera Clarice Martin.

RIVERS: And what was your date of birth?

MARTIN: 6/18/23.

RIVERS: And where were you born?

MARTIN: In a place called Natchez. It's a very historical place in Mississippi. My mother was a student at a Black college there, called Natchez College, I think is the name of it. She lived in a guardian household in Louisiana and wanted to get out of it. She gave me away when I was a month old to these same guardians, and that is something that I have never forgiven her for. I lived in Tensas Parish, the capital of which was Saint Joseph's. I would say that the population was probably fifteen hundred. If you counted all the chickens and the dogs, you might come up with two thousand. As a child, before I had to go and stay on my farm all the time, I lived in St. Joseph's with the mother of the female guardian. This woman that I lived with was nine years old when the slaves were freed, and she married a man who was a preacher. I had pictures of him—he always wore a top hat and that coat with a split in it that well-dressed people wore. He was a traveling minister.

When I was five, I was sent to be with her [Martin's mother]. I went in May and stayed until the following Christmas holidays. The male guardian came and got me and took me back to Louisiana. I didn't see her again until I was twelve. [After that] I didn't see her until I was sixteen, and by that time she was in California. I didn't trust that husband that she had. I was afraid of him because I knew he was going to molest me. So I got married at eighteen, 'cause I didn't know how else to get out of that house. I didn't know there was such a place as Phyllis Wheatley. I didn't know there was such a place as Sojourner Truth where I could have gone to live with a house mother, and I could have worked part-time and gone to school part-time. I didn't know how to do that. I didn't know enough about the city.

RIVERS: Do you remember having crushes or being in love with friends when you were young?

MARTIN: I had this best friend whose name was Camille, and she's the only person those guardians ever let come spend any time with me. We just had the grandest time. We just had a grand time.

RIVERS: Were you lovers?

MARTIN: Oh god, we just had a ball. We didn't know what to call it. We didn't even know what it was. We were just playing grown-ups.

RIVERS: So you get married when you're eighteen; tell me about that—you're in LA at the time . . .

MARTIN: I just couldn't figure out how to make my life any better as long as I was in that house, and they fought a lot, and that was terrifying to me. He [Martin's first husband] kept calling and coming to visit. He was trying to get this on another level. He was really heading towards sex. Well, see, in my head as a child growing up, all I ever heard the grown-ups say was "She's not going to be anything; she's going to be just like her mother." Well, I didn't know what that meant, but as I got older, I concluded that that meant that I was going to get pregnant. I was hell-bent that was not going to happen to me. I wasn't going to end up marrying somebody that I didn't want to marry. So when he got this relationship going off towards this sexual encounter, I just stopped dead in my tracks and froze up. He would take me to an outing and bring me back home and dump me and go see the other girlfriend who was going to play the game. I guess he really liked me, so one day the subject came up again, and he said, "Why don't we get married?"And I said, "Well, we can do that." So we ran away—we went to Yuma.

He went to the military when my baby was six weeks old. He had a first cousin who was a lesbian. Some of the women that she was running around with were girls that I had gone to school with. I was always begging her to let me go with them, wherever they would go. She said, "I'm not going to get into . . . no, I'm not going to do that." This was a diverse group; two of the girls that used to come to the house were white and had been in one of my classes when I was in high school. They would go out on Friday night or Saturday night. I don't know what they did or where they went, but they had a good time, and I wanted to go. Like a kid looking through the store window at a candy store. [My daughter's] memory is that I always had gay people around and [when] I had parties that were basically heterosexual parties, 'cause I'm married at the time, I invited my gay friends. I was always gay friendly, always gay friendly.

He [Martin's husband] came back in December of 1945, which was a total surprise. I didn't expect him to come home. I expected him to get out of the military, but I didn't expect him to come home as he had so many women all over the country, and one in particular that he was literally engaged to. She was a student at Tallahassee down in Florida or Alabama or somewhere, and I thought he was going to go and marry this person. So when he showed up in my door, I had to do a lot of tap dancing. I must say, I was a bit relieved because it was going to support my philosophy of my kid having two parents. Biggest mistake I ever made in my life.

[Here Martin briefly discusses sleeping with another woman in the mid-1950s after having her son in 1953 and leaving her husband in 1955.]

And then I just dismissed the whole notion. And then in the late fifties, I met this beautiful, beautiful Japanese woman [Kay] who had married an African American man during the war. He had been stationed in Japan and was from New Orleans. That's where he took her. It was a miserable, miserable time for her. She had two kids—a girl and a boy. [Martin's friend] Chuck said, "I've got this wonderful girl that I want you to meet—she really needs a good friend, and you make such a good friend." So he told her about me. She invited me to dinner and invited him, too. She called me at the office, and she invited me to dinner again, and there was just the two of us there. She talked about two women that I knew were lesbians. In the meanwhile, while I was there—she was a call girl—some guys called her to set up a date, and she didn't want me to hear this conversation. But I heard enough of it that I immediately knew what was going on, so I try and make her comfortable. I said, "Did you really want to confirm that date, because I can leave," to let her know it was okay.

So then, by the time I saw her the next time, she let her guard down. We talked about it, and I said, "I'm your friend and I'll be here now." We lived about eight miles apart, and she'd call me up sometimes. She'd get very, very depressed because she came from a very upscale family in Tokyo, and she would say, "Oh, if my mother knew what I was doing she'd just have a fit." She would call me sometimes at two or three o'clock in the morning. One night, Kay and I went clubbing; we went way up on Sunset [to a club] called the Moulin Rouge. The drinks were just lined up in front of me. I was trying to drink all these damn martinis, and I hate martinis. Well, by the end of the night, I got us this cab to go home. We got home. I got hysterical. We were at her house. I got hysterical, and she was in the process of comforting me, and the next thing I knew we were having mad sex. We were great partners, lovers, for almost a year.

[Discussing the circle of women that Martin got to know through Kay]

RIVERS: Most of these women were lesbians?

MARTIN: Yeah, yeah.

RIVERS: Was this when you went out with Kay and hung out with Mimi, Juanita, and Trudy? Did these women hang out in lesbian bars in LA? Was that part of the scene?

MARTIN: Sure, there was a bar on—I believe it's Sixth and Vermont or Eighth and Vermont—called the If Club. Then there was a really nice one on Melrose and La Brea called David. They were basically men's bars, but women were welcome because both of them served dinner. You could go there and have this great dinner with all this great atmosphere.

RIVERS: So you and Kay would go out to the clubs?

MARTIN: Yeah, we'd make this grand entrance . . . we'd always make this grand entrance when we go to these bars, and of course all the men were sending drinks. We'd just have them lined up. Kay couldn't drink a glass of lemonade—she turned pink.

RIVERS: And both of you would dress high femme.

MARTIN: Oh man, oh man. . . . We were dressed to the nines.

RIVERS: And were there a lot of butch-femme lesbians in these circles?

MARTIN: Oh yeah.

RIVERS: Did you all get hassled for being two femmes out together?

MARTIN: Oh yeah, "What in the hell are you, AC/DC?" whatever that was.

RIVERS: How did women explain to each other that they were in the life when they were around straight folks?

MARTIN: Well the first thing that you would do is say, "Have you ever been to such and such a club?" They had all kinds of signals—they had a certain way they wore a handkerchief—they would say, "Well, have you been to such and such a club?" They would wear their keys in a certain pocket—let them hang out, then all kinds of crazy signals. If you were a femme and you saw the person with the keys or the handkerchief or whatever, you'd just flirt. Yeah, you'd just flirt. There was a club in town in Hollywood called Peanuts. We went to Peanuts a lot because both straight and gay went there. They used to get some pretty good fracases going on in there, because the straight guys would come over.

RIVERS: So, I found myself wondering—thinking about—internalized homophobia. What that was like for you and Kay? You become lovers, and during that time Kay has two kids, you have two kids. What were your concerns about being around the kids? I mean, did you keep your love relationship totally separate from them?

MARTIN: Well, the oldest of the kids was my daughter, and she was old enough to be the babysitter for the other kids. So my two kids and I would get in the car, and we would go to Kay's house and then get them all settled for the evening. Then we would go out. And it worked, you know, I don't remember us ever talking about it and having major concerns about it. It was just—she loved my kids, and my kids loved her. My kids loved her kids; her kids loved my kids.

[Here Martin replies to a question I ask about the kids going with them when she and Kay spent time with other lesbians in the late 1950s.]

MARTIN: Well, you know, none of the rest of them had any. We were the two that had the kids, which also made us stand out because they weren't tolerant of the fact that we had kids. My sense of it was that the children were a bother. They decided on the spur of the moment, "Let's go do this." We had to think about what are we gonna do. They had no patience for that—there wasn't supposed to be any kids. And you know what? That's going on today. I've heard many lesbians say they would never get involved with a woman who had children. Even in later years, even after the revolution, I've heard lesbians say that if you got men and had kids and you weren't a real lesbian.

I used to do panels that we defined as lifetime lesbians—meaning lesbians who had never been married, who were insightful enough, strong enough, to go on with their life and let their sexuality take them where they wanted to go—with those who are so brainwashed by the mores of society that they did get married and have children. They would tell their stories. The lifetime lesbians have the notion that they are the heroines and that the ones that were naïve enough or browbeaten enough were the weak ones, and that they were superior to these people. My contention is that they are all heroines. They all had to live in a very dangerous place and to give up a lot. The ones who got married and had those children, when they decided to make that 180-degree turn—everything was at stake. That took a lot of courage because you had that sense of motherhood. You felt you had to protect those children. You couldn't go around making rash decisions and not include the children in the process. Whereas if you never got married, and you never had children, you only had to think about what you wanted to do and how much flak you wanted to take from society.

We knew that we had to certainly be careful and to keep the knowledge that we had kids very quiet, very quiet, because you never knew in that culture of call girls. It was very competitive, and you never knew who was going to use that information to destroy you—to turn your life upside down. [Here Martin discusses the first of two scares she had about losing custody of her children due to accusations of lesbianism.]

Yeah, well, that was when I was seeing Kay. Somebody that knew me saw me and Kay at a bar [the If Club]. It was somebody that he [Martin's ex-husband] knew. Even if I was dating a man, and he got the rumor, he would make a point of showing up at my house and acting as if he still lived there with the idea that this would chase the guy off. I said to her [Kay], "That was somebody who knew me when my husband and I were together and they are still in touch." Now my head was going a mile a minute. I thought he would use a pay phone and call them, and the next thing I knew I would be looking at his face. It was not okay to be publicized. You really kept it under wraps. As a matter of fact, in those years a few people that I knew who were in the lesbian community, they always found a gay man as an escort, and one that wasn't too effeminate so they would look real—women who had jobs that they didn't want to lose. My fear was first of all losing my kid, and the other part of that was the scandal was going to spill over on my job, and I could very well have lost my job.

[Here Martin discusses Kay's tragic death at twenty-nine, a year after they had met.] She died at the age of twenty-nine. She got sick; they took her to the hospital. They left her in the lobby for hours. By the time they gave her a room and got the doctor there, it was too late. She hemorrhaged to death. I was having a birthday party for my son. His birthday is in October. I had rented this merry-go-round and a clown, and she was supposed to come and bring her kids. My phone rang about noon. It was her housekeeper. Pinky said, "Vera, this is Pinky," and I said, "Well, how are you, and what's going on?" And she said, "Did you hear about Kay?"And I said, "No." She said, "Well"—this was on a Saturday—"I've been trying to get you since early yesterday," she said. "Kay's dead." Well, I dropped the phone and fainted. So we had a brief service for her and sent her ashes to her parents. Her ex-husband waltzed in and got the house and custody of the kids.

Oh, I wanted those kids so bad. She had specifically told a caregiver—Annette was her name—"Annette, if anything ever happens to me, I want you and Vera to take care of my kids." Annette really, really tried, but she had nothing to stand on because even if it'd been in writing, it wasn't going to help, because in reality, in the United States, she [Kay] was still married to Cesar. She just had a divorce out of Mexico, which was useless. [Here Martin discusses her marriage in 1963 to E., a man who she knew had same-sex relationships himself, to diffuse any custody threats from her first husband and to keep her job.]

When I got that rumor that he was thinking about going after me, I just ran in the closet and nailed the door. My daughter had gotten married at the end of her first year at Long Beach State, and the company had shipped them off to Columbus, Ohio. By the time they got back to California she was twenty—the baby was born when she was nineteen. At the time they got back, she was twenty. I was calling her two or three times a week in Ohio: "When you get ready to come home, please let me know that you are on your way. Don't go to the place. Come home—I will move out the very next day, and you will live here." Well, they didn't. The doorbell rings, and I go to the door, and there stands my daughter and my granddaughter and my son-in-law. Yeah, so the next morning I got up and called my office and said, "I have a family emergency, and I won't be to work for a couple of days." I went outside and started looking for an apartment. I left T. [Martin's son] at the house with R [Martin's daughter] because I didn't want him to have to change schools. When the word got out—their father—the rumors started again. So I had to hurry out, and every morning I would get out, get him dressed and take him to her house and let him go to school from her house to head them off, because at this point he was married again. All I needed to do was end up in court by myself with all this crap he could bring into court. And he's now married.

RIVERS: Did he have any idea at that time that you were a lesbian?

MARTIN: He must have because whenever he ran into me, he would make statements like, "I know what you're doing."

RIVERS: When you heard the rumors again that time when R got home, you were scared that he would bring that into it? That was about lesbianism?

MARTIN: Yeah, I was scared to death. I was scared to death, so I went over and got T. and all of his clothes and brought him over to my place. I would get up in the morning early enough to take him and dropped them off at her house. He would have breakfast with her and then walked to school from the house. In the evening, I would come by from work and pick them up and take them home. When I got married the second time, I married this man who'd been living in the closet all his life trying his best not to admit to himself that he was a gay man. I had done all the research I needed to do. I worked in the Civic Center for many years. I worked in vital records for many years in the recorder's office. So a short time after I met him and found out that there were three marriages already, I went downtown and pulled every one of the divorce papers and read them. Every damn one of them said "irreconcilable differences." That's always a buzzword for sexual incompatibility. I knew exactly what was going on. I knew exactly what was going on. There was a man that I am now still friendly with who worked on his job with him at that time that he was having a fling with. This is a white guy. I met him in 1962 before I really married E. He represented cover, and even though he would never admit it, I was a cover for him, too.

I would chide him now and then because I knew what was going on. When he died, I was cleaning out the garage, which was the place which he used as his workshop for the upholstery he did, because he did that beautiful tucking like on period furniture. It was the Louis XIV furniture—that was his specialty. He had more work than he could handle, because he had a regular nine-to-five, and he did this in his spare time. He spent a lot of time in the garage, and when he died, I found his batch of letters. Man, they were the hottest love letters you ever read in your life. But I never betrayed him. I never said a word to his family about it and never said a word. As a matter of fact, somebody called me one night from LA that knew me because they had met him and recognized him. He was at this club with one of the flings, and they called me up to tell me. I said, "Oh really? Well, tell him hello, and I hope he's having a good time." I knew he was going there. I thought it was all right because I was getting what I wanted. I had a male figure for T. who absolutely adored him. And I had somebody to go with me every time I had to go someplace in those different organizations that I belonged to. Everybody in the community thought we were the perfect couple.

RIVERS: So when you say that you slam the closet door shut in 1963 after that second scare, this is a question that comes up for me. How much of marrying E. was about, "Look, I just can't risk this—I have to . . ."

MARTIN: I didn't feel safe. I just was too much of a coward to risk having that custody thing come up again. I was working in the recorder's office. That was really a homophobic place, so I had to worry about the scandal of the custody suit and the scandal of the custody suit causing me to lose my job, not to mention the holy terror of losing my son. We got married in Vegas. We went in an entourage. He had a brand-new Thunderbird. [The] couple that was there the day that he first brought this up [getting married] had a brand-new Thunderbird. Boy, did we create a sensation when we pulled up in front of the Stardust Hotel to check in.[2]

Commentary

Malcolm X, in a 1964 speech, said, "History is a people's memory," arguing that reclamation of one's historical past was essential to liberation struggle. Without a clear historical self-understanding, he noted, groups fighting repression could not challenge dominant cultural paradigms that left them powerless.[3] This sentiment has been at the heart of scholarship on lesbian, gay, bisexual, and transgender (LGBT) history in the United States since the early 1970s. However, documenting LGBT historical presence in the United States is challenged by both the obscuring effect of homophobic repression and the difficulties inherent in looking backward across the sharp historical divide separating the pre-liberation and postliberation eras—one that includes changing definitions of sexual identity. Oral histories have been crucial in addressing these challenges and constructing pre-Stonewall LGBT histories in the United States, particularly social histories attempting complex portraits of everyday lives that lay outside heterosexual norms before the late 1960s. In this essay, I draw from my own work on the history of lesbian and gay parents and their children, focusing in particular on an interview I conducted with Vera Martin, to show how oral histories in pre-Stonewall LGBT history in general and LGBT family history more specifically illuminate historical intersections between race, class, gender, sexuality, and the family.

Oral histories have been a vital part of LGBT activism and community self-understanding. The importance of self-documentation itself is rooted in lesbian and gay liberation. The coming out story was a commonly understood marker of lesbian and gay life in the 1970s and an important part of a gay and lesbian liberation-era politics of visibility. The publication of collections of interviews such as *The New Lesbians* (1977) and *The Coming Out Stories* (1980) marked the focus on personal testimony in lesbian feminist and gay male communities of the period.[4] In addition, as LGBT history emerged as a field of research and community inquiry in the 1970s and 1980s, there was increased interest in chronicling the experiences of lesbian and gay elders. This grew out of a growing internal criticism within lesbian and gay liberation movements that they were too youth-oriented, as well as the despair of the first years in the struggle against HIV/AIDS. Books published in this era include *Quiet Fire* (1985) and *Long Time Passing* (1986).[5]

These oral traditions mirrored a reliance on oral evidence among early gay and lesbian historians such as Jonathan Ned Katz, Allan Bérubé, John D'Emilio, and Lillian Faderman.[6] During this period, LGBT archives nationwide became repositories for local and national oral history collections, and a number of regional oral history projects were founded.[7] In 1993, Elizabeth Lapovsky Kennedy and Madeline Davis published *Boots of Leather, Slippers of Gold*, an ethnographic history of butch-femme communities in Buffalo, New York, from 1930 to the late 1960s, based on the Buffalo Women's Oral History Project. A complex local history, imbued with a sense of respect for its participants, *Boots of Leather, Slippers of Gold* inspired the push toward oral history–based, community studies in LGBT history that followed its publication.[8]

In part, the importance of oral histories for LGBT historians reflects the specific historical character of homophobia: LGBT cultures have been, to a greater or lesser degree, underground cultures; sexual minorities have long hidden for fear of legal persecution and social condemnation or lived as social outcasts. People who frequented lesbian or gay bars in the 1950s or 1960s risked incarceration and loss of employment. This atmosphere led to traditions of code and guarded secrecy. One woman I interviewed, Annalee Stewart, who fell in love with her partner in Minnesota in the late 1950s, told me that although they had two close female friends they suspected were a couple, the four women never discussed their relationships with each other; in fact, when they adopted children in 1970, neither my interviewee nor her partner had ever mentioned their lesbianism to anyone else.[9] As a result of this kind of secrecy, historians have relied heavily on oral history to supplement the relatively sparse material record of gay and lesbian lives, particularly in the pre-Stonewall era.

The effect of this historical silencing and repression is particularly acute in the case of lesbian and gay family history. In the postwar era, media images and political voices emphasized a heterosexual, middle-class, nuclear-family model of domesticity in which women were homemakers and men were breadwinners. This strongly heterosexual culture elided lesbians and gay men and rendered lesbian mothers and gay fathers completely invisible. Mainstream society cast same-sex sexuality and desire as antithetical to parenting, which it understood exclusively as an outgrowth of heterosexual intimacy. Most lesbian and gay parents remained underground during these years, in contrast to the period following the emergence of lesbian and gay liberation movements. While documents exist that reveal parts of this history, they often provide only small glimpses of the struggles of lesbian and gay parents. For instance, while an arrest record might tell us that a man charged with "lewd vagrancy"—in this case a euphemism for same-sex sexuality—was a father, it tells us nothing about his fears of being ostracized from his children or the way he himself identified his own sexuality.

Oral histories help us understand how lesbian mothers and gay fathers were personally affected by homophobia. In a three-day interview, Vera Martin told me about her experiences as an African American woman raising two children in the 1950s, first in a heterosexual marriage and then while loving another woman. My discussions with Martin and with other lesbian and gay parents of this era illuminate the historical connections between reproduction and sexuality. By the late 1960s, lesbian mothers and gay fathers were fighting custody battles, and court records from this period reveal a powerful nationwide judicial bias against lesbian and gay parents. But without the recollections of lesbian and gay parents from the pre-Stonewall era, we would not know that many lesbian and gay parents during the immediate postwar era also lived in fear of being separated from their children. Through their life histories, we can see that the injunction against lesbian and gay parenting has been a central structural element of heterosexist prejudice for decades. It was, in fact, so strong that it was largely unspoken; the heterosexuality of the family was a naturalized cultural assumption until post-Stonewall communities openly challenged it. However, lesbian and gay parents of the pre-Stonewall era lived in contradiction to this assumption, and their recollections show us that they were acutely aware of their own marginality and the dangers they lived with during this period.

Understanding this experience allows us to put the modern struggle for LGBT parental and domestic rights in its proper historical context. Seeing the right to raise children as a fundamental civil right historically denied generations of lesbians and gay men complicates the argument that the concerted effort by the modern LGBT freedom struggle for familial, domestic, and marital rights is a recent, assimilationist, and homonormative one that contradicts the historical radicalism of the liberation era.[10] Rather, pre-Stonewall life stories of lesbian mothers and gay fathers show that these battles have long been at the heart of sexual minority experience in the United States. These histories contextualize the dramatic legal struggles of the 1970s and help us understand the place of domestic and family rights in today's mainstream LGBT freedom struggle.

Martin's story also illustrates how systems of prejudice against gay men and lesbians intersected with racism and classism and how reproduction has been socially configured through categories of race, class, gender, and sexuality. She described falling in love with a Japanese American woman named Kay in Los Angeles in 1958 and living in fear that her ex-husband would use her lesbianism to take away her two children. Like women in the later liberation era, this fear restricted Martin and Kay's activities, but unlike women in the 1970s, they had no lesbian mother activist organizations to turn to for help. In addition to being afraid of losing custody of her children, Martin recalled being afraid of losing her job as a county employee. These fears crystallized when an acquaintance of her ex-husband saw Martin and Kay in the If Club, a Los Angeles lesbian bar, in 1959. The couple stopped going out to lesbian bars after this incident. When Kay tragically died that same year, Martin was aware that she had no chance of raising Kay's children with her own, even though that was what both women explicitly wanted.

As lesbian mothers of color in 1950s Los Angeles, Martin and Kay were vulnerable to both heterosexism and racism. These struggles were not only with heterosexual society but within lesbian communities as well; Martin remembered that after the Second World War the two women experienced intense anti-Japanese animosity and a general attitude of jingoistic patriotism both on the street and sometimes in lesbian bars. The threat of unemployment was an ever-present factor in Martin's life as well. After leaving her husband in 1955, she was economically vulnerable, a situation compounded by her relationship with Kay. As a divorced mother in the 1950s, deeply concerned about maintaining her employment, racism, sexism, and heterosexism limited Martin's choices and made her afraid for her own survival.

Martin connected her early sense of the cruel illogic of racism with her acceptance of her own lesbianism. She remembered refusing to address white playmates as "ma'am" when they all reached the age of puberty and linked this early resistance to her ability to see through the homophobia she encountered in the 1940s and 1950s. "I have always had my own opinion, and I was never ever easily brainwashed," she recalled. Going to high school in Boyle Heights, after she migrated from Louisiana to Los Angeles at sixteen, taught Martin about the militarization of American racism against the Japanese, something that deeply affected her. She visited the internment camps frequently—particularly the one at Manzanar—and a hotel in Boyle Heights used as a temporary detention point, bringing supplies and listening to the internees' stories about their loss and fear. In the early 1950s, during Joseph McCarthy's anticommunism crusade, Martin struggled with her boss over a demand that all state employees take a loyalty oath. As a vocal union organizer and an African American woman, she faced intense scrutiny. As a result of her resistance, she was blackballed from some lucrative work for which she otherwise would have been eligible as a county employee. All of this was part of her commitment to live the life she chose for herself and to oppose the social condemnation of others.

By the early 1940s, Martin, whose husband was overseas in the military, was aware of a vibrant, butch-femme community in the Boyle Heights neighborhood of Los Angeles. She longed to be a part of it but was snubbed by her husband's cousin and her young, butch-femme crowd because she posed trouble as a married woman. Marriage often operated in contrast and opposition to women loving other women in the lives of Martin and her friends during this period. But women's lives crossed these boundaries and were much more fluid than that cultural opposition suggests. Martin remembered that a woman she lived with during the Second World War whose husband was in the military was having an affair with another woman from that same butch-femme lesbian community. She also remembered going to see Billie Holiday at the African American–owned Club Alabam with these women. This was all part of an urban emergence of an African American women's community that contributed to the growth of lesbian cultural networks in the war years.

Martin resolutely tried to keep her first marriage alive, motivated by a belief that her children needed to grow up with their biological father. In contrast to the way she lived other parts of her life, she stayed in a marriage that made her unhappy and took its toll in myriad ways. She had more than ten abortions in the years before their separation in 1955 because her husband refused to use birth control. She had already realized her attraction to women, and her married world was not completely separate from LGBT communities in Los Angeles; as a married mother in Boyle Heights in the late 1940s and early 1950s, Martin had parties that included gay men and lesbians, though she did not have a relationship with another woman before her divorce. She explains: "Oh, I didn't trust him. I did not trust him. My making the effort to stay with him had nothing to do with love; it had to do with fulfilling my commitment that I was going to make sure my kids had two parents—and hopefully their biological parents." She called this "the biggest decision I ever made in my life that was so wrong." Originally seeing marriage as the way out of her mother's house, Martin remained because she believed her children needed a nuclear family home.

Oral histories reveal the extensive pressure toward heterosexual nuclear family formation in the 1950s and 1960s as an important facet of the homophobia faced by lesbian and gay parents. Many lesbian mothers and gay fathers of this era saw no other option but heterosexual marriage. Some of them lived double lives and worried over getting caught or, like Martin, were divorced, had lovers, and existed both in and out of the queer world of the pre-Stonewall era. In an oral history done with Arden Eversmeyer in 2001, Barbara Kalish recalled falling in love with another woman in her local PTA and having an affair with her for eleven years while they lived two blocks from each other with their husbands and children. This queer suburban history is part of LGBT life in the

United States in the 1950s.[11] Vera Martin's story and other stories of nonhetero-sexual mothers of this era demonstrate the power of the heteronormative married ideal of the family and the ways it intersected with other systems of oppression to regulate those who sought to be independent in their reproductive, sexual, and economic lives. These regulatory and discriminatory forces are the historical predecessors of explicit cultural and political attacks on lesbian and gay parents and parental rights in later eras.

Oral histories of lesbian mothers and gay fathers of the pre-Stonewall era also show that postliberation categories of sexual orientation cannot be assumed to be transhistorical. Words and concepts that are common referents today meant different things in a queer world of the 1950s. For instance, Martin described how her ex-lover, Juan, who was strongly butch-identified, made fun of the fact that a newspaper article about Martin and her activism had called her a "dyke grandmother." For Juan, Martin explained to me, the word dyke could refer only to a butch, not a femme like Martin. Responding to Juan's taunt, Martin explained that after the emergence of a widespread lesbian feminist movement in the 1970s, the word dyke had been claimed by many lesbians as a badge of honor and that it no longer referred only to butches. These changes in language and self-representation point to dramatic shifts in the years directly following the Stonewall riots and the rise of large-scale liberation movements.

In our conversation, Martin, who raised children in a complex African American queer world of 1950s Los Angeles, and I, raised in a poor Native American lesbian feminist household, employed a shared vocabulary that included both the languages of lesbian feminism and the concepts of butch-femme. My own experience helped us speak about lesbian and gay parenting as a historical fact and about Martin's motherhood and her lesbianism as not mutually exclusive. An understanding of white supremacy, institutional and extrainstitutional racism, and the importance of freedom struggle history also underlay our conversation. All of these shared commitments and interests shaped the stories told and questions generated. When Martin told me that her lover Kay, a Japanese American woman, a lesbian, and a sex worker in 1959 Los Angeles, died after being ignored in a hospital waiting room for hours, there was a shared understanding between us that those things were linked and that this was not the story of an accidental death.

These shared epistemologies do shape the way we see the past, but as part of doing so, they also enable us to move beyond a post-Stonewall framework and to articulate a queer family history. In the early 1970s, definitions of sexual identity and community shifted radically after gay liberation and lesbian feminism demanded visibility for identities and communities that had previously existed underground. LGBT politics became centrally organized around a politics of coming out, of declaring one's sexual identity clearly and unequivocally. Before the advent of liberation politics, however, the lives of same-sex-oriented men and women were often much more complex than this politics of the closet might assume.

Oral histories can help us understand the complexity of these queer lives that could otherwise be invisible from a static, post-Stonewall perspective. Definitions of lesbian and gay as fixed and known identities fail to capture the ways that men and women in the postwar era often moved in and out of nonheteronormative communities. Martin, faced with her lover Kay's untimely death in 1959 and the increasing threat of a custody suit by her ex-husband, married a man, E., in 1963 as cover, for financial security, and to give her son a father figure. She was comforted by the knowledge that her new husband was a closeted gay man himself, though they never spoke openly of their sexuality to each other.

E.'s gayness made Martin feel safe. She believed he would never use her love for other women to threaten her job or custody of her son. She also still felt that her son needed a male role model, and E. and Martin's son got along well. This movement between a queer world and heterosexual marriage is part of LGBT history in the 1950s and 1960s, but it is visible only when Martin's history is read separately from post-Stonewall definitions of sexual identity. Although we used ways of thinking and speaking in our conversation that owe much to the liberation era, in our dialogue, Martin and I spanned that period of dramatic change, and the story moves historically beyond it. A shared sexual minority vocabulary informed our conversation but also allowed us to challenge binaries implicit in the semiotics of the closet. This process is essential for constructing a queer social history of the postwar years.

In 1963, Vera moved to Altadena, a suburb of Pasadena outside of Los Angeles. A trumpet player in the 1950s, E. was by then working in furniture sales. Martin had parties for the regional director of the civil rights commission and visiting African dignitaries she met as an organizer for African exchange students. In 1973, Martin finally came out for the last time and got involved in Los Angeles' lesbian and gay activism and community life: "I figured it was the right time. I can do this now, and I don't have to be concerned about the custody junk. I want to get out of this place . . . and if I'm going to do it, I'm already fifty, and it's time to get on with it." Martin went on to cofound Old Lesbians Organizing for Change (OLOC) in 1989. Throughout the 1980s and 1990s, she was an active advocate for women's reproductive rights and lesbians of color in the Los Angeles area.

Martin's life history captures shared moments in lesbian and gay history that would have been less visible in a history based solely on nonoral evidence. Blue Lunden, a working-class, white butch who grew up in New Orleans's French Quarter and, much later, a close friend of Martin's and member of OLOC, raised her daughter, Linda, within lesbian communities in New York's East Village, something we know about only because of an oral history with Lunden.[12] Although their circumstances were in some ways very different, Lunden and

Martin both feared for their custody rights because they were women who loved women.

In the 1950s, many parents lived queer lives. Like Martin, some men and women moved in and out of married life, while others raised children while remaining active in lesbian communities for decades. Vera Martin's story is exceptional in many ways, but she shared struggles around sexuality and the family with a whole generation. Hers is a postwar lesbian and gay family history, one intimately connected to the world after Stonewall by the custody courts, the backlash, and the move toward parental rights in the freedom struggle. But it is distinct from the liberation era as well and takes place at a time when categories of in and out were more porous and a lesbian could live married with children in the Pasadena suburbs.

The stories of men and women like Vera Martin, who realized their same-sex sexuality in the 1950s and had children, were very difficult. They are the stories of men living in fear that they would be caught in a raid and have to call their wives, possibly waking the children. Such struggles illustrate a fundamental homophobic injunction in American society that children be kept separate from LGBT life and that the family be always heterosexual. Oral history helps us see this and, at the same time, expand on earlier LGBT history by including child rearing as a critical part of 1950s lesbian and gay historical experience, connecting histories of the family and sexuality. The paths these lives took foreshadowed the lesbian and gay parental activism of the 1970s and 1980s and the lesbian and gay parenting boom of the last decades of the twentieth century. Oral history compels us to complicate our questions, along with the answers. It can enable us to see the intersections of sexuality, race, gender, and class with reproduction and offers us a more complex and richly rewarding queer history.

Notes

1. I would like to express my deepest gratitude to all of my participants for sharing their stories with me. In particular, I am thankful to Vera Martin and Annalee Stewart for making this essay possible by speaking with me about their life experiences.
2. Vera Martin, interview with author. Apache Junction, Arizona. September 22, 2006.
3. George Breitman, ed., *Malcolm X, By Any Means Necessary: Speeches, Interviews, and a Letter by Malcolm X* (New York: Pathfinder, 1970), 35–67.
4. Laurel Galana and Gina Covina, eds., *The New Lesbians: Interviews with Women across the U.S. and Canada* (Berkeley, CA: Moon, 1977); Julia Penelope Stanley and Susan J. Wolfe, eds., *The Coming Out Stories* (Watertown, MA: Persephone, 1980).
5. Keith Vacha and Cassie Damewood, eds., *Quiet Fire: Memoirs of Older Gay Men* (Trumansburg, NY: Crossing, 1985); Marcy Adelman, *Long Time Passing: The Lives of Older Lesbians* (Boston: Alyson, 1986).
6. Allan Bérubé, *Coming Out under Fire: The History of Gay Men and Women in World War Two* (New York: Free Press, 1990); John D'Emilio, *Sexual Politics, Sexual Communities: The Making of a Homosexual Minority in the United States, 1940–1970* (Chicago: University of Chicago Press, 1983); Lillian Faderman, *Odd Girls and Twilight Lovers: A History of Lesbian Life in Twentieth-Century America* (New York: Columbia University Press, 1991); Jonathan Ned Katz, *Gay American History: Lesbians and Gay Men in the U.S.A.* (New York: T. Y. Crowell, 1976).

7. Archives that began collecting large numbers of LGBT oral histories in this period include the Lesbian Herstory Archives (LHA) in Brooklyn, New York, and the Gay and Lesbian Historical Society of Northern California (GLHSNC) in San Francisco. Projects initiated under VOICES, the oral history initiative of the GLHSNC, include the Uncles Project (1990s), Go West Migration (1990s), Shedding a Straight Jacket (1990s), Fresno Project (1990s), Artists Project (1990s), McCarthy Project (1980s), and the Tede Matthews Project (1990s).

8. Elizabeth Lapovsky Kennedy and Madeline D. Davis, *Boots of Leather, Slippers of Gold: The History of a Lesbian Community* (New York: Routledge, 1993); original transcripts from the Buffalo Women's Oral History Project interviews are housed as a special collection at the Lesbian Herstory Archives, Boots of Leather/Slippers of Gold Special Collection 98–1. In an essay marking the twenty-fifth anniversary of the Stonewall Riots, Kennedy noted the importance of oral history to LGBT history, particularly in the pre-Stonewall era, in generating empirical knowledge, sharpening our understanding of queer subjectivities over time, and heightening our sensitivity to the interconnections between the two. Elizabeth Lapovsky Kennedy, "Telling Tales: Oral History and the Construction of Pre-Stonewall Lesbian History," in Martin Duberman, ed., *A Queer World: The Center for Lesbian and Gay Studies Reader* (New York: New York University Press, 1997), 181–98.

9. Annalee Stewart, interview by author, Minneapolis, Minnesota, October 19, 2006.

10. For an example of these arguments, see the introduction to the winter 2008 issue of *Radical History Review*. The editors claim that "the current focus within gay and lesbian movements and culture on the family and reproduction as vehicles for claiming citizenship and rights works to suture reproduction to a privatizing neoliberal agenda, rather than to disrupt nationalist and heteronormative ideologies." Kevin P. Murphy, Jason Ruiz, and David Serlin, "Editors' Introduction." These critiques of the mainstream LGBT freedom struggle are crucial but need to be tempered with an appreciation for the decades-long history of lesbian and gay parental activism. I would second the editors' emphasis on the need to interrogate much of the current politics of the family. In particular, I think the ways in which children of LGBT parents are being used as political symbols must be examined. However, I would argue that this current phenomenon is only one part of a larger genealogy that involves a contestation by multiple generations of lesbian mothers, gay fathers, and their children of the family as always already heterosexual. I chronicle this history in my book, Daniel Rivers, *Radical Relations: Lesbian Mothers, Gay Fathers, and their Children in the United States since the Second World War* (forthcoming, University of North Carolina Press).

11. Barbara Kalish, interview by Arden Eversmeyer, Long Beach, California, January 2001, OLOC.

12. Blue Lunden, interview by Quinn, December 1989. Blue (Doris) Lunden Special Collection 83–04, Box 1, Folder 2, Lesbian Herstory Archives.

4

SPIRALING DESIRE

Recovering the Lesbian Embodied
Self in Oral History Narrative

Jeff Friedman

**Oral history by Jeff Friedman with Terry Sendgraff, San Francisco,
California, November 12 and 28 and December 6, 1990**

*In response to effects of the AIDS epidemic on the San Francisco Bay Area dance com-
munity, I founded the Legacy Oral History Project in 1988 to record, preserve, and make
accessible the life histories of Bay Area dance community members who were at risk
from life-threatening illness. For the next six years, a volunteer staff and I recorded and
transcribed nearly fifty oral histories with dancers, choreographers, educators, critics,
and administrators, including narrators from classical, contemporary, experimental,
folk, theatrical, and commercial dance genres. The oral history interview with Terry
Sendgraff was recorded for three hours on analog audiotape over three separate sessions
in 1990. All interviews were transcribed and edited according to the University of
California–Berkeley Regional Oral History Office's formats and standards. Deposited
in 1992, the completed research transcript includes contextual tools and finding aids to
support future research. Interview tapes and transcripts are available for research and
public access at the renamed San Francisco Museum of Performance & Design.*[1]

JEFF FRIEDMAN: Tell us where you were born.

TERRY SENDGRAFF: I was born in Fort Myers, Florida, 1933. That's the west coast of
Florida. It was beautiful then, not so densely populated as it is now. I lived in
a beautiful home, I thought; wonderful gardens and lawns and trees and
flowers and a fishpond. Really a paradise. I thought my parents owned the
house, but they didn't; it was just rented. My father was a golf professional so
it was a home that was given to him as part of his job. It was near the golf
course so I also had the golf course as a playground.

I spent a lot of time outside rolling in the grass and even playing in the
hurricanes. I loved to swing—I had a big swing in the backyard—and I really
enjoyed moving. I can remember those days so clearly. The big winds would
come up, and I'd be out in my swing. If it was raining, I'd quit. When there are

hurricanes, there's a kind of calm. But you feel the pressure. I can remember as a child wanting to go outside. . . .

FRIEDMAN: Exciting! Was it a military town, Fort Myers?

SENDGRAFF: Yes.

FRIEDMAN: How many siblings?

SENDGRAFF: I had two older brothers, both ten years older than me. One was adopted and one was a stepbrother. I also had an older sister who was adopted. So that was Tommy and David, and Virginia. I don't think Virginia was at home the first year of my life. She moved to wherever she did, I don't know, and was not in contact with the family. I don't really know the circumstances of her leaving. I grew up and was in Fort Myers for about nine years, with my mother, father, and my two brothers.

Then there was the war—it wasn't easy to be a golf pro at the time—so my father managed to get some job in Pennsylvania. We moved to this coal town in Pennsylvania—New Castle. Incredible shock for me. It was very dreary compared to my paradise and was very depressing. Also the war and the atmosphere was depressing.

My mother was physically abusive to both my brothers. . . . My brothers went into the Navy, and so they left home. My mother and father separated shortly after that, I didn't really know the circumstances of that. All of a sudden he was gone. I was in a state of shock about the loss because I adored my father and my brothers. I continued to live with my mother, who was an alcoholic. Her alcoholism got worse and worse, and so my teenage years were pretty much dealing with that. My brothers and my father, I think, came home once, and then after that they didn't come back until I went off to college.

I was very close to both my brothers, actually one more than the other. Tom was really very special because he was a dancer too. . . . He'd dress me up so we could play—[laughter]—and dance—he really did teach me to dance! So he was a big influence, big influence on my life. He was also helpful in getting me into college. He felt it was very important for me to go to college, so in some way he helped to make that arrangement. My father contributed towards my education and I did work some, too, to go to college, but it was really my brother's guidance there, in that respect. I felt he deserted me when he left for the Navy, and then he got married and did his own life. So there was a strong emotional cutoff from my brothers and my father; it was an unhappy time. . . . I learned to swim before I could walk.

FRIEDMAN: Because you were on the coast?

SENDGRAFF: Because of the beach, yes. And diving.

FRIEDMAN: As a teenager, you were diving from the board?

SENDGRAFF: I went to a swimming pool, and I had swimming lessons and diving lessons. I was afraid of diving though, actually.

FRIEDMAN: High diving?

SENDGRAFF: Oh—I remember the first experience just diving from the side of the pool. It's like diving into the unknown. But then I did it, and I accomplished that and then moved onto the diving board, and then later, as a teenager, from the high board. It was my favorite activity in high school [in Pennsylvania]. Summer was going down to the lake where there was a diving board and [I would] just dive, get up out of the water, climb the board, dive again, just in again, out again. It was a big deal, and I was thrilled by the height and the physical activity. I'd ride my bike to the lake and ride home.

FRIEDMAN: You went to Penn State?

SENDGRAFF: Yes, and then I went to Penn State University and enrolled first in liberal arts, which I thought was going to be art! [Laughs] Well, there was no drawing and painting or sculpture in that at all; it was all very boring. I was not happy at college the first year, very, very unhappy. I think the loss of my family, even though I was not happy with my mother, was still—I was not secure. When I left home, I didn't have a good solid home to leave, so there's always this kind of gap, always missing the home and family that I never had.

[At college] I had this counselor-kind-of-housemother-person, a very spectacular student, who was given some honor to be a housemother. I was very fortunate because she was extremely bright and insightful and helpful, and she got me involved in a lot of activities, dancing in the Thespian theater group. So I became very active in the second semester and, from there on, throughout my years in college, I was involved in dance. I finished my school years with physical education/recreation, which was more up my alley and provided me with a social life as well as academics I could handle. . . .

So I went to California and studied with Betty Jones and Ethel Winter, [Martha] Graham and [José] Limón technique, and ballet. I also enrolled in a class with Al Huang, who was a Tai Chi and modern dance [master teacher]. He had combined these things, but his approach was process. It was like— wow!—I saw this other way. Shirley Ririe and Joanne Woodbury were there from Utah [teaching] Nikolais improvisation; here it is again, improvisation and process. So I found something that was strong for me, that I could feel comfortable in and excited by and creative and smart and because I was good at it. I was good at being spontaneous, and I liked their thoughtful approach to it. So that was California. I went back to my job in Arizona and I said, "I do not want to teach ballet anymore. I do not want to teach modern dance, this isn't working for me. I want to go see what's in California." Some students were [going to California] for the weekend in April, so I said, "Well, great! I'll go! Just check it out!" We went to see Anna Halprin's studio and watched the dancers, and I was just blown away, I really liked it. So I went back and quit my job. I had divorced by then, too, so I was ready for a new life. . . .

Then, I met Al Wunder and he was the right teacher at that time. He had worked with [modern dancer and choreographer Alwin] Nikolais; he'd been teaching for Nikolais for about eight years. Al is an incredible, special teacher in that he really encourages you—encouraged me—to find my own thing. Which wasn't easy, I fought him all the way, but we became lovers, and very best friends, and family, perhaps that was my first sense of family. . . .

At that same time I was getting involved in Gestalt therapy and a lot of the growth work including Feldenkrais movement. I would go towards these movements, schools of thought that were geared for personal growth and awareness, and away from technique. And yet, now I know how important the technique was for me. I'm glad I have it, I integrated it, and I was able to use it in a way that was right for me. I couldn't have done that had I kept studying *the* techniques [that is, Graham, Limón, Nikolais, et al.]. There was nowhere at that time, nowhere to take that technique and use it from the inside out. It always was so external, with mirrors and everything.

FRIEDMAN: You had those vocabularies, you had those techniques, you chose to play with them instead of . . .being formed by them?

SENDGRAFF: Yes, and seeing how we are also a product of our times and as well as helping create the times. That time of play, experimenting and performing, studio performing, was just right for me. . . .

FRIEDMAN: When you began to formulate Motivity, what were the roots of those ideas?

SENDGRAFF: Well, I knew I liked gymnastics. I liked the feeling of going upside down, and I liked the feeling of extending the body for what was clearly function. If you're going to do an aerial cartwheel, you've got to extend your legs. It wasn't point your toes and straighten your legs because it looked good, it had a purpose so you could feel it; I could feel that. It was exciting to do that kind of movement. . . .

I started to experiment with the idea of rolling safely because I'd been really scared [as a child in school]. You have to run and do this dive roll or something and—wow!—the neck and the head and my body didn't like that! So how could I do them smoothly? So I started to play with just very small segments of things. The idea of play was Al [Wunder's], and the idea of slow motion was Al Huang's Tai Chi work, and then Gestalt awareness also came in there—"What were you really experiencing in each movement?" So this style began to develop of doing gymnastics work very slowly and transferring the weight very slowly and doing a roll into weight on the hands, which [still might look like] a handstand or a cartwheel, but conceptually changed. Instead of thinking of these things as tricks, I started thinking of them [as] ways of locomoting, transferring weight in any way that I could get in this inverted work and do it safely, with care and awareness. At first, it was really hard. Now everybody's doing it fairly easily, but at that time I didn't see anyone doing it.

So, I was shifting then from the gymnastics I had known. Then Al's influence about how to play with motion. . . . At first I didn't know what he was talking about and I would get very annoyed—"Why doesn't he just give me something to do, tell me what to do," which is what I hated in the other classes [laughs], and now I was rebelling about this. But he was so patient and wouldn't budge from his approach because he knew what he was doing. It was developing and cultivating curiosity, . . . playing up and down: . . . when something's up, something's down.

Then I had this incredible experience with dance. For a while, when I came out here, I was trying to teach modern dance the way I had been taught. I was going to teach a class one night. I think there were maybe six or eight students in the new study, our little Berkeley Dance Theater gymnasium. I started to teach this class and I went blank. I couldn't think of any combinations. I couldn't get it together in my head. I had to stop the class and say, "I'm sorry, but I just can't teach this way anymore." And I never did again. It just didn't work. I was humiliated. I certainly went through a lot of wondering, "What am I going to do?"

I did continue to teach gymnastics, pretty much like I had been taught. But then that started to change, too, and then soon that wasn't working either. So I started to play with that. How could I play carefully and give people a chance to do what they could do; play with inverted work. So then I started to develop a whole way of teaching gymnastics that involved weight bearing and weight transference and conceptually looking at it differently. I was playing with motion. The combining of those two things, the dance and the gymnastics, for me was like combining axial movement and locomotive movements.

Then the trapeze work came in about a year and a half later. I had used high-flying trapeze at the YMCA in Denver when I was teaching in the early sixties. I had also done a piece with Al with the big swing on stage and a trapeze. So I had this great idea. I gathered four women who liked gymnastic kind of movements. I asked them to be in my birthday performance. I started working on a piece with trapezes, and I made some more and hung them up, unusually perpendicular to one another, and some very low to the ground, and I started using this same concept of transferring the weight slowly, how to move in the corners, fast or slow, bring your nose to your knees, all these odd ways of moving on the trapeze. It was amazing what started to happen, and that was the beginning. I saw this as totally fascinating to me—working on the ground and then working in the air. Then we started to work double-lifting each other, contact improvising work on the trapezes. That birthday performance was my forty-second birthday in which I announced that I was going to call my work "Motivity" and I introduced this piece as my first Motivity piece. And so that was the beginning. Yes.

FRIEDMAN: It's so useful to hear what the roots were, and the roots were deeply connected to all the things we've talked about in the past [interviews] and that you made that shift gradually until the point came, and then they began to move toward one another. . . .

SENDGRAFF: . . . Yes. . . .

Motivity founder Terry Sendgraff demonstrates the use of her single-point trapeze as an exploration of three-dimensional space. *Photograph by Deborah Hoffman*

FRIEDMAN: . . . almost inside you, in a cognitive way, intrinsically, and that the equipment came later as an instrument. I'd thought you'd say, "I found this trapeze and I liked doing that."

SENDGRAFF: [Laughs]

FRIEDMAN: . . . and of course [Motivity] has got a larger and more deep process through which it came to that point.

SENDGRAFF: Yes. The whole body of knowledge of Motivity is rooted in the work of Mary Wigman, Hanya Holm, [Alwin] Nikolais, [Rudolf von] Laban, and the early Gestalt psychologists and present-day Gestalt theory and therapy. That school of thought is a very rich body of knowledge. I think it's little understood by many, very misunderstood, often like Zen. It's basically simple in that awareness, the continuum of awareness is a meditation. So, I was applying that and not really even getting all the connections myself. . . .

I think that, as I teach now, it's still very much with the intention of bringing people to their own form. When you slow down and encourage the students to have awareness of themselves, then you have to take what you get. I've really become skillful at working with what's in front of me and sensing what to do. I teach totally improvisationally but know my material so well. It makes it

very exciting to teach that way because I really stay in the moment. I'm looking to see what's not happening and what is happening and where I can shift
if I need to. I teach like I would like to be taught.

Commentary

Cultural phenomenology is an interdisciplinary enterprise that studies the way
individuals use embodied experiences to ground and articulate their consciousness of the world around them. Cultural phenomenology as a field foregrounds
a conflict between figural and field perceptual modes of embodiment. The more
normative figural mode emphasizes singularity, fixedness, and serial perceptions. In contrast, the field mode uses a holistic approach emphasizing multiplicity, simultaneity, and change. Cultural phenomenologists highlight this
conflict between the two perceptual modes when representing embodied experience through documentary media such as photography, video, or written or
spoken narratives. For example, anthropologist Thomas Csordas brings oral
interviews directly into this discussion. Csordas reminds us that culture emerges
first from "bodily processes of perception." For Csordas, our world comes into
being as a consequence of being-in-the-world, a complex simultaneity of sensorimotor perceptions and our subcognitive awareness of ourselves as we *move*
through those perceptions. Regarding representation, Csordas notes, "There is
no special kind of data or special method for eliciting such data but [instead] a
methodological attitude that demands attention to bodiliness even in purely
verbal data such as written text or oral interview."[2] Extending Csordas's call for
attention to bodiliness, this essay locates that methodological attitude within
the oral history interview, moving away from a normative figural mode toward
a more embodied field of representation.

Legacy's oral histories directly access embodied experience through interviews with dancers. However, oral history narratives with dancers have proven to
be not, in Csordas's words, only "purely verbal data" but also embodied performances correlated to the particular being-in-the-world that emerges from a life
committed to dance. Those subjects' embodied aesthetic generates a narrative
style characterized by a finely tuned awareness of the body's multiple parts simultaneously and continuously moving through time and space. That these aes-
thetics are complex and difficult to analyze does not release us from attending
to their importance. Rather, dancers' oral histories reveal a narrative erotics that
acknowledges alternative storytelling modes and representations of embodied
reality that deviate from normative language.

A dance studies perspective provides an analytic framework within which
those alternative storytelling modes can be articulated. My study of dancer and
choreographer Terry Sendgraff's oral history interview exemplifies one such alternative narrative. This essay links cultural phenomenology with the embodied
practice of dancers to articulate the desires of subjects, like Terry, as they express

themselves outside the norms of narrative construction. For Terry, nonnormative desire is a form of queer storytelling that refuses categorization, and by studying her story, we are challenged to open our critical lens further to encompass their unique approach to self-representation through oral history.

During a difficult year in which I sustained back injuries while dancing on tour in Alaska, I took a sabbatical. Determined to reclaim my body from chronic pain and reduced mobility, I found Joah Lowe, a dancer, choreographer and physical therapist, who provided professional therapy. After six months, I returned to my regular work schedule. In December 1987, Joah visited his family in Texas for Christmas. Not knowing he had become HIV-positive, Joah developed a serious case of *Pneumocystis carinii* pneumonia and died a week later.

Joah's partner and his medical and dance communities were in shock, but together they put together a memorial service for him. We gathered at a local dance studio in San Francisco's Mission District and watched Joah's dancing image flicker distantly on a small video screen. I was angry at our loss and also the lack of documentation for Joah's career as a performer and choreographer. At that moment, I vowed I would do justice to the unseen, unheard, unfelt narratives of dancers' lives.

Within a year of Joah's memorial, I put together a plan for recording oral histories of dancers with AIDS. Under the auspices of Legacy Oral History Project, I began recording life histories with dancers challenging HIV and AIDS in the San Francisco Bay Area.[3] While engaged in my own community's struggle to respond to the AIDS epidemic, it became clear that HIV and AIDS were not the only risk factors interrupting the historical record. Elders and dancers with other life-threatening illnesses such as cancer were equally and sometimes more at risk. I expanded Legacy's project design to include multiple risk factors for selecting narrators. Under these new criteria, I became aware of Terry Sendgraff, a significant Bay Area dancer and choreographer then battling breast cancer.

I contacted Terry through her partner, Aileen Moffitt, and Terry agreed to record an interview with me for Legacy's collection. We all hoped that Terry would become a long-term breast cancer survivor (and twenty years later, she is), but by then, Terry had already had recurrences and undergone a mastectomy. Terry contributed an important narrative to Legacy's collection that diversified our collection in several ways: her multiple identities as a lesbian, as a survivor with non-HIV-related illness, and most important, her unique contribution to the San Francisco Bay Area dance and activist women's communities.

Terry's contribution to dance is Motivity, a unique amalgam of gymnastic tumbling work and aerial dance supplemented by trapezes and other equipment. By 2010, at least two generations of artists attribute their work as aerialist dancers and choreographers to Terry's movement aesthetic.[4] These artists recognize Terry and Motivity as generating a new field of creative inquiry focused on fully exploring the three-dimensional field of space through movement. While many artists and audiences think of Motivity as equipment-supported movement, it is in fact a more comprehensive inquiry into holistic embodiment. Based on her interests in Gestalt approaches to human development and psychotherapy, Terry developed a movement pedagogy based on supporting fuller movement expression. Movement begins on the floor, where the body yields to gravity without hesitation or injury. Informed by her early gymnastics experience, Terry developed more complex three-dimensional tumbling moves within a dance framework. She then encouraged use of vertical walls as support for movement, in addition to floors. As students evolved their skills, Terry created low-flying trapeze equipment to encourage more engagement with three-dimensional space. This equipment included one- and two-point rigging trapezes at varying heights that allowed a variety of movement and choreographic choices. Though students eventually developed virtuoso skills under Terry's training and guidance, she always kept her aesthetic vision focused on supporting embodied experiences that encouraged three-dimensionality at all levels, from simple floor-based movement to advanced and complex aerial choreography supplemented with a variety of equipment.

A caveat to this physical aesthetic was Terry's emphasis on group process that encouraged the evolution of movement communities. Key to this process was improvisation, keeping one's moving body fully engaged with his or her inner life, as expressed outwardly through movement. While Terry's early work remained inner-directed, her later work is concerned with community activism, especially where women fully embrace three-dimensional space. For example, Terry's performance work "Women Walking Tall" used waves of women and girls on stilts emerging from a large grove of trees at a local outdoor festival, ululating powerful and joyful agency as they pierced the upper reaches of space, many dancers looming over ten feet tall. Integrating feminist politics and activism with Gestalt psychotherapeutic theory, Terry's embodied practice activates three-dimensional space as a holistic approach to a life committed to connecting inner experience with outer action.

The feminist theorist Mary Gergen posits that narrators always tell their stories within normative structures laid out by social parameters, "paradigms deemed intelligible by their specific culture."[5] However, narrative theorists Rosenwald and Ochberg note that subjects conserve a certain amount of individual agency, where tension between their actual experiences and the social conventions invested in narrative production struggle toward resolution, but sometimes fail: "Desire (and the life stories in which it is represented) is inevitably shaped by the forms each culture provides. At the same time, desire strains against these forms. The silences, truncations and confusion in stories . . . point out to us . . . what else might be said and sought.[6]

Often social hierarchies overdetermine the interview event, especially between elites and nonelites. Perceived power differences between academic researchers and their nonelite narrators force lower status participants to construct an "official" story for the elite interviewer. Following discursive norms, subjects construct a narrative they believe the higher status interviewer wants and expects, instead of one reflecting their experience. Under these circumstances, the official story stretches to fulfill those norms and then begins to fray; the narrative fragments and the subject's desire for authenticity are revealed.

Although Rosenwald and Ochberg suggest the narrator is reduced to silence, this description is faulty. Fragmentation of a spoken narrative reveals and foregrounds nonverbal communication channels. Rather than silence, fragmentation of semantic text reveals a significant visual-kinesthetic component: the narrator's body continues to express itself. Oral history interviews are embodied performances with multiple channels of information delivery and reception. Fragmentation of oral history narratives reveals not only silence, not just a desire toward authenticity, but also embodied desire, a narrative erotics. Terry Sendgraff's oral history provides illustrations of these narrative erotics.

While verbal silence reveals the ongoing communicative erotics in an interview, this desire is not necessarily for a simplistically coherent narrative. Narrative theorist Elliot Mishler cites studies supporting the argument that "personal narratives serve a 'coherence' function, a teleological approach that chronologically lists specific events ordered around a problem requiring conflict resolution through action."[7] However, Terry Sendgraff's oral history resists simple coherence. Demonstrated by Terry's Motivity work, sensorimotor perception of the world emphasizes multiple and simultaneous experiences received through several perceptual modalities. This type of holistic perception of being-in-the-world produces alternative narrative structures to represent the narrator's embodied perception of reality.

By rejecting the fixed stages of developmental theory where "each stage build[s] on the resolution of earlier stages," Mishler offers an alternative option: "Identity changes in adulthood do not follow the fixed, linear path of a universal stage model. Their trajectories involve detours, recursions, embedded cycles, that are responsive to culturally framed and socially situated alternatives."[8] Mishler chooses distinctively embodied language to describe alternative narrative forms. He associates narrative production with an embodied journey that is distinctively nonlinear, keeping the story moving in cyclical turning and returning, a recursive spiral like Terry's aerial movement on the trapeze.

Both Gergen and Mishler find that these narratives disturb the norm, creating what postmodernist theorist Jane Flax calls a "reality . . . even more unstable, complex and disorderly."[9] Flax posits that representations of unstable realities emerge frequently in women's narratives. Gergen describes these narratives as "more fragmentary, multi-dimensional, understated and temporally disjunctive,"[10] paralleling a field mode of perception. In Terry's oral history, temporal and spatial disjunctions are, in fact, part of a larger narrative whole. This narrative is not so much destabilized as self-mobilizing, allowing fragmentation so that another kind of coherence can emerge.

There are similarities between the creative process and oral history interviews. Both are emergent processes involving a substantial amount of recursivity. Oral history topics introduced earlier in a recording remain unarticulated until the narrator returns to comment on this previous node of interest in the earlier narrative. Similarly, the creative process in dance and other artistic forms often remains opaque, even to the primary creator from whose mind-body the process emerges, until the work is staged or completed. Even then, after many performances, a work of choreography turns and returns on itself, revealing facets previously unknown. In Jeffrey Evans's study on choreographers' narratives, neither subject consciously wished to represent their life experience transparently; they resist producing a narrative that is clarifying, coherent and achieves closure. Rather,

> Their histories suggest that self-knowledge, traditionally understood as expressing oneself through words, need not proceed parallel with development . . . development proceeds with and without verbal self-understanding as persons clear a path to mediate the forces moving their lives.[11]

Evans emphasizes how the oral narrative's verbal expression circumvents the choreographers' desire. Both subjects are conflicted because "as we know from rhetoric and body language, the clearest words are often too simple to convey what an author intends or what an audience is able maximally to receive. For the artist, artistry is rarely the shortest distance between two points."[12] We are reminded of Mishler's cyclical narratives that embody a recursive turning away from Evans's citation of normative "straight" narratives.[13]

In Terry's oral history, two theoretical concerns intersect: Gergen and Mishler's nonfigural narratives and Evans's project where choreographers' embodied expression seeks to violate discursive norms by creating alternative forms of narrative expression. Based on my earlier description of Terry's three-dimensional movement aesthetic, her choreographic aesthetic helps us understand how narrative erotics emerge from oral history.

Quoting from my introduction to Terry's interview:

> Alone in a spotlight, Terry was working with a low-flying trapeze to extend her movement. Matching the trajectory of her body weight to the momentum of the trapeze, she suddenly spiraled up from the floor to the full height of the equipment's capacity and then down in one effortless motion. In that moment, Terry seemed to clarify the physics and metaphysics of the human body in motion. Some people believe the spiral represents basic form in nature: the center of plant spores, seashells, human muscle fibers, all seem to have adapted, incorporating function and the forces of external physics into spiraling forms of one kind or another. Terry, in that moment, seemed to have both understood that deep knowledge, become it, and showed it to us.[14]

This excerpt exposes the core visceral reality of Terry's performance, and the excerpts that follow are purposefully framed by an image of embodied movement.

First, Terry employs a narrative style that emerges from her dance aesthetic, grounded in her ability to fully occupy three-dimensional space. For Terry, this means emphasizing what her partner, Aileen Moffitt, calls "being":

> [Meeting with the board] was always more than business, because the business of "being" always comes first with Terry. For example, board meeting agendas were sometimes set aside to give each member an opportunity to check in on internal feelings; feelings were then shared with the group and affected the direction of the rest of the meeting.[15]

Terry's emphasis on the present moment is supported by her art practice: a Gestalt-based movement aesthetic that emphasizes holistic apprehension of three-dimensional space through the full sensorium. Terry says,

> Using technique from the inside out . . . gestalt awareness came in there: "What were you *really* experiencing in each movement?" Let's do something fast, let's do something slow, now incorporate those two. Play with the space between your nose and your knees and relate to the space between yourself and the wall, play with . . . working on the ground and then working in the air . . . . My first Motivity piece . . . involved using the floor, the walls, the trapezes and each other to move with, on, and against.[16]

Second, while being in the present, that is, "being-in-the-world," in relation to the external environment, Terry also accessed her internal emotional world, a "being-in-the-self," if you will. Consequently, her narrative style moves easily out of the figural experience of chronological time and the normal limits of geographical space because emotional coherency counts more in Terry's field of being that directly connects inner motivations with outer-directed action. By accessing full emotional connection to her sense of self, as a body "being-in-her-world," Terry creates her own coherent connections among diverse temporal and locational differences.

For example, during her narrative, Terry is able to leap from the present decade backward in time to the far past and thousands of geographic miles from her Oakland, California, present to her early childhood in Florida. Difficulties associated with her father's losing his job as a golf professional in Florida during World War II forced Terry's family to move to New Castle, a coal town in upstate Pennsylvania. For Terry, the move was "an incredible shock for me; It was just dreary compared to my paradise." Terry then makes an emotionally logical shift backward in time and returns to Florida to discuss a new but related topic:

> My mother was physically abusive to both my brothers. My brother's relationship to my mother was not very pleasant either. They were, of course, eager to go away from home.

Terry's narrative then shifts forward in time to her adolescent experiences with her brother Tom in their new home in New Castle, Pennsylvania:

Tom was very special because he was a dancer, too. He liked to dance and he used to dress up in costumes. . . . I remember that I did some sort of performance with him but mostly at home. I would stand on the stairway and jump off the stairs into his arms, and he would twirl me around and throw me up in the air and catch me!!—[now in present time and space] and so I can see why I like to fly.[17]

Immediately spiraling backward in time to her previous location in Florida, Terry recalls:

There are a lot of reasons why I like to fly. For my birthday, my brothers rigged up this wire that went from the height of one [tree in my backyard in Florida] down to the bottom [of the other tree]. They put this handle on [the wire] and a ladder up to the top of the tree, and then I would take hold of the handle and slide all the way down. . . . It was the biggest thrill! I pretended I was Wonder Woman![18]

Then, Terry finishes up with another shift forward in time as she completes her undergraduate degree in physical education at Pennsylvania State University:

I finished my school years [at the university] with physical education/recreation [degree], academics I could handle. I was so distraught, emotionally disturbed really, that I couldn't study. I didn't know how. . . .

Then, she briefly shifts back in time and space to her teenage years in New Castle, Pennsylvania:

I could never study in high school because I'd come home and my mother was drunk, so you couldn't study, the concentration is not there. I had no quiet environment because there was emotional abuse and some physical abuse, so it wasn't exactly conducive to academics. So, I didn't think I was very smart either.

In the next sentence, Terry returns to the Oakland-based present moment, with an alternative self-assessment: "Well, since then, I've discovered I'm very smart, I'm fine!" She immediately returns in time to Penn State University: "But, I didn't have a chance to develop in that way, so I had these doubts, a lot of doubts about myself, a lot of self doubt."[19]

Terry then moves into a virtuosic narrative performance, shifting fluidly back and forth between her past and present and between local and distance space. The interview with Terry had touched an inner nerve and, stricken with emotion, her narrative fragments and then recoheres into what I call a narrative spiral:

[Voice quavers, near tears] And just feeling all of the sudden, I mean, it's not all of a sudden, but—there it is—you know [pause, beginning to cry here]—family—[more crying, taking a few breaths as she cries]—just seeing everything flash before me—[pause, crying still]—just having finished the performance and being through this feeling so vulnerable; I feel pretty vulnerable. My brother's never seen me do what I do. I don't know if he's an alcoholic or not, I think he may be. His behavior is alcoholic.

Shifting immediately to local space and recent time:

[Tom and I] reconnected when he was coming to this area one time when I was doing a performance so I told him that I dedicated the performance to him. I thought he was in the audience because he'd said he was coming, and he never showed up. I didn't hear from him for about six months. He wrote saying he's sorry he didn't make it, but he had jet lag. I don't know what his real situation was, but that's typical of the way he is with me.

Shifting to past time: "because there was another occasion when he was going to come around Valentine's Day. . . . I was living here and he was going to come stay with us and he never showed up. . . ." And shifting again to present time:

So, talking about the family is difficult. I'm also studying right now for the [Marriage, Family, Child Counselor] exam. I've been focusing on these emotionally dysfunctional families with their alcoholism, and physical and emotional abuse. I think my family's been on my mind a lot [long pause] how does that play part in who I am and all of that.

FRIEDMAN: Have there been families that you've created for yourself?
SENDGRAFF: Well—[pause]—not really until now. Not really until I came out as a lesbian. The women's community and my partners have been more my family.

Shifting to past time and nonlocal space:

SENDGRAFF: I was married twice and it just wasn't right for me. I was not the wife type [laughs a bit], just wasn't right, trying to do a family in that way just didn't work. So, when I came out, I was so happy. It was just right, you know? It was like coming home to the home I never had. So coming out was a wonderful experience for me. Actually, my brother Tom is gay too. He came out when he was fifty-one years old. He has nine children. . . .
FRIEDMAN: Oh my!
SENDGRAFF: [Laughs] . . . and I came out shortly after he did, after he told me, although I always knew he was gay, I just always knew he was gay, I was not surprised. It coincided with my own coming out, so that was really a great celebration. Coming out in the seventies was like—what a great time [laughing] to come out.

Shifting to present time and local space:

The women's community is so special, and so supportive, and the community in general, Berkeley, the Bay Area, is supportive of Motivity, supportive of experimental work, period, supportive of trying to find yourself, to really figure out what you like—do your own thing![20]

The "fragmentation" of Terry's narrative, as it traverses time and space, signals where her embodied desire, especially as it approaches questions of personal and sexual identity for both herself and her brother, deviates from narrative norms. Rather than building a linear teleology enacting the agent-crisis-resolution narrative model, Terry spirals recursively back and forth in time and space to create an emotionally coherent three-dimensional geographical and temporal field of memory.

Analyzing the transcript twenty years after the interview, I discovered my own voice, as interviewer, responding to Terry's virtuosic narrative performance by trying to bring her back into chronological teleology: "Let's go back to going from Penn State to the next step and fill in."[21] This discovery reminds me that, when I first confronted Terry's verbatim transcript during the editing process in 1990, I attempted to reconfigure her three-dimensional narrative into a normative chronological teleology. After literally taking a scissors to the transcript, I have a distinct memory of looking at my living room floor covered with strips of paper, each with three or four lines of type. That sight convinced me I was eviscerating Terry herself. I stopped immediately and began listening carefully to Terry's voice and her nontraditional narrative style. In this essay, I pay my respects to Terry's indomitable voice and her embodied desire that resisted my original impulse to distort them into a normative narrative.

As stated in the essay's introduction, cultural phenomenology emphasizes embodied experience of the world. The emphasis is on using a field approach to perception. This field approach values the multiplicity of our world, where the simultaneity of experience and the ever-changing evolution of those experiences are hallmarks. The essay describes how figural norms reduce that life-world to a type of narrative where a series of discrete perceptions become fixed bits of experience along a linear progression. However, feminist and other perspectives on narrative support alternatives to this normative storytelling style.

Analysis of Terry's oral history interview reveals what may be called a narrative erotics, where her body desires to break open and expand the normative figural narrative. When Terry repeatedly returns recursively to her memories, her narrative moves forward and backward along a chronological time line, while also shifting between geographic locations. The result is a time line with linear movement in both directions, lateral geographic shifts among locations, and recursive circling among memories. These three movements, forward and backward linear, horizontal lateral, and circling actions, combine to create a spiraling narrative trace-form. A trace-form is not a fixed form but a movement signature that represents both Terry's ability to spiral recursively across time and space in her oral history and her spiraling aerial dancing. Terry's movement signature links her dance aesthetic and the oral narrative that represents her life in dance. The signature balances field and figure orientation. This balance is found in a dialectic between Terry's strongly-grounded belief system and feeling states and the multiple and simultaneous swirling world of embodied experience around her. The resulting balancing act is not stable or fixed, but a dialectic process emphasizing movement.[22]

Terry's movement aesthetic drives the emergence of her narrative erotics in an oral history format. Those erotics emerge from her desire to be experienced fully and wholly as who she is: an evolving woman, a dancer who moves, a lesbian engaged in activist change. Psychologist Elliott Jaques agrees with this hard-fought battle for balance between modes of perception, where he notes:

> Balanced oscillation between the poles of the [figure]-field duality is not simply there for the asking. *It must be worked for.* In particular it is the field dominant perspective which can be lost sight of. The object dominant perspective is strong, it pushes itself forward. It is the unbounded continuous field which is more difficult to keep hold of.[23] [my emphasis]

This dialectic suggests we need not choose between categorical figure and holistic field perception approaches, but that field orientation, in Jaques's words, must be worked for. This work is revealed in Terry's own aesthetic development. From her oral history, we learn Terry challenged figural norms in her own dance life, especially approaches to training. She struggled with a conflict between dance techniques that focused on discrete steps and tasklike accomplishments. In contrast, Terry preferred a fieldlike gestalt responsiveness to three-dimensional space, represented in her Motivity work. Eventually, Terry rejected the competitive and commodifying worlds of gymnastics and technical dance that emphasized the figural approach. Instead, she developed a movement aesthetic in Motivity that emphasizes three-dimensional space and recognizes contextual intention through improvisation techniques. Freeing herself from the figural approach, Terry forged her own three-dimensional style of teaching and dancing that emerges from her aesthetic interests. She describes resisting normative constraints:

> I think it was such a struggle for me having dance taught to me in such a left-brain linear way when it's just not my mode. The last modern dance class I went to was Phyllis Lamhut's. She came to Berkeley to teach a master class, and I thought, "After all that therapy and finding my own dance, now I could go back and I wouldn't care." Oh God, it was *awful.*
> *I had to* leave. I was so upset, *I had to* call my therapist.
> It was so *intensely* left-brain and she went *so fast,* explained everything *so fast.*
> When I left, I said, "I will never do this again."
> It's not *for me.*" Didn't work *for me.*
> I'm just *not—not—*it's *not* my mode, you know?[24] [my emphases]

This excerpt from Terry's oral history narrative represents how Terry's conflict balances figure and field modes, even at the most granular level of individual words and phrases. Semantic expression in Terry's oral history interview uses words to convey a figural approach to consciousness. Words are singular and fixed, using a serial one-by-one approach to representing experience. However, when all the embodied elements of speech are also taken into account, a field is revealed that surrounds words. For example, vocal production such as Terry's tone and volume provide a field context for words by expressing embodied intentions of emotion and emphasis. These field elements are received by a listener simultaneously with the semantic content of the word, emphasizing a balanced approach to communication. In addition to vocal production, other embodied aspects of Terry's verbal expression include movements of her facial expressions, posture shifts, and arm, hand, or other gestures. These movements provide another complex, simultaneous field context to the figural semantic content. Jaques notes:

> The idea that verbalization might emerge from the oscillating interaction of two modes of cognitive organization is a worthwhile proposition. We need to keep strong contact with our intuitive sense of *movement episodes* in an unbounded field—for without that contact, we lose our sense of purpose and we lose our sense of contact with the intentions and the purposes, the *desires and will*, which make human episodes human.[25] [my emphases]

In the semantic content of this text, we hear Terry rejecting norms in the dance field that emphasized figural consciousness. But in this text excerpt, I have deliberately emphasized where Terry's body breaks through the semantics through vocal volume and phrased repetition and rhythm. I use italics to show how Terry's words are highly inflected by her intense desire and will to resist the norms of dance training. The italicized rhythmic repetition of phrases reveals how Terry grows more frustrated, signalling her desire for a different mode of dance expression. This field of desire leads to Terry's characteristic fragmentation in the last sentence. As Ochberg and Rosenwald stated, the gaps between her words resound with desire, but not in silence, as they suggest, but in her body's yearning. This essay also shows that Terry's desire resounds beyond the level of semantic expression and its fragmentation; she resists narrative norms at the level of structure. She de-emphasizes the figural approach to narrative and reaches toward an embodied field consciousness in her desire to find balance in a narrative erotics. Terry demonstrates that work in her own words: "I'm just not—not—it's not my mode, you know?" Within that brief moment of fragmentation emerges Terry's ongoing, intense embodied desire to find and be herself, that is, being-in-her-world, being-in-her-self, and, finally, being-in-her-story. Representing embodied erotics in queer narratives is activist work. Like Terry, we can climb into the air, curve away from that straight line and explore the horizon of possibilities. Work for it.

Notes

1. In 1994, with support from the California Arts Council, Legacy proactively reached out to embrace the full cultural diversity of Bay Area dance for community members of Native American, African, Hispanic, Latina/o, and Asian descent. By 2001, Legacy had received funding support from many Bay Area and California private and community foundations,

as well as several grants from the National Endowment for the Arts's Dance, Service, and Heritage and Preservation programs. Although Legacy had been regularly depositing audiotapes, videotapes, and print transcripts in the San Francisco Performing Arts Library & Museum's archive, Legacy officially merged as a dedicated program of the library in 2001. With support from a Library Services Technical Assistance grant from the State of California in 2009–2010, Legacy's collection of approximately a hundred life histories were selectively digitized with a Web site presence at www.mpdsf.org. The author acknowledges Terry Sendgraff for her permission to substantially cite from the oral history transcript, Terry and Aileen Moffitt for their feedback in the writing and editorial process, Horacio Roque Ramírez and Nan Alamilla Boyd for their editorial guidance, and the J. William Fulbright Association for a Senior Research/Teaching Fellowship in 2009–2010, which provided time and space in Frankfurt, Germany, for completion of this essay.

2. Thomas J. Csordas, "Embodiment and Cultural Phenomenology," in Gail Weiss and Honi Fern Haber, eds., *Perspectives on Embodiment: The Intersection of Nature and Culture* (New York: Routledge, 1999), 147–48.

3. For additional archival sources on dancers with AIDS, see the Estate Project for Artists with AIDS (www.estateproject.org) and the Jerome Robbins Dance Collection's sound archive at the New York Public Library in Lincoln Center (www.nypl.org).

4. For additional practitioners of Motivity-based performance work in the San Francisco–Oakland Bay Area, see works by Joanna Haigood, Zaccho Productions (www.zaccho.org), Jo Kreiter, Flyaway Productions (www.flyawayproductions.com), Amelia Rudolph, Project Bandaloop (www.projectbandaloop.org), and Capacitor (www.capacitor.org). Other groups in the United States, such as Cycropia Aerial Dance Company and Frequent Flyers Dance Company, acknowledge Sendgraff as the important founding innovator of the now international aerial dance movement. See www.cycropia.org for a more complete list of aerial dance companies.

5. Mary Gergen, "Life-Stories: Pieces of a Dream," cited in George C. Rosenwald and Richard L. Ochberg, "Introduction: Life-Stories, Cultural Politics and Self-Understanding," 7, in George C. Rosenwald and Richard L. Ochberg, eds., *Storied Lives* (New Haven, CT: Yale University Press, 1992), 1–20.

6. Rosenwald and Ochberg, "Introduction," in *Storied Lives*, 7.

7. "The essential markers of the well-structured narrative in the Western cultural tradition [are] a temporally-ordered set of events" (Labov, 1972; Labov and Waletzky, 1967), coherence at several levels (Agar and Hobbs, 1982), and the basic agent-conflict-action structures (Rumelhart, 1975, 1977), all cited in Elliot Mishler, "Work, Identity, and Narrative: An Artist-Craftsman's Story," in Rosenwald and Ochberg, eds., *Storied Lives*, 35.

8. Ibid., 36–37.

9. Jane Flax, "Postmodernism and Gender Relations in Feminist Theory," in *Signs, Journal of Women in Culture and Society* 12:4 (1987): 643, cited in Gergen, "Life-Stories: Pieces of a Dream," 128.

10. Ibid., 132.

11. Jeffrey E. Evans, "Language and the Body: Communication and Identity Formation in Choreography," in Rosenwald and Ochberg, eds., *Storied Lives*, 107.

12. Ibid., 95.

13. Rosenwald and Ochberg comment on Evans's finding, where he suggests that "search for identity is in jeopardy when [narrators] are asked to give a transparent account of their commitments to an audience or interviewer." These subjects consciously act to "violate narrational norms," because embodied expression serves the choreographers better than the oral narrative. Rosenwald and Ochberg, "Introduction," *Storied Lives*, 11.

14. Jeff Friedman, "Interview History," in *Dreams of Flying* (San Francisco: Legacy Oral History Program collection, San Francisco Museum of Performance & Design, 1992), vii.

15. Aileen Moffitt, "Introduction," *Dreams of Flying*, iv–v.

16. Terry Sendgraff, *Dreams of Flying*, print transcript, 34.

17. Ibid., 3–4.

18. Ibid., 5–6.

19. Ibid., 8–9.

20. Ibid., 9–10.

21. Ibid., 11.

22. For more on embodied signatures in oral history narratives, see Jeff Friedman, *Embodied Oral History: A Laban Movement Analysis of Dancers' Life Histories toward Ontological Awareness*, unpublished dissertation (University of California-Riverside, 2003).

23. Elliott Jaques, *The Form of Time* (London: Crane Russak, 1982), 213–14.

24. Sendgraff, *Dreams of Flying*, 35–36.

25. Jaques, *Form of Time*, 221.

PART II
SEX

5

TALKING ABOUT SEX

Cheryl Gonzales and Rikki Streicher
Tell Their Stories

Nan Alamilla Boyd

Oral history by Nan Alamilla Boyd with Cheryl Gonzales, San Francisco, California, February 1, 1992; oral history by Nan Alamilla Boyd with Rikki Streicher, San Francisco, California, January 22, 1992

On February 1, 1992, I met Cheryl Gonzales at the Gay and Lesbian Historical Society on Sixteenth Street in San Francisco. We sat at a metal table in the archives and discussed Gonzales's memories of growing up in San Francisco. I was eager to meet her because I had heard from other narrators that Gonzales started going to lesbian bars in San Francisco as a teenager. I had gotten Gonzales's name from Sharon Tracy, who had co-owned the Highlander Bar on Potrero Hill in the late 1960s—an important venue as lesbian feminism evolved within the bar scene. Gonzales was also connected to Thelma Davis, whose oral history describes San Francisco's African American queer bar culture. In the interview that follows, Gonzales remembers her first foray into the bars via Maud's, the notoriously free-spirited Haight-Ashbury bar owned by Rikki Streicher.

Gonzales's and Streicher's oral histories, as well as Tracy's and Davis's, are among forty-five interviews I conducted in the early 1990s for my doctoral dissertation. This research led to the subsequent publication of Wide Open Town: A History of Queer San Francisco to 1965 *(University of California Press, 2003). While I worked on my dissertation and book, I also worked as a volunteer at the Gay and Lesbian Historical Society (now, the GLBT Historical Society), founding its oral history program, helping to manage the archives, and serving on the board of directors from 1992 to 1994 and 2003 to 2009. The oral histories, ephemera, and documents I collected have been deposited at the GLBT Historical Society as the Wide Open Town History Project.*[1]

FEBRUARY 1, 1992

CHERYL GONZALES: My first involvement with the gay community was, uh, the bars were really the only avenue for socialization, and so I had heard from a woman, one of my neighbor friends who was in the neighborhood, a gay woman who I became intimate with, that there were gay bars—that there were quite a few of them in San Francisco. Would I like her to take me to one? I was seventeen years old at the time, living with my grandmother at the time. My grandparents raised me. So I decided that sure. But basically I wanted to go on my own. I've always been a real curious and very independent person, and I wanted to do this on my own. I remember how she drove me up to Maud's, which was called The Study at the time. Basically, we sat in the car, and I just sort of watched people come in and out. I was really fascinated, so I proceeded to, uh, well, this was when I was in high school. So I went back on my own. I took the bus up there by myself, no, actually I took a taxicab and decided to venture in on my own without the accompaniment of this older woman who was twenty-one. She was an older woman at twenty-one, and I was seventeen. So I thought that was pretty far out.

So I walked in. I never even once thought about a drinking establishment and having an ID. It never even occurred to me. So my first time in I got carded. I thought, "This is real strange." And I remember there was a bartender named Jay. His name was Jayola, and he was a very small, little, diminutive man. He kept seeing me because I went back the next week. I thought, well, maybe he won't notice. I went in again, and I got carded again. I was very tenacious. So I was able to finally put two and two together, and I decided to get a fake ID. So I went ahead and got a fake ID. Illegally. My grandmother would have died, rolled over in her grave if she knew I did this.

NAN ALAMILLA BOYD: Where'd you get your fake ID?

GONZALES: Well, I don't want to say. Anyway, I went in and had gotten an ID. Or I knew that I could get in when there were other bartenders there that didn't know me. So I started hanging out and proceeded to meet other women, other gay women, older women. Very few were in their twenties. Then there was that whole issue, there was a whole emphasis on at that point in time, which would have been 1966, there was a whole emphasis on roles—defined gender roles. And it was real weird to me because I didn't really feel that I fit into either one, either category. I remember this one time where I sat down at a table, around the pool table, by myself, and this woman came up to me and asked me if she could join me. I was just petrified, but I said well sure. So she was really masculine. She was wearing a man's flannel shirt with a T-shirt underneath and real short crew-cut hair. Pretty similar to the way a lot of people are dressing now. It's real interesting. And desert boots. She came up to me and sat next to me, and we started talking and she asked me what I was. I thought well that's a real strange question. I said, "Well, what do you mean?" And she said, "Well, are you butch or fem?"[2] I looked at her, and I told her I didn't know. I mean that was really kind of a weird question to me. I just didn't answer. I don't even remember what I said, but I know I didn't define myself. I proceeded to go home with this woman, and it was just a disaster, an absolute disaster. Not the actual intimacy part of it, but just the dynamics of meeting this first person in a bar, and she turns out to be really, really into substance abuse. It was just a disaster. And what she had done was ended up calling my grandmother and telling her that she was sleeping with me. I was devastated. I just thought this was just bizarre. So I basically ended the relationship but proceeded to pursue my sexuality because that's what I wanted to do. Then I started meeting other people up at the bar—meeting other people that were a little bit more balanced psychologically.

Basically, the one thing that should be stressed as far as the bar community in the work that you're doing is that the bars were communities. They were families. It was a whole sense of, well, there was the cliquish component also, but there was a real sense of belonging. If you were having problems in your personal life or you couldn't make your rent, we'll say that as an example, people would really rally together. If someone had, i.e., breast cancer or something, people would set up funds. It was just a real sense of community. People played softball between the different bars. It's unfortunate, but I don't sense that happening now with the women's community. And a lot of women are getting clean and sober, which I think is wonderful, but there's not a sense of that closeness and that camaraderie.

BOYD: Maud's was the place that you spent most of your time?

GONZALES: Maud's, and then I went down to the Highlander, which is the bar that Sharon owned. That's where I really, say, cut my teeth on drugs—started doing a lot of psychedelics. And down there, I got involved in more of a, my friendships were much more solid. That's where I feel that I had more of a sense of family at that point in time. The Highlander was a wonderful place. People just sort of hung out together. It was more of a sense of family. People would be intimate with one another, and yet there were no strings attached. I can't say I had a real solid relationship with one person at the time, but I formed some really good alliances with women. There was a sense of nonmonogamy, but it was okay. People didn't get hysterical about it—it wasn't really defined. It was real interesting. There was a lot of, I mean people really slept around a lot. But like I said, there wasn't a sense that we had to get married or we had to form commitments right then and there.

BOYD: So the jealousies of sleeping with someone's girlfriend didn't happen?

GONZALES: I don't know about that. I never got involved with people that were in a couple. That's always been personally a taboo for me. I try to keep my life uncomplicated as much as possible. That's not to say that it doesn't happen, but I don't prefer triangles. I think they're messy. I learned by other people's mistakes. No, there was a real sense of, it was just indicative of the sixties. It was what was going on. Free love. That whole attitude was disseminated into the gay community.

BOYD: I have a couple questions for you. When you say intimate, you mean sex?

GONZALES: Sexual.

BOYD: Let's talk a little bit more about that and in particular back to this question of role-playing. Can you just describe that a little bit more for me?

GONZALES: What aspect of role-playing?

BOYD: Like when you first started going to Maud's, your first introduction into the culture, you learned about the fact that there were roles by someone telling you about it.

GONZALES: Right.

BOYD: But what did you learn?

GONZALES: What I learned. What I learned from it was I just sort of felt that, well, I go this way and then I go this way about it. I feel that there are certain attributes that people have—there are certain women that like to react and behave in certain ways. Their behavior and their psychological makeup may be much more masculine. They look at the world that way. But I think for me, myself, I was really caught in between because I never could play—although I passed in society. I work in a corporate job as a feminine woman, and yet there are parts of myself that are much more aggressive. I hate to align aggression with assertiveness, but I sort of felt that I was in between. I was always uncomfortable with having to pigeonhole myself. I was uncomfortable with the label of being a lesbian not per se of being a lesbian, but I've always been very uncomfortable with labels. I don't necessarily need to fit into the mainstream. . . .

The role thing was very difficult for me. I always ended up with seeming to be with women that were very, very into what they called stone butches. They were real tough, but I always tried to break through that shell. I was always attempting to soften them up because I always saw another side. But the image, the image that was portrayed in society was not that. So I would get real frustrated with that whole roles issue.

BOYD: So there were two roles?

GONZALES: Yeah.

BOYD: It sounds like you were sort of taking up a third role, right? So maybe there were three roles?

GONZALES: Um-hmm.

BOYD: Did you know other people like you who didn't participate in the role thing?

GONZALES: Yeah, I did. One woman I'm still in contact with who is in Colorado right now, she and Sharon are really the only two people I've kept in contact with through that whole period of time. She lives in Colorado, and she was just pretty much, we were both sort of in the middle. Basically, to this day she is still very much in love with me. Twenty-four years later, we've just had a real connection through that whole period of time. I saw her through a very hard drug period for her where she took a lot of acid and really flipped out, ended up back in a hospital in Oregon. I would write letters to her. I could say she was probably one of the few people who was in the middle. I keep saying "in the middle," and that sounds so boring, but in that place where roles were real weird.

BOYD: Do you think that other folks who were participating in butch-fem culture could recognize that there were people who were neither? I mean, was "in the middle" a social role that you could pick, as well as the other two?

GONZALES: Exactly. Well, you pretty much were forced to. Sexually, too, I think. I do remember having an affair with a woman, a one-night stand—many one-night stands. It was just real interesting because I just don't know, I'm in a couple right now, but I just don't know with the younger gay community, younger women, if they're that much involved in one-night stands. If they go out and just trick with somebody one night. I don't have any women in my life right now that are in their twenties that are single and that hang out. But that was the norm. I went home with this woman, and she basically, we were in bed, and she wore men's pajamas. I thought, "This is really strange." She didn't want me to touch her. She didn't want me to be intimate with her. It was like a really one-way relationship. But that was very acceptable. I mean it was like there were certain women that you didn't touch. An untouchable.

BOYD: So she would make love to you or have sex with you, but you couldn't reciprocate.

GONZALES: I think it was very much—this is just my theory—I think it was a parody. I think it was an emulation of the heterosexual world again, one more time. That it was a power trip, and it was a denial, a resistance to look at your own, to look at the soft person. But I mean I'm not judging, I'm just theorizing.

BOYD: In the bar, did people talk openly about sex and sexual behavior? Did you know what you were getting into before you went home with someone?

GONZALES: No. It wasn't pre—well, I was really naïve. I didn't know what to expect in the world. Up to that point, I hadn't had, well, with the woman in my neighborhood that I had been intimate with, it was all one way also. It's like I didn't know that there was any other way that I could, you know, possibly make love to another woman, and it could be reciprocal. So I sort of had no other frame of reference. So it was weird to me because I always felt you had to be different.

BOYD: How did you have sex when it was just one way?

GONZALES: Do you mean technique? I would say oral sex and digital, using hands. It was very mechanical. There wasn't any passion in it. I didn't feel passion. It was kinda strange.

BOYD: Were women using dildos at all?

GONZALES: No. Oh, actually there was one woman that I lived in an apartment building with. I lived in an apartment building right across from Sanchez and Market. There was a woman upstairs and the manager downstairs, and they were both best friends. I was sleeping with the woman upstairs, but I was extremely attracted to the manager. I remember going in to pay my rent one day, and there was this gigantic dildo sitting on her coffee table, and I was just blown away. I thought I had never seen anything like this before. What do you do with that thing? So that was really funny—I'll never forget it. I'm sure the expression on my face was just priceless. It was sitting on the coffee table.

But that was a whole different time in my life. But it was around the same time. I was living on my own.

This will blow your mind. That apartment that is still there on Sanchez and Market, I had rented for $70 per month. It was a wonderful apartment. That was in 1973. So between that period of time and the sixties I had gotten involved with, uh, I had started to do drugs. I had started to do psychedelics. I smoked pot. I never did hard drugs. I did an incredible amount of drinking, and I'm amazed that I lived through it with the combination of the drugs. I took some amphetamines. Basically during that period of time, I just had many affairs with people, and it was sort of like three months here, four months there, and then you just moved on. I never really wanted a relationship. So the whole atmosphere at that time was fine with me. It was fine. I didn't want commitment. I really can say that it wasn't until the seventies that my heart was really broken. I sort of came out of that nonmonogamy. . . .

It seems as though we've sort of made a circle. It's real permissible now, and this is a generalization, so correct me if I'm wrong, because like I said I'm not that involved in the younger women's gay community, but it seems like [today] it's very permissible for women to be very masculine and to wear their clothing that way. Clothing is definitely a statement. There's a certain negativism about lipstick lesbians. I hear that. "Oh, those lipstick lesbians." So there's that polarization. I've gone to a couple dances where I've watched women. There's a real acceptance again of the butch and fem: the butch wearing the tuxedo and the fem wearing the gown.

BOYD: Did that happen in the sixties?

GONZALES: Yeah. Oh yeah. There was a club out by the Cow Palace that was called Leonarda's, and it was a nightclub. Thelma Davis might have told you about Leonarda's because that's where I met her. Women were in drag. Women dressed in drag. It was definitely couples, and when you walked in, you knew who the butch was and you knew who the fem was. There was unspoken rules about dancing with someone's girlfriend. There was a lot of fights in the bars at that period of time. Coupled with alcohol, you know, it can be very violent.

Fems . . . were a possession. They were definitely a possession. I guess it's all relative. I never felt that the more feminine of the couple was really looked down upon. Definitely she had to stay in her place. It was really, uh, if you ever saw two, well, I don't know if you've heard this expression, ki-ki? Well, if two fems got together or two butches got together, it was like a shock. It was like wow, what a trip. Can you imagine? That was funny, too. It was funny. That was sort of like breaking rank. It was like, "You don't do that kind of stuff." Blah blah blah. So that was pretty much a rule, an unspoken rule.

BOYD: Was there a name for someone like yourself who refused to choose?

GONZALES: No. Probably "confused." I don't know. No, I don't think so. I would have probably been called fem.

Four male impersonators and butch performers relax between sets at Mona's 440, about 1945. Mona's was a popular lesbian bar in San Francisco's North Beach, and male impersonators drew both locals and tourists to the place. *Courtesy of the Wide Open Town Collection, GLBT Historical Society, San Francisco*

BOYD: Did people identify themselves as lesbians or butches or fems?

GONZALES: They never said lesbian. They said butches or fems. They never said dyke or queer. Lezzie. Lezzie was one. But I never heard dyke. Butch or fem or "that way." But I never heard the term dyke or feminist. Gay. Gay was something that was at one point in time made reference to both men and women.

BOYD: Were there other ways when you were coming out that you sort of acclimated yourself, or was it exclusively in the bars that you learned how to be?

GONZALES: Basically exclusively in the bars. That's really the only resource that I had. Then parties. People would leave the bar and go to someone's home. Friday to Sunday night, it was just doing drugs and parties and staying up all night and going to the softball game together and having meals together. There was that real scene. Showering at other people's houses and running home to get your clothes. It was just a real, everyone was on the move and everyone was playing. But it was very, the feeling was not one of doom. It was one of awareness and exploration. For my twenty-first birthday, I'll tell you about this. This will be a great addition to this interview. For my twenty-first birthday a real good friend of mine, a woman friend, gave me a birthday party in her home in Potrero Hill. The home had a swimming pool. She had constructed a birthday cake for me out of lavender cardboard and had written "Happy Birthday Cheryl" with joints, and the "i" in Birthday was dotted with amphetamines. So what happened through the course of the evening, the cake basically was smoked [laughs] and the "i" disappeared constantly. We just played all weekend. It was really a lot of fun. And when I say play, I mean we'd just sit and listen to music and trip out and drink. People would drift in and people would drift out. So that was quite an unusual twenty-first birthday. We got up the next morning and there were brassieres and panties all around the pool area where people had just thrown them. It was pretty wild. Pretty wild time. But real creative.[3]

Commentary

This essay is titled "talking about sex," but I should have called it "why wouldn't the women I interviewed talk about sex?" I pose this as a methodological question pertaining to the practice of oral history, but it has implications for thinking about lesbian and queer history as well. For instance, Elizabeth Lapovsky Kennedy and Madeline Davis's history of working-class lesbian communities in Buffalo, New York, *Boots of Leather, Slippers of Gold*, asserts that conversations about sex played an important role in the construction of bar-based lesbian identities in the 1950s. Beginning their research in the late 1970s, they assert:

> Discussion of sex was one of many dimensions of an increasingly complex culture. The instruction of newcomers even came to include sexuality. This public recognition of sexuality gave lesbians the support to affirm their own sexuality and explore new horizons. At the same time, the community's growing public defiance produced an increased concern for enforcing role-appropriate behavior. . . . Because roles organized intimate life as well as the community's resistance to oppression, sexual performance was a vital part of these 1950s standards.[4]

Through oral history methods, Kennedy and Davis were able to analyze butch-fem sexual roles and expectations, but also the role sexual pleasure played in the formation of a resistant postwar lesbian culture. Sex was integral to socialization and community formation, Kennedy and Davis argue, and narrators talked openly and candidly about the sex they experienced and its meanings. In the oral histories I conducted in San Francisco in the early 1990s, however, "lesbians" were unwilling to talk about sex.[5] Was this because the kind of community Kennedy and Davis document (a sometimes mixed-race, bar-based, and working-class butch-fem community) did not exist in San Francisco? Or does this outcome have more to do with my approach? If sex was an important structuring paradigm, why were the women I interviewed unwilling to talk with me about it?

In the early 1990s, I conducted oral histories with forty-five mostly cisexual[6] or nontranssexual men and women who had participated in some way in queer public life in San Francisco prior to 1965.[7] Most narrators I interviewed had been born in the 1920s or 1930s, and few are alive today. The pool of narrators included roughly one-third people of color, and more than half had actively participated in bar-based communities.[8] Strongly influenced by Kennedy and Davis's historical analysis, I was particularly interested in how sex roles affected the formation of queer identity and community across race and class. However, as the conversation turned to sex during the oral history interview or interaction, gay men would talk endlessly about the subject, but the lesbian/queer women I interviewed would not.

Gay men described in vivid detail the kind of sex they were having, the specificity of their attractions, and the minutiae of how to attract certain kinds of partners. They described how to negotiate certain kinds of sex and, more important, how racialized and class-specific social spaces like bars, parks, and parties were organized around the production of these codifications or microsexualities. Gay men had theories about the way sex translated into social power and how different kinds of desire (racialized, age-based, sex-specific, etc.) functioned as a fulcrum for new social and political identities. Lesbians and queer women, on the other hand, were mostly reticent and often resistant when it came to talking about sex. Most women did not offer up information about sex without being asked directly, and when I posed questions about sex, I was often acutely aware of their discomfort.

When lesbian/queer narrators did talk about sex, several different dynamics evolved. The first dynamic was that narrators would sometimes become judgmental of their own sexuality (or sex practices) or the sexuality of others, inviting me to collude in the perspective that some sex practices were somehow socially primitive or politically retrograde. This dynamic pulled me into a political space that reinterrogated sex-war ideology and drew certain sex-specific boundaries around the idea of lesbian community.[9] A second dynamic that emerged was that talking about sex invited a kind of flirtation. In these instances, the narrator would sometimes flip the conversation, asking me about myself and my sexual practices and positioning me as the sexual object or, in other cases, the titillated voyeur. This dynamic sexualized me, and it opened up the conversation in ways that were sometimes very productive.[10] A third dynamic I observed was that while some narrators were willing to talk about sex, they seemed particularly vulnerable and expressed concern about their authority, claiming that either they did not have enough sexual experiences to speak on the subject or they were unsure of "what I was looking for." This dynamic pulled me into a counselor-type role in which I felt compelled to reassure the narrator of her authority as a sexual subject.

When I started conducting oral histories, I had had very little training. In 1991, as a graduate student, I received a small grant from the Center for Public Service at Brown University to initiate an oral history project at the Gay and Lesbian Historical Society in San Francisco. The Historical Society's archivist, Willie Walker (1949–2004), gave me a handful of contacts, and Allan Bérubé (1946–2007), oral historian and MacArthur Prize–winning author of *Coming Out under Fire*, coached me through my first round of interviews.[11] Bérubé helped me generate a list of questions, reminded me not to forget to turn on the tape recorder, and allowed me to use his release form as a template. When I contacted people, many were anxious about talking about themselves and claimed that they had done nothing special with their lives. The idea of gay and lesbian history was fairly new at the time, and in the minds of many potential narrators, history seemed to center around politicians such as Harvey Milk, activists such as Del Martin, or famous drag performers such as José Sarria.[12] I explained that memories of everyday life were just as important as the lives of famous (or infamous) people, and these types of memories would help preserve the history of gay and lesbian life in San Francisco prior to 1965. I also explained that each oral history would become part of the Gay and Lesbian Historical Society's archives, and I brought a brochure about the Historical Society along with my tape recorder and release form to each interview.

Typically, I met narrators at their homes, where I thought they would be most comfortable. At first, I studiously followed a short list of questions: "when were you born?" "where did you grow up?" "when did you move to San Francisco?" As time went by, I became more practiced at the nuances of these complex interactions, and a loose structure emerged that was more conversational. In fact, after just a few interviews, I realized that the structure of the questionnaire limited the verbal exchange and seemed to restrict the narrator's authority, so I changed my approach and committed myself to trying to follow rather than lead the conversation. Initially, I had felt a certain professional duty to control the oral history interview, and I had a naïve (beginner's) clarity about the kind of information I wanted to cull from the interview.

With time, I lost that clarity. Narrators challenged many of the assumptions I brought to the oral history project. For instance, many narrators challenged my overdependence on the concept of identity, and many refused to use the identity-based categories (lesbian and gay) that framed the oral history project. Narrators also frequently challenged a progressive approach to historical change, arguing that "things were better" before the so-called liberation of the post-Stonewall era. Similarly, some narrators challenged the concepts of pride and liberation, noting the pleasures of social secrecy and surreptitious sex.

With time, my conceptualization of the oral history "interview" shifted to a conversation or collaboration, and by the end of the year and a half I worked on the oral history project, a method emerged where I started the taped conversation with a broad and open-ended question about the city of San Francisco. In an attempt to decenter identity construction, I started with: "Tell me about your relationship to the city of San Francisco. When did you move here and why?" and then I let the narrator lead as much as possible. Because the project was framed as a gay and lesbian oral history project, however, most narrators moved immediately to queer culture and community, describing their favorite bars or when and how they had met a particularly important lover. Through the course of the conversation, I tried to remember to weave in a few topics that were important to me, and one of them had to do with sex.

Two oral histories are emblematic of the dynamics that emerged in conversations with lesbian/queer narrators that ventured toward the topic of sex. The first, with Cheryl Gonzales, describes butch-fem roles, as well as her experiences at several different queer bars in 1960s San Francisco, especially Maud's, a lesbian bar near Haight-Ashbury.[13] Gonzales's narrative is richly conversational, and I remember that I had fun talking with her. I was particularly excited to find that she was willing to talk directly about sex. In the oral history we produced, I ask Gonzales to explain butch-fem bar culture and to describe the social meanings attached to certain gendered sex roles: How did she learn about butch-fem culture? Did fems have sexual agency? What kind of sex was going on? Was it possible to carve out an independent sexual role? Throughout the conversation, Gonzales maintains that she had a lot of sex and a lot of fun in the 1960s, and the culture that evolved around bars was a positive aspect of her life. However, Gonzales also asserts that she felt constrained by butch-fem roles. They felt "weird" to her, and she felt "naïve" and "in the middle." She notes that one-night stands and nonreciprocal sex were the norm at that time, but she expresses negative judgment of these dynamics and a concern that present-day (1990s) "gay women" do not engage in these activities. In other words, she seemed concerned that future readers of the oral history might judge her so-called promiscuity or the value of nonreciprocal sex. Finally, Gonzales concedes that she did not always enjoy the sexual interactions that positioned her in a passive or fem role, and she experienced these interactions to be "all one way," "mechanical," "strange," and "weird."

In this interview, I do more leading than following, despite my intentions. I'm excited that Gonzales is willing to talk about sex roles and sex practice, but as a narrator, Gonzales is on the young side of the cohort, entering the bars in the mid-1960s as a teenager. As such, she is relatively close to my age (fifteen years older). She is also a light-skinned and fem-identified Latina, like myself, and these factors contribute to a certain amount of overidentification and thus (I suspect) more casual conversation. Gonzales's age puts her a whole generation younger than most of the women-identified narrators interviewed for the project who entered the bar scene in the 1940s or 1950s, which may explain her willingness to talk more openly about sex. And while her racial and ethnic identifications do not register overtly in this excerpt—she does not verbally identify with Latina/o communities—her reticence about her own racial/ethnic identification mirrors her ambivalence about structured sexual roles, as well as her pleasure in the possibility of recuperating stone butches, trying "to break through that shell." For example, Gonzales's desire for a sexual place in the middle and her desire to pull stone butches back from their untouchability, which to Gonzales seemed like a radical—even pathological—polarization of sexual roles, may be a further expression of her ambivalence toward or resistance to the social structures that define race and sex. As Gonzales asserts, "I was uncomfortable with having to pigeonhole myself. . . . I've always been very uncomfortable with labels. I don't necessarily need to fit into the mainstream." More germane to the methodological questions raised at the start of this essay, however, are the concerns Gonzales raises about promiscuity and nonreciprocal sex.

Gonzales is conscious of her audience, her responsibilities as a historical narrator, and my role as a historian. For instance, there are several moments during the interview when she breaks through her storytelling to speak directly to me as a historian. "Basically," she interjects, "the one thing that should be stressed as far as the bar community in the work that you're doing is that the bars were communities." Here, Gonzales shifts from a story about one-on-one intimacy to clarify what I would consider to be a political perspective. She wants me to understand the important social role bars played in community formation. "They were families," she asserts, "there was a real sense of belonging." Historiographically, in the early 1990s when this oral history was conducted, the idea of bar-based communities performing a social good was not a popular perspective with regard to lesbian/queer history, and Gonzales goes out of her way to stress this point. At the end of the excerpt, for instance, before launching into the story of her drug-filled twenty-first birthday party, she states, "This will be a great addition to this interview," certain that this kind of story is appropriate for our oral history interview.

Gonzales is less certain about the story she wants to tell about sex, however. She expresses disdain for stone butches and decries nonreciprocal sex, yet she tells several stories that affirm her attraction to stone butches. Similarly, she is proud of her history of nonmonogamy and defends its meanings: "It was real interesting . . . [and] there wasn't a sense that we had to get married or form commitments right then and there." Still, she registers concerns about contemporary misunderstandings: "I just don't know with the younger gay community, younger women, if they're that much involved in one-night stands. If they go out and just trick with somebody one night. . . ." Gonzales includes this disclaimer prior to a story about a one-night stand she had with a stone butch whose use of men's pajamas was "really strange" and whose untouchability meant a lack of intimacy and a dissatisfying sexual experience. It is at this point in the interview when, trying to repeat Gonzales's words but, instead, sounding unnecessarily judgmental, I state, "So she would make love to you or have sex with you but you couldn't reciprocate." And Gonzales, perhaps following my cue, puts forward a theory of butch-fem sexuality that conflates nonreciprocal sex with heterosexuality and stone butch sexuality with "a power trip and a denial." While Gonzales is certain of her political position regarding the value of bar-based communities, and she is not afraid to proudly retell stories of free love and abundant drug taking (again, not popular topics in the Reagan-Bush era), she is less certain about the value of nonreciprocal same-sex sexual practices and, following my ambiguous comment (not at all my political point of view), likens stone butch sex and butch-fem sexuality to a parody.

The next excerpt is from a taped conversation with Rikki Streicher, a white, middle-class butch (not lesbian identified) woman, who, prior to owning Maud's, the Haight-Ashbury bar that Gonzales describes as a community, had spent a lot of time in queer bars in San Francisco.[14] For a while in the 1940s, Streicher had dressed in drag (stylish male attire), pimped for her sex-working girlfriends (that is, negotiated their sex for sale), and hung out with a rough crowd of butches and dykes in San Francisco's North Beach neighborhood. In the early 1940s, Streicher had lived in Los Angeles, where she had also spent a lot of time in queer bars. In this excerpt, I ask her about whether queer bar culture was a working-class culture, and we begin by discussing, again, butch-fem roles.

JANUARY 22, 1992

NAN ALAMILLA BOYD: So what about butch-fem lesbians?

RIKKI STREICHER: That's my generation. That's not Maud's. That's not the sixties.

BOYD: That's the fifties?

STREICHER: Forties and fifties, right. Butch-fem. There used to be, well, butch and fem, you wouldn't get—a dyke was low class. And I used to delineate between butches and dykes by, now this is really, this is Los Angeles and how it was then. Now, if you're going to try to do all these things, and I see all these other words and how they're applied, and I think, "I wonder who in the hell thought of that" because it's not true. Obviously, people with power are men. So the women that saw themselves as butches or dykes of today would emulate men. Then further down, I called them the industrial set. [laughs]

BOYD: Uh-huh.

STREICHER: [mocking] Uh-huh. I mean, you know, snobbery is snobbery, no matter what the generation.

BOYD: No! I'm interested.

STREICHER: So they perceived things on a fairly straight ahead and simplistic sense. And they emulated men.

BOYD: How'd you differentiate between the industrial set and the butches?

STREICHER: Well, a butch is a butch is a butch, I suppose. In that sense of the word. Then of course the industrial set, for instance, would hop up and hold the chair for the little lady. They would do all of [that], where you wouldn't get that [with a butch]. [It's like] the difference between a bar in Long Beach or Venice West . . . as opposed to say Tess' or out in the valley in LA. Out in Venice West you'd get this sturdy little group of Mom and Pops right? In Venice West you had, it was, well, somebody still took out the garbage. It was still the same, the same thing was going on except that nobody acted it out, basically. Then there was, then you get into the difference between oral versus manual, and that was a delineating factor in a way, too, you know.

BOYD: Tell me about that.

STREICHER: It's hard to, not having been a part of one half of this equation. It's
hard to really talk about it.
BOYD: Which part?
STREICHER: Well, I was hardly the industrial set, let's put it that way.

Commentary

In this somewhat fragmented conversation, Streicher explains that butch-fem
culture was a product of the 1940s and 1950s, not the 1960s, as Gonzales asserts,
and that within queer bar culture, both in Los Angeles and San Francisco, a multivalent butch-fem culture thrived. She differentiates butches from dykes, or
what she calls "the industrial set," which I understand to signify a working-class
culture or affect, and she explains that the industrial set "emulated men," practicing more stereotypically gendered gestures like holding out a woman's chair
while getting seated at a table. Streicher maintains, however, that most lesbian
relationships, even middle-class relationships, maintained gendered differences
("somebody still took out the garbage"), but class differences could be expressed
sexually, "oral versus manual." Streicher concedes, when pressed, that she was
more aligned with the butches or the middle-class nonindustrial set, and it is
important to note that when asked directly about her own sex practices, Streicher
backs away—"it's hard to really talk about it"—but implies that she practiced
oral rather than manual (digital or penetrative) sex.

Streicher perceives that I expressed a certain "snobbery" with regard to her
use of the phrase "industrial set." When I ask her about working-class culture,
she assumes that this kind of differentiation is a judgment used to criticize gendered role-playing, and she corrects my assumptions and defends working-class
cultural practices. She also states, as an aside while differentiating between
butches and dykes: "Now, if you're going to try to do all these things, and I see
all these other words and how they're applied, and I think 'I wonder who in the
hell thought of that' because it's not true." I understand this statement as a cau-
tion to me, as a scholar, not to make assumptions or create new language or
define things incorrectly. At the time of this interview, 1992, Streicher was current
on the scholarship in lesbian history and critical of the knowledge produced.[15]
Also, in other parts of our conversations, Streicher often turns the interview on
me, asking me direct questions about myself, challenging me, flirting with me,
and practicing some of the stereotypically gendered gestures she describes, like
holding the door open and, memorably, cleaning my sunglasses for me. Still,
Streicher never returned to the topic of her own sex practices—and I taped three
fairly long conversations with her.[16] This one short excerpt reflects the most
direct conversation we had about sex and sexual practices.

Rikki Streicher is an exceptionally important person in San Francisco's queer
history, and her insights shaped, to a large degree, the analysis I brought to the
book I ultimately wrote on this topic, but there was little information about sex

to be culled for the public record. And in the end, I did not include this point of analysis in my book.[17] I was not able to follow up on Kennedy and Davis's analysis of the important role that sex and sexuality played in the formation of lesbian culture and community in Buffalo in the 1940s and 1950s. Was this because a sex-specific culture did not exist in San Francisco's lesbian communities as it did in Buffalo? Was it that conversations about sex were not useful to the formation of queer culture and community? I don't think so. Rather, I would argue that in San Francisco, the value of certain sexual behaviors had changed so dramatically since the 1940s and 1950s that narrators were unwilling to disclose them. Butch-fem sexuality had become, in a sense, unspeakable in San Francisco.

Why? The most salient factors are the ideological structures of the oral history interview and the identity-based terms I brought to the larger oral history project. Narrators perceived the oral history experience to be a middle-class endeavor, and despite my effort to control this image, they perceived me to be both middle-class and a feminist of the kind that would judge the sexual role-playing prevalent in their generation. For instance, several narrators mentioned the differences between "digital" and "oral" sex, maintaining that lesbians of the 1970s-feminist variety practiced reciprocal oral sex while butches, dykes, fems, studs, and girls practiced a kind of retrograde and nonreciprocal digital or penetrative sex. For those who would talk about it, there was an almost unanimous disavowal of stone butches, as Gonzales maintains—even though these women were her primary sexual part-ners—and a strong disavowal of the use of dildos or other sex toys, though many women remember sex toys for sale in the bars, though "no one they knew" ever used them. There was a similar disavowal of sadomasochistic practices.

Most, if not all, of the women I interviewed were able to describe in rich detail the social nuances of butch-fem culture, but very few wanted to articulate how butch-fem culture influenced sex practice or how sex practice influenced butch-fem culture. Women, like men, were clearly engaged in fairly specific sex practices, as Gonzales's story exemplifies, but most of the women who agreed to discuss their experiences with me in an oral history (across race, class, and sexual culture) did not recount that these roles were liberating, healthy, pleasurable, or an important aspect of community formation. Most embraced a fairly stereotypical critique that equated gendered and sexual role-playing (that is, role-playing in and out of bed) with heterosexism and misogyny. And they expressed shame and disavowal at what they perceived to be prefeminist or preliberation-era sexual styles or behaviors. Cheryl Gonzales's narrative underscores these points in that as a self-consciously rebellious person, she recuperates bar life, promiscuity, and drug use but not the kind of nonreciprocal sex that was common among queer women in the 1960s.

Rikki Streicher is something of an exception in that she vociferously defends the integrity of a highly sexualized bar culture, though she is fairly mute about the role sex itself may have played in the formation of this community. Rikki Streicher is also an exception in her disidentification as a lesbian and a feminist. She's openly critical of 1970s-style feminists and scholars of any stripe and, for that reason, was, perhaps, less judgmental of butch-fem sexual styles, even though she wouldn't talk openly with me about sex. Streicher also would not talk about pimping or cross-dressing, though I asked her several times to describe these experiences to me. I learned about these aspects of her life from others, and while she hinted at them and, in fact, teased me with this information, she wouldn't discuss it openly with me. As with the other women I spoke with and despite her critical position, Streicher was conscious of her self-representation and aware that our interview would be transcribed and available to the public. Butches pimping or cross-dressing or fucking their girlfriends, digitally or otherwise, wasn't going to be part of the public record, at least not in a celebratory or recuperative sense. These practices are just too far outside the scope of middle-class sexual propriety.

The omission of sex talk during my interviews with "lesbians" reveals the limits of oral history as a method. In both its identity-based construction and its "public record" justification, the practice of lesbian and gay history making, or oral history making, is often perceived by queer narrators to be a middle-class endeavor, a political project aimed at social uplift. Indeed, oral history involves the self-conscious production of a particular kind of representation—a representation fit for public consumption. So while butches and fems, studs and girls, might have talked differently among themselves, when talking with me—a dissertation-writing grad student from an Ivy League institution—no matter how working class I was before college or how much I tried to follow rather than lead, and no matter how much I tried to disavow middle-class judgments of queer sex and sexuality, the production of knowledge about sex practice was limited to what narrators perceived to be permissible speech.

This does not explain why Kennedy and Davis were more successful at engaging their narrators in conversations about sex and sexuality, but it does follow up on a point that historian Kevin Murphy raises about queer oral history methods: the veil of homonormativity allows certain speech acts and not others; it polices our histories and renders the nonnormal impermissible.[18] Unbeknownst to me, the lesbian and gay oral history project, as I described it to possible narrators, suggested a kind of neoliberal or homonormative public memory that assumed the evolution of butch-fem sexual cultures into middle-class identity categories that worked to distance women, for example, from the pleasure of "digital" or nonreciprocal sex.[19] San Francisco, after all, was the city that gave birth to homophile movements. By the 1990s, the highly sexualized butch-fem cultures that existed in the 1950s didn't exist anymore and had, in many ways, been supplanted, first by the powerful rhetoric of gay and lesbian liberation movements and, second, by lesbian-feminist and identity-based movements that, over time, had become increasingly aligned with citizenship claims that shunned nonnormative sex practices. Keenly aware of power, the dykes who lived through the 1940s and 1950s and were around in the 1990s to tell about it challenged my assumptions in many ways, including my assumption that they would talk openly with me about sex. Where does this leave us as historians? It leaves us, perhaps, more cognizant of the many ways sex and sexuality function as vectors of political economy. In other words, as Foucault's writings have made clear, conversations about sex are never unmediated by the power relations that situate them in time and place.[20]

Notes

1. I want to thank Horacio N. Roque Ramírez for his insightful comments on this essay. I also thank Julian Carter, Mel Chen, Rebekah Edwards, and Don Romesburg for their critical readings and lively conversation.

2. In keeping with Kennedy and Davis, I prefer the spelling "fem" to "femme" in deference to its public rather than academic usage. See Elizabeth Lapovsky Kennedy and Madeline Davis, *Boots of Leather, Slippers of Gold: The History of a Lesbian Community* (New York: Routledge, 1993), 391.

3. Cheryl Gonzales, interviewed by Nan Alamilla Boyd, tape recording, San Francisco, February 1, 1992, Wide Open Town History Project, Gay, Lesbian, Bisexual, Transgender (GLBT) Historical Society, San Francisco, California.

4. Kennedy and Davis, *Boots of Leather, Slippers of Gold*, 194.

5. While "lesbian" often functions as an umbrella term to signify women who engage in same-sex sexual relations, I put the term in quotes because many of the women I interviewed did not identify as lesbian, even though they were actively engaged in same-sex sexual relationships and/or gender-transgressive communities; in fact, some narrators, such as Cheryl Gonzales and Rikki Streicher, used the term *lesbian* as an othering term to differentiate themselves from women ("activists," "feminists") who, like themselves, engaged in same-sex sexual relationships but expressed a different political understanding of those relationships.

6. For more on the term *cisexual*, see Julia Serano, *Whipping Girl: A Transsexual Woman on Sexism and the Scapegoating of Femininity* (Seattle: Seal, 2007).

7. In an attempt to prioritize the history of the 1930s, 1940s and 1950s, 1965 was the cutoff point for my oral history project. For more on why 1965 is an important turning point in San Francisco's (queer) political history, see Nan Alamilla Boyd, *Wide Open Town: A History of Queer San Francisco to 1965* (Berkeley: University of California Press, 2003), 1–19.

8. See ibid., 5–6, for a more thorough description of my method, terminology, and oral history narrators.

9. On post–civil rights movement sex-war ideology, see Lisa Duggan and Nan D. Hunter, *Sex Wars: Sexual Dissent and Political Culture* (New York: Routledge, 2006).

10. See Esther Newton, "My Best Informant's Dress: The Erotic Equation in Fieldwork," in Ellen Lewin and William L. Leap, eds., *Out in the Field: Reflections of Lesbian and Gay Anthropologists* (Urbana: University of Illinois Press, 1996), 212–34. See also the introduction to this book.

11. Allan Bérubé, *Coming Out under Fire: The History of Gay Women and Men in World War II* (New York: Free Press, 1990). For remembrances of Walker and Bérubé, see Terence Kissack, "In Memoriam: Willie Walker," *Perspectives: The Newsmagazine of the American Historical Association* 43, no. 5 (May 2005); and John D'Emilio, "Allan Bérubé's Gift to History," *Gay and Lesbian Review Worldwide* 15, no. 3 (May–June 2008): 10–13.

12. For more on Del Martin and José Sarria, see Nan Alamilla Boyd, *Wide Open Town*, especially chapters 1 and 4. See also Marcia M. Gallo, *Different Daughters: A History of the Daughters of Bilitis and the Rise of the Lesbian Rights Movement* (Seattle: Seal, 2006).

13. See the 1993 video documentary *Last Call at Maud's*, directed by Paris Poirier and distributed by the Maud's Project, 32A Horizon Ave., Venice, CA 90291.

14. Rikki Streicher, interviewed by Nan Alamilla Boyd, tape recording, San Francisco, January 22, 1992, Wide Open Town History Project, GLBT Historical Society.

15. For instance, Streicher had just finished reading Lillian Faderman's *Odd Girls and Twilight Lovers: A History of Lesbian Life in Twentieth-Century America* (New York: Columbia University Press, 1991), which, to her surprise, features a photo of the young Streicher on the cover.

16. January 22, 1992; March 4, 1992; July 25, 1992.

17. *Wide Open Town* explores the history of how queer bar cultures and communities developed an implicit political economy that challenged the more overt political ideology put forward by lesbian and gay homophile organizations. As such, it analyzes political culture more than sexual culture.

18. Kevin P. Murphy, "Gay Was Good: Progress, Homonormativity, and Oral History," in Twin Cities GLBT Oral History Project, eds., *Queer Twin Cities* (Minneapolis: University of Minnesota Press, 2010), 305–18. See also Nan Alamilla Boyd, "Who Is the Subject? Queer Theory Meets Oral History," *Journal of the History of Sexuality* 172 (May 2008): 177–89.

19. On links between neoliberalism and homonormativity, see Lisa Duggan, *The Twilight of Equality? Neoliberalism, Cultural Politics, and the Attack on Democracy* (Boston: Beacon, 2003).

20. Michel Foucault. *The History of Sexuality, Vol. 1: An Introduction.* (New York: Vintage, 1980), 3–49, 81–102.

6

PRIVATE LIVES AND PUBLIC HISTORY

On Excavating the Sexual Past in
Queer Oral History Practice

Jason Ruiz

Oral history by Jason Ruiz with Charles W. Paul Larsen, Columbia Heights, Minnesota, October 16, 2006

Charles Larsen, who likes to be called Chuck, spoke with interviewers Jason Ruiz and Ann McKenzie at the dining room table in his suburban Minneapolis home. This was one of dozens of interviews that we conducted as part of the Twin Cities GLBT Oral History Project, a collective of students, scholars, and activists interested in the queer history of Minnesota. Participants in this project were completely self-selected. Larsen, an older man who was quick to laugh but also showed a melancholy side during our long interview, responded to an advertisement in a local queer magazine. This excerpt, which focuses mainly on his sexual life, is part of a much longer interview that details— among other themes—how Larsen, an ordained minister, reconciled his spiritual calling with his sexuality in the 1960s and 1970s. Full transcripts of this and other interviews conducted by the Project are archived as part of the Tretter Collection in Gay, Lesbian, Bisexual, and Transgender Studies at the University of Minnesota. Several of these interviews influenced Queer Twin Cities, *an anthology edited by members of the Twin Cities GLBT Oral History Project (University of Minnesota Press, 2010).*[1]

JASON RUIZ: How did you learn about sex?

CHARLES LARSEN: Well, that's interesting. One day I went to the Aster Movie Theater on Hennepin Avenue. I think I was in high school. And I went there because they'd have two movies for the price of one, and it was real cheap. So I'm sitting there watching the movie, and I thought I felt some guy's hand on my knee. And I thought, *What's that?* And I thought, *Well I'm just curious. Let's just see what happens.* And so one thing led to another and another, and finally we were fondling each other. He invited me to go to his car, where he did fellatio on me . . . didn't know what the term "blow job" meant. I thought,

That's what it means! I had no idea. When I was sixteen, I'd saved up my money and went to Europe because that was after my junior year. After my senior year, I was going to join the Christian Brothers, and I decided that if I was going to see the world, I have to do it then. I went to France among other countries. I had been having sex with Dennis [a childhood friend] off and on. And that was about it. In Paris, some man took my hand, and when he shook my hand, he scratched my palm. I knew what that meant! How would I know? I did! I knew that had something to do with gay, homosexual. Of course, then it scared me, and I just walked away, but I knew what it meant. It was like . . . a signal or something. And that was amazing. I had no sex in the thirty days I was there. I was with a number of University of Minnesota students who were gay. And they were just carrying on like trash on the boat and in London. So while I knew I was having sex with Dennis, I wasn't like them. In fact, I was certain I was going to get married and then that would stop.

Ruiz: Could you back up a tiny bit and describe who Dennis was?

Larsen: Dennis was a childhood friend I met in the second grade. In about the seventh grade, we'd go over to his house after school and just started goofing around. We ended up having sex. He'd tell me we couldn't have sex because every time we do, it's a mortal sin. So he was supposed to wait for me to ask so it wouldn't be a mortal sin for him. I thought, *Screw that mess! It's not a sin!* As Catholics, you were supposed to confess masturbation. Well, that got old hat. The priest would just go crazy. I thought, *It's not a sin, just forget that.*

Ruiz: How would you have gotten that sense when so much around you would have been telling you that sex was a sin?

Larsen: Survival. To think that what Dennis and I were doing was a sin and I was gonna go to hell was too heavy to deal with. However, when I graduated from high school and entered the Christian Brothers down in Glencoe, I was totally celibate for thirty-three days because I knew that just wasn't the place to do it. But then I when I came out, I decided, *Well, now I can be who I am.* I didn't know what I was. I just knew I liked having sex with men. In July [of 1961] I went down to Glencoe, Missouri, with eighty young men to enter the Christian Brothers. . . . They're the equivalent of a nun. They're the male, nonpriest religious who teach. I felt I could do it. If you love God good enough, you just give up sex. But I went to the Christian Brothers to become a teacher. You'd go there to become a Christian Brother first, and then teaching came second. Well, I had teaching first, and I'd be a brother on the side, just say my prayers. Decided that wasn't going to work. The day I came out in St. Louis to get the train to come back to St. Paul, I stopped in a Methodist church. And I said, *Someday I'm going to be a Methodist minister.* I went back [to the Twin Cities] to go to the U.[2] Two years here at the U, I was a star in General College, but bombed out when I transferred into education. I failed Introduction to Teaching! So I [went] to St. Cloud, where I was an honor student for the rest of my career. You're dealing with a lot of farm kids who party [at St. Cloud

State University], and I didn't. I was a history major. And when I came to the Happy Hour, which was the big gay bar [in Minneapolis] in my day, I started seeing a number of my classmates from St. Cloud. I came to find out the entire History Club was gay! And I thought, *Darn it, I didn't know that*! But every weekend, I'd come home to work at the White Castle. So I never had sex up in St. Cloud in two years. I never had any type of homosexual anything. I was just there to study. And one day in November, I was walking from the little house where I paid $4.75 a week to rent this really teeny bedroom. It hit me. I don't know how it hit me, it hit me. I was going to be gay the rest of my life. This was not a phase. There was no right woman or girl. I was going to be gay the rest of my life. But I had a choice. I could be a good gay boy or a bad one. And I decided I would do my best to be a good one.

RUIZ: What did that mean to you, a good gay boy?

LARSEN: Not promiscuous. Not an alcoholic. The first time I walked into the Happy Hour, I looked around and thought, *Oh my*! I was like seventeen. I walked into the Happy Hour, saw what appeared to me to be drunks hanging out in this dark bar. I looked around and thought, *Is this how I'm going to end up? No! This is not how you're going to end up*. . . . This was in the early sixties. I walked in there, and it shocked me. I knew they were gays, homosexuals. And I guess I was one, but I didn't want to end up like that. And over the many years that I went to the Happy Hour, I rarely if ever met somebody to have sex—well, maybe five or six in seven or eight years. . . .

RUIZ: What drew you to the Happy Hour bar at the tender age of seventeen?

LARSEN: I wanted to see what gay people were like. My dad, one time—he was a cop—said, *Whatever you do, don't go to Rice Park because there are strange men there*. . . . From decoding, I realized they were probably homosexuals. Well, guess where I went. In the family car. And I'd pick up strangers. God, almighty, I ended up in a funeral home with a guy. He was driving a black Cadillac and dressed in a suit. I should have known! In that case, I followed him, and we go up to this funeral parlor. And I go, *Oh my God, this is going to be interesting*. Fools rush in where angels fear to tread, and I just followed him in there. We went to his bedroom, sort of made out. And I thought, *I'm not too interested in this*. He went into the bathroom, and I got dressed and I ran out of that room down a hall. And I thought, *Where am I? How do I get out of this place*? Well, I found my way out and came home. I'm amazed at some of the strange things and dangerous things I did.

RUIZ: How did you know how to cruise?

LARSEN: As a young person who was attracted to men, I obviously would usually stare at their crotch or their body language. If they had an attractive body, and they appeared to be friendly or whatever. It was just, I was just attracted to men. I guess I would just look them over, and if they'd look me over back, I guess you'd just see what happened.

RUIZ: What other dangerous things did you do?

LARSEN: Oh my. When I was pastor in San Francisco, the board of directors gave me a pass to the baths. They thought it would be nice for the pastor to relax. I didn't go to the baths that often. I enjoyed going to the parks. Lafayette Park in San Francisco was a gay paradise. When the sun went down, the few straight people who had been there during the day left, and it was ours. By ours, I mean forty or fifty gay men walking around in suggestive poses. And what I didn't realize was you'd follow them into the bushes, and there were these little clearings they'd made. And at any time there'd be forty or fifty men having sex all over Lafayette Park. And you'd just walk through and you'd see somebody and you'd follow them or they'd follow you. I left there in the end of '78 to become pastor in Houston. I left San Francisco one year before AIDS hit. And I would have been a goner. There's no way if I'd stayed there that year—the sexual activity would be six or seven contacts in a night. I had legal speed from a doctor in Florida, and I'd take one of those and a cup of coffee, and baby I'd go from eleven until six in the morning and just have a great time. What in the hell was I thinking? I realize now it's a miracle I'm alive. Some of the people I followed as a youngster or as an adult into their homes or down dark alleys or out in the middle of fields, I can't believe it. And how do you tell this, as a pastor, well, I wouldn't dare tell people half of what I've done. I wouldn't tell my partner half of what I've done. I'd tell him just enough and hope he's not as foolish as I was. At the time, I just thought it was great.

In San Francisco, I was considered a wallflower. They didn't know, I was such a sneak. I was the pastor, and I was real sweet and nice. Didn't go to the baths, didn't have a lover every week. But boy, I'd hit the parks. And I thought, *I can match anybody in that church*. At one time had a list I kept in a little book. It was like 150 in the course of maybe a year. It was just way out of hand. But San Francisco before AIDS was just wonderful. It was this wonderful place where everything happened to anybody. You'd go to the baths, and there'd be a hundred people. And literally just one after the other, walking through the halls, the doors would be open. They'd have orgy rooms. One of the church members got dressed, went down the bus stop to go to work, and some guy picked him up. So he went home with this guy and had sex and didn't go to work that day. That's what happened in San Francisco! Harvey Milk had his lover, and then he'd have lovers on the side. A lot of couples had open relationships. The prevailing thought was the only way a gay male couple can stay together is if they have an open relationship. One actually had three in their family. Somebody asked me once to perform a holy union for three people. I couldn't do it. I'm just so traditional. And yet I was doing things probably just as wild.

When I was pastor in Houston [I was] again a Goody Two Shoes. But at one o'clock, I would go to these bookstores. And, ugh, I'd go from one until maybe four, come home dead and get ready. One time the MCC pastors went to the Holy Land. We went through this park and I thought, *This looks hot*. But I didn't say anything. The other guys, the other—Troy Perry—some of the other guys went to the baths, which I missed. Oh, and they were bragging. One said, *I never got off the floor, and blah blah*. And oh, I missed it. And as soon as they were in bed, I went back to that park. I literally was in that park from midnight until six in the morning. I crawled back to my hotel—literally. Got to my room just as the others are getting up, and I said, *I'll be right there!* Had sex with all of these Hasidic guys. That was amazing. The black hat and the curls. So that was just, it was wild.

Ruiz: Why did you maintain a public façade of innocence?

Larsen: Because I was the pastor. And the pastor shouldn't be a whore or a slut. Even though a lot of the pastors were so comfortable with their sexuality. The congregation just knew that I was old-time. I was raised Catholic, so you're a little more uptight. That one little shit of a nun telling me I was different. So a little hypocritical in a way. I don't know, I just, I felt that my sexual life needed to be mine. Private. One time I remember [that a member of the] Houston church saw me at one of the bookstores and said, *Well, I guess you're human*. And I said, *Yeah, I am. Just keep your mouth shut*. He did.

[Chuck goes on to describe how he found the MCC while he was the pastor of a conservative church in Atlanta. After a while, we return to Chuck's young adulthood in Minneapolis.]

Ruiz: What was the social scene [in the Twin Cities] like at that time?

Larsen: It was hit and miss. The thing is, though, you'd go to the Happy Hour, and many times after closing, people would have parties. And that was a ball. They'd have parties in Uptown. I remember going to a couple. I didn't know the guy who was having it. You'd walk in, there'd be maybe thirty or forty people there. They're having sex. It was mind-boggling and was just very exciting. I didn't have sex there, but other people did. But it was a total, total subculture. You'd see some of those people on the street, and they wouldn't even acknowledge you. Everyone there was afraid of being exposed or blackmailed. You just didn't know who you could trust. Supposedly there were cops around, too. You didn't know if somebody was a decoy.

Ruiz: What were you risking if you would have gotten caught?

Larsen: Everything. You'd risk your career. I probably never would have taught again. As a Presbyterian minister, I would have been defrocked. I was scared I wasn't going to get through seminary because the Methodists were uptight. Now they have gay caucuses at Emory. I went to Candler School of Theology, and that's Methodist from the Florida conference. They're very strict. Yet every Friday and Saturday night, I'd go to the gay bars in Atlanta, all these guys from Alabama and North Carolina coming down. They were all so hot. One night I went to the motel with this one guy who had a friend who picked up somebody also. We got there first, did our thing, and we're sleeping. Well, his friend comes in with somebody, and they're just acting like white trash. It was so bad. So noisy. The next morning we wake up, I look over, it's one of my classmates who's the son of a Methodist bishop—and he screamed! There were fifteen gay seminarians in my class, but I was the worst. At that time I had dark hair, and I bleached it. I bleached it beyond God knows what. It would turn green sometimes. I didn't care! And I was the minister of youth at Jonesburg Methodist, and I got some speed. It was legal, and I lost all this weight. I was really good-looking. Had this hair that—I liked red, I liked blond. This one lady in the church, she said, "Chuck, what happened to your hair?" I said, "*Plenty!*" I was just a sassy little thing at the time. . . .

RUIZ: Where were you when AIDS hit?

LARSEN: I was in Houston. MD Anderson Cancer Hospital called the gay community leaders together. They said, *We have something new called "gay cancer" and we don't know what it is. It's starting in San Francisco.* And I'm going, *Oh my God, did I get out of there just in the knick of time.*

All of a sudden it went from gay cancer to AIDS. In the early days, it was horrible. We had twenty people in the hospital at some times. These were people I knew, loved. They'd be in the same floor, and with each visit you'd have to put on a gown, gloves, a hat, a mask. And then you'd put that down and go to the next room and same thing. It just wore me out. And they died and they died. They had the most horrible, horrible side effects. This one guy, his legs looked like they were petrified wood. It was just so horrible and ugly, and they were in such pain. It just appeared to be so hopeless. And it just kept on hitting. It just wouldn't stop. And I'm certain that was part—I was just so overwhelmed. I just felt so bad. I went to so many funerals. Half the time the parents didn't even know their son was gay. Glen, my partner, says, *You rarely show any emotion. You rarely cry.* I say, *Well, after all that I've been through as a pastor, I couldn't.*

RUIZ: You were about to take us—you decided to leave Houston and go back to San Francisco. How had San Francisco changed?

LARSEN: AIDS just was wiping out hundreds of people that I'd known. It was really something. Almost all of the really sexually active people—and these were the really pretty ones that had dates all the time, always with new lovers—all died. It was sad. I was like, *Well, it's good if you're not quite so hot and quite so active and don't have quite so many lovers and you'll live.*

[Chuck goes on to describe his professional life in San Francisco and his return to the Twin Cities in the late 1970s.]

RUIZ: Final question. Why did you contact us?

LARSEN: I think everybody would like to be remembered. For a lot of gay and lesbian people, that may not happen. Even though Glen and I have an extensive will and all this stuff and we're going to be cremated, it doesn't say where the ashes are going to go. I don't know where they need to go. As a gay person, I don't have a family that is going to want to visit my crypt or gravestone. And that's okay. Because most of the gay and lesbian, transsexual, bisexual folks won't have any of that. But in answer to your question, that's why I wanted something on record that at one time this gay person named Charles W. Larsen lived. And he was involved, and he attempted to make a difference in the gay community.[3]

Commentary

Gayle Rubin opened her now-classic 1984 essay, "Thinking Sex: Notes for a Radical Theory of Politics and Sexuality," with a simple but clear call: "The time has come for us to think about sex."[4] The author does not suggest that we think exclusively about sexuality (that is, the identities that we attach to sex), but, along with sexuality, she quite literally urges us to think about sex itself—what we do with our bodies for pleasure—and what sex means. What would happen if oral historians took up this call? This is one of the questions that I explored when I interviewed several dozen gay- and lesbian-identified men and over the age of fifty from 2004 to 2006. I conducted these interviews for the Twin Cities GLBT Oral History Project, which I had founded with Dorthe Troeften and Kevin P. Murphy with funding from the University of Minnesota.[5] Our intention was not to produce a comprehensive community history, as other projects had successfully done, but to create an archive of life stories that would help to remedy the dearth of oral historical evidence of queer life in the Twin Cities. Since the founding of the project, we have grown into a collective that includes undergraduates, graduate students, and faculty at the University of Minnesota.

At the time that we interviewed Chuck, our main goal in the oral history project was to capture the life stories of GLBT Minnesotans, so we kept our questions quite general. This allowed the interviewees to choose how to narrate their lives and, we hope, will allow scholars and community members with a wide array of interests to access and make use of the archived interviews. Of course, sex is an important part of most people's lives, so it became an important topic for our interviews. Despite the fact that many of our narrators tended to submerge sex within narratives of love and affection, it was clear that many of the men I interviewed considered it a driving force in their lives.

I reluctantly focus here on men's life narratives because my interviews with lesbian-identified women elicited mostly superficial discussions of sex. Queer women were more reticent than men in talking about sex with me. Gay men with whom I spoke inevitably turned to matters of sex in narrating their life stories, whereas women carefully detailed the emergence of their sexual *identities* and mostly avoided discussion of their sexual *practices*. This is undoubtedly due in part to my own perspective as a young queer man and my (misguided) reluctance to press such matters with women (and perhaps my eagerness to discuss the topic with men).

When I did discuss sex with the women I interviewed, it was most often used by the narrators to illustrate the bonds they shared with a particular partner rather than to illustrate their routes to erotic pleasure, so narratives of sex were often couched within the broader emotional histories that narrators constructed for themselves. In other words, they talked about (or around) sex as a way to describe their *relationships* with other women and girls—rather than to narrate their own drives for erotic pleasure. As I reread the transcripts of my conversations with the lesbian-identified women I interviewed, I could not help but wonder what might have happened if I had pressed for more information about these matters. For example, I interviewed a lesbian-identified woman named Lynda, who lingered for a long time on her first sexual experiences, with a German foreign exchange student who stayed with Lynda's family when they were both fifteen:

RUIZ: You described your relationship and your experiences with Krista as scary—simultaneously terrifying and exciting and very pleasing. What does that mean?

LYNDA: I mean the physical bond was . . . exciting—just to feel very connected on a deep level with someone that you really care about. And the fact that she was from another country and culture was very intriguing to me and she spent a lot of time with me and she was dependent upon me in a lot of ways and she was very sensitive to my feelings and I think that was really important. I hadn't really had anyone who was that sensitive and who understood that emotional side of me.

RUIZ: What did she look like?

LYNDA: She looked like total innocence.

More than forty years later, the ending of their affair (which led Lynda to become engaged to a man) still evoked powerful feelings for Lynda. She mentioned several times in our interview the importance of the "physical bond" and then couched that bond within an emotional narrative. I asked about Krista's physical appearance in the hope that it would remind the narrator of her physical attraction to her friend. Perhaps Lynda described her appearance as "total innocence" to suggest that their connection was beyond the corporeal, a way to suggest that she wanted to talk about love rather than sex. In this sense, she was actively constructing the narrative she wanted me to follow. Lynda was one of the few women interviewees who did—however obliquely—narrate their sexual pasts; indeed, many silences remain regarding how the women we interviewed found sexual pleasure with other women before they came to call themselves lesbians.

The silences around lesbian sexual practices have been challenged in a number of arenas inside and outside the academy. Cherríe Moraga and Amber Hollibaugh's discussion, published as "What We're Rollin' around in Bed With,"[6] challenged a lesbian-feminist audience to talk openly about lesbian and, more broadly, women's sex. In anthropology, Esther Newton has described the role that her own lesbian desire played in her ethnographic work among queer communities on Fire Island. "What else is going on between fieldworker and informant?" she asks. "Is 'the romance of anthropology' only a manner of speaking?"[7] Newton bravely explores this question through her romantic (though not sexual) involvement with an elderly doyenne of the Cherry Grove community. The research conducted by Elizabeth Lapovsky Kennedy and

Madeline D. Davis in Buffalo's working-class lesbian community deeply affects how we undertake oral history and queer history.[8] Kennedy and Davis's interests in what the lesbians they interviewed were "rollin' around with" enriches their analysis of butch-femme dynamics in pre-Stonewall Buffalo. *Boots of Leather, Slippers of Gold* helped to transform queer history into an intellectual field that takes lived (sexual) experience seriously as a site of inquiry.

However provocative and important these interventions have proved to be for lesbian history and politics, the experiences of many of us involved in collecting queer oral historical texts suggest that silences persist around female-female sexuality. "Silence," however, "can not be equated with *absence,*" according to historian John Howard. The task of the queer historian, Howard says, is to read the silences that surround sexuality as much as read what is spoken (or written): "Such reading, in order to offset the multitiered biases against queer historical inquiry, must assume from the beginning the *presence* of queer desire."[9] In the years that followed the important work undertaken by Kennedy and Davis, scholars interested in male-male sex have produced a small but important body of work that takes sex seriously as an oral historical field of inquiry, such as Howard's own work in *Men Like That: A Southern Queer History*, which was particularly successful in talking about sex with oral history narrators and exploring the matter of where, how, and with whom pleasure was sought. Perhaps more important, Howard demonstrates how sex illuminates a constellation of important matters beyond the erotic, including race, sexuality, and Southern identity.

Talking about sex means that we are asking oral history narrators to tell us their secrets, but does telling secrets mean telling the truth? We must not take for granted that talking about sex—even telling those sexual secrets that have been suppressed—will uncover the heretofore hidden truths of queer history. To the contrary, I want to read narratives of sex as the fallible, fragile texts that they are. I use the term *excavate* to frame this discussion because it works on two complementary levels: first, and quite simply, we must dare to talk about sex with those who tell us their stories; second, we must dig deeply into the stories that are narrated to us to ask how memory shapes the construction of the past. We must first gather the stories that are considered too vulgar or too personal by traditional modes of historical inquiry and then ask ourselves how these stories are constructed and what they *mean*—both to the individuals who tell us stories of their sexual pasts and, more generally, to queer history.

Sex is a particularly useful topic for oral history research precisely because queer people are socialized *not* to talk about it. Homophobia has meant, of course, that queer sex is both policed and silenced. As such, we are compelled to politely talk about our identities as if they can be easily separated from our erotic desires and practices.[10] Today, with the push for cultural inclusion and civil rights for gays and lesbians (and especially for same-sex couples), we must reassert the question of what it means to be queer, as the contributors of a special issue of *Social Text* have asked, and what sex has to do with queer identity and political formation.[11] These questions are especially timely as I write this article, for the legalization of marriage in California has been mired in discourse of "love" and "commitment." In this schema, gay rights are divorced from queer sex. Even as queer love and identity increasingly dare to speak their names, queer sex seems to be increasingly relegated to the personal and the private. Sex has been central to certain queer qualitative research practices—particularly those projects that engage with questions of AIDS and its prevention[12]—but it often plays a small role in analyses of community and identity formation. In this sense, talking about sex with our narrators helps oral historians unpack the nature of oral history as a mode of knowledge production. Practitioners of oral history are aware that oral history is an endeavor that is always at the mercy of memory and often subject to the desire (on the parts of both the interviewer and narrator) to tell a neater, cleaner, less shameful version of one's life. Sex is one location that makes it clear that what we get out of oral history is not *the* truth but *a* truth that is tailored by both the story the narrator tells and the countless stories she chooses to forget.

And sex is fun to talk about. As Newton, Kennedy, and Davis remind us, the role that pleasure plays in community-based research matters to both the researcher and the participant. Next I offer an in-depth look at the interview with Chuck Larsen that begins this chapter. Here, he remembered cruising a St. Paul park as a teenager:

> My dad one time—he's a cop—he said, "Whatever you do, don't go into Rice Park." "Why?" "Because there are strange men there." "What do you mean?" "They're strange." And from all the decoding and stuff, I realized they were probably homosexuals. Well, guess where I went. In the family car! And I'd pick up strangers. God almighty, I ended up at a funeral home with a guy, and we're down in this room next to the—and he was driving a black Cadillac and dressed in a suit. I should have known! And in any case, I followed him, and we go up to this funeral parlor . . . and I go, "Oh my God, this is going to be interesting!" . . . We went to his bedroom, sort of made out, and I thought, "I am not too interested in this," and he went into the bathroom and I got dressed and I ran out of that room down a hall. I thought "Where am I? How do I get out of this place?" Well, I found my way out and came home. I'm amazed at some of the strange things and dangerous things I did.

Not only did Chuck have a lot of fun as a teenager but also he seemed to find real pleasure in the context of our interview while recalling the sense of sexual power that he felt during his youth—the loss of which he later lamented. In stories like this one, Chuck described sex as a matter that was only difficult insofar as one had to find sexual partners and spaces to engage in sex. Although I think these stories demand more complicated readings, it is important to note that the pleasure that we find in sex is not merely in the moments when contact is made; part of the pleasure in sex is thinking and talking about it later, whether rehashing it with friends and lovers in the morning or telling our tales much later. In this case, Chuck's experiences cruising Rice Park forty years prior to our interview remain a source of pleasure and help him narrate the broader story of his life as a gay man.

Of course, sex can also be a painful thing to talk about, and memories of abuse, trauma, and regret have been common in the stories that we have collected for the Twin Cities GLBT Oral History. Although the moments these memories surface are painful for narrator and oral historian alike, they are equally crucial to tell. In the dozens of interviews I collected for the project, there were two moments in which narrators took me up on my offer to stop the recording because they were overcome by painful memories. In one case, a man in his late seventies recalled the death of his longtime lover. In the other instance, a lesbian-identified woman remembered being forced to give up a child for adoption when she was a teenager. Much more commonly, when it came to sexual trauma, narrators told me that they were driven to record their truth in its entirety precisely because they had held it in for so long. This makes our roles in the interview more complicated. Do we cause narrators undue harm by raising questions about sex? Should we more clearly delineate ourselves as historians rather than therapists? While taking these questions seriously, we must also remember that in oral history we do not consult with dispassionate archives; the moment of risk begins when we turn on the recorder.[13]

I interviewed Chuck in his suburban Minneapolis home in 2004. Project intern Ann McKenzie and I immediately loved Chuck, with his quick laugh and vivid memory. We sat at the dining room table surrounded by the bric-a-brac that he and his partner had collected together. Chuck was eager to tell us his life story, including details about the sex that he had throughout his life. Several vignettes from Chuck's sexual life illustrate the usefulness of sex to oral history; however rife with contradictions and inconsistencies, the story of how Chuck found and had sex illuminates a complex life story. My intent here is not merely to expose one man's sexual past, but to illustrate the important ways that sex structures knowledge about the self and the past. Although his stories do provide insight into the history of sexual practice, what interests me most is how we might *read* Chuck's sex stories (beyond what they explicitly say about practice) to glean insight into the epistemologies of sex, that is, the systems of sexual knowledge that shape how Chuck operates as a queer subject.

Chuck was sexually active as a child and teenager, having regular encounters with Dennis, a childhood friend. He remembered the casual way that it started ("just playing around") and the impact it made on both of them (their sexual contacts lasted for years). Chuck was adamant that, despite growing up in a deeply religious home, he felt no guilt regarding his activities with Dennis and his attraction to men: "He said, 'We can't have sex because it's a mortal sin,' and he was supposed to wait for me to ask so that it wouldn't be a mortal sin for him.

I thought, 'Screw that mess! It's not a sin!'" While I was interviewing Chuck, it was difficult for me to grasp how he now regarded his sexual past—an important question for his broader history as a queer person. At the same time he insisted he was not subject to Dennis's sense of guilt regarding their sexual contacts, Chuck also had serious concerns about his burgeoning sexuality. Was Chuck remembering a youth of careless abandon or was he, as the child of a strict and religious household, more repressed than his stories suggest? What role did sex really play in the production of Chuck's sense of self and his gay identity?

Of course, there was no single truth to Chuck's sexual past. Instead of vainly looking for such a truth, I had to learn to listen for and read the contradictions that made up Chuck's past. For example, when I asked him how he learned about sex as a child, Chuck said:

> Well, that's interesting! I went to the Aster movie theater on Hennepin Avenue. I think that was in high school, and I went there because they'd have two movies for the price of one, and it was real cheap. So I'm sitting there watching the movie, and I thought that I felt some guy's hand on my knee. And I thought, "What's that?" And I thought, "Well, I'm just curious, let's see what happens." And so one thing led to another, and finally we were fondling each other. And then he invited me to go back to his car where he did fellatio on me. . . . I didn't know what the term "blow job" meant. I thought, "That's what that means!" I had no idea.

Chuck's attitudes about sex, however, were not tinged exclusively with youthful curiosity. A few minutes later, Chuck remembered a trip he took to Europe as a teenager:

> In Paris some man took my hand, and when he shook my hand, he scratched my palm. I knew what that meant. How would I know? I did. I knew that it had some-thing to do with gay—homosexual—and, of course, then it scared me, and I just walked away. But I knew what it meant: it was like a signal or something, and that was amazing. I had no sex in the thirty days that I was there. I was with a number of University of Minnesota students who were gay, and they were just carrying on like trash . . . and I was sixteen. So while I knew that I was having sex with Dennis, I wasn't like them. In fact, I was certain that I would get married and then that would stop.

The narrator seemed to embrace his youthful curiosity in the movie theater (and, as we saw before, in the park and with Dennis) but shied away from sexual encounters in Paris and, he told me, throughout college.

Although he claimed that he was unashamed of his sexual behavior early in life, Chuck also distinguished himself from the queer people he knew in child-hood. He remembered being both attracted to and repulsed by queer people in his extended family in the 1950s, including a "diesel dyke" who was partnered with a femme cousin and a solitary rural uncle who fascinated the young Chuck. Ultimately, he described himself as feeling sorry for these queers because they seemed to him to be "very sad." When he developed a gay identity of his own as a teenager, he disidentified with such sexual outlaws and, more specifically, with abject queers that he saw at a gay bar in the city:

CHARLES LARSEN: It hit me. I was going to be gay for the rest of my life but I had a choice: I could be a good gay boy or a bad one. I decided I would do my best to be a good one.

JASON RUIZ: What did that mean to you—"a good gay boy"?

LARSEN: Not promiscuous. Not an alcoholic. The first time I went into the Happy Hour I . . . saw what appeared to be drunks hanging out in this dark bar. . . . I looked around and thought, "Is this how I am going to end up? No!" . . . But that's what I saw—these are my people, you know? You look both ways before you go in. This was in the early sixties. I walked in there, and it shocked me. I knew that they were gays, homosexuals. And I guess that I was one, but I didn't want to end up like that. And over the many years that I went to the Happy Hour, I rarely if ever met somebody to have sex.

Chuck first entered a gay bar at the age of seventeen. The story of Chuck at the Happy Hour suggests that he found no problem with his own same-sex attraction and activity but that he actively disidentified with the queers he found in the increasingly public gay scene in Minneapolis. This differentiation between a "good" and "bad" way to be a gay person set a pattern for his adult life, in which he struggled to portray himself as an upstanding citizen and leader while clandestinely engaging in sexual activity that he found embarrassing or shameful. The moment described in the bar establishes a theme that recurs throughout the narrative.

After several stints as a reluctant (and closeted) schoolteacher, Chuck finally resolved to fulfill his childhood ambition of a religious vocation. Although he was raised in a mixed Catholic-Baptist household, Chuck heavily identified with his Catholicism and entered the Christian Brotherhood in 1961. "I just felt that I could do it," he told us. "If you love God good enough, you just give up sex." It was not long, however, before Chuck realized that his sexual appetite was incompatible with the Brotherhood. He eventually found his way to Methodism, in which he was ordained as a pastor after college, and to the Metropolitan Community Church (MCC), where he spent most of his professional life.

His work with the MCC took him to San Francisco in the late 1970s, where he headed a church and found pleasure in the city's legendary cruising grounds:

I enjoyed going to the parks. Lafayette Park in San Francisco was a gay paradise. When the sun went down, the few straight people who had been there during the day left, and it was ours. By ours, I mean forty or fifty gay men walking around in suggestive poses. . . . You'd follow them into the bushes, and there were these little clearings that they'd made. And at any time there'd be forty or fifty men having sex all over Lafayette Park. And you'd just walk through and you'd see somebody and you'd follow them or they'd follow you. I left there at the end of '78 to become a pastor in Houston. I left San Francisco one year before AIDS hit. And I would have been a goner. There's no way if I'd have stayed that year—the sexual contact would be six or seven contacts in a night. I had legal speed from a doctor in Florida, and I'd take one of those and a cup of coffee, and baby I'd go from eleven until six in the morning. . .

Chuck again described his sexual life as wild and fulfilling, but with the caveat that his role as an MCC pastor meant that it was also hidden from the public that he served:

CHARLES LARSEN: I was such a sneak. I was the pastor, and I was real sweet and nice. Didn't go to the baths, didn't have a [different] lover every week. But boy, I'd hit the parks. And I thought "I can match anyone in that church!" . . .

JASON RUIZ: Why did you maintain a façade of public innocence?

LARSEN: Because I was the pastor, and the pastor should not be a whore or a slut. Even though a lot of the [MCC] pastors were so comfortable with their sexuality. The congregation just knew that I was old-time. I was raised Catholic, so you're a little more uptight . . . a little hypocritical in a way. I . . . felt that my sexual life needed to be mine. Private. One time I remember [that a member of the] Houston church saw me at one of the bookstores, and said, "Well, I guess you're human." And I said, "Yeah I am. Just keep your mouth shut." He did.

Chuck's description of his sexual life in the late 1970s echoed the paradox of shameless-but-hidden sexuality that he used in describing his experiences from childhood and throughout his adolescence. As Chuck told it, there were stark contrasts between what he did with his body for sexual pleasure, what he thought about sex, and how he talked about sex as a pastor and public figure. In other words, he quite literally did not practice what he preached. This is what haunts me about Chuck's life narrative. Was Chuck a producer of retrograde—even dangerously sex-negative—discourse by privileging love and commitment for gay couples in his sermons and then fucking indiscriminately at night? Given the spate of recent political and religious sex scandals, it is difficult to separate this discursive split from that of, say, Ted Haggard's. Or does he provide a model for sexual liberation in his nonchalant and guiltless approach to narrating sex? Perhaps Chuck lived a theory of homosexuality in which what one does with his or her body does not necessarily need to align with how he or she conceptualizes or narrates sexual meanings.

My goal here is not to reinforce Chuck's opinion that he behaved like a hypocrite for developing a public persona that was at odds with his sexual behavior, but to offer Chuck's story as an example of the fascinating tensions that emerge when we talk about sex in oral history. Chuck's role as an MCC pastor gave him political clout. For instance, he worked with Harvey Milk and represented the gay and lesbian community to the San Francisco Police Department by serving as an official advisor. This kind of influence depended at least partly on his ability to produce a public image of himself as a "good" gay person—the same desire that he had upon entering the Happy Hour bar almost two decades earlier. Sexual promiscuity, along with kinky sex, public sex, drug use, and a wide array of behavior that transgressed Chuck's status as a proper gay subject, was suppressed. We might read this as analogous to the gay and lesbian movement, which de-emphasized sexual freedom in favor of identity-based civil rights as it became more visible and viable. In that broader context, good behavior (or at least an artifice of good behavior) has been central to the claim for citizenship rights. It is compelling that, as an older gay man, his past "bad" behavior plays such an important role in his life narrative.

Consider the story of Chuck's sexuality in relation to Amber Hollibaugh's provocative comment, "The memory of our histories is often constructed to work as our conscience as well as to configure our secret desires."[14] We see in Chuck's narrative that the "memory of his history" conjures both his conscience's desire to be a "good gay boy" (when no models for such behavior existed) and his secret desires. Hollibaugh's strange turn of phrase—"the memory of our histories"—is apt here, for Chuck does not narrate an objective *thing* that we can safely call his history. Rather, all that Chuck, or any narrator, can offer us is memory. In this case, I have analyzed not Chuck's sexual history but Chuck's memory of his sexual history. This is the precise reason that institutionalized history has historically discounted oral history as a nonacademic, artsy-craftsy, and community-minded endeavor. It is also what makes oral history so valuable. I do not mean that oral history methods are valuable because they illuminate the history of queers—that such methods will allow us to simply write ourselves back into history, which was, perhaps rightly, the aim of the first wave of gay and lesbian histories that emerged in the 1980s and 1990s. Instead, queers who work as historians are uniquely positioned to radically transform how history is made by turning to the most subjective parts of ourselves to unpack who we are. Chuck is, after all, not only a queer subject but—vis-à-vis the choices he made when narrating his sexual life—also a theorist of sex. In other words, if we listen closely we can glean what Chuck thinks sex is and should be.

In "Thinking Sex," Rubin conceptualized "good" and "bad" forms of sexuality on a spectrum. Only the highest forms of good sex are granted access to the "charmed circle," but some queer erotic forms are closer than others to "good" sex. What is more, these erotic forms are not stationary through time and space but can oscillate closer to and further from the imagined center that the author establishes. Rubin, for example, noted that the 1980s saw certain forms of homosexuality shift closer to the center of the circle:

> As a result of the sex conflicts of the last decade, some behavior near the border is inching across it. Unmarried couples living together, masturbation, and some

forms of homosexuality are moving in the direction of respectability. . . . Most homosexuality is still on the bad side of the line. But if it is coupled and monogamous, the society is beginning to recognize that it includes the full range of human interaction. Promiscuous homosexuality, sadomasochism, fetishism, transsexuality, and cross-generational encounters are still viewed as unmodulated horrors incapable of involving affection, love, free choice, kindness, or transcendence.[15]

Although the thought of unmarried heterosexual couples inhabiting the "outer limits" of sexuality might seem like a quaint notion today, Rubin's essay has remained timely, for we can now see that society has more fully recognized that coupled and monogamous homosexuality "includes the full range of human interactions" and can therefore rightfully claim citizenship, rescued from the darkest corners of the outer limits. We certainly see this process at play in contemporary gay marriage debates: same-sex marriage proponents couch theirs as an argument for "love" and "commitment" while those working to "defend" "traditional" marriage argue that gay marriage would open the doors for those forms of queer sexuality that are further from the charmed circle (promiscuity, sadomasochism, fetishism, etc.) to move closer. Lisa Duggan characterizes the current political and cultural shift as "the new homonormativity," and her reading of it within the contemporary politics of neoliberalism has helped to reinvigorate the scholarly interrogation of the shifts that Rubin observed twenty years previously.[16]

By closing this chapter with the specter of homonormativity and its recent critiques,[17] I do not mean to suggest that queer sex has become normalized as gay and lesbian politics and cultures have gone mainstream. To be sure, queers have and will continue to find routes to pleasure and desire that transgress social norms—and the law (as well as other institutions set in place to police how we have sex and where we find it). Even so, the politics of homonormativity means that transgressive modes of sex and sexuality must be submerged so that a monogamous, gender-conforming, and upwardly mobile class of gay men and lesbians can enjoy the benefits of appearing "normal." As a result, LGBT identities are normalized at the same time that queer sex remains dangerous and—as in the case of Senator Larry Craig at the Minneapolis–St. Paul International Airport—increasingly under surveillance.

Most of the older queers I interviewed are heartened by the homonormative turn and see gay and lesbian civil rights and cultural inclusion as the markers of "progress." Many of our interviewees fought for such inclusions and went to great lengths to be—or appear to be—good gay and lesbian subjects. However we talk about queer sex in oral historical practice—whether we work to undo the silences around female-female sexuality, continue to talk about sex with older queer men, or look for new connections between gay and lesbian and other modes of dissident sexualities—we must excavate the sexual past to develop a clearer vision of queer histories, identities, and meanings that contradict normalization.

Notes

1. Special thanks to Aaron Carico and Adam John Waterman for advice on early drafts of this essay. I also thank Kevin P. Murphy and members of the Twin Cities GLBT Oral History Project for their guidance and support. This piece is dedicated to Chuck Larsen and the other men and women who talked about sex with me through the years.

2. Locals refer to the University of Minnesota as "the U."

3. Chuck Larsen. Interview with Jason Ruiz and Ann McKenzie. The Jean-Nickolaus Tretter Collection in Gay, Lesbian, Bisexual and Transgender Studies, University of Minnesota.

4. Gail Rubin, "Thinking Sex: Notes for a Radical Theory of Politics and Sexuality," in Carole S. Vance, ed., *Pleasure and Danger: Exploring Female Sexuality* (Boston: Routledge and Kegan Paul, 1984), 267.

5. Project intern Ann McKenzie accompanied me on these early interviews and contributed much to the initial success of the project.

6. See *Heresies* No. 12 (1981).

7. Esther Newton, "My Best Informant's Dress: The Erotic Equation in Fieldwork," in *Margaret Mead Made Me Gay: Personal Essays, Public Ideas* (Durham, NC: Duke University Press, 2000), 243.

8. Elizabeth Lapovsky Kennedy and Madeline D. Davis, *Boots of Leather, Slippers of Gold: The History of a Lesbian Community* (New York: Routledge, 1993).

9. John Howard, *Men Like That: A Southern Queer History* (Chicago: University of Chicago Press, 1999), 28.

10. This proved to be particularly challenging in the context of our project's focus on the Twin Cities, a Midwestern context where sex remains a taboo subject. I cannot help but wonder how the sexual dimensions of the project would have been different in a place with a larger population of older queer people (like Palm Springs, for instance).

11. David Eng, ed., "What's Queer about Queer Studies Now?" *Social Text* (2005): 84–85.

12. See Hector Carillo's *The Night Is Young: Sexuality in Mexico in the Time of AIDS* (Chicago: University of Chicago Press, 2001) for a wonderful example.

13. The question of risk was of particular interest to the Institutional Review Board at the University of Minnesota. We secured IRB approval for the Twin Cities GLBT Oral History Project even though the legitimacy of IRB oversight over oral history projects was (and remains) unclear. The IRB categorized the project as low risk.

14. Amber Hollibaugh, *My Dangerous Desires: A Queer Girl Dreaming Her Way Home* (Durham, NC: Duke University Press, 2000), 8.

15. Rubin, "Thinking Sex," 282–83.

16. Lisa Duggan, *The Twilight of Equality? Neoliberalism, Cultural Politics, and the Attack on Democracy* (Boston: Beacon, 2003).

17. See also *Radical History Review* 100 (Winter 2007).

7

GENDER, DESIRE, AND FEMINISM

A Conversation between Dorothy Allison and Carmen Vázquez

Kelly Anderson

Oral history by Kelly Anderson with Dorothy Allison and Carmen Vázquez, Guerneville, California, November 19, 2007

I recorded this joint interview with Dorothy Allison and Carmen Vázquez in 2007 as part of the Voices of Feminism (VOF) project at the Sophia Smith Collection, Smith College. The Ford Foundation–funded project was initiated in 2002 to document the full range of late-twentieth-century activism on behalf of women. Voices of Feminism video interviewed more than sixty women who identified as feminists, and some who did not. Our explicit focus was those previously left out of the historical record, including labor movement activists, poor women, lesbians, and women of color. Narrators include labor, peace, land-tenure, and antiracism activists; artists and writers; lesbian rights advocates; grassroots antiviolence and antipoverty organizers; and women of color reproductive justice leaders. These oral histories are extensive, ranging from four to twelve hours and taking place over at least two days. The full transcripts are available online at www.smith.edu/libraries/libs/ssc/vof/vof-intro.html.[1]

KELLY ANDERSON: What is butch-femme? Tell me about its history for you.

DOROTHY ALLISON: But it changes depending on where you're standing and when. How old are you, darling? [to Vázquez]

ANDERSON: You're both fifty-eight.

ALLISON: So we're grown-ups, more or less.

VÁZQUEZ: We are, honey.

ALLISON: Of an age. And you grew up in New York, right?

VÁZQUEZ: Yeah. I grew up in New York, in Harlem. I came from Puerto Rico when I was about five, spent about three years on the Lower East Side. And then my family got this great three-bedroom apartment in the General Grant Projects on 125th Street, in Harlem, and I lived in Harlem about fourteen years, and then moved to the Bronx.

ALLISON: When did you realize who you were?

VÁZQUEZ: Really, about five or six. There was a little girl, a little German girl that used to taunt me and I wanted to be with her. I wanted to play with her, I wanted to kiss her. I wanted to do all those things. But my first sort of conscious experience of sex and sexuality, of being something—I don't think *lesbian* was even a word that I knew—was when I was fifteen. I was in some home that I had been sent to for God knows what reason, because I was acting out. And in there, there was a sexual experience with a girl, where I definitely knew that that was not play. I was wanting to kiss that girl, and I wanted to get up on that girl and do all kinds of things to that girl. Still, though, it didn't have a name, and it was just, like, something that happened. Then there was another relationship, with someone that was about seven years older than me, also a femme, who hung out with other femmes. I was fifteen or sixteen.

ALLISON: You were a pet.

VÁZQUEZ: I was. I totally was. And I was taken in by these women, and it was mostly in their home. You know, they'd have parties, and I'd come, and I was the pet, and I was always the boy. Sometimes they'd take me out to, like, these places where you had to have passwords and stuff like that, and it was all very secret and very exciting, completely exciting. I would dress up in my shirts and ties and things, and they took good care of me. I mean, I was never in trouble because they took really good care of me, these girls. So that's—I mean, that's my formative experience of what it meant to love a woman and to be involved with a woman. It was a completely Puerto Rican subculture, these lesbian femmes. I didn't know that they called themselves anything.

ALLISON: There wasn't even the language.

VÁZQUEZ: There wasn't language that I can recall anyway, but they clearly were that—high femme at that, with the heels and the tight dresses. And we'd go to the dance clubs. And they'd all have to be worried about how much alcohol I consumed because I was sixteen years old, and they could be in a whole lot of

Dorothy Allison and Carmen Vázquez relax around Dorothy's kitchen table in Guerneville, California, after a long day of conversation. Their reflections on San Francisco during the AIDS crisis shed light on the complexities of lesbian culture and activism in the 1980s. *Photography by and courtesy of Kelly Anderson*

trouble, but somehow managed to avoid the trouble. Then, for me, there was not a conscious identity around butch, really, until I left New York. It was in San Francisco that—all of what I talked about earlier in terms of discovering a gay world and then a lesbian community.

ALLISON: And the language?

VÁZQUEZ: And the language. But the language then was, like, *lesbian* and *lesbian feminist*. I had no idea what people were fucking talking about. I honestly did not. And I did not have a word for myself that was the word *butch*. I knew that I liked lesbians who looked like my mother.

ALLISON: Yeah, okay. [laughs]

VÁZQUEZ: And were girls. Then some language did come around. Okay, so, like, "You're a butch, and you like femmes." And so then I started to incorporate some of that language. But in my efforts to try and find a social life and a political life, and to integrate into the lesbian feminist community, it was horrific. It was horrible, because I had no reference point. Flannel shirts.

ALLISON: Only if they've got a lace teddy underneath it.

VÁZQUEZ: Oh, baby.

ALLISON: I've dated some of those.

VÁZQUEZ: I mean, I couldn't even wear a flannel shirt myself [laughs], much less date a woman who was wearing one. So it was complicated. It was really complicated to try and figure out what was going on. And there was an awful lot of rejection, and there was an awful lot of, "What are you doing? You know, You're a traitor, you're"—you know.

ALLISON: Who would say you're a traitor? Family, friends?

VÁZQUEZ: No, no. White lesbians.

ALLISON: Oh for God's sake, yeah.

VÁZQUEZ: Feminists.

ALLISON: Yeah, I remember.

VÁZQUEZ: Take the tie off. What are you doing? And a real push towards an assimilation into more androgynous lesbian—whatever—presentation, even though that was still never who I was attracted to or who I ever fucked.

ALLISON: They always read as asexual to me, that whole androgynous thing.

VÁZQUEZ: Well, that's how I read it, too. So that's sort of about twenty years ago.

ANDERSON: How did you know who you were? How did you get to that point? [addressing Dorothy]

ALLISON: I figured out really quickly, when I was young, that I was just—in my mind, I was just queer and—no, we should use the word *weird*. I figured I was probably sick, I was probably crazy. But mostly what I figured was that I was wrong. I did not want to get married. I was not interested in boys. I was not interested in dating. In my family, it was like, Dorothy's not like that; Dorothy reads a lot.

But a lot of it was also protective, because I was getting raped on a regular basis. And by the time I got old enough and strong enough to counter that and more or less stop it, I found a place of safety, which was to be asexual. But that doesn't stop desire or fantasy or lust, so that a lot of my erotic fantasies centered on being trapped with girls in terrible situations in which I alone could rescue them by performing acts of enormous suffering.

· So then a lot of that became a lot of my erotic charge for most of my teenage years. I would fall in love with girlfriends, and I tended to fall in love with the more butch girls, although I did not have a language. I didn't have the word *lesbian*, except that I read constantly, and gradually—and then I discovered my stepfather's porn, and that's where I found lesbians. The things I knew about lesbians was that they were rapists and they had hairy nipples. It was porn that I was getting all my education from. I found that kind of a turn-on. Big mean dykes. Ooh, where are they? How can I find them? Then I went off to college and fell into a relationship with one of my resident advisors, and she was aggressive enough to be interesting, but she really wasn't my stuff, and to a certain extent, she was kind of androgynous. I fell in love with a Russian student, who was aggressive enough and butch enough to be more of my stuff, but not quite. It took me a long time. But meanwhile, I made do.

VÁZQUEZ: One has to.

ALLISON: One has to. And then I discovered, in the South, old dyke bars, most of which were in bad neighborhoods. And pretty quickly, that's where I started seeing women who were more my erotic charge. And they looked so good and so scary and, on some levels, were dangerous. Well, but quasi—mostly what I found out was that, when I found the butch girls, they just all wanted to marry me. [laughs] And I was supposed to do the laundry and the cooking and, you know, tie their ties. And I didn't want to get married. I had a horror of any kind of marriage entrapment.

One of the things that I ran into really quickly when I did start finding butch girls and having sex with them and dating them, was that they thought I was a slut. And I was, in terms of—I don't know about the Northeast, but in the Southeast, there's a real—there's a culture that disdains women who want to fuck around. A good femme lesbian finds herself a good butch, settles down, and plays house. I didn't want to settle down and play house. I just wanted to have a really great time and go home, or send them home if they came with me. And so that was problematic and troublesome.

After college, when I found the women's movement in Tallahassee is when I found the more lesbian feminist androgynous community, and that was—they read. You could talk. I could be a feminist and do organizing, but having sex with them was not satisfying at all, with a few exceptions. There were some good butches hiding under those flannel shirts, but they tended to be more working-class girls, and they tended to be older. And, without fail, they all wanted to marry me. So there would be these constant dramas.

So I had two lives. I had my lesbian feminist life. I lived in a lesbian collective. I was sleeping with a number of women in the collective, and it was okay. Mostly I was fucking them, because it just didn't work for them. To do me, you had to have sincerity. You know what I mean?

VÁZQUEZ: I do. [laughs]

ALLISON: But they did not know what I was talking about. So I would leave the collective and go to the pool hall and find sincerity, bring her home and then—interestingly enough, and problematically enough, especially when I moved further north—I was dating across color, because I found a better quality butch girl. [laughs] At least for a time. Because there was such a huge emphasis on androgyny among white lesbians, it became so asexual to me. And let's be clear, not much talent. Because it's my opinion that the secret to good sex is a willingness to be humiliated, and that means taking some risks. And they were all so hesitant and tentative, and that doesn't work.

VÁZQUEZ: They all talked about, why you are a lesbian is because it was safe.

ALLISON: For some of them, yeah.

VÁZQUEZ: Well, girl, that is not what sex is about.

ALLISON: No. And I had a huge bent towards being safe. I could organize a lot of safe, because sex was really problematic for me—because I had a lot of resistance to being helpless, but I eroticized it at the same time. So you really had to be committed to have sex with me.

VÁZQUEZ: And, you know, there's something else about a butch—well, for me. My understanding and sense of wanting to be with a woman and wanting to take care of her and wanting to please her had very little to do with expecting that they would cook or clean the house, or do any of that stuff. That was not part of the bargain. And I was never interested in femmes that were submissive.

ALLISON: Oh, honey, let's be very clear. I was not submissive.

VÁZQUEZ: No. I get that.

ALLISON: Unless you pushed it, and then I could become instantly submissive.

VÁZQUEZ: But you know what I'm saying? I mean, culturally, that was not a part of the deal.

ALLISON: No. We're talking about femmes with an enormous amount of authority.

VÁZQUEZ: Enormous amount of authority, independence, and attitude. And that's gotten me in trouble. But I was never looking for the one that would take care of me.

ALLISON: The little wife.

VÁZQUEZ: No. I was never looking for the little wife, and neither were the folks that I hung out with. Everything that I've just been talking about in terms of a sexual relationship that is charged—and, you know, that has changed completely for me, from, like, charged and I'm the one that's in charge—thinking that I was the one in charge. Thinking. [laughs] And I'm very happy that I'm not, but it took me a long time to figure that piece out and go, like, okay, so, really, why it works is because there is an exchange of power; that there is surrender and submission, but it's surrender and submission on both our parts. Who's in charge is not dependent on my identity as a butch or hers as femme.

ALLISON: And it shifts.

VÁZQUEZ: And it shifts, but that was not something that I understood consciously and could have even had language for.

ALLISON: Even once I understood it, I couldn't talk about it, right? What language did I have?

VÁZQUEZ: No. Twenty years ago, no. I could not have said what I just said. And it's evolved for me. And on a very personal level, erotically, it's been this very gradual sort of moving to a place where I understand that part of my desire to please her involves her ability and her desire to take me. That just was not— that little baby-dyke butch person, no.

ALLISON: Well, when I started finding those bars—starting in D.C., and then in New York—it was just like, I'd just sit with my mouth open. And I would date women who'd say, "You know, you mean well, but you spent too long in the women's movement. I mean, you'll never be as good at this as you would have been if you hadn't done that." And to a certain extent, they were right, because I have this whole rebellion against the expectations of high-femme drag. What would work for me is if we were going to be frank about how I can fetishize it. Then I could do it, and enjoyed it and could play with it, especially when I was younger.

Then, as I got older, I started to get annoyed at how much work this involved. But when lust is riding the tide, oh Jesus God. And those girls— man. I remember the first time I was in a dance bar in New York and they played "Thriller." All of a sudden, all of these women in tuxedo shirts, full suits, and girls in heels so high I couldn't see how they were dancing, hit the floor, and it was like, Oh mama. I'm going home to change clothes and come back. Presentation and courage. God, the sexual lure of courage, yeah.

But the lesbian feminist community actively, militantly rejected it and critiqued it and held contempt for it, which meant that a lot of my core stuff I either had to hide or battle for, and at different times I did different things. Early on, especially when I was young, I just took it as a given that there would be only coded ways in which I would be a genuine femme in the lesbian feminist community. That changed over time as I lost patience with them. Especially when I was in Tallahassee and I got some of my working-class butch girlfriends to come to events in the lesbian feminist community. You only had to treat one of my girlfriends bad once, when I became a terrorist. You know, you don't do that to a woman I've had sex with and admire and honor. I'll rip your throat out. So then I wasn't so good at hiding for a while. It got tricky. But it got bad and painful, and a lot of times I felt like a failed femme because

I couldn't live up to the expectations of the community that was my erotic community. Meanwhile, lesbian feminism was absolutely vital to my life, and the work was vital, and I'm meanwhile trying to get them to be just a little bit more accepting, make some shifts there. Dancing on razors all the fucking time. But to get them to actually look at their analysis and see the flaws. And it was all about class and getting them to register class. Well, it's larger than class, but class is a big piece of it.

VÁZQUEZ: The androgynous-whatever thing—that got so elevated and still is. I mean, I think that there has been a period of objectifying and glorifying male identity in women. You know, it's all well and good if you go out and articulate a defense of butch-femme, and if you can be titillating and you can talk about it and everybody loves it and there's an audience for it. But don't you fucking go and actually be that person and expect that you're going to have any real decision making or power in the movement, because you're not. This is not a movement that will tolerate male-identified people at its leadership. It never has and never will. So for me, butch-femme is so fundamentally and completely about an erotic signaling that that's what it is, folks. Here we are in the world and, actually, we fuck.

ALLISON: It's prudish. It's also prejudice, the same kind of prejudice that I found when I was a slut. The first thing I discovered is that in a lesbian feminist culture in New York, when all the shit hit the fan, all of a sudden I was again a slut. But I wanted there to be honor for sluts. I wanted respect. We're acting on desire. I believed that that was a feminist ideal. You know, autonomy of the body, autonomy of lust. Let's give it some respect and give it its place. But there was a triumph of this asexual androgyny that was really problematic for a lot of lesbians. I sometimes wondered if it wasn't the compromise made with heterosexuals in early feminism, but that's too nefarious.

ANDERSON: How do you defend or explain butch-femme to the younger generation who feel more at ease with the identities of trans or gender variant?

ALLISON: I don't think you explain; you model. You talk frankly about desire and your own history. That's the best way to do it, in order to get them to speak and to feel that they have a safe place to speak. But you have to be willing to be humiliated and to be wrong. I can't tell you how many times—I did a talk down in LA some years ago, and I knew not to answer the question when it was asked. I knew it was going to blow up on me. There was no way around it. And it was that same old question, which is, "Well, how do you feel about the transgender young?" And, "You know, I read something in which you said that you were dating a woman, and then she started to smell different, and you didn't want to have sex with her anymore." I was like, "Yeah, well, that's true. I am an old dyke. And if you smell like a boy to me, you step off of my erotic markers. And the moment when you do that transition, we can be friends and we can be a coalition, but we can't be fucking lovers. It's not happening." The immediate response was "Well, you are prejudiced against transgender people." I said, "Well, I don't have sex with them; they're not my stuff. I'm a dyke. I am a dyke."

But I can't stop thinking about it, you know. Because I'll train myself to be, in many contexts, a dominant femme, an aggressive femme, but that's not my stuff. My stuff—I want someone who can, you know, make me, take me; it's safe enough for me to give it up and go down and be taken. There is an exchange. But transgender people assume a different gender position in my matrix. Now that doesn't mean that doesn't have anything to do with their right to do this or be this or, in fact, all the cultural complications. I have enough libertarian in me that I actually do fight for the right of people to shift their gender and make those choices. Meanwhile, though, what I'm seeing happening to a lot of butch women is that, it's almost like a replication of the triumph of androgyny. It's the triumph of transgender, where all of a sudden young butch women believe that, Oh, there is no butch. There is male or female, and I'm going to shift the matrix.

VÁZQUEZ: And I do not accept the notion that the transgender experience is the be-all and end-all of what is queer transgression. In fact, when you make a decision that you will cross over and make the transition from male to female or female to male, you're entering the binary, baby. I don't care what anybody says, but it looks straight to me. I do defend completely the right of any individual who feels that they've got the wrong body. Go change it. But that doesn't make you queer. You know?

And I know I don't want the space that I occupy as a female-bodied person who does identify as male in many ways to be obliterated. I want the right to live in this female body as a male-identified person, and, you know, to the extent that that space gets shrunk, I get really scared and pissed off, honestly, because why should it be shrunk? What was the fucking point of feminism in the first place if it wasn't to create a space where women could make this decision about our bodies?

ALLISON: I meet a lot of young women, especially when I go to colleges, who are in some form of transition, are living not really as men, except that they present as men. So on the street, they get treated as men. That means that they step out of a lot of what happens to women in this culture. But meanwhile, they want to still be in the queer community, and they want the authority and position and—let's be clear—privilege that we have ascribed to butches in our culture, but they want to erase the concept of butches. Because they do want more—they want to be the primary. They want to be honored because they are gender outlaws, and in some way they have defined butch as not being outlaw enough. And that's where I get into trouble, because I grew up thinking that the bravest thing in the world is a butch woman, and the second most bravest thing is the femme. [There has to be] a more complicated discussion. Show me what is queer about what you're doing. And show me how, in fact, it's feminist, and what does it lay the groundwork for in the future?

This is where I get in trouble.

VÁZQUEZ: Well, it's also interesting that we're having this whole discussion, right? And some of what pissed us off thirty years ago was the androgyny thing. And now, you know, thirty years later, we're looking at the dissolution of butch-femme and the evolution of transgender-something.

ALLISON: Long ago I decided, if you're self-defining as a woman, I'm going to take you as a woman. If you're self-defining as a man, I'm going to take you as a man. I just think people have the right. What's troublesome is when they're self-defining as a man, but meanwhile they want to be taken as queer. I'm having some hard time with it.

VÁZQUEZ: And running off with our femmes, damn it. [laughter]

ALLISON: Or snatching up the good butches and marrying them. That's not an issue for you.

VÁZQUEZ: No, baby. [laughs]

ALLISON: And since I'm an old married bitch, it's not that big a deal. You know?[2]

Commentary

My lover, Carmen Vázquez, and I flew to San Francisco in November 2007 to spend a few days with Dorothy Allison in her home just north of the city. I had asked Dorothy to do an oral history with me as part of the Voices of Feminism project. It was the Voices of Feminism project that had introduced me to Carmen, with whom I had done an oral history in 2005. She joined me on the trip, in part, because I hoped that I could pair Dorothy and Carmen for an interesting conversation. They are both the same age, have similar political sensibilities, are both writers and activists, and both spent a fair amount of time in San Francisco and indeed overlapped there during the 1980s. Dorothy is as fervent a femme as Carmen is a proud butch. I was enthusiastic about the rich possibilities for a dialogue about gender, sexuality, and feminism across generation, race, and class.[3]

My particular interest for the Voices of Feminism project was in both restoring the central role played by lesbians in feminist activism and complicating the historical narrative regarding feminisms, gender, and sexuality. Specifically, I wanted to explore the silences and mythology around the conflicts over sexuality that erupted during the 1980s, what we now call the "sex wars."[4] Dating back to the early twentieth century, sexuality has often caused conflict among feminists, so this was something not entirely new. What were the race and class implications of the attack on radical sexualities, including butch-femme, sadomasochism, and propornography feminists? And what lessons have we learned from these internal tensions that we are now bringing to discussions and policy debates about women and sexuality, including transgender identities and practices? These questions led me to prominent feminist activists such as Cherríe L Moraga, Amber Hollibaugh, Minnie Bruce Pratt, Suzanne Pharr, Achebe Powell, Joan E. Biren, Virginia Apuzzo, Katherine Acey, and others, including Carmen

Vázquez and Dorothy Allison. The ensuing conversations with these narrators are rich and varied, addressing various topics in the context of lifelong negotiations over sex, gender, race, and class. I often begin conversations with childhood and proceed chronologically, although occasionally I have approached them thematically. This was the case with Dorothy[5]—she has written about her childhood extensively in her novels and memoir—and so our focus was her activism and sexuality. While I came into this interview, and all others, with a set of open-ended questions, I let her lead in many ways, gently keeping us on track but open to exploring the themes important to her.

In the course of my multiple-day interviews with both Carmen and Dorothy individually, we had covered many topics that I knew had rich overlap: surviving poverty and violence, finding the women's movement, practicing sexual politics within feminism, experiencing erotic culture and practices, and aiming for a clear understanding of self that was informed by race, class, and solid footing in butch-femme sexuality and culture. Moreover, they have a shared journey of moving from New York to California within five years of one another (late 1970s for Carmen, early 1980s for Dorothy), and both spoke of the struggle of adjusting to a West Coast community whose politics looked very different from those of New York. Dorothy's center of gravity was the leather community, and her activism was largely within the realm of culture at this time (after decades of work in women's centers and battered women's shelters). Carmen's focus was lesbian feminism and the San Francisco Women's Building. Despite these differences, both Dorothy and Carmen had encountered the classism and sexual conservatism that created much of the tension we now attribute to the sex wars of the 1980s.

By the time Dorothy, Carmen, and I sat down for a joint interview, Dorothy and I had spent the better part of three days together and had covered a lot of ground. Carmen and Dorothy had also spent some time together off camera as we all prepared for one last conversation before Carmen and I flew out the next day. In the excerpt included here, we began by talking about butch-femme and its meaning for them over time. They both told stories of young adulthood and realizing "who they are," shared their journeys through 1970s and 1980s feminism and the ensuing emphasis on androgyny and hostility toward butch-femme, and reflected on current debates within the lesbian community over trans identities. The excerpt represents the last hour of our taping and has been edited only slightly. We covered topics that have important and provocative implications for scholarship on feminist movements, particularly the interplay between sexuality and politics.

Representing a generation of butch-femme lesbians, including working-class women and women of color, Dorothy and Carmen's life stories offer important challenges to dominant narratives of liberation politics and sexual freedom. Committed to a radical politic that includes the right to self-definition and sexual expression, Dorothy and Carmen experience themselves as having been marginalized voices in women's movement leadership, middle-class lesbian feminism, and the neoliberal leadership of the LGBT community. In the interview, Carmen describes feelings of exclusion from movement leadership because of her insistence on a male-identified presentation, noting the community's enthusiasm for "titillating" conversations about power and desire yet a reluctance to place masculine women in leadership roles. Similarly, Dorothy describes the immense effort involved in maintaining a double life—of lesbian feminist organizing by day and the erotic culture of the bars by night. She reflects on the struggle to integrate her worlds, to bring butch girlfriends to her lesbian feminist collective, and to live up to the expectations for high femme within butch-femme culture.

These voices are important correctives to the mythology and scholarship on second-wave feminism. Not all self-identified feminists were adhering to the sexual ethos of androgyny or the prescriptive of reciprocal or vanilla sex. For these narrators, and indeed many others, erotic desire was born of a raced, classed, and gendered experience that in many ways collided with a mainstream, sexually conservative, feminist ideology beginning in the 1970s and that is now in an embattled ideological conversation with queer and transgender politics. It would be a mistake to assume that radical, prosex, or butch-femme sexualities disappeared in the 1970s or that lesbians with these sex practices rejected the language or imperative of feminism. Rather, women like Carmen and Dorothy and many others insisted on and claimed feminism as an identity and locus of their activism despite charges of being antifeminist, dangerous, or immoral by mainstream movement spokespersons.[6]

Other key themes emerge that potentially challenge the mainstream narratives of women's liberation movements: the range and persistence of lesbian activism within feminisms, the professionalization of the women's movement, butch-femme identity and culture versus the imposition of androgyny, and the persistence of race and class in the shaping of desire. We turned to the topic of transgender identities and the implications for categories of butch and femme for the last twenty minutes of our interview, and while their observations may be provocative, even problematic for some, the three of us felt it was important to bring a sense of history and a feminist analysis to an issue that is often veiled in silence. Through those lenses, historical and feminist, we were able to draw some important connections between generations. Dorothy and Carmen's navigation of feminism and gay liberation politics is a rich story that will provide future scholars and activists with new evidence of the complexities of sexuality, class, and feminism.

Those of us who collect oral history and, moreover, those of us who rely on oral history as primary sources know that this material is invaluable as evidence—evidence of our tenacity, our resilience, and creativity, sometimes of our very existence. The field of queer history is made possible, in large part, because we have been willing to speak—about violent pasts, the terror of homophobia and racism, our secret desires, our strategies for survival. But oral history is not just evidence—and we know this already, as practitioners and as students of the growing field on oral history methodology. Much has been written about oral history as a relationship, the self-reflexive piece of conducting interviews, and how to listen effectively and pay attention to this dynamic interaction. For the queer subject and narrator, we often delve into subject matter that other oral histories usually do not, including sexual identity and sex practices. It is not out of bounds then (and it may even be necessary) to ask about earliest sexual memories, awareness of difference around erotic desire and gendered behaviors, coming out and the vulnerability of exposure, and painful memories around family violence and incest.

Given the vulnerable nature of these topics, my intention was to create a safe environment where the narrator felt respected, trusted my intentions, and had a sense of control over the outcome of the interview. For me, one key factor in creating safety is reciprocity. Others have written about the usefulness of self-disclosure at the beginning of the relationship with the narrator, and I cannot overemphasize this, particularly in the context of queer oral history. I make a conscious effort to share something intimate early on to establish some level of vulnerability on my part. For example, because I am often not perceived to be a lesbian, I make a point of coming out right away. The femmes always read me as gay, as one of them, but butch women often do not. And once I do come out to them, it shifts our interactions entirely. However, what I choose to self-disclose is not uniform—it may be coming out, but often that is not necessary, so I may share that I have a young son, or that I am divorced, that I am from the South (an important detail for Southern narrators like Minnie Bruce Pratt, Suzanne Pharr, or Linda Stout because they often feel unfairly judged by Northerners), or that my lover is twenty years older than I am. Revealing something private about me creates connection and trust, and sometimes the narrator and I find a shared experience.

The existing literature on oral history methodology generally cautions against group interviews. Typically, and for good reason, we are coached to avoid having someone extra in the room, so many of us have shied away from using equipment that requires a technician in order to preserve the intimacy and authenticity of the two-person conversation. When I teach oral history to my students, I insist that they find a way to create that space—no taping in offices, no friends along, no extra relatives in the house, unless, of course, your narrator feels more comfortable with an ally for herself or it is impossible (and the conditions of interviewing are often out of our control). An interruption-free environment and an audience of one are optimal. This interview was not that. This may have cost us, but I also think it gave us opportunities. And as public intellectuals on topics of gender and sexuality, Carmen and Dorothy brought a comfort level to the conversation that allowed us to break with traditional oral history training.

For the purposes of this particular project, I believe a collaborative interview worked, and its success leads me to believe that group, or collaborative, interviews have the potential to be more productive than dyads in certain contexts. I approached the conversation as an experiment with very low stakes. The intention of the trip to California was to record Dorothy's oral history, and that had been accomplished. A taping with her and Carmen was a bonus. But I also had my concerns. Is it appropriate or ethical to interview your lover? Have we really tossed the notion of objectivity out the window? Is a group interview still oral history? And how could I be responsible to the dynamics between interviewer and narrator in this context? Because so much of the success of an interview depends on the interaction between the narrator and the interviewer, I was concerned that a trio might not work. I could not control the relationship between Dorothy and Carmen; what if it went poorly? Could I keep all of these factors in check and still be facilitating a reflective conversation that felt worthwhile?

Dorothy and I had been taping for a few days, and the three of us sat down together on the last evening of our trip to Guerneville. We were tired; Dorothy's partner, Alix, and her son Wolf were in the next room playing video games; the dogs were going in and out of the kitchen screen door. It was not ideal, and yet it was. Dorothy's kitchen felt relaxed and easy. We were familiar with one another since it was the end of our trip, we had spent time hanging out at the house with Alix and Wolf, and there was an open bottle of wine on the counter. And so we approached it as a friendly and informal conversation but with a clear sense of structure and agreed-upon topics for discussion. I asked them to compare their experiences in San Francisco during the 1980s, to reflect on their evolution sexually, and to discuss the politics around sex and gender within feminism at the time. While I remain fairly silent in the transcript of the conversation, I provided the opening framework for Dorothy and Carmen, and we had agreed on the agenda. During the course of the interview, Dorothy, Carmen, and I each take responsibility for the direction and focus of their discussion.

In this context, a collaborative model was successful and opened up new possibilities. The format was useful in sparking memories. The narrators often helped to fill in information for one another—names or street corners—and compared their recollections. In some ways, it was reading their distinct experiences of the lesbian community in San Francisco against one another that created a more cohesive narrative of fractiousness, professionalization, hostility toward butch-femme and sexual radicalism, and race and class privilege. Dorothy's tenure at *Out/Look* and leadership in the Outcasts dovetailed with Carmen's world of the Women's Building and political organizing to begin to create a piecing together of this decade in feminism and LGBT politics. My concern, though, was that trios can be a challenge—in any situation. In hindsight, I see that the way this trio worked was that within this group of three, there were many ways in which we became pairs. And it shifted throughout. This kept the power in balance during our conversation and prevented any one of us from feeling outnumbered and therefore timid or intimidated. For example, Dorothy and I have Southern roots, a femme identity, and motherhood in common. Carmen is a Puerto Rican butch from New York. However, Carmen and Dorothy are the same age and share the same class background. Carmen and I are lovers, but Dorothy and I had spent the last few days together. And Carmen and Dorothy can flirt. No side of the triangle ever became too heavy. This allowed us to get at topics that are intimate and controversial. Sex and desire are not easy to talk about—with lovers or with new acquaintances. We all had to take some risks to talk in a way that was honest and compassionate.

In an exchange about safety, submission, and power, Dorothy talks about butch desire to domesticate femmes and pushes back when Carmen calls femmes submissive. And she shares her desire for "sincerity," a lover who is assertive, dangerous. Carmen talks about the exchange of power during sex and the relinquishing of control. Both women take chances with one another and also begin to chip away at some of the silences around power, control, desire, and misogyny within butch-femme sexuality. While both Carmen and Dorothy have talked publicly about sex and sexual identity in the past, this interview covered new ground. For Carmen, I believe, her vulnerability and rethinking the erotics of butch-femme happened, at least in part, because of our intimacy. When we met three years ago for her oral history interview, Carmen and I talked briefly about her former lovers, and she shared a few sexual encounters. She was more self-reflective and open three years later, and it's logical. We were strangers in 2005. I was there to talk about politics and activism, and the gender difference between us—her butch to my femme—meant that we played out those roles with one another in the course of the interview. She was flirty and in charge, and I was the supportive listener. Our intimacy now has created room for a different and more vulnerable conversation.

While I am hesitant to generalize based solely on my own interviewing experience, I want to raise some questions regarding the role of gender in queer oral history. I have observed significant differences in my conversations with butch women versus femme-identified lesbians. In my experience, femmes are more apt to confide, to explore places of pain particularly around sexuality, and to talk more openly about past lovers and their own desire. Butch-identified women have been more reticent to discuss past relationships and sexual practices with me and tend to rely on butch-femme modes of behavior to shape our interaction—flirtation, gentlemanly gestures, more bravado, and less vulnerability. Can we apply what we know about gendered communication styles to lesbians? Does gender operate in similar or distinct ways? Was this a dynamic at work in this oral history? What if the interviewer was butch? Were Dorothy and I question askers and attentive listeners? Were Carmen's stories declarative and confident in a way that we ascribe to masculinity? Who was vulnerable or silenced? Did my femininity and/or my status as Carmen's lover open up space or close it down for either of them? In terms of our self-presentations, gender differences are highlighted—mostly in a flirtatious kind of way—but the performance of self is exaggerated by the presence of the other in the room. Does this raise questions about gender and authenticity, self and performance that look different in a queer context?

Although I was not conscious of it at the time of our taping, as I reread the transcript, I am keenly aware of the way that race dropped out of our conversation about sex and desire. This trio managed to create safety around class, desire, and gender but not race or racism. We talked about women of color and feminism in the first hour and cross-cultural desire at different times, but for the most part, race was only given tentative and indirect attention. Sticking to shared identities of class, generation, and butch-femme where Carmen, in particular, knew there was some common experience to draw on was safer. I regret that I/ we had not made race a more explicit part of our agenda for the evening, and I see that our silence echoes the larger community's inability to navigate discussions around race and queer desire.

Shared political sensibilities and investment in butch-femme sexuality led us to the topic of transgender and gender-variant identities. Grounded in current debates within the LGBT community over (relatively) new categories of identity, Dorothy and Carmen shared their reflections on the meaning of trans for butch-femme identity.[7] In her observations about the erotics and the politics of transmen, Dorothy asserts her support of self-determination for transgender people but acknowledges her erotic disinterest. Carmen echoes Dorothy's critical assessment of transgender expression and queer politics and asks, "What was the fucking point of feminism in the first place if it wasn't to create a space where women could make this decision about our bodies?" Both narrators offer important, though contentious, observations—grounded in history, experience, and a commitment to gender and sexual freedoms— that are often lost in an ahistorical queer discourse about transgenderism. And in this historical moment, our shared concerns over continued feminist backlash, the homonormativity of the LGBT movement, and an investment in butch-femme sexuality created something for us to push off of to carve out a political stance that was grounded in personal experience. We may think differently on this topic a few years from now, but its key contribution—indeed, that of any oral history—is capturing a sense of self, embattled as it is, in the moment.

Queer oral history is still in its infancy as a self-conscious methodology that explores some of the theoretical questions I have raised here, but not as practice. While social historians and community-based groups have relied extensively on oral history to create a narrative of the past, we are only just beginning to look critically at our methods. We are learning as we go—to take risks, to continue to challenge categories and assumptions, and to break silences about sex, gender, and desire. More important, the overarching questions queer oral historians raise as practitioners—the nature of memory, the construction of self, the meanings of history—continue to push the discipline of history in general in significant directions.

Notes

1. My sincere gratitude to Dorothy and Carmen for their time and trust. This Stonewall baby walks in the trail you blazed. And I offer my deep appreciation to the Sophia Smith Collection at Smith College for their broad and just vision of women's history that made this project possible.
2. Dorothy Allison and Carmen Vázquez, interview by Kelly Anderson, transcript of video recording, November 19, 2007, Voices of Feminism Oral History Project, Sophia Smith Collection, pp. 26–45.
3. This conversation was partially inspired by "What We're Rollin' around in Bed With: Sexual Silences in Feminism: A Conversation toward Ending Them," a dialogue between Cherríe Moraga and Amber Hollibaugh, more than twenty-five years prior, about race, class, and butch-femme desire. Originally printed in *Heresies*, the sex issue, in 1981, it is now reprinted in Joan Nestle, ed., *The Persistent Desire: A Femme-Butch Reader* (Boston: Alyson, 1992).
4. Barnard's 1982 conference, The Scholar and the Feminist IX: "Towards a Politics of Sexuality," represents the apex of the "sex wars" among feminists. Many of the papers presented there are collected in Carole S. Vance, ed., *Pleasure and Danger: Exploring Female Sexuality* (Boston: Routledge and Kegan Paul, 1984). For a broader view of the conflicts over sexuality during the 1980s and 1990s, see Lisa Duggan and Nan D. Hunter, *Sex Wars: Sexual Dissent and Political Culture* (New York: Routledge, 1995).
5. Although it feels informal and out of step with academic publishing, I've chosen to use the narrators' first names in this essay because it more accurately reflects the tone of our relationships and conversations with one another.
6. For testimony around the complexities of butch-femme culture and desire, see Nestle, ed., *The Persistent Desire*. For the history of a butch-femme community, see Elizabeth Lapovsky Kennedy and Madeline D. Davis, *Boots of Leather, Slippers of Gold* (New York: Routledge, 1993).
7. For an excellent collection of theory and testimony on queer politics and gender, see Joan Nestle, Clare Howell, and Riki Wilchins, eds., *Genderqueer: Voices from Beyond the Sexual Binary* (Los Angeles: Alyson, 2002).

PART III

FRIENDSHIP

8

FRIENDSHIP, INSTITUTIONS, ORAL HISTORY

Michael David Franklin

Oral history by Michael David Franklin and Dorthe Troeften with Carol, Minneapolis, Minnesota, June 24, 2005

Along with my colleague, Dorthe Troeften, I first met Carol, an eighty-two-year-old transgender woman, in June 2005 after she contacted the Twin Cities GLBT Oral History Project (OHP) at the University of Minnesota with the express interest of sharing her oral history. For approximately two hours that first afternoon, and in subsequent interviews in July 2005 and May 2008, Carol shared memories of her childhood, her friendships with transvestites in the 1960s, her thirty-five-year marriage, and her gradual identification as a transgender woman in the late 1990s. A Korean War veteran and printer by trade, Carol practiced cross-dressing throughout her adult life as she moved around the Midwest, and in the 1960s, she cofounded a Wisconsin chapter of the national male-to-female heterosexual transvestite sorority established by transgender pioneer Virginia Prince. Her oral history recounts memories of negotiating her feminine self with her male social identity and of forming friendships with other cross-dressers.

Approximately seventy oral histories have been gathered so far by the Twin Cities GLBT OHP. Once transcribed, they will be donated to the Jean-Nikolaus Tretter Collection in GLBT Studies at the University of Minnesota's Andersen Research Library. Carol's, as well as many other GLBT oral histories, are featured in Queer Twin Cities *(Minneapolis: University of Minnesota Press, 2010), a book that uses sexuality to chart connections between people's lives and the formation of urban spaces, political movements, social groups, and identities throughout the histories of Minneapolis and St. Paul.*

CAROL: Myrtle, I met, Myrtle was the first . . .well, we used to call ourselves TVs.
DORTHE TROEFTEN: TVs, yeah.
CAROL: The first TV I met. Well, she'd been doing it for years, too. And she came to visit me in Wilmer, and I, uh—

MICHAEL DAVID FRANKLIN: And I'm sorry, how did she, how did you get in touch with each other?

CAROL: Oh, they had, in the thing, letters to the . . .you could write to each other, and that's what we did.

TROEFTEN: How did you find them? How did you find—

CAROL: The TV magazine. *Transvestia* magazine. In some of the early ones, you'll notice in the back they had, you know, the names, and of course, you had to send it through the company and then they remailed them and so forth.

TROEFTEN: But where did you find the *Transvestia* magazine?

CAROL: Oh. Oh, yeah, that's—forgot that! I was, uh . . .come to the [Twin] Cities every once a month, I'd go home to my folks once a month and then I'd stay out there where I lived for two weekends. Well, I'd come down here, and I'd go to Shinder's, and all these places to see what I could find about cross-dressers and so forth. And this one day I saw this one, it was about some party who dressed, I don't remember if he dressed part-time or what, but I bought the magazine but took it back with me and read it, and there was *Transvestia* magazine, the party who started this, so right away I wrote for the magazine and got the magazine, and from there I wrote to this Myrtle and I wrote to this Sally. And first Myrtle came to visit me, then Myrtle told me any time I came through her town I should call her and we could have coffee or something, so I would do that. And she lived in Hutchinson, and she's not around anymore, and she's safe. But anyway, she used to put on shows at the National Guard Armory, she was with the National Guard, and they put on shows every year, and her and another guy were the old scrubwomen in the show. They'd come down with mops and buckets and so forth, and kind of got their two cents in the play, but they were dressed in a way that gave them an out there. And this Sally I met and she came to see me, and she was from . . .Big Lake. And we met in Saint Cloud, and visited and got to know each other better. And then from there I moved out of Willmar, and I was working out in Wisconsin and I get a letter from this party called Fran, who lived in Madison. And she was, I was the only other one in Wisconsin, and she invited me down and that, and so I went down and visited with her, and so we went to Chicago to a Transvestia meeting, and met, oh, ten people there, and from there we thought we'd try to get other people in for ourselves. We had, oh, I don't know, I'd say ten people come to meetings pretty regular. . . .

CAROL: Well, I went down to Madison on the Greyhound. As my original self. [chuckle] Anyway, we went to Chicago, Fran and I did, and we stayed—we went to this hotel where they were having their meeting down there. And I don't know, this Chicago chapter had a few meetings and Fran has been to them before, but we thought we'd go down and really see what they did and see if we could start our own. Of course, we didn't know where we could get any members from, but we came back and started our own. And we had, uh . . .let's see, there's Fran and me, and, uh . . .we got a party from Appleton whose name was Lynn. And we started out, the three of us would get together every month, and sit there and have a little meeting and what we were going to do. And then we decided we would make a little paper, so we bought a hectograph—mimeo, no, mimeograph, it was a mimeograph. And Fran did all the typing and that. And we'd do that and send it out to a variety of people, and then we got associated members. We had associated members from Ohio—which, we had Laura—and we had one from, uh . . .Indian . . .Indiana, and I can't think of her name right now. And we had several from Chicago, even, joined the associated club. Then we'd, you know, hear from them each month. They wouldn't be at the meeting, but if they come through town—I know the party from Ohio would come through town about twice a year, and stop, and be at the meeting, and then he'd stop here in Minneapolis and be here for a couple of days. And he did some big business here in Minneapolis with one of the big defense firms.

TROEFTEN: Hmm.

CAROL: And, uh . . .then, uh . . .we got more members—in fact I got a picture of some of the members we have—uh, had. And, uh . . .[sounds of Carol getting up from her chair to retrieve the picture]. . . .

CAROL: [standing away from microphone, searching for picture] And, anyway, uh . . .you know, when you want to find things, it's hard to find.

TROEFTEN AND FRANKLIN: [laughter]

CAROL: But I saw it in here, so I know it's here.

TROEFTEN: Maybe if you come over and sit by the microphone, you can look through while we talk. . . . Oh, there it is.

FRANKLIN: Oh, wow.

CAROL: And some, I don't know their names. I figured there's that one time, the last meeting we had, when we kind of closed up things after that. And it was this party's—I think it was this party's wife.

TROEFTEN: Oh yeah, you mentioned that. So we're looking now at a picture of eight . . .women—no, nine women.

FRANKLIN: Nine, yeah.

TROEFTEN: Dressed—

FRANKLIN: From March 1967, the photograph says. . . . And they're all dressed up. There's a row standing behind the sofa, with four ladies sitting on the sofa and five standing behind. It looks to be in a living room, possibly?

CAROL: Mmhmm.

FRANKLIN: Somebody's living room, and everybody looks, you know, very well put together.

TROEFTEN: Yeah.

FRANKLIN: Very well dressed. Very stylish.

CAROL: There's Virginia

TROEFTEN: Oh, there's Virginia

FRANKLIN: Oh, yeah!

CAROL: And this is the Fran from Wisconsin. And I think Fran, from my opinion, Fran was the big promoter of this thing in the early days.

TROEFTEN: Which one is you? . . .Yeah, okay, that's what I thought.

CAROL: And this is June. She's from Minnesota And used to live in St. Paul. She lives up north now.

FRANKLIN: Like, upstate? Up north in the state?

CAROL: Yeah, up north in Duluth.

TROEFTEN: Hmm.

CAROL: And, uh . . .otherwise, I know where this party [a TV in the picture] lives, and I'm going to give her a call some day. But she doesn't know me real well, so I just don't know. . . . I'm going to call her and tell her who I am. That I used to belong to Theta And she used to come to Minneapolis meetings, when we used to have Minneapolis meetings, she would come here. And, well, a lot of them would drive a far distance, because it was important to meet people from . . .and talk to them and so forth. So. . . .

TROEFTEN: So in the meetings, you basically got together, and . . .?

CAROL: We'd have a short little meeting. Then the rest was talk. People who wasn't used to this, you know, they—you'd fill them in and kind of get them

THE THETA GIRLS
EDWINA   LYNNE   GERALDINE   JUDY   FRAN   CAROL

Six transvestites sit primly along a brick fireplace during a sorority club meeting in Madison, Wisconsin, in 1963. A network of sorority clubs for male-to-female transvestites crystallized in the United States during the 1960s, thanks to the campaign of transgender pioneer Virginia Prince to educate the public about heterosexual transvestism. *Courtesy of the Tretter Collection, University Libraries, University of Minnesota, Minneapolis* on the right road, you know, that they weren't, they weren't all bad. [laugh] And so forth, and . . .

FRANKLIN: And would you socialize?

CAROL: You're like a therapist, you know? And yeah, you'd socialize, and we'd have a little lunch and coffee and that. . . .

FRANKLIN: I have another question, since I'm still so captivated by this photograph you've shown us. It's just so wonderful. But I noticed that you all look very middle class, and it seems like everybody, I would say, would be white. So do you remember any TVs who were not white, who were of another race, or possibly a class background or maybe they struggled to buy things?

CAROL: There was no TVs in the group that was any other race but white. But this Myrtle from Hutchinson corresponded with a TV years before, I don't know how she got—through some magazine she picked up. And she lived in Utah, and she was a b . . .a porter on the train. And she was black. And . . .so, I knew there was a black one who was there. Then there was talk once that they didn't think there was any Jews.

FRANKLIN: Who didn't?

CAROL: Well, like, articles. Nobody joined Theta and that who was Jewish. It was all Europeans, you know, and that. And then they thought this little celebration they have for Jewish boys—whatever they call it now, bar mitzvah . . .

FRANKLIN: Bar mitzvah, yeah.

CAROL: They thought maybe that's why they didn't fit into this TV thing, but then it turned out that they did. There was . . .finally ran into some Jewish men who were cross-dressers. . . .

TROEFTEN: How long were you involved with these groups? Did it end when that group broke up in Madison?

CAROL: Well, it kind of ended there. The meetings did. We did have some meetings in Minneapolis, at different motels here. One . . .this is kind of a funny thing. We held a meeting at the Fair Oaks, over by the [Minneapolis] Art Institute. Which is back in 1960s, you know? And that is where we had our meeting. We had a good turnout. We had several meetings there. But this thing today that they have, which is also from Virginia's group—I can't think what they call it now—they had their first meeting over at the Fair Oaks. I told the party that was doing the thing, "Well, you were the second ones there at the Fair Oaks 'cause we were there first." And this woman lives in a apartment house over there. Soph . . .Sophia? She's got such a funny name, I can't think of what it is. But anyway, I told her, "You live in this apartment house in the corner across the street, the house behind this one is where we first got together to do the job." So we got together about the same area So . . .

TROEFTEN: Did the people who come there have—did you feel like you had similar experiences to the other TVs that you met with? In terms of their lives—

CAROL: Well, I feel like—you mean, growing up experiences?

TROEFTEN: Yeah, or sort of, your . . . yeah—

CAROL: Oh, you mean I lived in poverty, and the other was rich? [chuckle]

TROEFTEN: Well, I was thinking—I don't know. I mean, I was thinking, you know, if you felt that was a place you could come and meet people who understood who you were because you shared something, or did you feel like you didn't, actually?

CAROL: I felt like it was a place you come and talk to people. A lot of them didn't know much because they were . . .well, everybody was just kind of finding out about everything. And I felt like at the time that I was one of the better posted people. And Fran was real good posted. She was—her and Virginia were corresponding a lot and that. In fact, they wrote a book, and I forgot the name of the book. But it's at the library, I know. So . . .but . . .a lot of people didn't— well, you're a guy who dressed. That's how they felt, a lot of them, you know. They're a guy, and I think there's a lot of guys today still think they're a guy who likes to dress as women. And, see, I don't feel that way. I feel like I am a woman, and I can't come out and say directly that I am a woman, but I'm a transgender woman, because I do have some of the other stuff, you know. But . . .the people came to the meeting, they were out there searching to find out stuff, and so forth. So . . .you have any books from the new organization out in California. They used to be Transvestia?

FRANKLIN: Is it . . .? I just, I'm totally blanking.

CAROL: *The Mirror.*

FRANKLIN: I'm sorry, what's that?

CAROL: *The Mirror.*

FRANKLIN: I guess not, no.

CAROL: I think they call it . . .I have some here. I only have a couple because I joined the club, and I quit the club, because . . .because I didn't think they were like the old days, you know.

TROEFTEN: Hmm. And when was this?

CAROL: Oh, I joined it maybe in the [inaudible, as Carol searches through papers] I don't know where I got [inaudible]. Anyway, Tri-Ess is what they call it. . . . I do have some other, and I'll dig them out and get 'em so you can use 'em. And these are—some of these are published papers from some of the clubs around town. This is from the Californ—the big membership, you know?

TROEFTEN: Mmhmm.

FRANKLIN: So you said that Tri-Ess and what you were involved in just wasn't like how it used to be in the old days. How is it different?

CAROL: Well, I don't—I just feel like that. Well, it could be that people are better posted on stuff and that. Maybe. And I don't feel that it's as sociable as it was.

FRANKLIN: Not as sociable?

CAROL: It's more antisocial, you know. It's more sociable back then—everybody'd talk to each other and that, and now it seems like you can go there and you can sit by yourself in the corner if you want to, you know.[1]

Commentary

What is the connection between oral history and friendship? Might the creation of oral history sometimes spark a friendship between interviewee and interviewer? If so, how can the evaluation of oral history as an incitement of friendship offer new insight into the university's regulation of relationships over which it claims jurisdiction? To put it another way, what happens to friendships born of oral history in an institutional context? And how can memories of friendships that took institutional form help us reconsider the institutional management of oral history as a method of knowledge production? Oral history lies at the intersection of two vectors of power within the university: the regulation of relationships and the administration of knowledge production. The oral history of Carol, a white transgender woman born in 1929 who lives in a subsidized retirement community on the outskirts of Minneapolis, clarifies these vectors of power.

This chapter weaves through Carol's memories, her reflections about her current living situation, and my interactions with her as a white cisgender gay man who represents a university-affiliated project. As this itinerary might suggest, "oral history" is defined here as both the resulting text and the process of producing the text. Because her remembered experiences across space and time cannot be neatly collapsed into one discrete identity, and indeed emphasize transvestite friendships as superior to marriage, Carol's oral history calls into question rhetorical deployments of "the GLBT community" in current national debates in the United States that frame gay rights in terms of marriage and military service. Carol's interview convincingly showcases oral history's unique potential among ethnographic methods to bring people together across divisions of age and identity for transformative interactions: in this case, oral history's potential is produced through an interviewer and interviewee's shared commitment to interactively illuminate queer and trans experiences, lives, and histories specific to the Twin Cities region.[2]

Carol's oral history is useful for addressing questions about the connection between friendship and oral history because more than forty years ago, via a magazine named *Transvestia*, she befriended other transvestites in the Midwest and formed a sorority-like social club. It is also useful because over the last thirty years, Carol has moved away from identifying as a transvestite and has come to identify as a transgender woman. Historically, the university has played a central role in producing knowledge about unconventional gender expressions that we now readily categorize as transgender. A culminating point of this history was the introduction in 1980 of the psychopathology Gender Identity Disorder into the third edition of the *Diagnostic and Statistical Manual of Mental Disorders (DSM)*. This entry into the DSM was the outcome of the study of transsexuality in American universities since the 1960s, and it effectively concretized the medicalization of cross-gender identification. Some twenty-five years later, it is this diagnostic category that impels the institutional review board (IRB) at the University of Minnesota to view transgender research subjects first and foremost as people who embody a medicalized mode of difference. Hence, when Dorthe Troeften applied in 2003 for approval to collect transgender oral histories, the IRB declared her project to pose greater than minimal risk to research participants because of its interpretation of their gender difference as pathology. The research reviewer made suggestions as to how she should minimize risks for potential participants, and after such changes, the project was given approval. Because its ethical code is calibrated by a historical precedent of institutional violence against marginalized communities, such as the infamous Tuskegee syphilis study, the IRB assesses all human research with a primary goal of minimizing risk.[3]

This is not to say that the IRB is wrong to concern itself with risk, or imply that beneficence is ignored, or to argue that an ethical recalibration around social change would automatically make for a progressive IRB. Rather, Carol's oral history presents us with an instance that contradicts the IRB's general outlook about the risks posed by transgender oral history. Because her current living situation in a heterogendered retirement community requires her to present herself daily as a man, the friendship that has emerged between Carol, Dorthe, and me as a result of our interviews has empowered Carol to express herself more *as* Carol. To put this another way, Dorthe and I have served as a positive outlet for Carol's gendered self-expression at a time in her life when she seems to have little encouragement along these lines. These expressions have occurred through her everyday interactions with Dorthe and me: when she has greeted us at her apartment door dressed in a new skirt and blouse that she then proudly discusses in her oral history, when she has told me over the phone about her latest public excursions, or when she has hinted that she longs for friends who understand her as she is. The interpersonal elements of creating her oral history have catalyzed her everyday life and buttressed her will to make changes in how, when, and where she presents herself as Carol and to whom she discloses her transgender identity.

A dynamic between transvestite and transgender becomes apparent when we look at Carol's oral history through the lenses of friendship and institution. On the one hand, Carol's oral history proffers memories of cross-gender practices and friendships that coalesced around and within a transvestite social club in the 1960s. On the other hand, Carol shares her frustrations, enthusiasms, and memories with Dorthe and me, representatives of an institutionally vetted transgender oral history project. Each instance presents us with a different constellation of institution, gender formation, and friendship: friendship among transvestites in a sorority and friendship among a transgender oral history participant and her university-affiliated cisgender interviewers. Pinpointing that moment in Carol's oral history when she believes she ceased to feel that she was a transvestite or began to feel that she was transgender (not necessarily the same moment, I know) is beside the point. And although Carol's life could be used to analyze the therapeutic and medical establishments' impact on the development of her gender identity, this approach marginalizes the significance of her friendships in this process.

Instead, Carol's oral history provides a basis for theorizing the connection between friendship and oral history in institutional contexts. Each connection between friendship and oral history demonstrates different ways that an institution mediates sexuality to elicit a particular kind of gendered subject formation. As institutions, the transvestite social club and the IRB seek to elicit and represent the cross-dresser and the transgender oral history participant. Neither club nor IRB represses gender expressions that jar dominant conventions of femininity and masculinity, but rather seek to incite and manage these expressions to form hegemonic subjects supportive of a particular social order. Indeed, *Transvestia* and its attendant community, including Carol's social club, sought to fend off the specter of homosexuality by presenting male-to-female transvestitism as heterosexual devotion to women and femininity. And the IRB originally rejected Troeften's bid to interview trans people critical of the medical establishment by insisting that she use more neutral language to recruit a broader array of research subjects, all in the name of objective research.

These examples signal two different moments of the productive regulation of gender identity and expressions. Yet, through her activities with the social club, Carol formed profound friendships, and within the constraint created by the IRB's risk management, a friendship has developed through oral history. These friendships are embedded within and enabled by their sheltering institutions, but they also exceed them. A paradox emerges, then: friendship is cultivated between male-to-female heterosexual transvestites and between an elderly transgender oral history participant and her interviewers by those very conditions of institutional regulation that seek to salt the earth of transformative relationships to uphold hegemonies. Ultimately, it is this enduring quality of friendship that illuminates how the interface of institution and friendship can paradoxically aid in the production of new social movements and new ways of positioning oneself in relation to society.[4]

To examine the links between oral history, institution, and friendship, we should first review Carol's oral history for the details of her life up until her participation with the Midwestern transvestite social scene. Carol remembers her experiences as a Korean War veteran who regularly "dressed up" in feminine attire, as she puts it, throughout her childhood and adolescence in upstate Minnesota. During the 1950s, when she was in her twenties, Carol moved between small towns in Minnesota and Wisconsin. In these towns, she worked as a printer, a trade she acquired in the Army. One weekend a month, she would visit her family, who had known about her cross-dressing since her youth and who even would see her dressed in women's clothing around the house at times, but speak nothing of it.

Another weekend a month, she would drive to Minneapolis, where she spent much time dressed up in public, strolling through stores and streets. During one of these forays, while shopping in a downtown bookstore for material about others like her, Carol found an issue of the magazine *Sexology* that featured an article about transgender pioneer Virginia Prince and the male-to-female hetero-sexual transvestite social network that she was trailblazing across the United States. Included in the issue was an ad for the magazine *Transvestia*, the nerve center of Prince's movement.[5] At this moment, the idea of transvestism entered Carol's life as a socially viable identity and practice. She purchased *Sexology* and sent off for *Transvestia*, which regularly included editorials by Prince, an array of photographic and written reader contributions about the vicissitudes of Cold War heterosexual transvestism, and a personals section for readers desiring cor-respondence. Through this section, Carol struck up friendships with fellow transvestites in Minnesota and Wisconsin. In 1961, she relocated from a small town in Wisconsin to Minneapolis to be, in her words, "more free" to be Carol. Soon after her move, she coestablished in Madison, Wisconsin, with one of her first transvestite friends, Fran, a club that was part of Prince's national social network for heterosexual transvestites. Because of the sorority-like structure of Prince's network, Carol and her friends' club in Madison was called the Theta chapter.

When Carol speaks about her life before her introduction to the transvestite social scene, she gives an impression of solitude. This impression resonates with her current living situation as a transgender woman having to pass herself off daily as a man. As an adult in her twenties, she would drive to hotel rooms in neighboring towns to dress alone and in anonymity. These moments of solitary expression occur throughout her life and are especially pronounced now that she lives in a heterogendered communal setting, when once again her car is refuge from the gendered demands of her daily life. It is notable, then, that she describes her Army service during the Korean War as central to shaping her cross-gender identification. Reflecting on her military experience, she comments on her transformation:

> Well, you know, during my life I was not really a leader. Kind of set back. Don't take control, or [I would] be shoved a little bit and that. But then came that great day when I went to the United States Army, and I became a leader. As long as I was in the Army, I was somebody, not nobody. I was one of the important enlisted men there. So that's on leadership, you know? And then I come out of the Army and I kind of slid back. Well, I knew I wasn't a female impersonator, but . . .so my leadership kind of slipped, you know. But . . .then you read a little more, and then you find out about the transvestites. Well, I'm a transvestite. Then, as time goes on, then you find out there's more than just transvestites. There's the transgender, and transsexuals, and so forth. Well, I decided I was transgender because I want to be Carol, a woman, and I want to live that way, and I don't have any desire to be a transvestite.[6]

In this passage, Carol makes a connection between leadership skills acquired during military service and the process of cross-gender identification. She makes this connection following a discussion about her dual roles as vice president and coordinator of entertainment at the retirement community. Expressing frustration about the lethargy of the retirement community's social scene, Carol associates her inability to freely dress as a woman with her visibility as a leader to whom fellow residents look for direction and diversion. She comments at length about the staidness and homophobia of many of her fellow residents and how previous conversations with them convinced her that the retirement community was a hostile and potentially unsafe environment for her to present herself as Carol. In short, the friendlessness that Carol experiences, coupled with the surveillance she feels as a well-known resident, foregrounds the previous quotation. The gendered dimensions of her life in the retirement home, in which she is expected to serve as a leader due to her outgoing personality and desire to connect with others, invoke her memory of the gendered expectations of her service during the Korean War as "one of the important enlisted men."

It is no accident, though, that this quotation links Army service to the transformation of a nobody into a somebody who becomes a transvestite. By doing so, it indicates how military service is an intensely heteromasculine realm that a male-bodied person who feels cross-gender desire would experience differently. Indeed, Carol's memories about the Army recur throughout her oral history but are not prominent. She credits the Army for her trade skills and her leadership skills, but she does not, for instance, reminisce about serving in Korea, fighting against communism, or spending time with Army buddies. This is certainly due to Dorthe's and my focus on other aspects of her life and probably to Carol's thematic priorities in her narration. When remembering her Army service, though, Carol focuses on stolen moments of cross-gender expression:

> I took my basic training and schooling in—which was Fort, is Fort Gordon, Georgia, now, but was Camp Gordon. And this desire we have, you can't keep a cap on it. So one day I was in town on pass, and I got a few clothes and that, and went over to this little hotel and got a room there for the night, and dressed and went out for a little while, but not, not long. But I could say I've been dressed in Augusta, Georgia . . . And then I ordered, when I was in Korea, I ordered some clothes from Sears. And I went down and had my picture taken with them on, I dressed and had my picture taken. I thought. . . . So that was another time. So I've been dressed in Korea, too. Old Klinger, he's not the only one.[7]

Carol does not express regret over having to contain her gender expressions to the hotel room and the photographer's studio. At plenty of other moments in her oral history, she narrates habits of clandestinely dressing in "dumpy little town[s]."[8] In every memory shared, including those about the Army, she is matter-of-fact about the need for discretion when she dressed.[9] And even with her current living situation, her frustrations stem not from having to leave the building if she wants to have a social life as Carol, but rather from the ignorance of those people whose lives are braided with hers because of their coresidence yet separate due to homophobia and transphobia.

What is telling about these memories, then, is her silence about friendships during her experience in the Army that set her down the path of personal transformation. Historically, war has been a crucible for male soldiers' relationships, which the military has sought to commandeer. In an interview titled "Sex, Power, and the Politics of Identity," Michel Foucault comments on "the problem of friendship" in the West that first makes its appearance during the sixteenth and seventeenth centuries. Namely, the rise of social institutions such as the military, universities, and the medical establishment in this era correlated with the reining in of potent relationships between people, relationships whose everyday intensities of pleasure, camaraderie, joy, and devotion were at odds with the institutional quest for power:

> For centuries after antiquity, friendship was a very important kind of social relation: a social relation within which people had a certain freedom, certain kind of choice (limited of course), as well as very intense emotional relations. There were also economic and social implications to these relationships—they were obliged to help their friends, and so on. I think that in the sixteenth and seventeenth centuries, we see these kinds of friendships disappearing, at least in the male society. . . . The army, the bureaucracy, administration, universities, schools, and so on—in the modern senses of these words—cannot function with such intense friendships. I think there can be seen a very strong attempt in all these institutions to diminish or minimize the affectional relations.[10]

Friendship's life in the modern institution is contradictory, according to Foucault. On the one hand, friendship is necessary for the institution's survival as a social entity that benevolently and productively governs people. Yet, on the other hand, the institution regulates and discourages friendship because of its capacity to dilute allegiance, to spark affections between people that defy the mechanical heart of institutional protocol: "Institutional codes can't validate these relations with multiple intensities, variable colors, imperceptible movements and changing forms. These relations short-circuit it and introduce love where there's supposed to be only law, rule, or habit."[11] Put simply, the management of friendship has become a necessary balancing act for institutions, the deft handling of a substance volatile yet vital to institutional hegemony.

This balancing act between institutional imperatives and affectional relations becomes prominent when Carol remembers her participation in the Midwestern transvestite scene. After returning to the United States from Korea and traveling from small town to small town throughout Wisconsin and Minnesota, Carol's life began to flourish in 1961. After moving to Minneapolis for greater freedom to express herself as Carol, she became very involved with the Theta chapter. Its monthly meetings, hosted by Fran and her wife in their Madison home, drew ten regular members as well as a number of occasional visitors. At meetings they would gather dressed and socialize alongside those wives or girl-friends who knew of and accepted their partners. (One of these wives eventually included a woman who married Carol in 1964. She initially accepted Carol's transvestism, and soon after their marriage, they began having children.) Mem-bers would discuss the responsibilities of the club, including the publication of a monthly newsletter contributed by Theta members and their wives, as well as news from other chapters in the Midwest. Occasionally the group would submit contributions to *Transvestia*.[12] According to Carol's memory, Virginia Prince vis-ited the Madison club on at least four separate occasions while traveling through the Midwest, and once Carol and her wife had Virginia to their Minneapolis house for lunch.

Due primarily to the anger of one member's wife, who threatened to go to the police, the Theta chapter disbanded around 1967. According to Carol, Fran feared the social and legal repercussions of exposure if the wife reported the meetings to the authorities:

> And then in one of the meetings one of the guy's wives, one of the TV's wives was really mad about this thing [the collective transvestism]. So that was the end of the meeting for Fran in there. Fran had the meeting at her home all the time. And, so she said, "I can't do this anymore because I don't know what would happen if she turned me in, and I'd have—the police would be out here."[13]

Because of the club's disbandment, and because of Carol's own marital prob-lems that centered around her wife's growing disapproval of transvestism now that they had children to raise, Carol's participation in this scene waned in the late 1960s. She attempted with friends to initiate a similar group in Minneapo-lis; it met several times but never quite got off the ground. By the early 1970s, she had lost contact with most of her transvestite friends. A certain solitude returned to her life. She continued to dress up in private with brief public out-ings over the following two decades, but only when her children and wife were out of the house. Indeed, in her oral history, Carol recalls a fight in 2000 that erupted when her wife unexpectedly came home from work to find her dressed up, a fight she says that signaled the moment the marriage was over.[14] During the 1980s and 1990s, she would infrequently visit various transgender social groups in the Twin Cities but never became a regular member because of her wife's protest and her dissatisfaction with the groups' dynamics, which she felt were inferior to those of the Theta chapter. Carol comments on one such group: "I joined the club, and I quit the club, because . . .because I didn't think they were like the old days."[15] In 2000, around the time Carol separated from her wife after thirty-five years of marriage, she moved into the retirement com-munity and got a letter from her therapist certifying her as a transgender woman.

Carol's friendships and her involvement in the cross-dressing scene in the early 1960s provided her with a template through which to express her cross-gender desire via a transvestite identity. In short, she achieved a social intelligibility distinct from the solitude of her life before moving to Minneapolis and after the Theta chapter disbanded. This intelligibility was brought about by the network of friends that grew within the shelter provided by the institution of the social club, yet at the same time this intelligibility was formulated by the national campaign of Virginia Prince.

The magazine *Transvestia* was central to this campaign. Through *Transvestia*, Prince provided to "males who are fascinated by feminine attire . . .an outlet to express their feelings and a medium of contact with others of similar persuasion."[16] Disputing the popular rationale that typically smeared transvestism as pathological, she denied any underlying motives of immorality and asserted the harmlessness of the majority of male cross-dressers. Yet, despite her trenchant critique of the widely circulated misconceptions about transvestism, Prince's advocacy was not for everyone. Living in a paranoid Cold War environment in which intertwining fears of a communist conspiracy and the insidiousness of homosexuality intensified the state surveillance and persecution of self-identified homosexuals and homophile organizations, Prince had to regulate her rhetoric as a transvestite activist advocating for a practice long deemed symptomatic of sexual perversion. Motivated to differentiate transvestites from homosexuals, she appealed to the dominant ideology by casting transvestism as a normal variation of human behavior. Such a claim on normality in effect separated gender expression from sexual desire while attempting to evade any taint of deviance commonly attributed to homosexuality. Indeed, Prince's carefully deployed contention that rigid concepts of gender and sexuality should open up to incorporate male-to-female cross-dressers paradoxically necessitated a dependence on heterosexuality and marriage, two components central to the heteronormativity responsible for the stigmatization of transvestism.[17]

Carol mentions in her oral history how club meetings were occasions to socialize with other transvestites. Despite the indispensability of wives and marriage in Prince's politics of respectability, wives in Carol's oral history are mentioned only in passing in the context of the 1960s scene. Carol focuses far more on her friendships and activities with other transvestites than she does on wives. Thus, even though Prince's campaign was the occasion to initiate the club, marriage in Carol's memory is overshadowed by transvestite friendships. This can be seen in two moments. One is that of the wife whose threats forced the club's closure. But another moment directly shaping the course of Carol's life is how she came to marry her wife. Carol remembers how before the Madison scene she would end her dating relationships with many women before they became serious because she "knew what [she] was going to do" if she married: continue to dress up and express her feminine self and possibly seek sex reassignment surgery.[18] As she grew older, she did not pursue transsexual health care services, as she had initially thought about in Korea when she first learned about Christine Jorgensen in 1952. Instead, she "listened to other drummers" and pursued a life of heterosexuality.[19] In 1964, at age thirty-five, after she had been involved with the Theta chapter for three years, Carol told the woman she was dating at the time about her transvestism. The woman supported her and accepted it, and feeling she ought to marry but not knowing what to do, Carol turned to her married transvestite friend Fran for advice. Fran was in favor of marriage to a woman who accepted her companion's transvestism. Yet, even this description in Carol's oral history is immediately followed first by speculation about whether Fran's marriage survived and then by a litany of complaints about the "miserable life" that marriage for Carol proved to be.[20]

Carol is adamant that her friendships were platonic and she knew of no members whose identities were overtly sexual in a way at odds with Prince's campaign. Indeed, the heterosexual accord that underpinned her experiences and more broadly the community imagined via *Transvestia* contrasts with a moment in the oral history when she discusses her dissatisfaction with more recent groups she has encountered. Specifically, she disapproves of these groups' greater permissiveness with respect to sexual expression, as indicated when she showed Dorthe and me one group's catalog of trans personal ads in which a trans woman's self-presentation was overtly gothic and sadomasochistic.[21]

This disapproval gains greater clarity in light of a memory of a femme lesbian Carol encountered when she and a few transvestite friends from Wisconsin attended a meeting of a Chicago-based chapter in 1960. She recalls a white, cisgender woman whose glamorous femininity and sexual unavailability excited all in attendance:

> There was one gay girl who attended the [Chicago] meeting, who . . . she was dressed to the heights of fashion: nice skirt on and blouse and heels. And everyone says, "Gosh, how can she be gay?" . . . And some guy who was a cross-dresser—he was an older guy. He was wearing a suit at the meeting, and that. But he was a cross-dresser, and he rented an apartment for her to live at so he could go and dress every so often.[22]

The desire of a femme lesbian would have been understood as taboo for the conjugal transvestism of *Transvestia*, yet she signals the adulation of white middle-class femininity so vital to Carol's transvestite friendships and so decent in appearance compared with the risqué personal ad. Thus, as Derrida has said that every text proposes an institution,[23] *Transvestia* and its contents gave rise to wide readership and a network of social clubs united in the cause of sanctioning transvestism as a normal heterosexual practice. Carol's oral history, on the other hand, recalls a space in which self-exploration, acceptance, and support flourished in the form of friendship. Carol's memories very well may stray from her actions and feelings at the time described, but nevertheless, they demonstrate how friendships exceed the institution built by Prince, even as they emerge out of and coalesce around that very institution.

The friendship that has developed between Carol and me cannot compare with those of her past, but it still has productive effects in both of our lives in ways not accounted for by the IRB. Unlike her past friendships, our friendship is not one of shared sexual identity and gender expression: I am a cisgender gay man and she is a transgender woman who does not identify as gay or lesbian despite her attraction to women. In our conversations, Carol's only comment ever about gay men has been to disapprove of the sexually explicit attire reported in local news coverage of the Twin Cities Pride Parade, arguing that such behavior further stigmatizes sexual and gender minorities. Yet, I believe that in addition to a source of encouragement, I have become part of her effort initiated in 2000 to articulate herself as a transgender woman. When she shows me her letter from her therapist confirming her as a transgender woman, or when she talks with an acquaintance from the University of Minnesota's Program in Human Sexuality about her contribution to the OHP and the publication of this chapter, I get the impression that her intention is typical of many of the other transgender people I have interviewed for the OHP: to contribute to defining a regional transgender history not steeped in the medical history that compels the IRB to define Carol as an at-risk subject. Carol finds validation for her transgender identity not by emphasizing a personal history of cross-gender identification, but by stating for the official record a public history of transvestite friendships in Madison during the 1960s.

Moreover, my discussions with her on and off the record, in her small apartment or over the telephone on those random, occasional nights one of us checks in on the other, have served as a reassuring and elucidating contact for me in a time in my life when I am finishing graduate school. But more to the point, in talking with Carol about her friendships and everyday experiences, I feel that they find an unexpected affinity with recent losses of mine: the untimely death of my mother in 2006; the severe deterioration of my grandparents' health and their passing in 2009. These deep losses that I feel daily have for me a strange communion with the longing that Carol has expressed for friendships in the past and currently, on the oral history record and off it. I seldom discuss the details of my personal life with Carol only because the occasions of our discussion in the service of institutional business of the OHP invites her to speak about herself. And I understand that our friendship is not outside of power, that it quite literally inhabits the confessional mode as theorized by Foucault. Yet even within this vector of power, our friendship has emerged around the creation of her oral history, the midwifing of her life's narration that she drives but that Dorthe and I redirect and refocus through our questions and words of encouragement.

If the university is increasingly becoming the domain for the administration of sexuality in the competitive arena of global capitalism, I suggest that in its cracks the contradictions of unlikely friendships can proliferate.[24] Foucault asserts: "We live in a relational world that institutions have considerably impoverished.

Society and the institutions which frame it have limited the possibility of relationships because a rich relational world would be very complex to manage. We should fight against the impoverishment of the relational fabric."[25] *Transvestia* gave rise to a transvestite community charged with a heteronormative hegemony and regulatory of suspect desires and practices, yet also contradictorily gave rise to profound affections recalled at length that have created an unlikely friendship more than forty years later. Oral history has the potential to enrich our relational fabric through the shared articulation of queer and trans lives.[26]

Notes

1. Carol, oral history interview, Twin Cities GLBT Oral History Project (Minneapolis, June 24, 2005), 4–20.
2. As explained in her book's introduction, it was Miranda Joseph's participation in a gay-lesbian San Francisco theater group and its members' uncritical deployment of identity in the theater's administration that informed her critique of idealized notions of community. Conversely, it is the coming together of people across identity—in mutual affect, cause, or need—that helps give practices of community their truest transformational potential. Miranda Joseph, *Against the Romance of Community* (Minneapolis: University of Minnesota Press, 2002), vii–xxxiii.
3. I explore this at length in "Calculating Risk: History of Medicine, Transgender Oral History, and the Institutional Review Board," Twin Cities GLBT Oral History Project, ed., *Queer Twin Cities* (Minneapolis: University of Minnesota Press, 2010), 20–39.
4. My thoughts about the paradox of friendship, institutions, and oral history have benefited from Judith Butler's assessment of the paradox of the diagnosis of gender identity disorder: namely, that submission to this diagnosis constrains a trans person's autonomy even as it permits access to resources and social recognition otherwise out of reach. Judith Butler, "Undiagnosing Gender," in *Undoing Gender* (New York: Routledge, 2004), 75–101.
5. Robert Hill, "'We Share a Sacred Secret': Gender, Domesticity, and Containment in *Transvestia*'s Histories and Letters from Crossdressers and Their Wives," *Journal of Social History*, 44, no. 3 (2011): 729–750.
6. Carol, oral history interview, Twin Cities GLBT Oral History Project (Minneapolis, July 8, 2005), 42.
7. Ibid., 8–9.
8. Ibid., 8.
9. One major thread running throughout the oral history was Carol's solitude and discretion in the towns she lived in before moving to Minneapolis. One figure who reappears throughout her oral history is that of the landlady. She describes how she would typically rent a room in a house and how she would dress when the landlady was away. Sometimes she might present herself dressed as Carol to the landlady with the story that she was practicing a stage performance for a play in a neighboring town. She recalls this story working the several times she used it. Indeed, this story diffused a potentially disastrous encounter Carol had one day with a new landlady in the late 1950s. The landlady came home unexpectedly to find a "strange, medium-size woman" leaving the house. She approached this woman, they spoke, and ultimately the woman revealed herself to be the new tenant practicing a theatric role. The landlady had connections with the town's newspaper and told her contact about the incident. Soon after, Carol was approached with the request for permission to report the incident. She reluctantly agreed because she feared refusal would raise suspicions and feed gossip. Roughly fifty years later, this clipping now hangs on Carol's wall, framed and accompanied with a picture of her from this period. The clipping (with names changed) is reproduced here:

"Who in the world is THAT?" wondered Irma Bublitz to herself as she drove up her driveway to the garage and caught a glimpse of a strange, medium-size woman wearing a stylishly short green print dress open her front door and step with slow, studied care down the stairs in white, ridiculously high-heeled shoes. The stranger's jet black hair, worn quite bouffant, fairly bounced, however, when she sensed she was being observed and swerved to retreat on her nearly unmanageable heels to the porch once again.

"I thought Jerry said that printer wasn't married," Irma silently fumed as she banged the car door shut and stalked to the porch to demand an explanation from the woman who awaited her there.

Her uninvited guest was the sister of the new printer, George Mueller, she informed Irma and she had just arrived in town to see her brother in his new location.

After her brief introductory sentences, she became strangely monosyllabic in her replies to the questions Irma plied, and her bejeweled fingers nervously twitched at her enormous earrings as she evaded the queries which were becoming more and more pointed.

Finally, with a slight shrug, she asked, "Can you take a joke?"

"Well, I suppose I can as well as most people," countered Irma. "Why?"

Without another word, the woman pulled off her wig and introduced "herself" as the new printer at The Monitor office, and Irma's new roomer. He further explained that he was a member of an amateur play cast at Grantsburg, and since he had been alone in the house had decided to practice dressing for the part and walking in the high heels he was required to wear.

After a rollicking good laugh together, Irma, considerably relieved, and her new roomer sat down to get acquainted.

10. Michel Foucault, "Sex, Power, and the Politics of Identity," in Paul Rabinow, ed., *The Essential Works of Michel Foucault, Vol. 1: Ethics: Subjectivity, and Truth* (New York: New Press, 1997), 170.
11. Michel Foucault, "Friendship as a Way of Life," in Rabinow, ed., *The Essential Works of Michel Foucault, Vol. 1*, 137.
12. Every issue of *Transvestia* had a TV cover girl whose picture graced the cover and whose autobiographical story was featured. Fran is the cover girl for the December 1963 issue: *Transvestia*, 3, no. 24 (1963): 2–14.
13. Carol, oral history interview, 5.
14. Ibid., 26.
15. Ibid., 20.
16. Virginia Prince, *Transvestia*, 1, no. 2 (1960): 1.
17. For an overview of Virginia Prince and her work, see Hill, "'We Share a Sacred Secret'"; Richard Docter, *From Man to Woman: The Transgender Journey of Virginia Prince* (Northridge, CA: Docter, 2004); *Virginia Prince: Pioneer of Transgendering*, ed. Richard Ekins and Dave King (Binghamton, NY: Haworth, 2005); Susan Stryker, *Transgender History* (Berkeley: Seal, 2008).
18. Carol, oral history interview, 10.
19. Ibid.
20. Ibid., 24.
21. Ibid., 29–30.
22. Ibid., 18.
23. Jacques Derrida, *Eyes of the University: Right to Philosophy 2*, trans. Jan Plug (Stanford, CA: Stanford University Press, 2004), 101.
24. Roderick Ferguson "Administering Sexuality; or, the Will to Institutionality," *Radical History Review* 100 (Winter 2008): 158–69. For more background on the ascendance of corporate imperatives in higher education since the 1970s, see Sheila Slaughter and Larry L Leslie, *Academic Capitalism: Politics, Policies, and the Entrepreneurial University* (Baltimore: Johns Hopkins University Press, 1997), 1–22; Christopher Newfield, *Ivy and Industry: Business and the Making of the American University, 1880–1980* (Durham, NC: Duke University Press, 2003), 167–94; Marc Bousquet, *How the University Works: Higher Education and the Low-Wage Nation* (New York: New York University Press, 2008).
25. Michel Foucault, "The Social Triumph of the Sexual Will," in Rabinow, ed., *The Essential Works of Michel Foucault, Vol. 1*, 158.
26. The concept of friendship as a shared affect and practice is inspired by Thomas Roach Jr., "Shared Estrangement: Foucault, Friendship, and AIDS Activism" (PhD diss., University of Minnesota, 2006).

9

GAY TEACHERS AND STUDENTS, ORAL HISTORY, AND QUEER KINSHIP

Daniel Marshall

Oral history by Daniel Marshall with Gary Jaynes and Graham Carbery, Melbourne, Victoria, Australia, August 6, 2008

The Gay Teachers Group (later Gay Teachers and Students Group) was formed in Melbourne in 1975 and led a public campaign around homosexuality and schooling. It is best known for its seminal self-help educational publication, Young, Gay and Proud *(1978).[1] In 1979, Victoria was heading toward an election, and suddenly the booklet and the GTSG became subject to intense media and political attack. Newspapers in rural marginal seats took up activist campaigns against circulation of the booklet. Fundamentalist Christian groups, such as the Committee to Raise Educational Standards and Citizens against Social Evil, mobilized supporters and petitioned the premier to curtail the use of any material depicting homosexuality in any way in any school; the holding of any meeting associated with any homosexual group; and the establishment of any support groups for gay and lesbian teachers and students. In response, the premier ordered an investigation, and in March 1979 the minister of education issued an edict to all secondary school principals directing them "to ensure that copies of books seeking to foster homosexual behaviour are not available to children."[2] The GTSG broke up toward the end of 1980.*

This interview excerpt draws on two oral histories I recorded over the course of one day in August 2008 with Gary Jaynes, cofounder of the GTSG, and Graham Carbery, spokesperson for the group and, later, founder of the Australian Lesbian and Gay Archives (1978). They are lovers. These oral histories narrate the story and the scandal of the GTSG from two personal perspectives.[3]

Gary Jaynes: I wasn't an activist; I would have been, if anything, more like a
 bystander at Gay Liberation in 1972 when I went along to the meetings . . . the
 ideas were very exciting to me, but . . . there was a big tension between those

ideas and what seemed possible in my working life [as a teacher]. . . . [By] '74, Gay Lib seemed at a pretty low ebb in Melbourne. . . .

So Laurie Bebbington suggested that activists organize a National Homosexual Conference "to try and put some oomph back into the gay movement," says Gary. It was held in Melbourne in August 1975. Other people, such as Helen McCulloch (a teacher), were also keen to organize gay teachers, and the Gay Teachers Group was formed at the conference with the initial task of writing a manifesto.[4]

JAYNES: The aims were twofold. One was the protection of the job rights of gay teachers, and simultaneously we wanted to do something to make for a better curriculum in the educational experience for young gays coming out. . . . [Our efforts] got a kick along around about June the following year, when the Australian Union of Students, and again Laurie Bebbington, organized a National Homosexuals in Education Seminar, which drew both teachers and a lot of tertiary students. There were a few school students, but mainly tertiary gay and lesbian students. . . . Our manifesto had been finished and had been submitted to unions, and the first union to take it up was [laughs] the Primary School Teachers' Union, of all of them. . . .[5]

DANIEL MARSHALL: Why was it first?

JAYNES: I think it was just chance, I don't think there was anything sinister in it. [laughs] No. But in retrospect it looked as though it could have been almost a suicidal timing, 'cause you would have thought primary school—gay teachers becoming public in a primary school union forum might have looked pretty off.

But I think wherever we'd have made our début, I think it would have been a bit controversial. And in a way it was probably good to have the primary school one out of the way 'cause it paved the way for a fairly easy reception within the other two teachers' unions, which represented high school teachers and technical school teachers. . . .

MARSHALL: Graham, can you talk a bit about your motivations for being involved with the group?

GRAHAM CARBERY: Well, my motivation was because of my relationship with Gary. . . . If I'm being brutally honest, I mean I was reluctant because I'm more conservative by nature I think. I agree with many of the aspirations of people who are involved in activism and so forth, but I haven't always felt comfortable in being involved, but because of my relationship with Gary, I would help him and I would do things and I got involved. I could see the logic of me being the public face for *Young, Gay and Proud* because there was no one else who was in a position to do it, and so I felt an obligation really to do it, but it wasn't an onerous obligation, I certainly don't regret any of that. . . . I was aware that it was significant. I mean I think we were all aware what was going on, what we were involved with, it was big picture stuff. . . .

JAYNES: Planning for *Young, Gay and Proud* began in 1977 but '78 was a pretty intense year politically for a few reasons. There was a whole focus internationally on issues of homosexuals and children that got expressed initially through the Anita Bryant campaign in the U.S. and that got reported in a very prominent way here, and I think that added some sense of urgency to get *Young, Gay and Proud* out, that we didn't feel as though we could go on the back foot. It was far better to be assertive about those issues to do with homosexuality and children rather than cower. . . .

CARBERY: At the end of '77, during the school holidays, I went overseas to England, America, and Canada. I've still got the little diary that I kept while I was away, and I was only looking at it not so long ago. It was absolutely amazing when looking back on it how much I put in, I mean I hardly had a spare moment. I certainly didn't go cruising for sex, which is one thing I thought I might do while I was away, but I didn't. I was really busy; I was meeting people, groups, and so on. It was an incredibly busy time, and I gathered a heck of a lot of information, a lot of literature which, because we were starved of things, there wasn't stuff being produced here and we were coming across things like the *Advocate*, *Gay News* from England, the *Boston Gay Community News*, the *Body Politic*, *Christopher Street*, which were really interesting publications. So when you went overseas and [had] been involved in activism, you were hungry for whatever you could get to find out what was going on and what you could pick up. Some of the stuff that I brought back was relevant to the book. We got a lot of feedback from people overseas, and I made some really useful contacts, particularly at the *Body Politic*. Gary Ostrom, who did some of the illustrations, he was very supportive and cooperative. . . . I went on demonstrations in Canada against Anita Bryant, and Mary Whitehouse, when I was in London. . . . So there were things going on internationally about gays in education which fitted in and motivated us. . . .

JAYNES: It felt like gay teachers were really in the front line if there was to be a backlash, which looked imminent, particularly when some of the initiatives in the U.S. started getting rolled back. . . . And so much of the U.S. gay movement's gains had flowed to Australia, we thought their defeats might, too. . . .

MARSHALL: So what do you think were the most successful things the group did? Was it publishing *Young, Gay and Proud*?

CARBERY: Well, to me I think yes because it was a first, it was breaking new ground. . . . We wanted to write something in language that was different to the language that had been used before, that used "us" and "we," instead of "them" and whatever, and it covered the issues I think that young people at the time would have been interested in. . . .

JAYNES: I think the work with the unions was pretty important . . . [and] we got that done really in two years.

CARBERY: That was amazing really when you think about it; it was so quick.

MARSHALL: What do you think enabled that?

JAYNES: I think that first generation of gay lib activists, a lot of them were moving into the education profession, not necessarily teachers but sometimes in support services, and I think that gave us a real strong, behind-the-scenes presence to get . . . motions up to AGM.

CARBERY: They were persistent; they were dogged.

JAYNES: They were pretty skilled activists, a lot of them, by that stage.

MARSHALL: When you think back on that time, is there a time when you felt really great about the work?

JAYNES: Well *Young, Gay and Proud*, my main memory of it was relief. I was expecting prosecution as a possibility.

MARSHALL: How long were you concerned about the possibility of prosecution?

JAYNES: After about the first three months, I thought we were fairly safe. So I don't know that I felt particularly jubilant about *Young, Gay and Proud*.

CARBERY: Because I suppose when you're involved with something for a long time and after awhile it becomes, you just want to get it done and so on, so I can see what you mean by relief. At the time I don't remember any, but looking back now, I think the fact there were 10,000 copies printed, that's a hell of a lot of copies, and despite . . . I mean, I know they say as soon as you ban something, you make it a best seller, but it was a bloody good effort to get rid of those.

JAYNES: I felt really on a high after that third union adopted the antidiscrim [policy] . . . which was the VTU, the primary teacher's union, the most conservative, I felt we'd really achieved something at that point. . . . We were involved at that time with law reform, too . . . and around 1978, it seemed we were doing much better with our education efforts through GTSG than we were with law reform.[6] . . .

MARSHALL: Elsewhere, Gary, you've mentioned that adoption of antidiscrimination policies in teachers' unions in Victoria was a lot easier to achieve than getting sex education programs to include fair treatment of homosexuality. Do you have any thoughts as to why that was more difficult?

JAYNES: At the time my view . . . [was that] I think there's a lot of sympathy for gay students in schools at the level of not wanting them to be bullied, but I think a lot of that sympathy sort of stops at the point where open discussion of homosexuality to the broader student population is suggested as a remedy to that bullying. Well, that's how I saw it then, I don't know the extent to which that's true now . . .

MARSHALL: Did you have any mentors?

JAYNES: No, we didn't. . . . I think that's a difference between then and now, too, because there wouldn't have been too many middle-aged activists, hardly any experienced gay advocates, or whatever you want to call them. There were a couple who were older in Society Five, but they weren't really activists. . . . Whereas now you could imagine that there's a whole generation of older gay men and lesbians who've had activist experience who might be able to play some sort of mentoring role in organizations. But they weren't there then . . .

MARSHALL: What was difficult about your work with the group?

CARBERY: Oh, the bureaucracy, having to deal with the director general and politicians, and I mean you could understand, anything to do with children they're always very protective and so talking about sex. . . .

JAYNES: Yeah, I felt that we'd been stymied once that directive went out [from] Laurie Shears, and we couldn't do much about that.

MARSHALL: Were there other reasons why the group stopped?

JAYNES: No, there were other reasons.

MARSHALL: Can you talk about that?

JAYNES: Like most activist groups, we were relying on the energy of half a dozen or so people. I became involved with other things from the end of 1979, other key people also moved on to other involvements, and the group didn't have ready replacements.

CARBERY: We just ran out of steam. . . .

MARSHALL: What do you think prevented that renewal, especially given that the group sought to involve students as well as teachers, so it had a model, I guess, that could theoretically have promoted some renewal?

JAYNES: Yeah, I see your point; it didn't happen, no. The student activists tended to come in for projects, like they were there when we needed to get *Young, Gay and Proud* printed or distributed or defended, but some groups like CRAC[7] out at Monash and the AUS people were similar; they'd help when we needed money to do something but there wasn't a continuity there. . . .

MARSHALL: Do you feel that the gains made by the group were compromised or wound back to some extent in Victoria because of public anxieties around homosexuality and pedophilia, especially around 1982 and 1983 with the *Alison Thorne* case?[8]

JAYNES: I do.

MARSHALL: Can you talk about that a bit? In what ways?

JAYNES: I just think it became much harder to publicly raise [the] issue of homosexuality in young people. The blurring of the issues became just too daunting I think. . . .

JAYNES: Don't forget that the group had already dissolved by then; it wasn't as though it dissolved because of that debate emerging. But having emerged, I think it did silence the rational discussion of those issues of young people, homosexuality, and consent, and virtually to this day. . . .

JAYNES: . . . There were other attempts at forming gay teachers' or gay youth workers' groups. Context was one of the other, although that didn't come until the '90s. . . . I think the other big change by 1998 was the emergence of PFLAG as a force. I think that at least put young people on the agenda but sort of vicariously, though, not in a direct way.

CARBERY: Groups like Minus 18 and that, they must have had an impact. If students, because many of the people who belong to that are students, if they find their way, that emboldens some students to come out at school or to do things which have a gay or lesbian emphasis, like going to a dance with a same-sex partner or something like that. I mean that sort of thing does happen but it's not organized, it's not a group that's pushing it, sort of thing. It seems as though society can handle it when individuals do that sort of thing, it's when things become organized, there's an organized push, that seems to be the really threatening thing doesn't it? . . .

MARSHALL: Can you talk a bit about the legacy or the influence of the work with the group and *Young, Gay and Proud*?

JAYNES: I'm not sure. I don't know that there is one. I mean there have been other subsequent efforts, I suppose, and each effort makes subsequent efforts a bit easier. . . .

CARBERY: Someone has to be first. Someone does something, and it gets criticized for its deficiencies, but people build on it, and *Young, Gay and Proud*, I think, was successful because it did reach a lot of people, it sparked a lot of debate and would have given people confidence, maybe not immediately but certainly into the future to do other things. And not just in Australia, as we say, overseas as well because in other countries there were attempts of doing something like *Young, Gay and Proud* so in some small way it was a positive. . . .

JAYNES: Well, the American edition's gone through umpteen editions. I just think contemporary equivalents of it in Australia won't necessarily borrow directly from *Young, Gay and Proud*, but I think it helped pave the way for later efforts.

MARSHALL: How do you feel now about the group and about *Young, Gay and Proud*?

CARBERY: Well, it's a different era, I mean it's a lifetime ago. But I'm certainly pleased that I had some role to play in it. You'd like to think you've been involved in things that have been positive. . . .

JAYNES: Yeah, I mean compared to, say, with law reform, it's very different isn't it, like the law reform is a very tangible outcome for the effort. But I think there were risks to be taken that were worth taking. The benefits were a bit intangible, but I think there were some. . . .

MARSHALL: Was there a reason why both of you stopped being active around issues to do with schools and gay issues?

CARBERY: Well, my time was taken up with the archives, that's where I moved. And as you get a bit older, too, I just didn't have the energy, I was slowing down a little bit. I suppose I just wanted to focus on one thing.

JAYNES: I was in a job where I virtually couldn't, I was told that I couldn't reconcile gay teachers' activism publicly with that role. Activism around gay legal rights was seen as okay, but not around issues of education.

MARSHALL: When were you told that?

JAYNES: About 1980.

MARSHALL: And what was your response to that?

JAYNES: I wasn't very happy about it, but I complied with it.

MARSHALL: And looking back now, how do you feel about that?

JAYNES: It's a very complicated story, and the center I was working for was under a lot of political attack in 1980 in its own right over sex education, and I think the complication of my activism around gays in education, even though undertaken in a private capacity, was seen as the straw that broke the camel's back.

MARSHALL: And you'd been involved for a long time with the group before 1980, was there something that happened in 1980. . . .

JAYNES: Yeah, there was. There was to be a ministerial advisory committee formed on health and human relations, and the center I worked for was very heavily represented in it, and it was to produce a set of guidelines for the future conduct of human relations in Victoria. I think it was by the end of that year, and in country Victoria there was this enormous backlash against sex education, and a lot of the backlash centered around personalities, including me, in their work at that center. . . .

MARSHALL: Do you feel any sadness about progress slowing in the 1980s after so many great achievements had been managed in such a short period of time with the group?

CARBERY: Things always go in fits and starts, though, don't they. It's never a continual push or movement.

MARSHALL: Gary?

JAYNES: Oh, it was a grim decade, there was no doubt about it.[9]

Commentary

Oral history can be a powerful methodology to enable intergenerational enquiry and negotiate intergenerational queer kinship. Reflection on how oral history as a method might help build relationships with older gay and lesbian activists stems from a critical and political interest in gay liberation activist expertise. In particular, this chapter explores oral history from the perspective of developing cross-generational solidarities and engaging with experiences accrued through the battles of the 1970s to enrich contemporary political and cultural activity in Australia.

Friendships, collaborations, and mentoring relationships between queer young people and queer adults are a crucial part of any future-focused queer culture-building project.[10] However, despite some limited exceptions, such relationships are made impossible by a profound and generalized fear of any contact between homosexual adults and children. My critical interest in my interviews with Gary Jaynes and Graham Carbery, two key members of the Gay Teachers and Students Group, was not only to explore a history of resistance to this dominant policing of queer young people and queer adults but also to reflect on how oral history itself can contribute to that process of facilitating relationships between older and younger gays and queers.[11]

I was introduced to the GTSG and the educational pamphlet *Young, Gay and Proud* while reading Andrew Lansdown's memorably titled polemic *Blatant and Proud: Homosexuals on the Offensive* (1984).[12] Here, Lansdown rails against the distribution of the educational booklet to students in Australian high schools. Lansdown quotes the booklet's advice to "young novices" to not panic if they find anal intercourse "a little hard," because "like anything else that's new" it may be that they just need "to practice a bit for the pleasure to come through."[13] His response is predictably condemnatory:

> Homosexuals themselves[14] not[e] how they had to "change their outlook" before they could adopt and/or maintain a homosexual identity. Some have strongly desired to be homosexuals; but many have *learned* to be homosexuals (and *all* have made a choice). It is not improbable, then, that children who are subject to "positive" education on homosexuality will be "positively" influenced by such education.[15]

In this passage, Lansdown strategically sexualizes the pedagogical relation by associating the practice of anal sex with "learning" how to be a homosexual. This tactic demonstrates an exemplary move of mainstream homophobia in that it renders the pedagogical promotion of homosexual rights coextensive with the intention to sexually penetrate male adolescents. This tactic plays a key role in the policing of contact between queer adults and youths, especially males. The horrifying specter of pedophilia is invoked to oppose and suppress the development of any queer-affirmative dialogue between the generations. Significantly, the imperative to separate queer adults from queer young people is motivated not only by an expectation of adult homosexual predation but also by the construction of adolescence as a period in which one's sexuality is malleable. Debbie Epstein and Richard Johnson gloss this profound social fear in *Schooling Sexualities*:

> One of the primary ways in which we understand the sexual in contemporary society is through recourse to discourses of the biological or the natural. In a theory of development which is based on notions of ages and stages (phases), one of the questions which causes anxiety to some is the notion that some girls and, maybe more so, boys could have their development "arrested" during a "homosexual phase" through contact with lesbians and gays. In this context, being gay or lesbian is seen as potentially contagious. Indeed, some of the anxieties about lesbian and gay teachers derive from this notion, which is then reinforced through the idea that adolescence is a time of massive change and uncertainty.[16]

Extending this observation by Epstein and Johnson, it is clear that there is an important relationship between the meaning of adolescence as developmentally incomplete and the meaning of homosexuality as an arrested or failed development. Indeed, the threat of homosexuality has been routinely employed to tell the story of adolescence and its fragile relationship to development. Likewise, the vulnerability of adolescence is a key feature of cultural stories about homosexuality. Understandings of homosexuality and adolescence are routinely bound together with understandings of development, reflecting the way they are mobilized to simultaneously express and carry broad and profound anxieties over the very nature of growth and development. It is these powerful and pervasive homophobic views of adolescence and homosexuality that form the context for my interest in the transgressive and queer-affirmative potential of intergenerational oral history.

As familiar stories about the dangers homosexual adults supposedly pose to young people demonstrate, homosexuality is commonly described with close reference to adolescence for the main purpose of emphasizing the extent to which homosexuals and young people should be physically kept apart. In *Moral Panic*, Philip Jenkins considers the twentieth-century conflation of (particularly male) sexual deviation with sexual crime. Jenkins argues that over this time a cautionary psychopathological narrative that conflates homosexuality with pedophilia has emerged as a familiar way of considering any possible relationship between the adult homosexual and the adolescent. This illustrates the ironic way in which cultural stories designed to argue for the segregation of homosexuals and young people do so by repeatedly talking about them together. Jenkins quotes from a 1951 *Psychiatric Quarterly* editorial as proof:

> The adult homosexual . . . is in a stage of arrested psychosexual development; he is not far above the child level. . . . If most homosexual adults are attracted chiefly to other adults—which is debatable—many are still attracted to children; and more still are attracted to adolescents. The impulse to seduce [adolescents] is, like homosexuality itself, characteristic of arrested development.[17]

In this sense, the only relationship between the adolescent and the adult homosexual that was imagined to be possible was a sexual, pedophilic one. The strength of this view, a view that routinely crowded out alternative visions of queer intergenerational relationships, is further demonstrated by the commonplace conflation of homosexuality and pedophilia[18] Significantly, the homosexual's alleged desire for the adolescent represents not only an indication of his outward threat but also a symptom of his internal psychology: to desire adolescents as subjects in development is in itself an act of arrested development. In this way, situating the adolescent as the exemplary object of homosexual desire sustains the popular homophobic contention that homosexuality itself is a developmental aberration. The cultural prohibition against queer intergenerational friendships and mentoring relationships then stands as an expression of a homophobic construction of the homosexual adult as the always-already pedophile and the queer youth as the always-already victim. In political and social policy terms, these views drive anxieties in education about "exposing" students to gay and lesbian curriculum and nonheterosexual adults. In this context, intergenerational queer oral histories offer the promise of intervening in or rupturing these dominant ways of thinking about and regulating homophobic conceptions of adults and young people, and the relationships they share, by providing new contexts for speaking, relating, and knowing.

Importantly, my perspective on the operation of these sanctions is further informed by my own adolescence: a personal mourning for the queer young people and adults I never knew. Their phantom possibility was dissolved by an injunction against the existence of homosexual young people and a prohibition against intergenerational contact. This is not to say that the injunctions and prohibitions managed to totally wither the queer possibilities of my adolescence, but they indeed worked to great effect.

This personal lament has fostered a politicized curiosity. How can we use oral history to deconstruct the old, sad, and untrue stereotypes of homosexuals (and especially gay men) as pedophiles and queer young people as victims? And how can oral histories work as sites that claim the possibility and importance of non-sexual intergenerational relationships? Can oral history function as an important part of a queer culture-building project for the future? These questions led me to my interviews with Gary and Graham. In this context, oral history works as a queer method on two levels. In terms of content, it examines a history of activist efforts in the field that document communication and education between older and younger generations. In terms of method, it actually brings together younger and older people.

Unsurprisingly, growing up in the 1980s meant that HIV/AIDS had a profound, structuring impact on my understanding of homosexuality. It came to literalize and symbolize the loss of potential queer relationships. Moreover, because of the ongoing immeasurable cost of HIV/AIDS, I cannot imagine how any queer experience of mourning cannot in some way be shadowed and informed by the pandemic. As Simon Watney has written:

> HIV has in many respects served to reconstitute homosexuality and identities founded upon homosexual desire. This reconstitution involves many overlapping elements, from attitudes toward sex, toward illness and death, mourning, and so on. It informs the totality of our social and psychic lives in ways that we hardly begin to understand.[19]

Watney writes about an "international unity" felt by gay men that is "forged in relation to our direct experience of protracted illness, suffering, loss, and mourning, together with the cultural solidarity we obtain from what has always been a diasporic queer culture."[20] In Watney's sense, mourning refers to literally grieving for and burying friends, lovers, and strangers. In my own experience, mourning related to AIDS is tied to a more generalized sadness and anger about the losses of affectional relationships that homosexuals have endured, of which AIDS is perhaps the cardinal sign.

Without seeking to distract from or diminish the physical loss of life connected to HIV/AIDS, the erasure of queer childhoods and denial of queer intergenerational mentoring relationships represents a historical loss that defines some contemporary understandings of homosexuality. Of course, this is not to say that queer childhoods and intergenerational mentoring relationships do not exist, but that their likelihood is the target of active opposition. For this reason, active resistance is required, and oral histories have often been employed as acts of resistance in histories of sexualities. In my work with Gary and Graham, oral history became a shared moment that allowed us to grieve together for that which has been lost while also building a relationship in the absence of those intergenerational ties.

Thus, queer oral histories build a presence in the absence of queer intergenerationality, both in my personal life and in the broader epistemological field of Australian history and culture. In content, I focus on the active efforts to build educational networks between gay teachers and gay students in the 1970s and early 1980s to raise awareness of the history of this struggle. In method, too, I use oral history work to actively build intergenerational relationships. The method of personal interview has a natural synergy with my political and critical interests in researching and building and rebuilding activist efforts to forge intergenerational queer networks because it methodologically relies on intimate and personal processes of interaction, knowledge transfer, and trust. In this way, my use of oral history draws explicitly on some of the foundational gay and lesbian oral history research, such as Kennedy and Davis's *Boots of Leather, Slippers of Gold*. This book had its genesis in the late 1970s, and it involved the development of intergenerational networks between students and community elders to produce a collection of oral histories of older lesbians in Buffalo, New York.[21]

Slightly predating these efforts by Kennedy and Davis, Gayle Rubin began to lay the conceptual groundwork for thinking about what might now be described as intergenerational queer kinship in "The Traffic in Women: Notes on the 'Political Economy' of Sex" (which, incidentally, was published the same year that the Gay Teachers Group was established).[22] I use "kinship" in a loose and unmoored sense, taking up Rubin's challenge to transform kinship into something other than a mechanism for the circulation of women as property. Drawing on Judith Butler's argument that "the topic of gay marriage is not the same as that of gay kinship," I use kinship in a more expansive way to reflect on how oral histories might be able to help us imagine a broader range of possible queer relationships.[23] Using Butler's description, kinship practices can refer to a broad variety of relationships "that emerge to address fundamental forms of human dependency, which may include birth, child-rearing, relations of emotional dependency and support, generational ties, illness, dying, and death (to name a few)."[24] Importantly, however, while Butler uses kinship to reference a broad range of (often) sexual relationships (broader than is currently accommodated under the heteronormative gay marriage model), I use kinship not to refer to sexual relationships but to nonsexual, supportive relationships that can develop between queer young people and queer carers, parents, teachers, uncles, aunts, adult friends, elders, older adolescents, and mentors—and, most pertinent for the sake of my argument here, multigenerational sets of oral history participants. I bring this (nonfinite list) of relationships together under the unstable term "queer kinship."

In "The Traffic in Women," Rubin influentially argues that dominant models of kinship crucially rely on normalizing ideas about "gender, obligatory heterosexuality and the constraint of female sexuality."[25] "Feminism must call for a revolution in kinship," she writes:

> The kinds of relationships of sexuality established in the dim human past still dominate our sexual lives, our ideas about men and women, and the ways we raise our children. But they lack the functional load they once carried. . . . Human sexual life will always be subject to convention and human intervention. It will never be completely "natural." . . . Cultural evolution provides us with the opportunity to seize control of the means of sexuality, reproduction, and socialization and to make conscious decisions to liberate human sexual life from the archaic relationships which deform it. Ultimately, a thoroughgoing feminist revolution would liberate more than women.[26]

A world away in Melbourne, the Gay Teachers and Students Group was attempting this very task of "seizing control" and exercising "conscious decisions" to intervene in the conventional operations of heteronormative families and schooling and their reproduction of heterosexist and misogynist ideas about gender, relationships, pleasure, and family. What comes into focus in the work of the GTSG is what might be described as an early attempt at building queer kinship ties. Significantly, however, without the relational data one gathers about the GTSG through the interactive, conversational mode of oral history, it would be difficult to gain insight into the kinship dimensions of the GTSG's work.

At the base of the group's project was a radical vision of queer kinship in which gay adults and gay children could develop educational relationships around mutually sharing experiences of living nonheterosexual lives. For example, the group's publication, *Young, Gay and Proud*, sought to achieve this by drawing on antioppressive education techniques to circulate gay-affirmative information to young people. The group's process (i.e., the work of the collective) sought to promote queer intergenerational interaction by creating a collectivist space in which gay adults and young people could collaborate and learn from each other. The oral histories I conducted echo this process. By recording and making available Gary's and Graham's stories, this work assumes an educative role, designed to promote an awareness of Australian histories of queer kinship networks. By interviewing Gary and Graham, my methodology has promoted intergenerational interaction, echoing the GTSG.[27]

Returning to Butler again, and recalling my earlier reference to the exemplary homophobia of the 1951 *Psychiatric Quarterly*, queer intergenerational kinship is under routine threat and challenge:

> In an interview with Jacqueline Rose, the well-known Kleinian practitioner, Hanna Segal, reiterates her view that "homosexuality is an attack on the parental couple" (210), "a developmental arrest" (211), and she expresses outrage over a situation in which two lesbians raise a boy (210). She adds that she considers "the adult homosexual structure to be pathological." When asked at a public presentation in October of 1998 whether she approved of two lesbians raising a boy, she answered flatly "no."[28]

Butler argues that to counter these attacks "with an insistence on the normalcy of lesbian and gay families is to accept that the debate should center on the distinction between normal and pathological."[29] What is required, in Butler's analysis, is "a more radical social transformation," which becomes available "when we refuse, for instance, to allow kinship to become reducible to 'family.'"[30] If, instead, we choose to limit our politics to the normalizing goals of gay marriage and gay parenting, we lose the capacity to imagine, let alone build, queer kinship structures that don't fit a heteronormative mold of social relationships:

> If we decide that these are the decisive issues, and know which side we are on, then we have accepted an epistemological field structured by a fundamental loss, one which we can no longer name enough even to grieve. The life of sexuality, kinship, and community that becomes unthinkable within the terms of these norms constitutes the lost horizon of radical sexual politics, and we find our way "politically" in the wake of the ungrievable.[31]

Patrick McCreery offers a similarly pessimistic account of contemporary (American) gay and lesbian emphases on normative models of gay families and gay parenting, critiquing how this ironically resurrects the child protectionist politics for which beauty queen and antigay activist Anita Bryant is perhaps the most pervasive cultural icon. He calls for a "progressive reconceptualisation of the family," although it is not clear from his analysis how such a reimagining should progress.[32] Intergenerational queer oral histories and the unstable queer kinship relations that fall out of those shared experiences might be one humble, tangible way to reimagine the new modes of relationships that Butler and McCreery call for.

In contrast to political preoccupations best exemplified by the notion of gay marriage, the set of relations embodied in queer oral history work provide a promising nonnormative reconceptualization of kinship structures. While queer kinship through oral history is still structured around a fundamental loss—the loss of queer childhoods and queer mentors—it is not a loss that, like gay marriage, holds our future hostage to questionable norms. Instead, it provides a context for collective grieving and imagining, embodied through the questioning and narrating of the oral history exchange. Also, by foregrounding the practice of oral history as a potential site for the development of queer kinship relations, queer oral history extends Butler's critique of normative kinship structures. Queer kinship is founded on and mobilized by the constitutive loss of queer childhoods and intergenerational relationships, so it provides us with a "way" (to use the term in Butler's sense) to pursue a queer politics that acknowledges a broader set of supportive relationships than is often included in conventional appeals to notions of marriage and family.

Oral history was influentially employed by feminist, gay, and lesbian activists and researchers in the 1970s to produce people's histories, grounded in lived experiences of ordinary people. These oral histories were conducted as interventions in the academy, protesting the omission of nonheterosexual experience and challenging familiar narratives about the threat of homosexuality. Drawing on this heritage, the oral histories with Gary and Graham represent a methodological intervention that challenges homophobic prohibitions of queer intergenerational contact while expanding beyond normalizing concepts of gay-affirmative kinship ties. Moreover, queer oral history as a research method addresses Rubin's call for revolution and Butler's grief for a lost radical politics through its privileging of the relational and personal over the official and hegemonic. Indeed, to some extent, all oral history is a little queer in the sense that it calls into question institutional knowledge by prioritizing people's memories.[33]

This understanding of oral history as an intervention implicitly relies on a politicized interpretation of silence: queer oral history seeks to make audible those voices and narratives that might otherwise go unheard. However, just as sexual difference cannot be collapsed into a simple in-out binary, so, too, does queer oral history eschew a rudimentary silenced-voiced binary. The told story expresses its own silences. The interpretation of oblique references and silences has played a major role in research on the history of sexuality. Indeed, when a queer critical project is routinely preoccupied with identifying and analyzing the omissions and occlusions in any given representation of sexuality, as well as how power regulates what can be articulated or represented, the silences often prove most instructive. However, in the context of oral history analysis, the silences draw together at once the epistemological and the methodological concerns of the exchange. Oral history is not only about the transmission of information but also about the respectful tending of relationships. By observing silences, omissions, and gaps, queer oral history research establishes itself explicitly on a deliberately fractured foundation: it does not present a complete, universalized narrative. Indeed, as this chapter has discussed, a key political motivation for queer oral history work is its desire to challenge universalizing narratives of homosexuality (e.g., the predator), and its methodological accommodation of multiple narratives is surely as much a part of this intervention as the content of the histories themselves.

At one point during the oral history, I asked Gary and Graham why they had stopped being active around issues to do with schools and gay issues. In Gary's response, he speaks of being given an ultimatum at work and being personally attacked for his activism in a public campaign. He and I had discussed this matter outside of the context of the oral history, and I knew this was all he wanted to say. Unlike desktop research, oral histories are moments of both research and relationality, of kinship, and so my role as researcher was guided as much by care as by curiosity, both hanging in careful balance.

Everyone has memories that are hard to tell. It is no surprise that in asking Gary and Graham to recount their involvement in a political movement that drew considerable attention and scandal that some aspects of that story might be too raw to tell. To be honest, for a brief moment I felt frustrated at not being able to access all of the relevant information. But what my frustration brought into focus for me was that you cannot extract information through an oral history as if the other person were simply a database. As Joan Nestle reminds me, "The histories of one generation cannot always be made accessible to the other."[34]

The silences in the oral history speak to the fact that despite the recent explosion in queer youth cultures, adult homosexuals can still feel intensely and unfairly policed in relation to their ideas about and contact with young people; LGBT adults carry the burden of surveillance and anxiety. Queer youth cultures are impoverished by the absence of relationships with adults. These examples demonstrate the importance not only of telling the history of groups like the Gay Teachers and Students Group but also of nurturing queer kinship ties through activities like multigenerational oral histories. Multigenerational oral histories can defuse the toxic suggestion that friendship and mentoring between queer adults and young people is somehow a cover for or step toward child abuse and pedophilia.

The human element of oral history research means that while it is research oriented it is also relational, and in my case it was part of an attempt to build queer intergenerational relationships in method and content. From this perspective, my expectations of Gary and Graham were influenced as much by my desire to display affection and care (as a worthy response to their generosity and trust) as it was by my intellectual interest in pursuing silences and questions left hanging. But because queer oral histories foreground historical silences and do not claim to provide a whole story, they promote a productive skepticism about the completeness of any given historical narrative. Further, there are always other versions to look to (not least the official ones, important because they help dramatize the differences, departures, and exclusions). For this reason, these queer oral histories, like the broader work of queer culture-building, are still a work in progress.

Notes

1. An Autonomous Collective of the Melbourne GTSG, *Young, Gay and Proud* (An Autonomous Collective of the Melbourne GTSG: Melbourne, 1978).
2. L. H. S. Thompson (Minister of Education) and L. W. Shears (Director-General of Education), "To principals of secondary schools," March 19, 1979.
3. I would like to acknowledge Gary Jaynes and Graham Carbery for their enormous generosity in allowing me to undertake this project and for providing invaluable assistance in

countless ways. I would also like to thank Joan Nestle, who provided helpful comments on earlier versions of the chapter. The oral histories recorded here were undertaken as part of a broader research project, *Beyond Homophobia*, which I undertook with Lynne Hillier and Anne Mitchell. I would also like to thank Annamarie Jagose and Clara Tuite, who provided comments on earlier versions of some of the ideas I discuss in this chapter; and I would like to thank Nan Alamilla Boyd and Horacio N. Roque Ramírez, as well as Nancy Toff, for their helpful editorial advice and assistance.

4. This is an edited excerpt of two oral histories recorded on August 6, 2008, at La Trobe University. The first interview was with Gary, and the second was with both Gary and Graham. Throughout the drafting process, I have liaised extensively with both of them, and they have provided corrections. Added text is indicated in [brackets] and ellipses refer to the omission of words. Italics refer to sections that have been paraphrased. My questions are edited and rephrased for brevity. The sequence of comments has been changed to suit the logic of the excerpt. Gary and Graham are both happy with this representation of their comments.

5. This union, called the Victorian Teachers Union, was the first to print the GTSG's manifesto but the last to adopt an antidiscrimination gay rights policy at an AGM.

6. Throughout the 1970s, activists and lobbyists, including the Homosexual Law Reform Coalition, were involved in efforts to decriminalize homosexuality, resulting in the passage of a bill in December 1980 that decriminalized some aspects of homosexuality. See Graham Willett, *Living Out Loud* (St Leonards, New South Wales, Australia: Allen and Unwin, 2000), 149–56.

7. The CRAC (Community Research Action Centre) was based at Monash University.

8. In 1983, a controversy erupted over Alison Thorne's alleged support for pedophilia. She was removed from her teaching role in a Victorian school.

9. Gary Jaynes, interviewed by Daniel Marshall, digital recording, Melbourne, Victoria, Australia, August 6, 2008, held at the Australian Lesbian and Gay Archives. This interview has been edited by the author; Graham Carbery and Gary Jaynes, interviewed by Daniel Marshall, digital recording, Melbourne, Victoria, Australia, August 6, 2008, held at the Australian Lesbian and Gay Archives. This interview has been edited by the author.

10. I use "mentoring" cautiously and a little uncomfortably—it risks naturalizing relationships between adults and children in which the learning is unidirectional, when the type of relationships I seek to value are those in which adults and children learn from each other in a nonhierarchical way.

11. Personal narrative, including oral history, has been employed effectively in lesbian, gay, and queer scholarship to document histories of sexuality and resistance. See, for example, Joan Nestle, ed., *The Persistent Desire: A Femme-Butch Reader* (Boston: Alyson, 1992).

12. Andrew Lansdown, *Blatant and Proud: Homosexuals on the Offensive* (Cloverdale, Western Australia: Perceptive, 1984).

13. Ibid., 25. In the original passage in *Young, Gay and Proud* that Lansdown is selectively quoting from, the authors acknowledge that not everyone will enjoy anal sex because it may not be "your thing" (see An Autonomous Collective of the Melbourne Gay Teachers and Students Group, 41).

14. Demonstrating the disempowering intent of his argument, Lansdown arrogates the right to speak for homosexuals in the first chapter of the book, which he calls "The Homosexuals' Self-View."

15. Lansdown, *Blatant and Proud*, 25–26, original emphasis.

16. Debbie Epstein and Richard Johnson, *Schooling Sexualities* (Buckingham, England: Open University Press, 1998), 151.

17. Cited in Philip Jenkins, *Moral Panic: Changing Concepts of the Child Molester in Modern America* (New Haven, CT: Yale University Press, 1998), 62.

18. Jenkins provides one example: "Mid-century dictionaries and medical texts defined *paederast* in terms of both 'boy-love' and anal sex and gave *sodomite* as a synonym, so that English usage thoroughly supported the identification of homosexuals and paedophiles" (Ibid., 62).

19. Simon Watney, "AIDS and the Politics of Queer Diaspora," in *Imagine Hope: AIDS and Gay Identity*, 130 (London: Routledge, 2000).

20. Ibid., 126.

21. See Elizabeth Lapovsky Kennedy and Madeline D. Davis, *Boots of Leather, Slippers of Gold: The History of a Lesbian Community* (New York: Routledge, 1993), xv–xvii.

22. Gayle Rubin, "The Traffic in Women: Notes on the 'Political Economy' of Sex," in Ellen Lewin, ed., *Feminist Anthropology: A Reader* (Malden: Blackwell, 2006). Originally published 1975.

23. Judith Butler, "Is Kinship Always Already Heterosexual?" *differences: A Journal of Feminist Cultural Studies* 13, no. 1 (Spring 2002): 14.

24. Ibid., 15.

25. Rubin, "The Traffic in Women," 94.

26. Ibid., 100–101.

27. And this process has occurred over some time, which is not to say that it took a long time to gain the trust to conduct the interviews, but that we had already built friendships over a number of years as volunteers at the Australian Lesbian and Gay Archives. Queer archives, like the process of queer oral histories, has played a crucial role in providing a material site for the development of queer kinship ties. Importantly, however, the intergenerational relationships among me, Gary, and Graham are necessarily different than those fostered by the GTSG, as we are all adults. In many ways, queer intergenerationality loses its capacity to electrify concern when "youth" are out of the equation. So, while I acknowledge a relationship between the ambitions of the GTSG project and the design of my small oral history project here, I am also aware of the important differences.

28. Butler, "Is Kinship Always Already Heterosexual?" 39.

29. Ibid., 39–40.

30. Ibid., 40.

31. Ibid.

32. Patrick McCreery, "Save Our Children/Let Us Marry: Gay Activists Appropriate the Rhetoric of Child Protectionism," *Radical History Review: Queer Futures* 100 (2008): 188; see also 202.

33. See, for example, Kennedy and Davis, *Boots of Leather, Slippers of Gold*, 15–26.

34. Personal communication.

10

SHARING QUEER AUTHORITIES

Collaborating for Transgender Latina and Gay Latino Historical Meanings

Horacio N. Roque Ramírez

Oral history by Horacio N. Roque Ramírez with Alberta Nevaeres (aka Teresita la Campesina), San Francisco, California, 1996

On April 19, 1996, the male-to-female (MTF) transgender performer Alberta Nevaeres (1940–2002), better known in San Francisco and especially in the city's Latino Mission district as Teresita la Campesina, met me to continue recording her life history, a process we had begun earlier in the month. This recording began, like our first interview earlier that month, with Teresita singing into the audio recorder as classic ranchera *song tracks played in the background. Our conversations were part of a growing project on queer Latina and Latino life in the city, which I had begun a year earlier as a small study on queer Latina and Latino activists organizing around HIV and AIDS prevention. As someone who was openly HIV+, Teresita had become a client of several Mission neighborhood health agencies. At these venues, she was known for being quite loud in her singing, joking, telling tall tales, and laughing. Through all of these actions, she contextualized queer life in the 1990s by comparing it with earlier decades.*

The following excerpt requires some explanation. In it, Teresita recalls her arrest for being "found out" as a "drag queen" (the word of the day), somebody having outed her for not being a "real woman" when she was working in Stockton, California, a semirural town ninety miles east of San Francisco. She then details the intricacies of gender identity, queering both the English and Spanish languages, back and forth, as she describes the drag queens and gay men of the 1960s. In "queering" language, Teresita spoke back and forth between English and Spanish, not careful to use the proper terminology of the day in either language (say, "transgender" or "transgé-nero") and instead harking back to earlier terms used to denigrate, police, and generally stigmatize queer populations, especially transgender women and men. "Drag queen" (and its Spanish-language version "vestida"), "sex change," "operada" (literally "operated," meaning, having gone through a sex change surgically)—these and other terms used liberally but also strategically made listening to Teresita's narrative quite a multilingual, multigender, and multivalent endeavor.[1] *Teresita and I shared such a multilingual exchange in Spanish, English, and "Spanglish," an impromptu mix of English and Spanish, in which we borrowed liberally from both linguistic codes in ways not discernible to listeners who are not able to move so easily back and forth between the languages. That she and I were also openly queer (I as a gay Latino) allowed us to further queer our exchange, although she did most of talking as I tried to follow along. That both of us were bilingual but, most important, spontaneously conversant in Spanglish was one of the main reasons that she and I communicated so well, something a solely English- or Spanish-speaking oral historian would not have been able to grasp in her narrative style and the subtleties of her gender play.*

The transcribed narrative appears first, almost verbatim. Bilingual readers, and especially those familiar with Spanglish, will appreciate the exchange. By contrast, the English-speaking, non-Spanish-speaking reader may want to go directly to the second, fully translated version of this transcript. The former will see a queer sense of Spanish and Spanglish in the ways that gender—so basic to Spanish language terminology—was

Alberta Nevaeres—better known in San Francisco and especially San Francisco's Latino Mission District as Teresita la Campesina— at a friend's home in the Mission around 1978. *Photograph by and courtesy of Dan Arcos*

queered in Teresita's recollections. In describing how she was outed for being a maricona, *for example, she is queering the Spanish* maricón—*"faggot"—by turning it female—* maricona, *to mean more generally "queer." Similarly, the common Mexican-Chicano pejorative term* joto *for "faggot" often became* jota, *but also the diminutive* jotito *or* jotita *("little faggot") as a term of relative endearment. To discuss gender identities and meanings in the 1990s in reference to life in the 1950s and 1960s, when "drag queen" denoted what later became transsexual and transgender, further complicates terms denoting genders and sexualities and how they are understood today. This 1990s queering or regendering of nouns and pronouns from earlier decades was part of Teresita's style. Since she was an illiterate singer (she could sign her own name only with very poor pen-manship), voice and language were particularly important for her. Teresita had a knack for recalling geographic details and names, but she also strategically introduced phrases, especially of the rhyming kind. For example, she described her youthful appearance as "bella como una camella"—literally, as beautiful as a female camel. Moreover, as she clarified particular statements, her thinking was more in Spanish than in English, making it that much more complicated to mix both languages and all genders. In many ways, she was always producing a bilingual text, constantly offering phrases in both languages. Fi-nally, the richness of her narrative derives from the challenge of following her re-creation of other voices. She often performed (reenacted) conversations she had decades earlier, and because those recollections usually involved multiple voices, she was performing a multivoiced queer history, whether in song or in oral history.[2]*

TRANSCRIPTION 1: UNTRANSLATED, BILINGUAL SPANGLISH VERSION

HORACIO N. ROQUE RAMÍREZ: What was working in the bar like?

TERESITA LA CAMPESINA: I was working there as a woman.

HORACIO: How was it?

TERESITA: I was working with nothing but nationals. They would pick cotton and berries. And I would work behind the bar, and I would sing to them. There was gay people that used to come there from the fields and some of them you could tell. They didn't know [about me], but [some] knew me from LA. One, a female [said], "Oh, that's a drag queen! I know her from LA. Her name's Alberta!" And she went and told. See, and even in our own kind, you have to look out who your friends are 'cause your own kind will give you away. It was some sissy punk, lowlife, working in the fields, didn't have shit going. And I'm working there with falsies, looking *gorgeous*, like a sunset, bella como una camella, trabajando como una hembra con todos los machos, chupando verga, engañando a los hombres—pos claro que le hiba a dar [celos] al joto— era flamboyant—le hiba dar coraje. Y me conocía Y jué y les dijo a todos que yo era maricona Entonces yo tenía una amiga que se llamaba Carmen—se llama Johnny. Him and his old man are still together. They've been together twenty years. So I got *him* a job in the field. And I says, "Este es mi amigo Juan. Le dicen Carmen." He was tall but looked effeminate, con la mano caida pero grandote. And so I got him a job there and she always loved me. I haven't seen her in years. So anyway, when I went to jail, when I got busted, she got that fucking queen that told on me, she says, "You motherfucker, Margie [Margarita; Teresita] is good people. Why did you do that to her? She's a sister. Como eres gacho." They beat the *shit* out of him.

HORACIO: Really?

TERESITA: *Yeah*, that's what I was told. That Carmen—he beat the fuck out of that queer. Lo golpió 'cause she went and told that I was a drag queen. *I* was never no angel 'cause nobody is, nobody is perfect. But you know when the bar owner wasn't there I would give Carmen beers and my friends, the little whores. They would come in and I would give them free drinks on the house y todo. And I was just in my young youth, twenty-five years old. I was there when Kennedy died. What year did Kennedy die?

HORACIO: Mmhh . . . I forget. . . . '63? Maybe I'm wrong.

TERESITA: Okay, well around there. I want you to hear this story. So that, I used to look at myself and feel sorry for the prostitutes and all that. There was a black lady there; they used to call her "Tomato." And after a while I used to see these women *cry* and all that, how hard it's for women and selling their vagina and everything.

HORACIO: In Stockton, at the bar.

TERESITA: Yeah and I—

HORACIO: What was the bar called?

TERESITA: La Ocua And I would give her drinks. So one day—everything in this world ends; it's got the beginning and its ending. I saw this real tall man, named Chita, and he used to do Greta Garbo. That's what he told me. And I'm working in drag, okay; he doesn't know I'm a drag queen. But I noticed. I could tell he was gay as a fruitcake: big eyes and all that—very, la mano caida, hand down, very swinging [at] the hand. And I didn't say nothing. And she was working in the fields. [lowering her voice] And then, I was alone with her and she would *looook* at me, and we started talking. And she *looooked* at me and everything. So she came up real close, y dijo, "¿Cómo te llamas?" Dije, "Me llamo Alberta pero me dicen Margarita" Dije, [whispering] "Ven par acá; I'm a drag queen." Y dijo, "¡Ay, eres manita!" Dije, "Sí, siéntate. Tómate un trago. ¿Quieres un wine?" Dijo, "Me caes *bien*. Pareces *mujer*. Estás bella" Digo, "¿Y tú, cómo?"—Dijo, "Pués a mí me decían La Chita Yo me vestia de mujer y hacía drag como la Greta Garbo!" Y él ya era grande, señor, se razuraba y todo pero tenía razgos muy femeninos, that I could tell, like that. Entonces yo . . . como siguiendo mi carrera en la vida de homosexual y lo que llaman ahora transgender, me ponía muy sad. Y me enseñó retratos Jué a su cuarto. She lived in a room. Showed me—this fucking bitch looked *fantastic*! Drag has been here since day one! ¡Se miraba como una *hembra*! ¡He was in *show* business! ¡Hacía la Greta Garbo! Entonces dije, "Híjola."

Entonces me decía la Carmen, Johnny, "Oh Marge, you got a good heart." I said, "Girl, that's not it, it's just that, you never know en qué pachos vamos a quedar." Y yo le regalaba tragos y me decía, "Yes," decía la Carmen, "you have a good heart, girl." Y yo le decía, "Sabes que, this person, this man y me enseñó retratos de él y todo." Y me pongo a estudiar. Y yo estaba joven todavía, fíjate, veinticinco años, y él ya pasaba los cuarentas. Dijo, "Hay que ser buena con él. Es jota, es jotito pero es buena gente." Y so. Y ella le gustaba tomar Burgundy wine. It was only twenty-five cents. Y Vermouth. [whispers briefly] Dije, "Porque mira, vamos hablando claro." Y es que yo me entiendo mas . . . hablando en español porque yo pienso español. And I could speak both languages. Dije, pos esta jota me enseñó sus drag pictures, y ponte a pensar, "No sabemos, girl. Hay que ser bueno con él." Fíjate y yo ya era así. "Que tú te vas a ver como ella some day. Mira que bella era. And I'm a drag queen, girl. [her voice breaking, emotionally] Y yo estoy vestido de mujer. Y él es mi clase. Y es jotita y sufrida y tal. But I like her." "¡Uuuu, como eres! Como te quiero, Margarita" y todo. No, no pues que yo me miraba como ella así. She went and looked like the way I—she probably already passed away. God rest her soul in peace. We have lost a lot of brothers and sisters. Tal vez ya falleció. Pero siquiera tuve ese corazón, reconocer que todo se acaba. Uuu, la jota me gloriaba, me daba cosas del fil y todo. [I said] "You don't have to do that." Y le decía a las otras jotas, "Look out for her, *cuídala*. Es buena gente. She's good people." [raising her voice] ¡'Pa que veas! So that carries me.

HORACIO: Great friendships.

TERESITA: Hm hhmm.

HORACIO: Gente que no se olvida.

TERESITA: Y yo mirando todo eso, dije, "Quién sabe si me voy a mirar así cuando yo esté vieja." Todabía no había hormonas ni implants, ni facelifts, ni de nada como ahora. Por eso les digo a muchos que quieren vivir como mujer. Aunque no te cortes abajo y quieres andar vestido de mujer con tetas—you can always remove that. Por lo menos arréglate la cara y todo. Todo se acaba. Go in style. Porque, if you are gonna live as a woman y tienes razgos de hombre y estás medio feminine, have your face done, fix your features, that's why they have doctors. That's the reason I talk to you that way because: if you're gonna do something, do it right! Don't do it half-ass.

Ya que yo no me corté abajo porque yo no creo en eso. Yo ando vestido por la vida como una mujer porque es parte—como un uniforme. Es como un hábito. Porque yo soy hombre y mujer. Yo recibo; yo no doy. *Pero* ya que no me corté abajo porque yo creo en los Siete Sacramentos del Altar. Porque yo sé que aunque yo nací, yo nunca voy a quedar como una mujer. Yo respeto cada quien que hace eso. Si se quieren hacer—pero nunca van a quedar como una mujer perfecta. So, por eso me quedé hombre—por eso yo me nombro *hombre* y mujer. That's why I call myself a male female. Because I am *not* gonna cut that off. No way in hell am I gonna be like a perfect woman. They could adopt, they're never gonna have a period. See, when I talk to a lot of friends of mine that have the sex change—I had, not fights but we have argued, and I have offended them.

So, I *respect* them but I'd rather just not even talk about it, 'cause that is *my* feeling. See, once that feeling is gone, you know what I'm saying? And if you know you like to masturbate, like *I* do, and I like to play with my cock daily, and I like my titties sucked, and I like to jack off, honey—I'm *not* gonna make a mistake. 'Cause see, God makes no mistake. We are women of the *mind*. Though we are not women from gender, but you *are* a woman mentally, though you are a man and you got everything of a man. But your mind thinks woman. But you don't have to cut off, and cut off the feeling, if you know what I mean. That's a psychological and it's a very big step. Because once it's gone, it's off. So, knowing myself mentally, I kept the family jewels and I'm still Teresita, known as Alberto Nevaeres. I am still the man and the woman. *Thank you*! Case closed. [thunderous laughter] Soy *única*. *Unique*! I'd rather be unique, but no. That's part of life. Oh, I was going to do it a long time ago. I was a good candidate. When they told me that I was gonna be like a brand new Cadillac—*and no motor in it?!* I'd rather keep this old jalopy, I still have a lot of sparks. And a way of putting it in a *comical* way. But you know, I'd rather make a joke and laugh at it than insult. But to each his own. . . . [in a quiet voice] ¡A ver qué dice!

TRANSCRIPTION 2: TRANSLATED ENGLISH VERSION

HORACIO N. ROQUE RAMÍREZ: What was working in the bar like?

TERESITA LA CAMPESINA: I was working there as a woman.

HORACIO: How was it?

TERESITA: I was working with nothing but nationals. They would pick cotton and berries. And I would work behind the bar, and I would sing to them. There was gay people that used to come there from the fields and some of them you could tell [they were gay]. They didn't know [about me], but [some] knew me from LA. One, a female [said], "Oh, that's a drag queen! I know her from LA. Her name's Alberta!" And she went and told. See, and even in our own kind you have to look out who your friends are 'cause your own kind will give you away. It was some sissy punk, lowlife, working in the fields, didn't have shit going. And I'm working there with falsies, looking *gorgeous*, like a sunset, *bella como una camella*, working like a woman with all the machos, sucking dick fooling the men—of course, the faggot was—he was flamboyant—going to be angry. And he knew me. And he went and told everyone that I was a *maricona*. So then I had a friend named Carmen—his name is Johnny. Him and his old man are still together. They've been together twenty years. So I got him a job in the field. And I says, "This is my friend Juan. They call him Carmen." He was tall but looked effeminate, with a limp wrist, but really big. And so I got him a job there, and she always loved me. I haven't seen her in years. So anyway, when I went to jail, when I got busted, she got that fucking queen that told on me, she says, "You motherfucker. Margie [Margarita; Teresita] is good people. Why did you do that to her? She's a sister. You're such a fucker." They beat the *shit* out of him.

HORACIO: Really?

TERESITA: *Yeah*, that's what I was told. That Carmen—he beat the fuck out of that queer. She beat him up because she went and told that I was a drag queen. *I* was never no angel 'cause nobody is, nobody is perfect. But you know, when the bar owner wasn't there I would give Carmen beers and my friends, the little whores. They would come in, and I would give them free drinks on the house and everything. And I was just in my young youth, twenty-five years old. I was there when Kennedy died. What year did Kennedy die?

HORACIO: Mmm . . . I forget. . . . '63? Maybe I'm wrong.

TERESITA: Okay, well around there. I want you to hear this story. I used to look at myself and feel sorry for the prostitutes and all that. There was a black lady there; they used to call her "Tomato." And after a while I used to see these women *cry* and all that, how hard it's for women and selling their vagina and everything.

HORACIO: In Stockton, at the bar.

TERESITA: Yeah and I—

HORACIO: What was the bar called?

TERESITA: La Ocua. And I would give her drinks. So one day—everything in this world ends; it's got the beginning and its ending. I saw this real tall man, named Chita, and he used to do Greta Garbo. That's what he told me. And I'm working in drag, okay; he doesn't know I'm a drag queen. But I noticed, I could tell he was gay as a fruitcake. Big eyes and all that, he's very—limp wrist, hand down, very swinging the hand. And I didn't say nothing. And she was working in the fields. [lowering her voice briefly] And then, I was alone with her and she would *looook* at me, and we started talking. And she *looooked* at me and everything. So she came up real close. She said, "What's your name?" I said, "My name is Alberta but they call me Margarita." She said, [whispering] "Come here; I'm a drag queen." I said, "Ay, you're a girlfriend!" She said, "Yes, sit down. Have a drink. Do you want some wine?" I said, "Listen, I like you. You look like a woman. You're beautiful. And you, what is?—" She said, "Well, they used to call me La Chita. I used to dress like a woman and do drag like Greta Garbo." And he was already older, a gentleman and shaved and everything. But he had very feminine features, but I could tell. So then, I . . . like continuing the life profession of a homosexual and what today they call transgender, I would get very sad. And he showed me portraits. She went to his room. She lived in a room. This fucking bitch looked *fantastic*! Drag has been here since day one. She looked like a woman! She was in *show* business. She did Greta Garbo! So then I said, "Damn."

So then Carmen, Johnny, would tell me, "Oh Marge, you got a good heart." I said, "Girl, that's not it. Just that, you never know in what state we're going to end up." And I would give her drinks and she would say, "Yes." Carmen said, "You have a good heart, girl." And you know what, this person, this man who showed me portraits of himself and everything—so I study him. And I was still young, okay, twenty-five years, and she was already over forty. I said, "You have to be nice with him. She's *jota, jotito* but a nice person." And so. And she liked to drink Burgundy wine. It was only twenty-five cents. And Vermouth. [whispers briefly] I said, "Look, let's talk straight." I communicate better . . . speaking Spanish because I think in Spanish. And I could speak both languages. I said [to Carmen], "Well this *jota* showed me her drag pictures, and think about it, we don't know, girl. You have to be nice to him." See, I was already like that. [I said,] "And you are going to look like her some day. You know how beautiful she was. And I'm a drag queen, girl. [her voice breaking, emotionally] And I am dressed like a woman. And he is my kind. And *jotita* and suffering and such. But I like her." [Recalling Carmen speaking] "Ooo, how you are! How I love you, Margarita" and everything. No, no, it's that I already was seeing myself like her. She went and looked like the way I—she probably already passed away. God rest her soul in peace. We have lost a lot of brothers and sisters. But at least I had the heart, recognizing that everything ends. Ooo, the *jota* had me on a pedestal, she would bring me things from the fields and everything. [I said,] "You don't have to do that." And he would say to the other *jotas*, "Look out for her, *take care of her*! She's good people." [raising her voice] So there—so you can see! So that carries me.

HORACIO: Great friendships.

TERESITA: Mm hmm.

HORACIO: People you don't forget.

TERESITA: And seeing all of that, I said, "Who knows if I am going to look like that when I am old." There were still no hormones or implants, or facelifts, or nothing like today. That's why I tell many who want to live as women. Even if you don't cut off down there and you want to dress like a woman with tits— you can always remove that. But at least fix your face and everything. Everything ends. Go in style. Because, if you are gonna live as a woman and you have masculine features and you're somewhat feminine, have your face done, fix your features, that's why they have doctors. That's the reason I talk to you that way because: if you're gonna do something, do it right! Don't do it half-ass.

Since I didn't cut off down there—because I don't believe in that. I walk around life dressed like a woman because it's part—like a uniform. It's like a habit. Because I am man and woman. I receive; I don't penetrate. *But* I did not cut down there because I believe in the Seven Holy Sacraments of the Altar. Because I know that even though I was born—I am never going to look like a woman. I respect everyone who makes that decision. If they want to—but they are never going to look like a perfect woman. So, that's why I stayed as a man, that's why I name myself *man* and woman. That's why I call myself a male female. Because I am *not* gonna cut that off. No way in hell am I gonna be like a perfect woman. They could adopt—they're never gonna have a period. See, when I talk to a lot of friends of mine that have the sex change—I had, not fights but we have argued, and I have offended them.

So, I *respect* them but I'd rather just not even talk about it, 'cause that is *my* feeling. See, once that feeling is gone, you know what I'm saying? And if you know you like to masturbate, like *I* do, and I like to play with my cock daily, and I like my titties sucked, and I like to jack off, honey—I'm *not* gonna make a mistake. 'Cause see, God makes no mistake. We are women of the *mind*. Though we are not women from gender, but you *are* a woman mentally, though you are a man and you got everything of a man. But your mind thinks woman. But you don't have to cut off, and cut off the feeling, if you know what I mean. That's a psychological and it's a very big step. Because once it's gone, it's off. So, knowing myself mentally, I kept the family jewels, and I'm still Teresita, known as Alberto Nevaeres. I am still the man and the woman. *Thank you*! Case closed. [thunderous laughter] I am *única. Unique*! I'd rather be unique. But no. That's part of life. Oh, I was going to do it a long time ago. I was a good candidate. When they told me that I was gonna be like a brand new Cadillac—*and no motor in it?* I'd rather keep this old jalopy, I still have a lot of sparks. And a way of putting it in a *comical* way. But you know, I'd rather make a joke and laugh at it than insult. But to each his own. . . . [in a quiet voice, excited, referring to the recording] Let's see what it says![3]

Commentary

This essay explores the multiple roles and positions Teresita and I shared in relation to one another—the shared authorities, in Michael Frisch's apt phrasing—and the specifically queer gendering of language that made that sharing particularly powerful, though not always perfect, given our different generations. That sharing began when we first met in the fall of 1994 in the lounging area of a queer Latino HIV agency (Proyecto Contra SIDA Por Vida, or simply "Proyecto"), continued at public community events, extended into simply spending time together, and later led to publications in which I considered her life, especially after her death.[4]

Frisch's concept originated as a cautionary injunction to avoid the two poles of public history: the supposedly legitimate, professional, and credentialed historian, most often working in private through her writings and teaching, and rarely coming up for air and conversation with the public outside formal institutions; and the alternative—some would say oppositional—new forms of public history evidenced in community-based studies, grassroots video and filmmaking, and popular theater, where the voices of oral history find a new legitimized role. Aiming for a relationship between the two, sharing authority encompasses "a synthesis" between them, assuming that all interested parties involved can come together in and out of institutions for a conversation about the production and consumption of public histories.[5] However, the kind of synthesis Frisch envisions might benefit from a more accurate understanding of the consumption of historical research, especially its public presentations and publications.

In my queer and academic life, I have variously shuttled between the poles that Frisch describes, however unconscious I was of the conversations and tensions between the two. In 1994, I landed at the University of California, Berkeley, through an intercampus exchange program for graduate students, my home department then being a doctoral program in Latin American history at the University of California, Los Angeles. That program was quickly losing its appeal, especially with my newfound consciousness as a gay Latino. Heading to Berkeley was also an excuse to be next door to San Francisco, that presumed gay mecca and, luckily for me, then in the midst of profound queer Latina and Latino organizing that was usually, but not always, tied to HIV and AIDS prevention work. Thus, while I was reading 400-page history texts for my studies, I was also meeting fellow queer Latino activists and elders (those in their forties, in the context of the first waves of deaths from AIDS, and some even in their fifties). That's when Teresita, as a grassroots public historian who did not let go, pushed herself on me. Eventually, the trick was for me to find a balance and a relationship between that rich and still living oral history and the more sedate but also attractive ideas about gender, sexuality, race, and their historical intersections in the Department of Comparative Ethnic Studies, from which I eventually earned my doctorate.

In my analysis of a shared queer authority, I follow Linda Shopes's astute explication of Michael Frisch's concept but, again, with distinctly queer twists. Shopes delineates four key issues: that "collaborative oral history . . . is long haul work"; that "collaborative work is personally and intellectually demanding, requiring an ability—even the courage—to deal with people and situations that can be difficult"; that "because collaborative oral history projects are frequently linked to broader social goals . . . they inevitably raise the 'objectivity question'"; and finally, that the "biggest challenge . . . [is] analyzing the interviews gathered and presenting them as published scholarship."[6] Each of these four key issues is exemplified in the oral history work I conducted with Teresita.

The excerpt that accompanies this essay suggests many of the issues Teresita was committed to putting down on tape, on paper, and on video, and the wide scope of topics Teresita and I covered in our oral history work suggests a mutual commitment to the kind of "long haul" approach Shopes describes.[7] Teresita's own life was quite a long haul. She was a survivor in many senses: as a young *mexicano* queer teen disowned by his blood family to make it on his own in the racialized policed streets of Los Angeles, surviving through various forms of labor (bartending, singing, sex work) in various cities before that mythical queer historical marker of 1969, Stonewall. She survived into the 1990s and by her early sixties began to benefit somewhat from the availability of effective antiretroviral medicine.

The issues and topics we covered included queer life—but especially transgender life—in a rural, working, poor region of the United States in the 1960s and the dangerous politics of passing and of being found out or outed, which entailed jail time and forcibly regendering the guilty party to her or his "appropriate" sex, as Teresita experienced at least twice when her long hair was shaved. She also explained the close parallels between transgender and nontransgender sex-working women who shared marginalized, policed, often nonwhite, working-class spaces. In one telling instance, she recalled the joy and pride of recognizing a transgender self in the 1960s in meeting Chita ("Tomato") from an earlier, unknown, or unrecorded history of drag queens and performers who had made history, one largely unknown. She alluded to the related unknown queer future (in seeing the suffering in Chita and identifying with what may be her own future as an aging drag queen) for transgender women like herself, who in the 1960s had no certainty about what her life would be decades later, long before any recognition of the legitimacy of their lives. Teresita was especially conscious of the experiences of bilingual, bicultural, transgender *mexicanas* and other Latinas like her, straddling two intersecting stigmatized minority positions: one racial/ethnic, the other gendered/sexual. She was aware of the politics and possibilities for sex change, based not only on individual preference but also on economic and historical possibilities. And finally, Teresita, as someone living with AIDS, stressed the importance of remembering and recording in the 1990s her history of pre–gay liberation queer/trans life to establish how radically different survival was then as compared with the possibilities for gay Latino men like me, living in a time of post–gay liberation movements and with access to health care.[8]

This last point was essential for Teresita in establishing her transgender Latina authority, that is, to force openly queer people like me in the 1990s—those in our teens, twenties, and thirties—to recognize who she was and where she had been. She referred to herself as a pioneer, an artist (recognizing that she was lucky to receive *"un don de Dios"*—a gift from God—of a naturally powerful singing voice), and a *mexicana* proud of her roots but who had to hustle to survive when faced with her blood family's homophobia, street policing, forcible institutionalization at the former Camarillo State Mental Hospital to receive electric shock "treatments," marginalization within the mainstream and largely transphobic gay and lesbian rights movements, and (later in life) HIV and AIDS.

She insisted on this multipronged authority as often as she could, whether in the street, in restaurants, on the bus, or in any community setting—especially whenever she felt ignored. And she took me along for the ride, because she had found in me an interested party for the truths she was telling.

Indeed, the rides I took with Teresita for several years were not always easy, and I was often required to play along with her performance requirements. She controlled the situation most of the time. During our first recording session in her cramped room in the low-income Mission Hotel, she played a videotape, thus becoming the story of a story. It was a singing performance she had done at the request of a gay Latino neighbor. He asked her to sing for his gathered guests, and she acquiesced despite being exhausted from *"una noche muy fuerte, ya comprendes la pasión y la ternura y el ardor, pues me sentía que ya ni me podía levantar"*— "a very heavy night, you understand, passion, tenderness, and ardor, so that I barely could get up." Prior to this first interview, I had shared only public spaces with Teresita, but here, speaking to me from the privacy of her bed, she was probably testing me to see how comfortable I was with the subjects at hand. Teresita was probably also flirting with me, especially with her slow, suggestive, and seemingly exhausted voice. I was still testing the waters of how to conduct oral history at this point, so my discomfort was probably visible to her, but we both went for the ride.

Shopes's second key issue points out the demanding nature of oral history work, and Teresita's oral histories demonstrate not only her queer courage to talk and listen but also my own commitment. Structured along different axes of education, gender expression, sex, sexuality, HIV status, age, and class, these interviews demonstrated that the queer authorities I shared with Teresita were not always easily determined or democratic. We each had our own intentions, motivations, and goals, yet we both wanted to historicize queer Latina and Latino desires. In looking back, I am surprised how difficult it was to get her to sit down with me in a quiet, private place to record. Teresita was clearly performing—literally and figuratively—her queer history for me, a considerably younger queer with a university affiliation but someone who took the time to be with her, allowing her to take me to the bars, homes, and restaurants frequented by some of the few remaining queer old-timers. She probably did not usually have the patience to sit down for a formal recording, preferring instead to perform her story live by taking me to places and situations where others could vouch for her life and talents. In introducing me to the many firsthand witnesses of her accomplishments, each of whom confirmed her own narration, Teresita made her authority all the more profound.

Teresita's crassness, her often foul mouth, and her direct confrontational style at times shocked me and embarrassed me, and there were times when she would not stay in a place where she did not feel comfortable, especially after getting into an argument with someone. Her sex life was also quite public—she was infamous for having been arrested more than once in Reno for soliciting, for example—but this public persona was not one I was ready to address. For instance, one day when I was driving back to my apartment in Oakland from San Francisco, as I was entering the freeway ramp I noticed "an older woman" provocatively dressed, seemingly waiting for someone to pick her up. I was embarrassed when I recognized the woman in question, and I made sure she and I did not make eye contact. I was trying to be more sex-positive then, but Teresita was quite far ahead of me.

Even though Teresita's sex life was no secret—she boasted, as the excerpt shows, that she had fooled many men into believing she was a "real woman"—at the time I was still uncomfortable with this facet of her life. Our shared queer bilingualisms were definitely our joint, shared strengths: together, we queered English and Spanish, perverting their respective uses. I was happy to share this queerly gendered Spanglish with Teresita. Part of the reason I was so attracted to her was the larger-than-life tall tales she could spin at any moment, even though I was also uncomfortable when she would boast in public about what she had done with whom and when, not always respecting the privacy of all the parties involved.

The intimacy I shared with Teresita produced a kind of queer reciprocity and a feeling of social and political responsibility suggestive of Shopes's third key point, in which she describes collaborative oral history work as a project "linked to broader social goals" and worries that "they inevitably raise the 'objectivity question.'" This was certainly true in my relationship with Teresita. For instance, both Teresita and I met in the historical context of AIDS—she as someone who was HIV-positive, and I as someone collaborating with an agency to support educational, sex-positive grassroots movements—and learn how to remain HIV-negative. Even if we came of age in different generations, we were both queers, and our politics generally matched, especially because I cared so much about her generation. She was Latina and I am Latino, Spanglish-speaking, so we had our priorities about whom to visit first and try to record—other queer Latinas and Latinos. We also both had our own criticism of the AIDS service industry—recognizing that the bulk of the funding generally provided jobs with benefits for those already better positioned by race, class, and education in society, rather than the more marginal (the homeless, the illiterate, transgender women and men of color, for example). Thus broader social goals clearly encircled our concern with HIV and AIDS, health and survival, including how neighborhood agencies could support queer homeless youth, the unemployed, those with less access to education, and queers of color of all stripes (not just Latinas and Latinos), who even in San Francisco remained isolated and at risk for different forms of substance abuse. Although I never felt the need to refer to my oral history work as "activist scholarship," any sense of objectivity in my work slowly diminished.[9]

While my larger oral history project was progressing with modest funding support, I was also trying to complete my dissertation. I began to teach during my last years of the doctoral program, and I made the decision to focus on my writing, complete my degree, and then figure out what lay next professionally. As a result, I began to see less and less of Teresita and others in the community. Teresita would still call me regularly, often leaving outrageously campy messages on my answering machine, but my visits with her grew less frequent. I did send her an invitation to my graduation, which she took very seriously, showing up on time for the program, well dressed and ready for the occasion. That night, she was also part of my extended family, accompanying my parents and the rest of my family to a Chinese restaurant where she "behaved" by not using foul language, but not before displaying her powerful singing voice in the short car ride to let them know who she really was. My late father (who died at age ninety-three in 2010) and seventy-six-year-old mother always spoke of her voice with deep affection and respect; they also understood what it meant to me when Teresita passed.

One of the last times Teresita and I met together was at a restaurant in the Mission where mariachis—many of whom knew her—roamed for potential customers. Unlike the classic Teresita who had hustled for money for decades—sometimes mixing love with the erotic pleasure of song—this time *she* paid the mariachis to accompany her in several live songs and for a sumptuous Mexican shrimp dinner for us. She immediately became the center of attention with her unannounced performance as she sang her history. This was the homage she was giving *me*, someone who had cared to listen to the memories of her life as a bilingual queen who never quite fit into any one place. The customers were stunned by the powerful voice of this tall and big-framed singing *mujer*, but they had no sense that this moment would be one of the very last impromptu cultural performances of this queer pioneer, who was slowly dying. I played second fiddle in moments like these, the much quieter, much younger oral historian, too preoccupied with research. But Teresita was just too queer and too loud, and I was just too hungry for queer Latina and Latino history, for us not to engage in an eight-year, on-and-off dance toward the end of her life. This was also the beginning of my queer consciousness, and it was important to share the respective authorities we claimed: she, the elder, illiterate, but much more knowledgeable and thus savvier about street life for queers—and especially queens of color like herself—and me, the much younger, street-dumb intellectual committed to following her life.

Finally, to address Shopes's fourth key issue in sharing authority, the challenge of publishing the scholarship requires equal parts patience and persistence. For a recently hired tenure-track professor whose oral history–based dissertation was slowly becoming "the tenure book," I struggled to get pieces of my years-long community research into public circulation. I tried to balance professional and community-based publications, but ultimately the former won, leading to a painful and rocky tenure review process. But an uneven collaboration remained. For instance, whenever I could, I got Teresita funding to perform at the university. Even more important, and returning to Frisch's link between oral and public history, Teresita was by far the center of attention during a very successful fund-raising anniversary celebration for Proyecto, where she sang classic mariachi songs with a live mariachi on a stage in front of hundreds of community members from different agencies that rarely came together. As part of this multimedia performance, I prepared a PowerPoint presentation and projected images and brief oral history quotes behind Teresita on a large screen as she sang. Thus the collaboration and representation of queer Latina and Latino public and oral history was sung, seen, and read.

I want to believe that Teresita vested unspoken authority in me—through her constant phone calls, in taking me around the city to visit bars and restaurants to meet the elders, in sharing quite intimate and painful memories about her family—which I claimed days after she died. I knew from our recordings and from community gossip that she had a long-standing and conflicted relationship with the owner and the manager of the one remaining (as of 2010) gay Latino bar in the Mission. She particularly disliked this place because she felt it was symbolic of gay bars that made money off transgender performers but failed to acknowledge their important history and contributions. In fact, she had been banned from this bar for at least five years, and she did not mince words about how she felt about the bar, its owner, its manager, and the illegal sexual activities she claimed took place there. In the final minutes of our oral history together, she claimed to have told the owner and manager the following during a fund-raiser at the bar:

> [Quoting herself] "Let me tell you something you two gay cocksuckers: the day that I go, because we *all* have to go sooner or later, you're not going to make no money off *my* ass . . . after the way you treat your own kind." I said, "You're not going to make *one* penny," I said, "and I'm going to make sure that it's in a power of attorney. So you could make money off my *bones*? After everybody that's cared or didn't care that loved me? You may not like me, but you cannot take the love away from other people that loved me, just because you feel that way and you hold a grudge. You're not going to make any money off me."

When it came time to organize the community fund-raisers for Teresita's burial and other related costs, I spent several days with other community members coordinating all the necessary pieces: where we would hold fund-raising events, what agency would handle the money, where to print the funeral and mass announcement cards, and so on. During one of these meetings, an activist commented that he had been approached by this gay bar to hold a fund-raiser in her memory. Faced with this request, I responded, "No way." I quickly grew angry at the possibility that in death Teresita's transgender body would be used yet again for other people's purposes. My sharp response surprised the activist, as I had earned a reputation as a community member and scholar who tried not to take sides (at least openly) in intracommunity conflicts. But this moment to me was different; I felt the need to stand my ground, claiming all the authority I could on Teresita's behalf.

Oral historians often have a false sense of equality in the notion of sharing authority, but some of us benefit much more than those we interview. As researchers, we do give back; many of us have devoted years, even decades, to projects with minority, marginalized, and neglected historical communities—queer, women, people of color, the working class, immigrant (especially the undocumented), those suffering from natural and unnatural disasters, and those at any of these intersections—and the commitment counts for a great deal. Although I am still confused about who benefited the most from the authority I shared with Teresita, I do think in retrospect that I did give back to her, not in any monetary way but in time, friendship, and respect. I cannot deny that at that stage of her life I held advantages over her: health, maleness, professional status, sometimes owning a car. Despite the impossibility of a truly democratic shared authority, Frisch's notion deserves appreciation and careful application as we aim for more egalitarian projects on behalf of publicly consumed histories, especially those aiming for social change.

Teresita's life and death have haunted me for years for the connections we had and did not have as queer subjects from different historical periods and for the differences in privilege. She repeatedly took her story back to the historical place of the drag queen, especially the nonwhite drag queen, but she also introduced me to nontransgender gay Latino men and Latina lesbians who provided me with other pieces of the history I wanted to know and share. And we both knew at some level that the queerly gendered shared authority of Spanglish brought greater equality to our relationship and our lives. My friend Ricardo A. Bracho once observed that Teresita was my method; she embodied my methodological approach to community-based oral history because oral history was so basic to Teresita's survival. Ironically, she would never be able to read anything I would write about her in any language, so my giving back continues to this day by writing about the significance of her life.[10]

For instance, I have written about Teresita as a "living archive" of queer Latina and Latino history—perhaps as an organic intellectual in the Gramscian sense. I have also written about her centrality as an artist to give voice—literally—sound, history, and visibility to all Latinos in San Francisco and as someone who forced us to keep the memory and the reality of HIV and AIDS alive.[11] I have written about Teresita as someone whose oral history is to be publicly consumed alongside portraits of a time when she was in better health and as a transgender body (male-to-female in her case) at the center of queer Latino history both in English and in Spanish. Finally, I have written about her as someone who queered the Spanish language both in songs (and very classic rancheras at that) and through her never-ending storytelling. In queering Shopes's four key issues and in consideration of Frisch's notion of sharing authority, my relationship and research with Teresita proved to be yet another example of how oral history and public history can come alive.[12]

Notes

1. A useful exposition on the relationship between gay Latino studies and mainstream (white, Eurocentric) queer theory is Michael Hames-García, "Queer Theory Revisited," in Michael Hames-García and Ernesto Javier Martínez, eds., *Gay Latino Studies: A Critical Reader* (Durham, NC: Duke University Press, 2011), 19–45.

2. I would like to acknowledge the late Teresita la Campesina for allowing me to record part of her life history and for introducing me to key members of an elder generation of queer Latinas and Latinos, Nan Alamilla Boyd for her leadership and wise comments in this collaborative project, Kathy Nasstrom for sound editorial advice, and the anonymous reviewers for their suggestions. Some of the stages for the research discussed here were supported by a small research grant from University of California, Berkeley's former Chicano/Latino Policy Project; a University of California Institute for Mexico and the United States (UC MEXUS) dissertation completion grant, and a University of California, Berkeley, Graduate Humanities dissertation grant.

3. Alberta Nevaeres (Teresita la Campesina), audiotape recording, San Francisco, California, April 27, 1996. Recording and transcription in author's possession.

4. Horacio N. Roque Ramírez, "Teresita's Blood/La Sangre de Teresita," *CORPUS: An HIV Prevention Publication* 2, no. 2 (Fall 2004): 2–9; "A Living Archive of Desire: Teresita la Campesina and the Embodiment of Queer Latino Community Histories," in Antoinette Burton, ed., *Archive Stories: Facts, Fictions, and the Writing of History* (Durham, NC: Duke University Press, 2005), 111–35; and "Memory and Mourning: Living Oral History with Queer Latinos in San Francisco," in Paula Hamilton and Linda Shopes, eds., *Oral History and Public Memories* (Philadelphia: Temple University Press, 2008), 165–86.

5. Michael Frisch, *A Shared Authority: Essays on the Craft and Meaning of Oral and Public History* (Albany: State University of New York Press, 1990), xxi.

6. Linda Shopes, "Commentary: Sharing Authority," *Oral History Review* 30, no. 1 (Winter/Spring 2003): 105–8.

7. San Francisco–based gay Chicano activist, videomaker, and journalist Valentín Aguirre also wrote, produced, and directed "Wanted Alive: Teresita La Campesina" (San Francisco, 20 min., video), part of the city's 1997 Tranny Fest Film Festival.

8. An earlier related discussion on the relationship between lesbians and sex workers is Joan Nestle, "Lesbians and Prostitutes: An Historical Sisterhood," in Nestle, *A Restricted Country* (Ithaca, NY: Firebrand, 1987), 157–77. In comparison to Teresita's marginality, it is also worth considering the one encountered by the better known, Stonewall-era MTF transgender Venezuelan-Puerto Rican activist Sylvia Rivera (1951–2002). See "Sylvia Rivera Talk at LGMNY, June 2001 Lesbian and Gay Community Services Center, New York City," *CENTRO: Journal for the Center of Puerto Rican Studies* 19, no. 1 (Spring 2007): 116–23.

9. I was not able to reciprocate as fully as I could have—or should have, I realize in hindsight—with someone with the historical knowledge of Teresita. During our second recording, Teresita pointed out her desire to try to reconnect with her blood family in Glendale. The last time she had seen them had been during her mother's funeral in the early 1980s, and at that event, some of her family members openly welcomed her as a transgender woman, though not all, especially not an older brother who insulted her by suggesting that because she was HIV-positive, they would have to cremate her body after her death to avoid contagion. Despite her stories of family separation and reunion, Teresita still felt the desire for this trip, one that I could have facilitated financially, even with my very modest graduate student means, but I did not prioritize this trip on her behalf.

10. For an earlier discussion of a public memory and art gallery event in the Mission, months before Teresita died, which she herself could not read, even though it was based on her oral history transcripts, see my "Memory and Mourning."

11. I address some of these historical politics around AIDS in "Gay Latino Histories/Dying to Be Remembered: AIDS Obituaries, Public Memory, and the Gay Latino Archive," in Gina M. Pérez, Frank A. Guridy, and Adrian Burgos Jr., eds., *Beyond El Barrio: Everyday Life in Latina/o America* (New York: New York University Press, 2010), 103–28.

12. I thank Augusto F. Espiritu for suggesting, during a presentation about Teresita's life at the University of Illinois at Urbana-Champaign, that many of her qualities and daily interventions in numerous community sites evoke the characteristics of the organic intellectual.

PART IV

POLITICS

11

DANCING WITH STELLA, LOS ANGELES DAUGHTERS OF BILITIS PIONEER

Marcia M. Gallo

Oral history by Marcia Gallo with Stella Rush, Los Angeles, California, March 15 and 19, May 2, May 21 and 22, November 17, 2002

In 2002, Stella Rush was among the first of the former members of the Daughters of Bilitis (DOB) to respond to my request for an interview for my dissertation, a history of the organization and its role in modern lesbian and feminist activism. A series of telephone conversations before we met in person provided me with an auditory awareness of Rush's method of recounting her experiences. Our talks further underscored the significance of establishing an interview context for all of my narrators that gave them the freedom not only to describe their social and sexual activities in DOB and other arenas of their lives in the 1950s and 1960s but also to articulate the feelings those activities evoked. Stella Rush motivated me to create a flexible mix of methodological approaches to doing oral histories.

Our first conversation took place on March 15, 2002; we talked for about thirty minutes. That and subsequent telephone conversations before and after we met in person on May 21 helped me in two important ways: first, as a researcher, talking informally with Rush aided me in the process of creating a list of questions to ask other narrators. A second benefit was an awareness of Stella Rush's "verbal choreography," the seemingly random turns and spins of her storytelling. Within one conversation, she would reveal a range of disparate feelings, people, events, and their meanings; in later talks, she often repeated certain memories, particularly those involving her intimate relationships and her search for spirituality, self-love, and knowledge. It became clear that her conversational denouements shed crucial light on the emotional, as well as cultural, experiences of other nonnormative young women of the 1950s.[1]

MARCH 15, 2002 (VIA TELEPHONE)

MARCIA GALLO: Hello, Stella! How are you? Is this a good time to talk?

STELLA RUSH: It's fine.

GALLO: I have some basic questions—your birthday, where you live—

RUSH: I'll be seventy-seven soon! I have an April 30 birthday—I live near LA—forty miles south. Did you know that Dr. Vern Bullough is now doing a book?

GALLO: Really? I'll have to find out more about that—

RUSH: Your name is Mar-CEE-ah? I knew a Marcia—Marcia Herndon. She was into anthropology of music—University of Maryland. Lived with Billye Talmadge.

GALLO: Where did the name you used in DOB, "Sten Russell," come from?

RUSH: Well, see, the "ST" was for "Stella"; the "EN" was for "Ben."

I would make fun of being butch by signing "Ben" sometimes. That came when I met Joan Corbin, "Corky Wolf" was her partner. [She was known as] Eve Elloree—she staffed the magazine at ONE Institute. Since 1953, I was on the periphery. I first got connected to the gay movement through ONE. I worked in civil service during the "moral turpitude" days. I gave $100 to ONE and it helped me get in.

I had read *The Well of Loneliness* and thought, "Oh God, I'm not." I couldn't identify at all—didn't want to be "this" or "that."

GALLO: How did you meet Sandy [Helen Sandoz, her partner of more than thirty years]?

RUSH: I met Sandy as part of the DOB contingent—she was of great importance to both the San Francisco and Los Angeles chapters—she signed her real name for the charter.

GALLO: What was the gay scene like in those days?

RUSH: At the old If Club—that was a bar in LA, mostly women's, some men. And "tourists"—including my church group—we'd go there after services, men and women. We were Young Unitarians. So that's how I started—I went to the gay bar after church.

I was cutting off half my sexuality as a gay person. I lasted a day as a femme and about three days as a butch—

GALLO: How about mixing butch and femme?

RUSH: No, that's ki-ki. And that was a no-no. I was potentially bisexual if I wanted to go that route—I liked the freedom—and it was a big deal about how you made love, who did what. I can make love with a man—and I had boyfriends in college—but I was a virgin at twenty-three! Only one I knew in my crowd. Can you please send me a picture?

GALLO: Uh, a picture of myself? Sure.

RUSH: And a list of questions—

GALLO: Okay. I'll do that. Maybe this is a good time to stop.

MARCH 19, 2002 (VIA TELEPHONE)

RUSH: In January 1957, there were plans to start an LA chapter. But I was into the gay movement and with ONE from 1953 on—I was living with Joan Corbin ("Eve Elloree") in 1955—we were together when I met Sandy, I can't remember where she was. Oh, we met in a committee at the 1957 ONE Institute—she was part of the contingent of Daughters there for *The Ladder*. Now, you asked about names. I have no problem with the anonymity thing—it's pretty much an open thing with me—and it's okay to name Sandy. Joan may be dead as well. I would like to see what you write.

GALLO: Of course. I'll send you a draft.

RUSH: I thought Sandy was the moon and the stars—but at one point she said to me, "Stella, you got published before I did." But at the ONE Institute, I looked across the table and saw Phyllis Lyon. I leaned over and said, "Didn't I know you somehow?" Phyllis said, "Like from where?" I said, "Well, like maybe University of California?" She said, "That must have been a long time ago," and I said "Not that long ago—1945–47." I was a freshman—she was a junior or senior—a minute thing, but on the *Daily Cal* [newspaper] staff, because she was one of the wheels. I said, "Weren't you so-and-so on the *Daily Cal*?"

[At the ONE Institute meeting] Sandy kept getting bored and going to the bar—they sent me after her to keep her from getting in trouble. There was the Prodigal Son—Sandy was like the Prodigal Son. It was so typical of Sandy— she'd make a lot of protestations, she'd gripe and growl, but she'd be there when you needed her—she was doing all this stuff out of friendship, but she had a lot of complications. She was a Reluctant Dragon—but her service to *The Ladder* and to DOB in general was monumental. She was hard to know—a

Stella Rush at her typewriter at home in Los Angeles, about 1953. She contributed original essays and served as roving reporter for the pioneering American homophile magazine *ONE* throughout the 1950s. *Courtesy of Marcia Gallo*

very private person—but I kept learning things at parties when she would drink. I was a two-to-three drinks max kind of drinker—they'd say, "Let's put Stella to bed" and keep on going.

So I first got to talk with Sandy at that bar—she was perfectly delightful, very funny. But we got onto this butch-femme thing that existed in bars—she hadn't come across it until she got to San Francisco. She had fallen in love with a teacher in college and came out in that rarefied environment. She was dressed in a nice suit when I met her—she hadn't had to deal with the harshness and arbitrariness; . . . that system wasn't any good unless you accidentally fit in. Her birthday was November 2, 1920. Sandy was dubbed the butch—in SF any way—otherwise she was just herself. But see, I liked to dress masculine and she liked to dress masculine—this put us at cross-purposes. She was fascinated by me 'cause she'd not met one like me—back in those days, you know, Del was the butch and Phyllis the femme, of course—and dressed to match. Sandy was very funny, intelligent, graduated with a BA in psychology. I had three years of college—was lacking three units of social science or civics for my degree. I went to night school, Saturdays, extension courses—tried to get serious about it. I worked in civil engineering department (as civil engineering assistant)—had to get past an arch feminist. She wanted to know why I wanted to be a planning assistant and make less money? Here I was going to ONE at night and we were catching some trolley—getting from downtown LA—and I made a comment about a woman as president and got into trouble—

GALLO: Tell me more about Joan.

RUSH: Joan was ONE's artist. You know, maybe if you try to do any part of this story, you should use people's magazine names. Had loved her about a year before it happened—she broke up with her partner of eight years; and I was with her about two years. It was during that period that I started writing poetry. They were "Ann Carll Reid" (Corky Wolf), who was editor of ONE, and "Eve Elloree" (Joan Corbin), the staff artist of ONE. They were a couple, working on ONE magazine.

That's enough for now.

MAY 21 AND 22, 2002 (STELLA RUSH'S APARTMENT IN WESTMINSTER, CALIFORNIA)

GALLO: OK, Stella, to start, I just want to get the chronology right. . . .

RUSH: My birthday is April 30, 1925. It was 1953 when I got involved with ONE magazine and after that learned about DOB. I met Sandy, Del, and Phyl in 1957.

But it was 1960—at our DOB convention in LA—that I got less fearful, used my work name tag even though civil servants were subject to California laws. . . .

I graduated from high school in 1943—Dorsey High School, West Adams district in Los Angeles; from 1943–45 I was at North American Aviation as an aircraft draftsman trainee; then I went to the University of California at Berkeley for two years.

In the second semester there, I got a scholarship—I was the daughter of a World War II vet—it was the Alice Unkhart scholarship. I worked in the lab while Oppenheimer was there, washed out glassware with sulfuric acid. Met Phyllis Lyon at the *Daily Cal* (UCB newspaper)—she was a wheel—a junior. . . .

In 1947 and '48 I was at UCLA and joined the Unitarian church in LA—and there it was rumored that I was "queer" and I didn't know what that meant. I was twenty-three, involved with men—like Mac (a boxer), a good guy, I think we were engaged; . . . anyway, I dated him—he asked if I was gay, too!

In 1948 to '50, the witch hunts were on; in 1949 I worked at Firestone Tire as aircraft draftsman, fell into the If Club in LA—didn't know it was gay. I met a young black officer, fell in love with him; . . . he wrote poetry and later taught at San Francisco State and at Berkeley. You know at this time they were burning the KKK cross in the hills of Berkeley, . . . the FEPC law was being fought for. . . .

GALLO: That must have been horrifying.

RUSH: I was mad all the time in the 1950s. . . .

GALLO: Tell me more about Sandy.

RUSH: June 7, 1987, was when Sandy died, she had been sick for two years.

Sandy and I hit it off instantly—she grew up in Oregon, in a small town near Eugene and got her degree in psychology from Reed College. Her mother was an immigrant from Sweden, came with her family to U.S.—very poor. Sandy's mom got a job as maid to the Beldens, they were well-to-do—upper middle class. Sandy's mother was related to Sandoz, the pharmaceutical people—they invented LSD. Her father was a railroad man—came through town, had a roll in the hay with her mom—Sandy paid for it for the rest of her life. Sandy's father returned to town and married her mom. Her mother left when Sandy was nine months old—she was taken to a TB institution.

Helen Jane Sandoz was Sandy's full name—she met her father when she was eighteen years old.

Reed didn't let her graduate with her class because she was nice to Japanese American schoolmates—wrote letters to them after they were sent away, with chess moves included, and the FBI started investigating.

Del and Phyl dragged Sandy into DOB and to Sacramento to incorporate the organization. When we met, I was lovers with Joan—she was an artist for ONE Inc. Sandy came along in '57—courted me like crazy—sent books, letters, complimented me. November 2 was her birthday. I wrote a piece in *The Ladder*, a thinly-veiled love poem to Sandy. I . . . in DOB, couples usually acted in unison, but I didn't, and Sandy didn't like it.

MAY 2 AND NOVEMBER 17, 2002 (VIA TELEPHONE)

GALLO: Let's talk about the Prosperos, okay? How did you get involved?

RUSH: Religion was very much a part of Mom's life—and mine, too, until I was eighteen. I was very bored by Protestantism, I had read enough, studied enough and couldn't accept that God concept, so I broke with religion. I was more lost and lonely when I decided I didn't believe in God anymore—my mind has been on this all my life. But I joined the Unitarian Church in Berkeley and then Los Angeles, with a lot of young people to whom the God concept isn't important.

It was a strange Unitarian group in LA—believed in doing good, primarily humanist. It had a lot of Jewish people, kids fleeing Orthodox Jewish families and Reformed Jews fleeing their Reform synagogues—lots of diverse creatures. And it was right in the middle of the witch hunts [of the 1950s]—the spectrum was anywhere from atheist to agnostic.

In 1955, I had an emotional crisis in my life because what I thought was my true love was having a sexual relationship with the last person I had been with—I couldn't understand it. I couldn't understand an affair in the middle of a brand new love affair. I was homicidal and suicidal at that time. During this time I had a transcendent experience of being lifted out. I saw a book— *How to Use the Power within You* [1955]—in a bookstore and thought, "Gee, if there's any power in me I'd like to get at it. . . . " The authors were Claude M. Bristol and Harold Sherman. It was the only thing that helped me at that time.

I finally found the integration of things I believed—philosophy and practice—with the Prosperos a few years later, but you had to stay in the cult. Prosperos still exists today—it's limping along.

Sandy and I were in the Prosperos—1965, 1970 most active. There were all kinds of students—mostly rebels, agnostics, atheists, freethinkers. It brought me back full circle to where I'd begun. Sandy and I were in our late thirties and forties when we were most actively involved. [Prosperos' founder] Thane [Walker] gathered archetypes from all over the world. He was a great deal older than we were—may have been born in 1900. Thane was a Teacher with a capital *T*. He was handsome—a white-haired gent—based in Hawaii [for many years] but born and raised in the Midwest. There were groups throughout the nation, in a great many states, with a center in Georgia It would be characterized as a New Age sect or cult. Thane was about "right thinking in the abstract." He came looking for us—he reached out to homosexual groups because he thought it [his teachings] would help them.

Thane studied to be a psychiatrist and got the M.D.—Jung was his favorite psychiatrist. But he quickly got off onto the religious path instead.

Thane's sex lecture was the thing that won over anybody with a hole in their life. He said that androgyny was the epitome—knowing, appreciating, using masculine and feminine sides of self. He was in Germany in World War II—ended up in jail for a while there, working on these principles when there. He wrote pamphlets—"I Watched Hitler Do Black Magic" is one of them. Thane was a student of Gurdjieff's but we didn't really have that kind of school. He was greatly influenced by him and his thinking, had been part of Unity, and he borrowed from all the offshoots of the day—Ernest Holmes, Emmett Fox, the Fillmores, and Physical Miracles.

In San Francisco, in LA, where we met, he sent his teachers in to talk to us, always sent beautiful women to our meetings. The name The Prosperos was very symbolic. It followed the Shakespearean characters in "The Tempest"—Caliban in the dungeon was symbolic of ancient animal-like instincts that we have that can be destructive, Ariel was the bright fairy sprite. The symbolism was gleaned from all over the world, but he kept trying to keep it to what Anglo-Saxon white Protestants could understand. Thane taught us a five-step exercise in right thinking in the abstract.

GALLO: Were many other DOBers involved, too?

RUSH: We were drawn into this circle of people by Billye (she was a wheel in the group), and Del and Phyl. We were drawn in to this magic teacher (very human) and they were going for it hook, line, and sinker—they were talking a whole other language.

It was rather marvelous—there were miraculous results; Billye was able to get rid of long-standing guilt or grief over her mother. We would write out a situation and apply rules of syllogisms that Plato did:

> "Truth is that which is so,
> that which is not truth is not so,
> therefore truth is all there is."

This was called "translation." We needed to practice to see the spiritual connotations in that. In translation classes, we shared writings, and there were workshops as well. But the ultimate was RHS—Thane called it "releasing the hidden splendor." Translation alone only takes you so far. He used the archetype of Joseph and his brothers—forgiveness and getting rid of guilts and self-hatreds.

Prosperos was a home for those of us who weren't able to go back to our churches . . . but it did cause disagreements among people in DOB. Billye took to it so strongly that she tried to teach it at our meetings. Our leaders got hooked on it—and Billye was full of the holy zeal.[2]

Commentary

Started by four lesbian couples in San Francisco in 1955, the Daughters of Bilitis initially was a secret social club for women. The eight founders, including Del Martin and Phyllis Lyon, purposely chose a reference to a fictional female lover of the ancient Greek teacher and poet Sappho as a way to screen their new group from unwanted scrutiny by a hostile heterosexual society. They reasoned that any woman who recognized the name Bilitis would have been "on the qui vive," or knowledgeable about lesbian life. The year DOB began, *Songs of Bilitis*, a book of erotic poems purportedly written by Bilitis to Sappho and "discovered" by French poet Pierre Louys in the late nineteenth century, was enjoying a renaissance among readers of paperback novels with queer content. Despite recurring debates about its awkwardness and difficult pronunciation over the next fifteen years, the Daughters maintained their allegiance to their strange, secretive name. In many ways, it is a reminder of their organizational roots in the midst of a Cold War culture of cunning codes and clever deceptions; it also reflects a wariness of exposure and misinterpretation on the part of the early DOB activists that lasted well beyond the life of the organization itself.[3]

Despite the metanarrative they created about themselves and DOB, by the early years of the twenty-first century, Martin and Lyon insisted that the insights of other Daughters were crucial to any accurate history of their organization, and Stella Rush's name was at the top of their list. Still largely unknown outside of gay circles in Southern California, she had been one of a handful of women at the epicenter of post–World War II gay organizing in Los Angeles, the birthplace of the U.S. homophile movement.

Rush is intriguing not only because of her longtime involvement in the lesbian and gay movement, as well as the tangle of personal relationships that propelled her activism, but also as a working-class white woman with a history of social justice awareness and activism. She articulated a youthful racial consciousness through vivid memories of being separated from Japanese American classmates after the attack on Pearl Harbor and recounted similar experiences that she said her longtime lover, Helen Sandoz, had had as a high school student. "It was the first time that I was really aware of the cost of being different, even in this great country of ours. How could this be happening in the land of the free?"[4] She easily made connections between systems of oppression, be they racial or sexual. It took no prompting for her to link the internment of her school friends with the harassment and arrests of other people in Los Angeles— black, bohemian, or queer—as she described bucking the tide of postwar conventionality in the late 1940s and early 1950s: "I was mad all the time in the fifties . . . [news about] homosexuals leaving the State Department, witch hunts for Communists. . . . And then there were the civil rights struggles in LA—we discovered that we didn't have any more rights than in the South. . . ."[5]

Rush began her gay activist life by writing "Letter from a Newcomer" for *ONE* magazine. Formed by a small group of men and women who split off from the pioneering Mattachine Society, ONE, Inc., focused on presenting educational workshops, as well as publishing a monthly magazine. Rush was first introduced to the group by a former girlfriend who took her to a party; meeting ONE leader Joan Corbin, with whom she soon fell in love, motivated her to get involved.

Although the relationship ended in heartbreak for Rush, Corbin had encouraged her to write about her experiences of the gay scene in and around Los Angeles in 1953. Her first-person account brought a great deal of response and encouraged Rush to continue writing. She published articles in ONE from 1954 until 1961, using the pseudonym Sten Russell.

She also was instrumental in the expansion southward of the Daughters of Bilitis. After DOB unveiled its monthly newsletter *The Ladder* in 1956, she became the "Los Angeles Reporter," recording the meetings and conferences organized by ONE and Mattachine. A meeting at a conference in 1957 led to a long-distance love affair with Sandoz, followed soon after by Sandoz's move to Los Angeles.

Sandoz was integral to DOB's development, yet she, too, is not well known among queer activists today. Daughters of Bilitis founder Phyllis Lyon remembers, "Sandy was one of the only lesbians we knew in San Francisco when we moved from Seattle. We visited her and her partner once, I think, and that was it. They were living in the hills of Marin, and Sandy's partner wanted nothing to do with DOB." Lyon continues, "Sandy got involved after they broke up, and she stayed with it for the next ten years or so." Sandoz was one of the first members

Using the pen name Sten Russell, Stella Rush was one of the first women to become actively involved in the homophile movement. In addition to her work with ONE, she cofounded the all-female Daughters of Bilitis chapter in Los Angeles in 1958. *Courtesy of ONE National Gay and Lesbian Archives*

of the Daughters of Bilitis. Using "Helen Sanders," her DOB pseudonym, Sandoz became the group's third president in 1957 and also served as editor of *The Ladder* from 1966 to 1968.[6]

Born in 1920 in Corvallis, Oregon, Sandoz attended Reed College during the early years of the war. She was the only daughter of a Swedish immigrant single mother, who supported herself and her daughter by working as a maid for a well-to-do family. Like Rush, Sandoz's mother was ill and often hospitalized throughout Sandoz's youth. Her father, though well-connected and wealthy, played no significant role in her life.

An energetic, independent woman, Sandoz moved to Alaska after college on a civil service assignment, then to Washington, and back to Oregon, where a serious traffic accident inspired her to look for a career that would not involve sitting for long hours. She learned sign printing and, by the mid-1950s, had found her way to San Francisco, where she soon met Del Martin. Within months of moving to Los Angeles in 1958, Rush and Sandoz held the first of many years of DOB meetings in their Silver Lake home. Sandoz died in 1987, but, even in 2002, Rush often spoke of her as if she were still a strong and vital presence in her life; her absence was palpable.

Although Rush's stories often careened wildly—from her relationships with Sandy and her mother, to the problems with Christianity, to her passionate crushes on both men and women—they were always riveting; our relationship evolved via many intricate verbal "dances" performed during four years of conversations. One step forward . . . two to the side . . . three back . . . then a sudden dip and a dizzying turn: the experience of following her lead revealed a great deal of information and insight that was crucial to understanding the beginnings of lesbian activism in post–World War II America It also illuminated a larger truth—the rhythmic nature of oral history.

Adapting to the storytelling choreography of a narrator is a crucial component of interviewing. With Stella Rush, it often was necessary to relinquish overt control and preconceived notions yet maintain the momentum of the project. She rewarded such agility with a great deal of openness, mountains of memories, painfully honest assessments, and juicy tidbits of gossip. The relationship that developed between us went beyond that of researcher and narrator; we experienced what Gesa Kirsch has called "the dynamics of friendship and friendliness as understood in the context of feminist fieldwork."[7] Further, the relationship was fueled by desires: a shared desire to work together in crafting a good story, as well as the strangely intense attraction between us. Although separated by more than twenty-five years in age, and eons apart in our disparate experiences of living openly as lesbians, we had a sisterhood of sorts, tinged by sensuality. Throughout the initial and follow-up telephone conversations, the in-person meetings and taped interviews, and finally the back-and-forth review and editing of the manuscript, a process also evolved that was active and engaged. It was then replicated, with very minor differences, with other primary narrators.[8]

However, the conversations with Stella always were different. They would often center on what Kirsch refers to as the "seemingly abstract, impersonal questions [that] could lead interviewees to reveal deeply personal, emotionally charged information—as if to a friend."[9] Rush's accounts of her experiences as a homophile activist often included such "emotionally charged" memories. For example, her symbiotic relationship with her mother and her mother's increasingly debilitating mental and physical illnesses were incorporated into her narrative. Although at first the unexpected sharing of such intimacies made for uncomfortable conversations, it soon became clear that they were very important to her; they illuminated how she felt her life choices had been circumscribed. Rush described the feelings she wrestled with when she was unable to continue her studies at UC Berkeley because of her mother's need for care and instead, after being summoned home to Los Angeles, completed her third year of college at UCLA in 1948. She then dropped out and went to work for Firestone Tire and Rubber as an aircraft draftsman, a line of work she would continue for years, and rerouted her search for independence by becoming an active member of the First Unitarian Church of Los Angeles.

Soon Rush began to explore whether her attractions to women meant she could be gay. The lesbian subculture in postwar Southern California and other major metropolitan areas was centered in a handful of gay bars and "explained" in a few books about homosexuality. She described both options as problematic: the bars put patrons in danger of police raids, and the books were hard to find and usually depressing. Rush said that what she read "convinced her that the lifestyle of gay men and women meant living a series of lies."[10] Her experience of a police raid on a Venice Beach bar in 1949 reiterates her sense of secrecy and futility:

I was scared to death, standing there shaking. This cop asked me to identify myself, so I hauled out my driver's license and said that's me. "Where do you work?" "I don't have a job." You don't know. You don't want to argue with a policeman or anyone who has a gun and a billy stick. I didn't give them any reason to take me down to the station. At the same time, I wasn't going to help them. The whole thing with me was not to argue with them about anything if I could help it. . . . The police officer told me, "You should cooperate with us," and I answered, "I would, sir, if I knew what you wanted."

Actually, there were about four times I had to talk with cops, and most of the time there was a good cop–bad cop scene. . . . The most difficult ones were not the gay bar raids but were being stopped by the police about race, like the time my partner Bea and I were taking a black man home from choir practice. I was ready, if I had to, to go to jail for the right of free association with others and to take a stand against race discrimination. I was a member of ACLU and could see what the ACLU could do about it—that is, for the racial discrimination. I wasn't prepared to go to jail about the homosexuality issue because, as far as I could see, gays didn't have any civil rights and ACLU didn't have anything to offer. It took a lot of work and education before the ACLU took us on—they had to get to know us and to read a lot of our stuff.[11]

Her reference to the American Civil Liberties Union is another example of the rewards that came from following her lead during the interview process. It initiated discussions of the importance of ACLU chapters—in Los Angeles, San Francisco, Chicago, Philadelphia, and Washington, D.C., among other cities—to homophile activists and became a hallmark of interviews with other DOB and Mattachine narrators; Rush provided a clue to the organization's significance that had not been readily apparent. So, too, did her memories of her search for a spiritual home.

One of the most jarring verbal turns occurred when she suddenly recounted a religious conversion experience she had had in the 1950s. It led to Rush describing many details about The Prosperos Society, which she, her lover Sandoz, Lyon and Martin, and a number of other early gay leaders in California joined. In 2002, no other DOB narrators were as willing as she was to discuss the group, which was led by Thane Walker, a charismatic teacher who claimed to have studied with Gurdjieff. Prosperos emphasized group and individual empowerment exercises that would lead to self-love and knowledge; Prosperos teachers and mentors believed that all people combined both masculine and feminine energies and that through special exercises and the study of spiritual archetypes, people could release repressed emotions and heal themselves from self-doubt, guilt, and despair. In the early 1960s, before both the creation of alternative gay religious institutions like the Metropolitan Community Church and the recognition by mainstream religions of the importance of ministering to gay people, The Prosperos Society provided a sanctuary for some Daughters; in hindsight, however, some of them treated it as somewhat of an embarrassment. Rush's longtime involvement in the group did not blind her to some of its problems, although the ways she initially described her search for spiritual answers were bound up both with her strong ties to her mother and with the devastating breakup of the love affair that launched her into homophile activism.

Rush continued her involvement with Prosperos until the early years of the twenty-first century. It was as significant to her as her years of gay activism and thus formed an integral part of her narrative. Yet, again, without a methodology that allowed for her sometimes surprising conversational turns and the unexpected spins of her particular storytelling choreography, many of Stella Rush's most closely held secrets would not have been shared. The "implicit social contract" that was established in the interview process was validated not only by her informed consent but also by an understanding that we were engaged in a joint project.[12] But bridging the inherent power relations between researcher and narrator to build the trust such engagement relied on required creativity and new methods.

Using nontraditional methods as an oral historian usually means climbing out of the archives, temporarily setting aside the secondary literature, and confronting the fear of interviewing real live people and forming close relationships with some of them. It means facing all the concomitant challenges such "asymmetrical interactions"[13] inevitably pose, including illness and death. The exultation of excavating intimate memories is, as Horacio Roque Ramírez has expressed, "intermittently at odds with the sadness, anger, and fear over the content of those memories."[14] Yet queer historians must be prepared to face the pain as well as the pleasure that comes from probing into our narrators' psyches and sexual experiences.

Writing about her oral history interviews with women and men who had been part of ACT UP (AIDS Coalition To Unleash Power) in New York in the early years of the pandemic, Ann Cvetkovich foregrounds the intersections between trauma and activism. She reminds us that, as queer historians, we "grapple with the ways sexual trauma and queer trauma can be relegated to invisibility by distinctions between private and public trauma, often a gendered distinction, and by structures of homophobia." Her work is especially insightful for oral historians who must take into account "this nexus of mourning and militancy" that frames activist work against "systems of violence, oppression, and exploitation." Further, as was true for many Daughters, the narrative of organizing against AIDS "is a story of activism structured around the intensity of friendship—a friendship that combines romance and collective work. These are intimacies shot through with longing and loss, and they are the foundation of activism's affective power."[15]

The experiences of homophile activists of the 1950s are refracted through the cultural complexities of early Cold War America, a complex time of paranoia and persecution. It also was a period of possibilities, when challenges to the status quo were mounting. Yet for lesbians and gay men, whose emotional desires were deemed pathological, their sexuality classified as diseased, it is not unusual to hear the echoes of trauma in the stories they tell, in the spaces between the shared erotic secrets and pleasures. Although their experiences were not, and could not have been, the same as those waged by AIDS activists thirty years later, what is similar for both groups is the linkage of sexual trauma and queer trauma. Both forms of organizing were necessitated by the enforced trauma of invisibility. "One of the hardships faced by gay men in the 1980s was the lack of public attention to the deaths and losses of AIDS because of the homophobic dismissal of those who were not seen as innocent or average citizens. Traditional forms of mourning were often denied, compounding the trauma of loss, or funerals kept the dead closeted, erasing the grief of lovers and friends," wrote Cvetkovich. However, in sorrow and angry defiance, Cvetkovich reminds us, "Gay communities also reinvented rituals of mourning, producing new forms of public funerals that incorporated sexuality and camp." Mourning was turned into militancy, and a new form of queer activism was created.[16]

These insights are crucial to incorporate into our experiences of oral history. Reliance on a mixed methodology may be instinctive as well as informed for many of today's historians of sexuality, who can draw from feminism and social history, as well as queer theory. Further, it is customary in oral history practice to include methods such as meeting narrators where they are, literally and figuratively, whether the setting is living rooms and kitchens, a restaurant or bar, or a quiet corner in an assisted living facility. There also seems to be a shared recognition that some of the best stories often come when the recorder is turned off and a more relaxed atmosphere encourages reflection. What is less acknowledged is that, sometimes, the memories that an intimate setting can bring forward—of former lovers, lost friends, and still-fresh emotional wounds—bring nervous laughter, long-suppressed tears, or tense silences. How these wounds are treated is crucial not only to the success of the interview but also to the integrity of the experience.

The ability to create the space for intimacy within the context of queer oral history is as important as any other methodological practice. As feminist oral historians noted in 1987, "If we see rich potential in the language people use to describe their daily activities, then we have to take advantage of the opportunity to let them tell us what that language means."[17] Such an imperative is even more compelling when encouraging narrators to share deeply felt, and often closely guarded, erotic and emotional secrets. In recording and interpreting the experiences of some of the first American women to publicly affirm their love for other women, it has been essential for researchers to establish a strong bond of trust and to check their presumptions about the nature of sexual identity, love, and loss. Narrators like Stella Rush, who saw themselves as lifelong sexual outlaws regardless of their racial, socioeconomic, or citizenship status, will reward those researchers with whom they can "dance": who pay attention "to the vernacular and to the mundane patterns of life," and who give credence to those stories that go beyond the standard tropes of contemporary sexual identity and experience.[18]

Notes

1. As always, I am grateful to Stella Rush for sharing her life stories, and to my partner Ann Cammett for sharing her life. My thanks also go to Nan Alamilla Boyd and to Horacio Roque Ramírez: it is a privilege to have worked with both of them. Further, I acknowledge the contributions of my colleagues and graduate students at UNLV, particularly those whose incisive questions and comments during our "Oral History: Theory and Practice" classes have helped me concretize the notion of "verbal choreography."

2. Stella Rush, Westminster, CA; interview transcripts in author's personal files. My conversations with Stella—as well as interviews and e-mails of varying lengths with nearly three dozen other former DOB activists I communicated with from 2002 to 2006—formed the basis for *Different Daughters: A History of the Daughters of Bilitis and the Rise of the Lesbian Rights Movement* (New York: Carroll & Graf, 2006; Berkeley, CA: Seal, 2007). Transcripts are being readied for deposit at community-based LGBT archives throughout the country.

3. For primary sources on the Daughters of Bilitis, see Del Martin and Phyllis Lyon, *Lesbian/Woman* (New York: Bantam, 1972); Kay Tobin and Randy Wicker, eds., *The Gay Crusaders*

(New York: Paperback Library, 1972); Vern Bullough, ed., *Before Stonewall: Activists for Gay and Lesbian Rights in Historical Context* (New York: Haworth, 2002).

4. Rush interview, March 27, 2002.

5. Rush interview, May 21, 2002.

6. Phyllis Lyon, San Francisco, CA, May 15, 2002; interview transcript in author's personal files.

7. Gesa E. Kirsch, "Friendship, Friendliness, and Feminist Fieldwork," *Signs: Journal of Women in Culture and Society* 30, No. 4 (2005): 2164.

8. In addition to extensive archival research, there were many conversations, interviews, and e-mails with five primary narrators: Phyllis Lyon and Del Martin, Barbara Gittings and Kay Tobin Lahusen, and Stella Rush. Not only were they always willing to verify other members' accounts of events, correct mistakes, and clarify interpretations but also each offered different perspectives on the development and growth of the organization, as well as the reasons for its demise.

9. Kirsch, "Friendship, Friendliness, and Feminist Fieldwork," 2164.

10. Judith Saunders in Bullough, *Before Stonewall: Activists for Gay and Lesbian Rights in Historical Context*, 138.

11. Ibid.; Rush interview, November 17, 2002.

12. Kirsch, "Friendship, Friendliness, and Feminist Fieldwork," 2164.

13. Ibid., 2165.

14. Horacio N. Roque Ramírez, "My Community, My History, My Practice," *Oral History Review* 29, no. 2 (Summer–Fall 2002): 88.

15. Ann Cvetkovich, "AIDS Activism and the Oral History Archive," *The Scholar and Feminist Online* 2, no. 1 (Summer 2003): www.barnard.edu/sfonline.

16. Ibid.

17. Kathryn Anderson, Susan Armitage, Dana Jack, and Judith Wittner, "Beginning Where We Are: Feminist Methodology in Oral History," *Oral History Review* 15 (Spring 1987): 111.

18. Nan Alamilla Boyd, "Who Is the Subject": Queer Theory Meets Oral History," *Journal of the History of Sexuality* 17, no. 2 (May 2008): 186.

12

"YOU COULD ARGUE THAT THEY CONTROL POWER"

Politics and Interviewing across Sexualities

Martin Meeker

Oral history by Martin Meeker with Quentin Kopp, San Mateo, California, April 16 and 17, 2007

Quentin Kopp is a former member of the San Francisco Board of Supervisors, an elected member of the California State Senate, and a judge for San Mateo County Superior Court. The interview that follows focuses on Kopp's years in San Francisco politics and his observations on the changing political landscape in that city. The interview demonstrates how oral history can be a powerful tool to help establish new perspectives on the queer past—in particular, demonstrating what can be gained by interviewing across lines of sexuality (that is, gay interviewing straight) and across lines of political ideas and policy positions. The interview with Kopp not only adds important factual information to the well-rehearsed narrative of gay political achievement but also forces a reconsideration of some of the most foundational mythologies of the gay movement in San Francisco. In one particularly revealing exchange, Kopp paints a fascinating portrait of Harvey Milk, the politician who was assassinated in 1978. Kopp's description should help historians add complexity to the dominant image of Milk as a martyr and a gay liberationist by contributing a more robust picture of him as a politician, with all that word implies.

MARTIN MEEKER: The San Francisco Human Rights Commission, which was created in '64, was charged with enforcing local antidiscrimination laws in housing and employment dealing primarily with race-based discrimination. In April '72, the Board of Supervisors voted to add sexual orientation to the nondiscrimination ordinance. Do you recall that coming up?

QUENTIN KOPP: No. I don't even know how I voted. Do you know?

MEEKER: No, I don't know. I was going to ask you! [laughter]

KOPP: I'd be interested to know how I voted. [Upon reviewing the transcript, Kopp added the following note: "I did vote for it."]

MEEKER: I'd like to know your perspective on why this legislation was able to be passed?

KOPP: Probably pressure, lobbying from gays—

MEEKER: So who would be lobbying, individuals or groups?

KOPP: Individuals, people I'd become friends with or at least acquaintances who I'd see around City Hall.

MEEKER: Do you remember any of those people?

KOPP: Gosh, I don't now. I remember there's a fellow who had a shoe store on Market, Larry, and I can't remember his name. I don't see him in town now. So that group has become more strident than it was.

MEEKER: Meaning?

KOPP: Well, there are more, and they occupy positions in power throughout San Francisco government. In fact, people argue, and you could argue, that they control power. But these were earnest people, they were active in SIR [Society for Individual Rights, a gay rights organization]. I met Harvey Milk, for example, I think in 1975, because he ran for supervisor and I'd see him on the stump. And I just can't remember the names now.

MEEKER: I found your discussion of Harvey Milk in your previous interview interesting because the way that he's usually written about in literature is more in a heroic sense, right? But you didn't talk about him either as a hero or a villain, but merely as a politician.[1]

KOPP: Oh, he was. He was as good a finagler as you could imagine, and he would devote full-time to finagling. I don't know what the camera shop brought in, although that's become legendary, but he was some finagler! And in '75, he'd get up and make speeches, and he'd say something that wasn't right! And I can remember at least once in the Mission District pulling him aside. I'd say, "Look, that's not correct! Here's what is correct!"

MEEKER: Do you remember what that was about?

KOPP: I don't remember the issue or the problem. I knew he's no threat to me as a candidate, he's not going to come close to finishing number one [in the at-large election for the Board of Supervisors], but he was a good schmoozer. When I think now of what I did in '76 for him, and then I'll bring us up to '77 with him, if that's at all interesting: He ran for the Board of Supervisors in '75, and he wasn't at the tail end. He probably finished around tenth, eleventh. Well, there were six seats up that year, and it went me first, Molinari second, Mendelsohn, I think Ron Pelosi finished fourth, and either Terry François or Bob Gonzalez finished fifth and sixth, respectively. I think Terry finished sixth. But so Harvey finished whatever, eleventh, tenth, and then so he started coming around committee hearings. Well then, oh, George Moscone was elected mayor in 1975, so now it's going to be a liberal sweep, radical sweep, and Moscone appoints Harvey to the Board of Permit Appeals.

MEEKER: That's a choice commission appointment?

KOPP: Yeah, that's a strong commission, because you hear appeals from every-thing, building permits, this, that, the other. So then in '76, George is out of the State Senate, so John Foran is going to run for the State Senate [Moscone's former seat]. And the Burtons [Phil and John] really had nobody for that election, because it picked up a part of San Mateo County already by 1970 in that reapportionment, and I remember there were a couple of people inter-ested. Bill Schumacher was on the Daly City Council, I think he ran. But Foran then vacates his Assembly seat, and Harvey Milk announces he will run for that Assembly seat against Art Agnos. But George Moscone and Leo McCar-thy must have cut a deal like this: okay, John Foran moves to the Senate, and that's what they did, sure, because Agnos was McCarthy's chief of staff. That's what they did, and then Agnos would be elected to the Assembly.

MEEKER: So wait, spell that out for me. What was the deal you think that happened?

KOPP: Well, the deal is this: George Moscone is elected mayor, he then vacates the Senate seat. Foran was in the Assembly. And Foran vacates the Assembly seat, and then Agnos moves into the Assembly. Well, Harvey Milk wants to run for the same Assembly seat and says so. As a result George Moscone an-nounces publicly that if Milk runs for the Assembly, he will be taken off the Board of Permit Appeals as punishment. The appointment term was four years, but it was not a fixed term, you could be yanked at will. So Moscone threatened to yank Milk from the Board of Permit Appeals.

I made a public statement that it's outrageous the mayor would do this—the policy position was that it would be a conflict to have somebody running for office while sitting on this commission. So then Milk files his candidacy for the Assembly, and Moscone promptly fires him, and I promptly endorse Milk against Agnos and helped him.

MEEKER: Then what were the politics, if you will, behind your endorsement of him?

KOPP: It was 50 percent indignation over treating the guy that way, and maybe another 50 percent with Leo McCarthy, because Leo and I were estranged, and that began in his '65 campaign when he lost to Moscone. I lost enthusiasm for that campaign because of Leo's personality, and he never tried to help me po-litically. When I ran in '71, for example, George was by then associated with the Hanson Bridget Law Office, and I went to see George. You try to get everyone's endorsement, and George was friendly, and George had carried a bill to help my father, and I knew George as a young lawyer and he was always a good guy to be with, in North Beach or elsewhere. So here was a deal which Leo had arranged, obviously, with George and the Burtons. So 50 percent of my en-dorsement of Milk was attributable to not part of either. I'm not part of Burton/Moscone/Brown, I'm not part of Leo McCarthy or John Foran, for that matter, and in later years, all of that was mended. But in any event, I endorsed Milk. He

Quentin Kopp (left) campaigning for Harvey Milk during his run for the California State Assembly, with labor leader Jack Goldberg (right), at San Francisco's Wharfside Restaurant, May 8, 1976. *Photograph by McLeod, San Francisco* Examiner *Photographic Collection, the Bancroft Library, University of California, Berkeley*

came close; I was with him election night, for example. He came close to pre-vailing. So then he runs once they get this district election, 1977 in the fall.

MEEKER: Can we hold, pause there for a second? And get you to discuss the 50 percent motivation that was contra-Moscone?

KOPP: Yeah, the Burton machine, it was a collective machine to me.

MEEKER: Well then, there are push and pull factors in everything, and it seems like might there also have been a motivation that Milk represented a new voting constituency in San Francisco and that you were seeking those votes?

KOPP: There might have been, but I don't remember. I remember Leo and I being on the outs. I'd had experience with Agnos. Now I remember him, and Richie Ross, who humiliated me out in the Bayview one night in 1975, and I was car-rying water for Feinstein who was president of the board, and I was chairman of the Health Committee. It was the sewers service project. I remembered Agnos pretty good, and to this day I don't know why Leo ever embraced him, as a friend of mine observed, "A great mistake in judgment."

MEEKER: So with supporting Milk, it was more a case of "the enemy of your enemy is your friend"?

KOPP: Yeah, and then half of it was the principle. Milk shouldn't have been fired. So now we get to district elections in the fall of '77—we didn't pay enough attention to that district election initiative, we being Barbagelata, Feinstein, me, Molinari, so it passed.

MEEKER: Well, it had been on the ballot before and been defeated, yes?

KOPP: Yeah, in '72 it had been on the ballot. In fact, there were three different versions. Voters rejected them all. Ron Pelosi played a part in at least one of them, and so did John Barbagelata and I.

MEEKER: You were opposed to it in '76.

KOPP: Yeah.

MEEKER: Why?

KOPP: Because we knew who was behind it, and who would come with it.

MEEKER: And who was that?

KOPP: The Community Congress, Calvin Welch, Nancy Walker. I can't remember all the names. Jeez, I'll come back to them.

MEEKER: What was the Community Congress?

KOPP: Well, you got to look that up in history. They began meeting around I think '72. Take a look at the *Bay Guardian*'s old files, they covered them. And they came out of that Alvin Duskin movement, anti–downtown development. Sue Hester was in it. I think Arnold Townsend was, too; he's a minister now and has been for a number of years. I think Harvey Milk was part of it. So we knew what it meant, you were going to get radicals on the Board of Supervisors, and we did! We sure did!

MEEKER: Then when he ran in '77, did you endorse him?

KOPP: No, because the only supervisor I ever endorsed was Barbagelata in '73 against Feinstein.

MEEKER: And you must have run again in '77. Everyone had to, right?[2]

KOPP: Yeah, I ran, and I was unopposed, so that's another story. And so I got about 22,000 votes, which was the highest. Everyone else had opponents, including Feinstein, which leads to another story, and she got about 10,000. Dan White got 5,000, and Harvey probably didn't get much more, because there were about five candidates in his district. Terence Hallinan ran, Bob St. Clair ran. I've forgotten who else. Oh, there was a lawyer, a gay lawyer. What was his name? Rick something.

MEEKER: Stokes?

KOPP: Stokes.

MEEKER: He ran, too.

KOPP: Yeah, he ran. So two nights after the 1977 supervisor election, we were up on Grant in North Beach. La Pantera was the restaurant, and they had kind of a street closing. Anyway, I got sick, and I wound up with appendicitis, it got infected, and I was in the hospital almost two weeks. And that's when Feinstein started putting together the votes to be president, even though I'm supposed to be president on the board.[3]

But let's forget that for a minute. She would bug me to come up and visit me, and I didn't want to listen to her. But Harvey came up to the hospital, and I let him, and he was already wheeling and dealing about the president this and that, and who was going to be board president. To shorten the story, John

Barbagelata had an idea that I cut a deal with Feinstein, and he would play on her emotions by saying she'd been rejected by her party twice, '71, '75: "You don't think the Burtons were going to let you be Mayor, do you?" '71, '75: And she had tried in '76 to get a job under [President] Carter. I'd written a three page letter for her. I wonder where that letter is, it must be in the National Archives. Oh, God! [laughter] Feinstein was bereft of any political future, so Barbagelata would play on her emotions so she'd endorse me for mayor against Moscone [in the next election year, 1979], and in the meantime I'd let her be president of the board. While I was in the hospital, and then home another two weeks recuperating, she got this Dan White, if you can believe it, she got him.

MEEKER: How so? What do you mean by that?

KOPP: She got his support. She lined up his vote.

MEEKER: To be president?

KOPP: Yes. So then John Barbagelata gets this meeting after I could get around, with Nelder, François, John, her, and me, and the deal is that she promises to endorse me for mayor in the 1979 election, and I promise to support her to be president of the Board of Supervisors, which probably means bringing in Lee Dolson, Ron Pelosi, and Bob Gonzalez. She'd already pretty much had Molinari. The lefties wouldn't vote for me, meaning Ella Hill Hutch, Harvey Milk, Gordon Lau—

MEEKER: Carol Ruth Silver.

KOPP: Carol Ruth Silver. But the others would. Those who came from the old board would all vote for me, and Lee Dolson would, and Dan White would, too.

MEEKER: What, then, happened between '76 and '77, when you were endorsing Milk, and then '77 when he wouldn't vote for you for president, even though you were the top vote getter?

KOPP: Well, nothing as such happened. Harvey was an operator. I remember I endorsed White. I endorsed two candidates in whatever that district was, because I remember one was a Palestinian, Waddie Ayoob, who I knew from hanging around the old deli out there, just hanging around San Bruno Avenue. So I endorse two or maybe three candidates. There was a woman who I liked who had been around City Hall. And I think I may have endorsed two in another district. But I didn't endorse in Milk's race because Bob St. Clair by then was a friend of mine. There was a woman, I'm trying to think of her name, who was nice. She later ran for treasurer. Clint Reilly put her up to it, and she put herself in hock with the mortgage—thank you, Clint—and lost, got blown out! [laughter] So I endorsed maybe in two, three districts. Anyway, whatever it was, I let Harvey come over to the hospital, and he's talking, he's wheeling and dealing, all that stuff.

Anyway, to bring it on home, Dan White had only one issue. That was to stop Mount St. Joseph's, up there on University Mound in the Portola, from being turned into a home for delinquent children. It was a home for unmarried mothers that the Catholic Church ran [University Mound Ladies Home], but there were fewer and fewer unmarried mothers, right, with birth control and everything. Feinstein promised that day of the vote, the endorsement would be by April first. So now she's the president, and now this Mount St. Joseph issue comes to us.[4] I've forgotten how it got to us, maybe it was a rezoning ordinance of some kind. And, of course, Dan White loses, and Harvey Milk votes no [thus allowing the property to be rezoned in favor of the youth facility]. And Harvey had probably dangled White into thinking he might vote against the rezoning [instead Milk voted for it]. Feinstein voted against it, and I voted against it, and Dan White, maybe Lee Dolson, and that was it. Dan White got wiped out. I remember White came across—he sat on the other side, he came over to my chair, and he says, "You're right, the leopard never changes his spots." Because I told him, "Milk isn't going to vote for this. He can't! He's liberal/radical!" That was Harvey. And then after that, Harvey was always wheeling, dealing with this, that, and the other thing. The pooper-scooper ordinance, which was fine, but who the heck cares? It's not going to change the world, but it got him a lot of press. Oh, he was a shrewdie. He was a shrewdie political wheeler-dealer. The problem was you got a nut on the board. His name is Dan White, and there was always something about him in his eyes. He came down to me in that campaign, and came down to my law office to get my endorsement, and I did eventually endorse him. But there was something that was strange about him. And, of course, I knew people, friends of mine had gone to high school with him—it was predominantly black even then—and he'd get in fights, and he was just crazed. And Barbagelata had the same sensation of him. John was no longer on the board, he'd have nothing to do with district elections, thought he was "off," too. And then, of course, what added to it was White playing footsie with Feinstein. He had no business from a political philosophy standpoint being with her, so it made him suspect, and it caught up with Harvey. That's why he killed him, because Harvey had lied to him, probably, or if he hadn't lied, he'd misled him to such an extent. And then Dan White works up all this. He sees the voting patterns, he sees how Harvey votes, and it caught up with him. I'm not condoning it, in case anybody looks at it, but that's what happened. It's like what happened at Virginia Tech yesterday.[5] You get people who are crazed, right? Who would ever think that someone would bring a gun into City Hall![6]

Commentary

The history of sexuality is regarded by many as an oppositional history, and lesbian, gay, bisexual, and transgender *oral* history even more so. For those among us who conduct interviews with lesbians and gay men, not only do we hear stories of discrimination and resistance but also we *expect* to hear those stories. After all, for a lesbian or gay man to have lived through and even thrived in decades past, especially in the decades before Stonewall, her or his life becomes an act of bravery in itself. And while historians may disagree with some of the opinions or political positions we hear expressed by our interviewees, we tend to see these individuals in a heroic light. This approach has produced many important interviews and a large number of path-breaking works of scholarship. It has enabled historians to uncover long-forgotten forms of resistance among a group of people who appear in the historical record—to the extent that they appear at all—primarily as victims: victims of police raids on bars, purges in the military, and defamation on the newsstand. Yet, this approach of interviewing gay male and lesbian elders in a quest for heroes has produced myths and meta-narratives that, while based in fact and containing truth, provide yet only part of the story.

Oral historians seeking to gain new insights into the history of sexuality are only now on the verge of making the most of this methodology. Oral history can be a powerful tool in moving beyond the static discrimination-resistance para-digm, and much insight can be gained by interviewing across lines of sexuality (that is, gay interviewing straight) and across lines of political ideas and policy positions. For instance, the interview I conducted with San Francisco politician Quentin Kopp in 2007 explores a number of issues related to the formation of a gay and lesbian political bloc between the 1960s and 1980s. Kopp's responses not only add important factual information to the well-rehearsed narrative of gay political achievement but also force a reconsideration of some of the most foun-dational mythologies of the gay movement in San Francisco. In one particularly revealing exchange, Kopp paints a fascinating portrait of Harvey Milk as a hard-nosed politician adept at the art of horse-trading and quite the opposite of the dominant image of Milk as a grassroots activist solely concerned with giving his people hope.

My interview with Kopp was conducted over two consecutive days in the spring of 2007 and took place in the judicial chambers of the San Mateo County Courthouse, where Kopp has served as a judge since 1999. The interview ran for about four hours, and the finished transcript was nearly 25,000 words; the por-tion of the transcript included here is not quite 3,000 words. The interview was conducted as part of an ongoing, albeit intermittent, interview-based research project on the development of minority-based politics and political constitu-encies in San Francisco between the 1960s and 1990s. The project began with a series of eight interviews examining the history of the San Francisco Human Rights Commission (HRC).

Founded at the height of liberal civil rights activism in 1964, the HRC was the city commission charged with enforcing municipal fair employment and housing ordinances. The commission initially addressed the problem of black-white inequality in the city, but its work soon expanded to become the site at which groups seeking protection from discrimination would go to have their voices heard. These meetings witnessed some of the first proposals for antidiscrimination legislation in the United States designed to protect homosexuals. In conducting interviews with former commissioners and staff members, it became obvious that it was impossible to examine the work of the HRC in isolation from social movement activists, politicians, and bureaucrats. After all, it was often the activists who brought new or persistent issues before the commission, bureaucrats who administered the public policy implications, and politicians who engineered the city's response, or lack thereof, to the problems raised. So, I began to widen my net and seek interviews with others active in San Francisco's civic sphere.

Because I was particularly interested in the 1972 inclusion of sexual orientation as a protected category in San Francisco's municipal administrative code (under the same chapter that created the HRC), I sought to interview the politicians who carried that legislation to passage: Terry François and Quentin Kopp, then both members of the city Board of Supervisors. François had died in 1989, never having been interviewed on the subject. Kopp, on the other hand, was still alive and already the subject of a long and substantive life history interview conducted by the California State Archives, which nevertheless did not touch on this particular topic.[7] I resolved to interview Kopp about it. But Kopp is a complex historical figure, and my desire to interview him hinged not only on his role as a gay rights pioneer but also on my prior knowledge that he was widely reviled by San Francisco's gay community because of his reputation as an anti-gay conservative.[8] Kopp, then, seemed to me a key and necessary witness to the transformation of politics not because he was another gay hero but because he probably had lost rather than gained status as result of the ascendancy of a gay power bloc in San Francisco. In a 2001 interview, Kopp acknowledged as much: "I was running for reelection to the board of supervisors [in 1984]. That was the most disappointing election of my career, because not only didn't I run number one . . .but I ran number three. . . . I'd put a lot into it, campaigned hard, but the demographics of the city were ever changing. I made a couple of utterances to the press that were used against me, one on the gay parade for a reporter with the *New York Times*."[9] In my interview with Kopp six years later, he was more pointed in explaining his declining political fortunes: "[Gays] occupy positions in power throughout San Francisco government. In fact, people argue, and you could argue, that they control power." Despite his advocacy of gay rights early in his career, then, Kopp might be expected to provide a fresh, idiosyncratic view of gay politics that a politician or bureaucrat who gained power in the context of gay political achievements from the 1970s onward would not offer.

Quentin Kopp was born in Syracuse, New York, in 1928 to a middle-class Jewish family: his father owned a drugstore, and his mother was a homemaker. After attending Cornell as an undergraduate and then Harvard Law School, Kopp moved to California by late 1955 to start his career as an attorney. Like many young lawyers seeking to establish themselves and build connections among local politicians and businessmen, Kopp began to participate in local politics. The first campaign on which he worked was the successful run by Democrat Stanley Mosk for California attorney general in 1958, a historic election in which Democrats swept candidates into most statewide offices, including governor (Edmund Brown). Democrats also won majorities in both houses of the state legislature for the first time since 1891.

Many today view the 1958 election as a turning point in California politics that established the Democrats as the party of urban liberals, while the Republicans became identified with suburban conservatives.[10] But the rise of a newly powerful Democratic party in California also brought about a new generation of leaders who nurtured competing power bases that subscribed to sometimes wildly different political positions. In San Francisco, for example, a generational and ideological battle was being waged between those Kopp described as "conservative," former New Deal Democrats and the upstart liberal politicos who gathered around Phil Burton, a towering figure in San Francisco politics first elected to the California Assembly in 1956. Kopp's place in this knotty mix of personalities, allegiances, and positions was complicated. In San Francisco, Kopp never fit within the Burton camp, and, after the 1958 election, he banded together with a small group of what might be called moderate Democrats, including, among others, Ron Pelosi, Leo McCarthy, Eugene McAteer, and John Foran. This group quickly established itself as the alternative to the more liberal wing of the party that coalesced around Burton. In Democratic primary after primary, Kopp's group squared off against "the Burton machine," and they split victories: George Moscone emerged victorious in 1966 in his state senate campaign against Leo McCarthy, but then Leo McCarthy beat out a Burton-sponsored candidate in 1968 for a seat in the California Assembly. By 1968, however, Kopp was estranged from both the Burton and McCarthy camps and thus started to blaze his own path.

During the 1960s, Quentin Kopp was a bit player in San Francisco's political contests, but he ran successfully for election to the Board of Supervisors in 1971. He won a seat in that body but with something less than a clear mandate: he came in sixth in an election in which the six top vote getters won seats on the board. Shortly into his first term as supervisor, in spring 1972, Kopp did something that in retrospect appears surprising. He cosponsored legislation to add sex and sexual orientation to the city's antidiscrimination ordinance. And this is where the section of the interview transcript included here begins. During Kopp's tenure on the Board of Supervisors, through 1986, he was one of its most prominent and visible members; he also was rightly regarded as one of the more conservative yet idiosyncratic members. In his 1975 reelection bid, Kopp garnered the most votes and thus, by tradition, was elected president of the Board of Supervisors. He then opposed the movement by neighborhood activists to switch supervisor elections from citywide and at-large to district elections; he and his colleagues won the first referendum on this, but lost when it came up again in 1976, thus paving the way for Board of Supervisors district elections in

1977. The 1977 elections ushered in a new group of supervisors, including Harvey Milk and Dan White, Milk's future assassin, who were more attuned to neighborhood interests.

The 1977 supervisory election was important for reasons other than, but still related to, the election of Milk and White. With the beginning of district elections in the city, all eleven city supervisors would have to stand for election in 1977.[11] Many of the veteran supervisors decided not to run again in 1977, given the changed circumstances, but Kopp was not among them. Instead, he was the sole candidate in the 1977 election who ran unopposed in his district, thus he garnered nearly twice as many votes as the next nearest district victor, Dianne Feinstein. Tradition, but not law, provided that the candidate who received the largest number of votes would be elected board president. But with the election of many first-time candidates who were selected on the basis of neighborhood commitments rather than long-nurtured political connections, the rules of the game had apparently changed. Kopp explained that after some election night joviality he was rushed to the hospital for abdominal pain. It turned out he had appendicitis, which put him out of commission for several days. Just as he was recovering and planning his return to the field and postelection maneuvering, he came down with a postoperation infection and thus needed additional surgery. By the time he finally was released from the hospital, it became clear that others were positioning themselves to be elected board president, chief among them Dianne Feinstein and Gordon Lau.

As a result of an oft-repeated but little-documented political compromise, Kopp opted out of the competition for the board presidency and instead supported his sometime rival Feinstein. According to Kopp, he approached Feinstein with an offer: in exchange for his support of Feinstein's run for board president, Feinstein would agree to not run for mayor in 1979 (she had previously run in 1975) and instead support Kopp in his bid for mayor in that election. If the deal in fact happened, it is one that would come to haunt Kopp for the remainder of his career in politics, for it probably marked both the high-water mark in his political influence and the moment at which his fortunes began to recede. What transpired over the next two years not only pushed Kopp to the margins politically but also forever changed the landscape of politics in San Francisco—and affected politics nationwide.

Early in the first terms of Harvey Milk and Dan White, a zoning question came before the Board of Supervisors that was a key item on White's agenda. According to oral accounts, Milk apparently hedged his bets and left White with the impression that he would vote along with White. But when the question came up for a vote, Milk voted with the majority in favor of rezoning, thus voting against White. Shortly thereafter, White resigned his seat on the board. The mayor accepted his resignation, but ten days later White, feeling pressure from those who elected him in the first place, sought to rescind his resignation. After some consideration, the mayor refused, and White was out. Almost immediately, White returned to City Hall, but this time to exact revenge on the two officials he felt had wronged him: Mayor Moscone and Supervisor Milk. Using a revolver, which he reloaded several times, White assassinated each man in his office, then escaped. Later that evening, on the steps of City Hall, Supervisor Feinstein announced to the world that the mayor and the supervisor had been killed and that the chief suspect was White. Precisely one week later, Feinstein was named mayor of San Francisco by vote of the Board of Supervisors.[12]

In the face of two political assassinations, an account of the fate of a single politician's career may seem irrelevant and insensitive, but the impact of these events on Kopp and the constituency he represented was important. With Feinstein's ascension to the mayoralty in late 1978, she became well positioned to run for that office in the upcoming 1979 election. But if Kopp is to be believed, Feinstein already had agreed not to run for mayor that year and to, instead, endorse Kopp. Tragic circumstances had changed that arrangement, though, and besides, backroom deals were necessarily unofficial and unenforceable, even if they were the lifeblood of city politics. So, while Kopp ran a vigorous campaign for mayor in 1979, he finished second to Feinstein, who went on to become the longest serving mayor in the city's history before moving to the national stage with her election to the U.S. Senate in 1992.[13]

Much of Quentin Kopp's political biography can be gleaned from published sources. While I was certainly interested in learning more about what Kopp thought were memorable aspects of his political life, then, I sought him out for a different purpose: I wanted to interview him because he seemed to me the San Francisco politician who lost the most with the rise of a gay political constituency in the city. I hoped to discover through the interview if Kopp concurred with this notion. I wanted to capture his explanation for these changes, and I looked to gain insight into the career of a politician who went from a supporter of gay rights in 1972 to, within a few years, a figure reviled by the very gay community who benefited from his legislation.

Given Kopp's complex historical relationship with the gay community, I presented my project to him in the broadest frame possible while still being true to my research goals. I invited him to participate in a project on politics in San Francisco history that would "focus on the politics of minority group political constituencies and their influence upon policies, appointments, and elections from the middle 1960s into the 1990s." I also told him that I had read his long interview conducted under the auspices of the California State Archive and that I wanted to ask in-depth follow-up questions and to raise a few issues not covered in that interview. In all of these goals, I was honest and forthcoming. I did, however, omit a few things. I did not mention that my main research interest was in the development of gay political constituencies, that most of my publications are in the field of gay and lesbian history, and that I myself am gay. I had no interest in deceiving someone who generously donated time and energy to my project, but I also felt that if I communicated all the details I may have primed Kopp to respond in a certain manner. In particular, I was afraid that if he knew more about me or my research agenda, he might bow to social convention and provide banal or polite answers to questions about the gay electorate—or perhaps answer no questions at all. Instead, I wanted Kopp to be frank, to be the independent voice for which he has become so well known. Of course, Kopp could have easily searched my name on the Internet, had he thought my background or specific interests relevant to the interview—and while I suspect that he did nothing of the sort, I cannot tell for sure. In interviewing Kopp about the rise of the gay electorate, I wanted to present myself as nothing more than the inquisitive historian, interested in the arcane people and events of California's political history. And while I make no claims that I got the "truth" out of Kopp, I do think that he provided an interesting and provocative outsider's perspective on the emergence of gay politics in the 1970s.

I did not bring up the question of the gay electorate until near the end of the second hour of the interview.[14] And I eased our way into the topic, asking him about civil rights activism and the creation of the San Francisco Human Rights Commission. I pointed out that the work of the commission started to change in the early 1970s when sexual orientation was included as a protected category. And while he did not recall how he voted during the course of the interview, he spoke about San Francisco's gay community as yet another minority political constituency. Kopp noted that prior to running for supervisor, he spoke on behalf on another candidate before the Society for Individual Rights (SIR), San Francisco's largest gay organization in the second half of the 1960s. In this and other sections of the interview, he showed that he did not much like these meetings, which he claimed were attended by people who tended to denounce the speaker, if they were not outright "fanatics." But Kopp also emphasized how attending the meetings of political clubs and other organizations was a key way in which candidates could reach out to self-defined political constituencies and attempt to communicate ideas to which the assembled would be especially receptive.

Appealing to political constituencies was certainly one way in which Kopp and his colleagues gained access to elected office. But time and again, Kopp returned to the power of personal and political relationships in explaining the chances at success or failure for a politician or a piece of legislation. Accounts of the centrality of personal relationships to politics are especially plentiful in oral history interviews. The scores of interviews on California politics at the University of California at Berkeley's Regional Oral History Office provide just one collection of this type. In the complete transcript of my interview with Kopp, stories of backroom deals to earn endorsements or to sabotage an opponent's campaign are abundant. Kopp explains that it was largely due to personal relationships with gay activists, including SIR leader Larry Littlejohn, that inspired him to carry the city's first gay rights legislation. But in the excerpt included here, the most interesting account of politics and personal relationships comes by way of San Francisco Supervisor Harvey Milk.

According to Kopp, Milk's adeptness at deal making and finagling was the source both of his success and his ultimate demise. The picture that Kopp painted of Milk was profoundly unlike the image of martyr, saint, and hero that he gained since his death. It was also substantially different from his reputation as a grassroots gay activist who, in his most famous speech, implored, "You got to give them hope!"[15] Kopp, in contrast, talked of Milk's career as a political narrative, and most certainly not as a story of a prophet or a savior or even a gutsy gay activist. To Kopp, Milk was first and foremost a politician, and not much more: he was a politician "on the stump," a "finagler," a "schemer," a "schmoozer," an "operator," and a "shrewdie." One might quickly dismiss these characterizations as homophobic or slanderous or, more likely, as easily discounted because they came from the mouth of Quentin Kopp, a man described more than once as a curmudgeon. And indeed, these are probably accurate ways to label Kopp's speech.

But I believe that historians of sexuality, and of gay and lesbian history in particular, can gain a great deal by paying closer attention to the words of politicians like Kopp, for they provide an added and I think necessary dimension to understandings of how homosexuals went from a despised group bereft of any political power in the 1960s to a group that gained civil protections against discrimination and elected its own representatives to public office in the 1970s. Much of the current literature on this transformation emphasizes the role of grassroots activists and social movement organizations.[16] And while activism, street protests, and the gay movement played an undeniable role in the process, those forces alone cannot explain the massive transformations that occurred. Personal relationships, political endorsements, backroom deal making, and, indeed, finagling were instrumental in bringing about the successes of the gay movement in the 1970s.

Perhaps the most instructive anecdote delivered by Kopp on this account addresses his endorsement of Milk in his unsuccessful 1976 run for the California State Assembly. In 1976, Kopp was the president of the Board of Supervisors and thus one of the most prominent politicians in the city. He also was regarded as an independent voice who appealed to diverse segments of the electorate, including homeowners, civil libertarians, and the sizable minority of San Franciscans who disliked and distrusted the Burton political machine. Short of an endorsement by a leader of that machine, an endorsement by its chief adversary provided Milk with the best chance to win the Democratic primary and thus the general election in this heavily Democratic district. But as Kopp makes clear in my interview with him, his endorsement of Milk had very little, if anything, to do with his support of Milk the man or his political agenda. Kopp explained the conditions under which he made his decision:

George [Moscone] is elected mayor [in 1975], he then vacates his [State] Senate seat. [John] Foran was in the Assembly. And Foran vacates the Assembly seat [to run for Moscone's senate seat], and then Agnos [seeks election] to the Assembly. Well, Harvey Milk wants to run for the same Assembly seat and says so. [As a result] George Moscone announces publicly that if Milk runs for the Assembly, he will be taken off the Board of Permit Appeals [as punishment, because Moscone and Agnos were both part of the Burton political machine]. . . . So [Moscone] threatened to yank him [Milk from the Board of Permit Appeals]. I made a public statement that it's outrageous the Mayor would do this. . . . So then he [Milk] does file his candidacy for the Assembly, and Moscone promptly fires him, and I promptly endorse him [Milk] against Agnos and helped him.[17]

When asked why he ultimately decided to go with Milk, Kopp responded, "It was 50 percent indignation over treating the guy that way, and maybe another 50 percent with Leo [McCarthy], because Leo and I were estranged." I then asked him if his endorsement was a case of "the enemy of your enemy is your friend," and he replied, "Yeah, and then half of it was the principle. [Milk] shouldn't have been fired [by Moscone]." Kopp added, "I was with him election night, for example. He came close to prevailing." Although Milk did not win this election, he garnered a substantial portion of the votes cast, as Kopp claimed, and thus established himself as a legitimate political contender, whereas in his previous runs for office in 1973 and 1975, he was considered marginal. This new legitimacy, combined with the transition to district elections in the 1977 supervisory race, translated into Milk's first, and only, victory.

Kopp's account of Milk is a necessary but heretofore absent element of the larger story about the emergence of a gay electorate in the United States. Kopp's anecdotes point to the fact that it took someone, Milk in this case, to actually do the work of schmoozing, finagling, and scheming as a politician within the established political order to firmly establish the fact of gay politicians and political constituencies. In this revised, political narrative of Milk and his career, we find a man who is motivated by the creation and maintenance of political connections—and who was willing to make deals and trade endorsements with San Francisco conservatives Quentin Kopp and John Barbagelata This transcript also provides insight into the character of Kopp and goes some distance to explain why a conservative Democrat carried one of the nation's first gay rights ordinances and became an early supporter of Harvey Milk. But in a larger sense, the interview sheds light on how gay rights legislation and gay politicians made it onto the urban political agenda in the early 1970s and on how forging personal and political relationships was a key—indeed, necessary—factor in casting such laws and electing such individuals.

Methodologically, as a historian approaching Kopp revealing general (i.e., nongay) rather than specific (i.e., gay) interests facilitated the kind of frank exchange of ideas that in fact transpired. But this is not to say that I consider this interview or even this slightly furtive, anonymous approach without pitfalls of its own. In reviewing the transcript, I was disappointed to discover so many instances when I failed to ask key follow-up questions or directly probe the reasoning behind some of Kopp's more curious or outlandish statements. I attribute this partly to the fact that I consider myself merely a student in the field of San Francisco political history and was not precisely attuned to everything Kopp said that ran counter to established narratives. But I must also admit that I feared pushing the question of gay politics too hard out of concern that I would be seen as an advocate or activist—again, I worried that he might become less than candid or flatly uncooperative. With Quentin Kopp, this particular interview strategy paid off.

By bringing the study of gay politics out of the exclusive realm of social movements, gay and lesbian oral historians gain crucial analytic insights. Because oral historians engage with living history makers, they create new opportunities to view gay political leaders as complex figures, even to the extent of seeing them as something that many gays have not allowed them to be: *politicians*—those who work within the state power structure in the arts of compromise, deal making, patronage, and constituent creation and appeasement. Moreover, just as queer theorists claim that outsiderness is conducive to making important critical insights into the history of gender and sexuality, those, such as Quentin Kopp, who look from the outside at queer history can offer productively disruptive insights into queer history as well. Thus, by interviewing individuals who might not confirm our well-established heroic narratives—figures who may sit well outside our personal comfort zone or political orbit—queer oral historians become better situated to push the boundaries of historical discourse beyond those metanarratives that have become comforting in their power to confirm a surety of right and wrong, just and unjust, liberal and conservative.

Notes

1. In a separate interview conducted in 2001, Kopp suggests that Harvey Milk attempted to make a deal with mayoral candidate John Barbagelata in which, it was presumed, Milk would offer his endorsement of Barbagelata against George Moscone in the mayoral runoff in exchange for an unspecified commission appointment. According to Kopp, Barbagelata rebuffed Milk's overtures. Whether accurate or not, this assertion that Milk would enter into a pact with archconservative (at least in San Francisco) Barbagelata provides a counterpoint to images of Milk as a grassroots activists or a martyr to the cause. See Quentin Kopp interviewed by Donald Seney (California State Archives, State Government Oral History Program, 2001), 200.

2. With the passage of district elections for the Board of Supervisors in 1976, one result was that every seat of the board was declared vacant, so incumbents were forced to run again but this time specifically in the district in which they resided.

3. By tradition, the supervisory candidate who received the most votes in the election would be named president of the board by his or her colleagues on the board.

4. To clarify, Kopp here argues that Feinstein was able to garner Dan White's vote for her board presidency bid in exchange for her support of White's effort to block the rezoning necessary to establish the youth facility in his district.

5. This interview was conducted on April 16, 2007, one day after an emotionally disturbed student shot students and faculty at Virginia Tech University.

6. Quentin Kopp interviewed by Martin Meeker, Regional Oral History Office, Bancroft Library, UC Berkeley, April 17, 2007.

7. See Quentin Kopp interviewed by Donald Seney, California State Archives, State Government Oral History Program, 2001.

8. Gay activists point to Kopp's 1980 quip about lesbian activists Del Martin and Phyllis Lyon as evidence of his homophobia On the occasion of their thirtieth anniversary, the Board of Supervisors voted on a commendation for the women, but when it was Kopp's turn to vote, he voted no, adding, "Toleration: yes; glorification: no." Quentin Kopp interviewed by Donald Seney, California State Archives, State Government Oral History Program, 2001.

9. Ibid.

10. On the 1958 election, see John Jacobs, *A Rage for Justice: The Passion and Politics of Phillip Burton* (Berkeley: University of California Press, 1995).

11. Previously supervisors were elected citywide in odd years, each for four-year terms; for example, in 1971, six supervisors were elected; in 1973, five were elected.

12. On the events leading up to the assassinations and the murders specifically, see Randy Shilts, *The Mayor of Castro Street: The Life and Times of Harvey Milk* (New York: St. Martin's, 1982).

13. Throughout the 1970s, while still a registered Democrat, Kopp inched to the right of the political spectrum in San Francisco. Although he detested Nixon and never voted for Reagan, he also fought against school desegregation busing programs and supported California's Proposition 13 "tax revolt" initiative in 1978, which is credited with keeping property taxes low in the state and condemned for defunding public schools. But in liberal San Francisco, Kopp's rightward drift did not play so well. After losing to Feinstein in 1979, Kopp was reelected to the board again in 1980, when the city dispensed with district elections in large part due to the tragedy of White's murder of Moscone and Milk, which many saw as attributable in some way by the excesses of community-based politics. In the 1984 supervisor election, Kopp's fortunes sank lower, as he came in third in a field of six elected to the board. Realizing that he was becoming unelectable on a citywide scale in San Francisco, Kopp resolved to run for the California State Senate in a district that included the more conservative western edge of the city but also bedroom communities to the south in San Mateo County. By the time he was elected to this office in 1986, he had left the Democratic Party and registered "independent," but he largely steered clear of hot-button social issues and instead became an expert in transportation and an advocate of high-speed rail in the state. He served in the State Senate as an independent until 1998.

14. The entire transcript is available at: www.lib.berkeley.edu/cgi-bin/roho_disclaimer_cgi.pl?target=http://digitalassets.lib.berkeley.edu/roho/ucb/text/kopp_quentin.pdf.

15. On Milk, see Shilts, *The Mayor of Castro Street*; also see Rob Epstein, dir., *The Times of Harvey Milk* (1985).

16. For examples of literature that emphasizes the power of social movement organizations and grassroots activists, including those associated with the bar culture, see Nan Alamilla Boyd, *Wide Open Town: A History of Queer San Francisco to 1965* (Berkeley: University of California Press, 2005); John D'Emilio, *Sexual Politics, Sexual Communities: The Making of a Homosexual Minority in the United States, 1940–1970* (Chicago: University of Chicago Press, 1983); Marcia Gallo, *Different Daughters: A History of the Daughters of Bilitis and the Rise of the Lesbian Rights Movement* (New York: Carroll and Graf, 2006); and Martin Meeker, *Contacts Desired: Gay and Lesbian Communications and Community, 1940s–1970s* (Chicago: University of Chicago Press, 2006).

17. Quentin Kopp interviewed by Martin Meeker, Regional Oral History Office, Bancroft Library, UC Berkeley, April 17, 2007.

13

DON'T ASK

Discussing Sexuality in the American Military and the Media

Steve Estes

Oral history by Steve Estes with Brian Hughes, Washington, D.C., January 25, 2005

This interview with Brian Hughes, an American veteran of the wars in Afghanistan and Iraq, was part of the Veterans History Project run by the Library of Congress. As a historian at Sonoma State University in northern California, I conducted the interview with Hughes over the phone. At the time of the interview, Hughes had recently completed four years of service in the U.S. Army (2000–2004), and he was living in Washington, D.C., where he worked as an intern on Capitol Hill. The Hughes interview was one of more than fifty interviews that I conducted with gay and lesbian veterans who served from World War II to the wars in Afghanistan and Iraq. These interviews ultimately were published in the book Ask & Tell: Gay and Lesbian Veterans Speak Out *(University of North Carolina Press, 2007).*[1]

STEVE ESTES: I'm going to start with a question I asked you a second ago; that is, when and where were you born?

BRIAN HUGHES: Born in San Francisco, California, on the second of June, 1978.

ESTES: Okay, and what did your parents do for a living?

HUGHES: My father runs a company for private hospitals in England: psychiatric clinics and drug rehab.

ESTES: Is your mom alive?

HUGHES: She is. She does not work, currently.

ESTES: Why did you decide to go to Yale for college?

HUGHES: Yale accepted me.

ESTES: [chuckles] That's a good answer.

HUGHES: And when I visited the campus, that's when I realized that this was really the place I wanted to go. So, it was a good fit for both of us.

ESTES: What did you major in there?

HUGHES: My major was math and philosophy.

ESTES: Can you talk about your first couple of years there? What it was like?

HUGHES: Well, when you get there—it was a great time. I got there in—'96? Would it have been? Yeah, sure, the fall of '96. I guess I first came out the Christmas of '96, back home, in California, and when I came back to the campus, I came out to my friends. So I'd been openly gay for over three years— three and a half years, before I enlisted in the army.

ESTES: How did your parents react to you coming out?

HUGHES: They took it very well; they are very open-minded folks. I came out through my sister, and it was really very easy. The whole family is really very accepting.

ESTES: Did you actually grow up in San Francisco proper?

HUGHES: No, I grew up in London. At the age of two, when I was two, 1980, we moved to London, and so I grew up there and lived there for sixteen years before coming back to college in the states.

ESTES: How do you think growing up in London affected you?

HUGHES: It's a fantastic place to grow up. Traveling all around Europe is like driving to Florida from D.C. You drive eight hours and you're in Italy. It was wonderful.

ESTES: Let me see—why did you decide to join the army after being at Yale for three and a half years or so?

HUGHES: Right, I dropped out towards the end of my senior year to enlist. There were a combination of factors. I wasn't ready to graduate in some sense. I felt that I needed some sort of practical, real-world experience before I actually went out into the real world. I felt that I needed the mental and physical discipline that I would get in the army, as well as, you know—I knew it would be very immediately rewarding. I knew I would be doing something worthwhile. The call of duty was also strong in that sense. I felt that military service was one of the duties of citizenship, and something I had to do. As to why I chose to do it before graduating rather than after graduating, because for all the earlier reasons I listed, I wanted to do my time as an enlisted man rather than as an officer, and if I had a degree, I felt the temptation would be too strong to go to OCS [Officer Candidate School] and get a commission.

ESTES: Why enlisted?

HUGHES: I felt the work would be more interesting and better and more physical. I sort of needed a break from more intellectual pursuits and wanted to get down and get my hands dirty.

ESTES: Gotcha. How did your family and friends react to you joining the military?

HUGHES: They were very upset. My family in particular was very upset, probably because we don't really have much of a history of military service in our family; you have to go back to World War II to find folks who served. Partly, also, because I'm gay and they felt that the army was not really a friendly place for gay people. The murder of Barry Winchell was just a year or two before,

After serving in Afghanistan and Iraq as an Army Ranger, Brian Hughes put down his gun and wielded his story in the battle to repeal the "Don't Ask, Don't Tell" policy. *Courtesy of Steve Estes*

and still very much a part of the public consciousness.[2] My friends were also surprised, but less so because I was right there on the scene to be able to explain what I was doing, whereas my parents found out long-distance.

[We spoke about Brian's decision to enlist as an army ranger and the rigors of ranger school. He was completing this training in September of 2001.]

ESTES: Can you talk about—take me to that morning when you heard about the attacks on the World Trade Center and the Pentagon.

HUGHES: Yeah, we were in an airplane hangar on our way to a training mission with a foreign nation: we were going to do a joint mission. We stopped over in an air hangar, and our first sergeant gathered us together and said, "All right, guys, terrorists have crashed two planes into the World Trade Center. The buildings have collapsed. We think they were Islamic terrorists." We didn't believe him, of course. We thought, "Oh, okay, this is part of the training scenario. Instead of going where we were going, now we're going to go somewhere in the Middle East and train with Israeli forces or something." [laughter] But then we rigged some radios together, and we got the BBC World Service, and we figured out that in fact, yeah, [laughs] the World Trade Center had been hit. So we were stuck there, where we were, for a week or so, until we could get back home. So then, we just carried on training, as usual, because we knew that within a short amount of time, we would be deploying some where, for something. Sure enough, before the end of the year, a contingent of rangers was in Afghanistan.

ESTES: Right. Tell me about when you first learned you were going to Afghanistan: what went through your head?

HUGHES: Well my first tour to Afghanistan—although rangers started going in '01 at the beginning of the war—my first tour was just after I graduated ranger school in '02. I went September through December–January of '02. By that time, it was my turn [laughs] to fly to Afghanistan. So I felt very ready to go, because I had just gotten through ranger school, and I knew exactly what I was and wasn't capable of. I felt very well prepared, and I was going with a great team, with a great platoon, with a great group of soldiers. I wouldn't say I was exactly looking forward to what I was going to do, but I was ready for it.

ESTES: What were your first impressions of Afghanistan and its people?

HUGHES: Let's see. [thinks for a bit] There's a certain desertness to the area of Afghanistan where I was. Water is a scarce resource there, and up in the mountains, they have these very complex irrigation systems that they've built, to drive their farms. Yeah, it was surprisingly barren. I thought it would be a little more fertile. Bagram [Air Base] in particular was very depressing. It's a great big plateau, actually quite beautiful, until you realize why it's such a completely empty plateau, and it's because most of the area has not yet been cleared of mines. There are mines just everywhere, land mines all over the place, and you just can't walk out of designated areas. So that made a strong impression on me I think.

ESTES: And the people: did you get to know any of the people there?

HUGHES: Well, there was a strong language barrier obviously. They're very hardy, with a *d*, people. They have a very strong sense of themselves and what they accomplished in the Soviet war. Every little village that we drove through there had, in the town center, a burned-out, rusted-out old Soviet tank that they had dragged in as sort of the monument in every village square. I think that's quite telling.

ESTES: Can you describe—you might only be able to do this in general terms, and that's fine—can you describe search patrols that you had to go on when you were in Afghanistan?

HUGHES: Most of our patrols—well no, we did both mounted and unmounted patrols. So we would walk through the mountains, and we would also go on HMMV patrols along sort of major routes, and some minor routes [chuckles] [. . .]

ESTES: *Really* minor?

HUGHES: Well, the concept of road out there is an interesting one.

ESTES: [Chuckles] Right.

HUGHES: So, yeah. We were conducting mounted and dismounted patrols in search of men, weapons, and equipment. In other words, looking for terrorists and munitions, which we found.

ESTES: Both?

HUGHES: Yeah, all kinds of things.

ESTES: Uh huh. Did you ever take fire?

HUGHES: Yes. We were shot at. Our base camp was mortared and shot at with rockets from time to time. And then, our patrols would also take fire from time to time.

[Because Brian was unwilling or unable (for security reasons) to tell me many specifics about his missions in Afghanistan, we quickly moved on to his time in Iraq.]

HUGHES: We might have staged late February [2003], but certainly we were there in March. My first incursion into Iraq was actually the night of April first, for the Jessica Lynch rescue.[3] We staged in Nasiriyah like the day before. It was tremendously quick, though. Between the staging, planning, and executing our mission, all within twenty-four hours of my chain of command being alerted.

ESTES: Well, okay, give me the blow by blow that you give everybody on the Lynch rescue mission, and then we'll talk.

HUGHES: Sure. I was a member of the special operations task force that rescued Private Jessica Lynch. Specifically, I was a member of the team that was detailed to retrieve the other nine Americans from the site.

ESTES: Okay. And the other nine Americans were alive?

HUGHES: No.

ESTES: That's what I thought. Okay, so—and you knew this going in?

HUGHES: Uh, yeah, we thought they were in the morgue, though. It turned out they were in shallow graves just outside the compound. . . . We did what we had to do. . . . I will say this: it was an amazing display of teamwork. Everyone pulled together and did exactly what they were comfortable with, and got the job done in a tremendously short amount of time. We were on schedule. We got out on schedule, despite having to dig up the Americans instead of retrieving them from the morgue.

ESTES: Right. Now, there's been a lot of media critique of that: of the Lynch rescue and how it was portrayed immediately afterwards. Do you have any comment on that or any thoughts about it?

HUGHES: Yeah, well, we were sort of distanced from that, because we were still in Iraq for several months while all these reports were coming out. I understand, though, that there were reports that we were carrying blank ammunition and that the whole thing was staged. I can't really speak for any of the other units that were involved, but you know, we were shot at, and when you think of the fact that we were running short of cargo space coming over from the States to supply us with water, it seems very unlikely to me that there were any blank rounds in Iraq at all, let alone blank rounds taken on a combat mission behind enemy lines. So I—yeah, I have serious reservations about those reports.

[Laughter]

ESTES: Okay.

    [Laughter]

HUGHES: I was carrying live ammunition.

ESTES: All right. [Laughter] And running from live ammunition it sounds like. . . . What was the rest of your service in Iraq—your tour like?

HUGHES: Then, after Nasiriyah, I moved up to Baghdad and conducted patrols out of Baghdad International Airport. Again, these were all mounted patrols, and we were doing a variety of search missions: again, men, weapons, and equipment mostly. So, you know, we found, again, plenty of all of those.

ESTES: Okay. Um, let me see. [pauses] What was the morale like amongst the troops in your unit, when you served in Iraq?

HUGHES: Great. Morale was great. We were an elite, special operations unit, with everything that entails: all the camaraderie, all the high morale, and all the high proficiency. So yeah, it was a great group of guys—great group of guys.

ESTES: Can you talk about friendships—I mean, you don't need to talk about individual soldiers by name, or anything like that, unless you wanted to—but can you talk about friendships that were forged?

HUGHES: Yeah, they are going to last a lifetime. That's the nature of the beast, you know. Shakespeare was not wrong when he talked about a band of brothers, and we're not wrong to keep it in the cliché of the language of today. It's true. The men you fight with under those conditions are your brothers, and nothing can ever change that.

ESTES: Can you talk a little bit about how "Don't Ask, Don't Tell" affected you— or what it was like serving under "Don't Ask, Don't Tell" before you were on tour—on a tour of duty in Afghanistan or Iraq; I mean when you were back in the States?

HUGHES: Uh huh. Well, I was back in the States frequently between tours also. I don't know, I was [pause] serving as a soldier and I was closeted and [pause] I don't know what exactly it is you want me to say. [laughter]

ESTES: I don't have anything I want you to say. I just wanted to give you a chance to talk about "Don't Ask, Don't Tell" and what you think about it.

HUGHES: Okay. Well I would say then that, you know, I knew what I was get- ting into beforehand, because I was openly gay when I enlisted, and I knew I would have to stay in the closet if I wanted to keep my job, and I found that I did in fact want to keep my job. It was something that I loved doing, and it was something I felt I ought to do, and those things didn't change over the four years of my enlistment. So I never really wanted to come out in that sense, because I wanted to keep my job. On the other hand, because of the close friendships that I was forming, I did want to come out to my friends, to my brothers, because—[has trouble finding the right words] ironically enough, the closer we got, the more I felt that was a wedge between us, that there was this large aspect of my life I wasn't sharing with them, and that was preventing me from bonding as fully and as effectively as I could have with them. Um, so after a couple of years I started to feel a little isolated by my homosexuality, and by the fact that I couldn't talk about it, that I couldn't share that aspect of my life with these guys. So I became more and more withdrawn, more and more antisocial in a lot of ways, and that was unfortunate, I think. I would have had a much fuller experience in the army if I had been allowed to serve openly, and as a result, I might have even been a more effective soldier. I don't know, but certainly in terms of unit cohesion, I would have experienced more unit cohesion had I come out, not less. . . .

[We spoke about Brian's second tour in Afghanistan and his promotion to sergeant. After Brian left the army in 2004, he decided to come out publicly as a gay veteran.]

ESTES: Ok, cool. So let's fast-forward a little bit: why did you decide to come out publicly and—well, let's start there. Why did you decide to come out publicly?

HUGHES: Uh, well, I was well convinced and remain convinced that "Don't Ask, Don't Tell" is positively bad for our national security, as well as being unnecessarily discriminatory. And so, I felt that I was actually in a unique and strong position to help bring that to public consciousness. And I was so advised by a number of other former service members that had come out, by my family and friends, and we decided it was the right thing.

ESTES: What was it like to be the center of attention—I guess in some sense, to continue to be the center of media attention because of this?

HUGHES: Uh, another eye-opening experience. As I've said, some reporters report more than you would like, and some perhaps a little less than you would like. [chuckling] But, it's very gratifying to receive the attention, and you just hope that you can get the message out—not that I have much of a message, but that you can make an impact on people. One of the overriding reasons why I came out publicly was because in the winter of 2003, three flag officers came out: General Kerr, General Richards, and Admiral Steinman. And these were the first flag officers—they were retired, but the first flag officers to come out. And that made a very strong impression on me; it was on the front pages of a variety of papers, and I felt that if I could make some slight impression, as they had made a large impression on me, that I would be doing something worthwhile, so I did. I received an overwhelmingly positive response as a result. They warned me actually that I would receive a lot of negative mail, and that hasn't happened at all. And the response has been overwhelmingly positive and uniquely positive: I haven't received *any* hate mail.

ESTES: That's good. I'm surprised, but pleasantly surprised.

HUGHES: Yeah, well so was I! [laughter] I wasn't looking forward to reading the other stuff. But it never surfaced.[4]

[At the time of the interview, Brian had just graduated from Yale, and he was working as an intern for a California senator in Washington, D.C.]

Commentary

Gays and lesbians have long served in the U.S. armed forces, but their official exclusion before the early 1990s mandated silence and secrecy. In one sense, President Clinton's 1993 "don't ask, don't tell" policy simply made this silence official; it was a new paint job on an old closet door. But in another sense, debates about lifting the ban on gay military service shattered the silence, making public discussions about sexuality central to considerations of military policy. My interviews with more than fifty GLBT veterans revealed that "Don't Ask, Don't Tell" both silenced *and* elicited conversations about sexuality by active-duty personnel. Beyond the military, the controversial policy stimulated much more discussion of sexuality and service by military veterans and political pundits. In fact, "Don't Ask, Don't Tell" became a metaphor for addressing silence and hypocrisy in other political and cultural contexts. Though I believe that both the policy and the metaphor are flawed, "Don't Ask, Don't Tell" created a unique opportunity to analyze the ways silence and speech are deployed on the topic of sexuality not only in the military and in oral history interviews with gay veterans but also in the American media.[5]

Many gay rights advocates welcomed the public debates around lifting the military ban in the early 1990s, but the focus on sexuality in the services created frustrating and frightening situations for many gays and lesbians in uniform. Signed into law in 1993, "Don't Ask, Don't Tell" prohibited the military from asking questions "concerning homosexuality" as part of recruitment or induction into the armed forces, and it allowed gay and lesbian Americans to serve as long as they did not openly admit their homosexuality or demonstrate a "propensity or intent to engage in homosexual acts."[6] This policy was a political compromise between those who wanted to keep homosexuals out of the armed forces and those who wanted to lift the ban entirely. Yet it was also a tacit recognition of the fact that gay troops had long served in the armed forces and in every military conflict the nation fought during the twentieth century.[7] Sadly, the men and women most directly affected by "Don't Ask, Don't Tell"—gay and lesbian military personnel actively serving, along with their families—were unable to testify openly about its effects. This was more than political; it was personal. In day-to-day interactions with friends, superiors, and even family members, "Don't Ask, Don't Tell" required a skillful navigation of silence to hide homosexuality. "What did you do last weekend?" or "Are you seeing anyone?" might seem like innocent questions, but for gay and lesbian military personnel, they took on the weight of interrogation even in friendly conversation.[8]

Such conversations called for more than silence. They often required the creation of fake heterosexual identities. Alan Steinman, a gay flag officer now retired from the Coast Guard, told me that a promotion to admiral left him feeling particularly vulnerable as a confirmed bachelor. As a result, he placed a personal ad in a Washington, D.C., area magazine during the early 1990s seeking a female partner. "It said, 'Gay Senior Executive seeks . . . female companion for meeting social obligations.'" With this cover, Steinman's sexuality was never openly questioned, and he remained close friends with this "partner" at the time of our interview, long after he left the service.[9]

Patty Duwel was not about to risk a lifelong career in the Navy when rumors about her sexuality began to fly. She had married the gay brother of a friend to hide the fact that she was a lesbian. When she learned that she was being investigated, she later told me: "I grabbed the guy I was married with. He even put his boxers on and pulled his jeans on. He wanted to look really butch. And we tromped into the XO's [executive officer's] office and I said, 'I hear I'm under investigation for being gay, and I don't appreciate that!'" Going on the offensive may have saved her twenty-year career.[10]

For combat veterans, the silences and subversions were particularly painful. Brian Hughes, whose interview appears here, forged lifelong friendships with his buddies in the Army Rangers. "The men you fight with under those conditions are your brothers," he explained, "and nothing can ever change that." But still, because of "Don't Ask, Don't Tell," Hughes felt that he had to conceal part of his identity from his comrades the entire time they fought together in Iraq and Afghanistan.[11]

Despite the potential consequences, other veterans I spoke with—particularly younger ones and enlisted personnel—told me that conversations about sexuality were nearly unavoidable. In fact, they often resulted in coming out to close friends in the service. Lisa Michelle Fowler, a veteran of the first Gulf War, found that coming out to herself was actually more difficult than coming out to her best friend in the army. "She didn't believe me at first because . . . you know, I've been playing this straight role. Soon after that she believed me. . . . And she loved me even more for it, I think."[12] Steve Boeckels, a 1996 graduate of West Point, told me that rumors about his sexuality circulated in his unit until 1999, when he finally decided to come out to his roommate. "I told him I kind of was bisexual," he remembered, laughing about it later. "He basically said, 'All right . . . why didn't you tell me sooner?'"[13] Robert Stout recounted a similar coming out experience that happened in 2002.

> At that time, all my pronouns were changed. "He" became "she," and the guy I dated at the time, I gave him a feminine name. So my team leader was asking me about her/him. And so we get talking and it eventually got to the point where I thought, "Wow! This is just not worth it. It's too much of a pain in the ass." And so I'm like, "Hey Sarge, she's a guy." And the only thing he said after that was, "Wow! I need a cigarette." He got done smoking a cigarette and he goes, "Damn it! That means my wife was right." And it's just like: "Wow! Okeydokey, I'll play your game." And shoot, after that we never had any trouble.[14]

The coming out story is often the metanarrative of GLBT oral history interviews, regardless of the particular focus of the researcher. The centrality of this narrative seems especially prevalent in interviews undertaken since the gay liberation movement, as coming out has become the foundation of public identity and political liberation.[15] Alan Bérubé heard the coming out narrative so many times in his interviews with gay and lesbian veterans of World War II that he incorporated it into the title of his groundbreaking book, *Coming Out under Fire*, with all of the meanings that the phrase implied.[16] Bérubé argued that the social movement accompanying wartime mobilization and the homosocial worlds of military service provided the cultural space for gay and lesbian service personnel to claim their sexual identities. Although my own interviews certainly support these conclusions, I would add that both the age of Bérubé's interviewees at the time of their military service and the oral history method so crucial to Bérubé's study might have underscored or even overemphasized the importance of coming out to the stories he heard. Bérubé understood that wartime service was a traditional rite of passage that paralleled the maturation process and self-awareness of coming out. For GLBT military veterans, telling Bérubé (or me) about "coming out under fire" became part of the more time-honored coming of age narrative that has long been central to war stories. We might ask, then, whether military service in World War II was unique in creating opportunities to come out or whether oral history interviews focusing on other coming of age rituals in American society (attending college, being bar mitzvahed, having a quinceañera party, etc.) would similarly elicit coming out stories.

Given its centrality to modern GLBT identity, the coming out narrative is one story that was explicitly proscribed by "Don't Ask, Don't Tell." Perhaps because of this and also because my interviewees knew I was asking about gays in the military, they would often begin their stories with the coming out narrative, even when I did not ask directly about it. (Before the official interviews began, about a third of the interviewees asked about my service and sexuality. I am the son of a Vietnam-era veteran but have never served myself. This did not present a problem for any of the interviewees. When I told the interviewees that I am a bisexual man, married to a woman, this occasionally raised eyebrows or elicited jokes about bisexuality simply as a way station on the road to coming out. In the end, these brief and frank discussions seemed to put the interviewees—or in this case, interviewers—at ease so that they could speak more candidly about their own service and sexuality.)

My strategy in most of the interviews with GLBT veterans was to start the conversations with the traditional military narratives or "war stories" and only later move on to sexuality. Though it may have been a naïve or misguided strategy, I thought that starting with the war stories, a narrative tradition as old as history itself, would set the speakers at ease. I also hoped that this structure would highlight for readers or listeners (whether they were straight or gay) the fact that these interviewees were just normal veterans who had done their duty regardless of their sexuality. On one level, this interview strategy was an abject failure, as many of my interviewees told their coming out stories early on and wove the story of their sexuality into the narrative of military service. This was true of World War II veterans and veterans of the Iraq War.

My third question to William Winn, a veteran of both World War II and Korea, was about his parents being high school sweethearts. Though I had not asked about his sexuality here, Winn smoothly segued from a discussion of his parents' romantic relationship to a delicate explanation of coming out. "I found that somewhere after my thirtieth birthday," Winn recalled, when "I had an intense friendship with a young man my own age and one thing led to another and then I found out, as I had suspected during my Korean War experience, that my ability to tolerate society was much more in the masculine vein."[17] The question that elicited Brian Hughes's coming out story was simply: "Can you talk about your first couple of years at Yale?" When interviewees did not address sexuality early in the interview, I would later ask them how their sexuality affected their military service. Because sexual identity and coming out were often woven seamlessly into the narratives of these veterans' lives, it was difficult to separate these topics from the war stories I had hoped to focus on. Perhaps it was futile to even try, thus underscoring the problematic nature of "Don't Ask, Don't Tell."

The primary argument for retaining "Don't Ask, Don't Tell" was that open discussions of homosexuality would undermine unit cohesion. The assumption was that such conversations would jeopardize camaraderie between gay and straight troops. All of the veterans I spoke with agreed that such camaraderie is absolutely necessary for combat effectiveness, but they questioned the assumption that simple conversations about sexuality would sever the bonds forged by military service. In fact, conversations about (hetero)sexuality have long been an integral part of the bonding process. This was particularly true in the years before the gender integration of the U.S. military in the 1970s. As one Vietnam combat veteran told me, this was one reason why R&R ("Rest and Relaxation" or "Rest and Recuperation") was just as stressful in its own way as combat duty for gay troops. "That's where being gay is really frightening," Michael Job told me. "Because every guy who goes on R&R comes back with these fuck tales about how many women they screwed. Now, as a gay person you have to make up these stories, so I was well aware of that."[18]

In the wake of gender integration of the armed forces, such conversations continue, despite concerns that they create a hostile environment bordering on sexual harassment. Because of the ban on gay service, such stories of heterosexual exploits put military women in the proverbial Catch-22, leaving them vulnerable to male sexual advances to "prove" that they were not lesbians.[19] The various branches of the military, particularly the service academies, have recognized this as a problem and have tried to address it since the 1990s.[20] Still, given the tradition of (hetero)sexual boasting in the military, it is not surprising that any discussion of homosexuality was seen as somehow dangerous to unit cohesion and morale. Words, in this case, could stand in for sexual advances and fraternization, because they have had this power in a heterosexual military context. Yet if it is possible for identity proclamations and sexual propositions to be separated in a heterosexual context, this should be possible in a homosexual context as well. As Brian Hughes explained, being able to tell his buddies that he was gay would have strengthened their bond of friendship, not weakened the band of brothers. Brian wished to tell his buddies about his sexuality not because he wanted to fraternize with them, but because he wanted to be honest. Trust was such a crucial part of the bond among soldiers and so integral to the military code that it was tough for Brian to hide this part of his identity from the other men in his unit. He did so, because he was a good soldier and that was military policy, but the price of this policy was alienation, not unit cohesion.[21]

Though Brian Hughes did not come out while he was in the military, many of my other interviews revealed that asking and telling went on in the military despite the official silence imposed by "Don't Ask, Don't Tell." The consequences of these conversations varied from unit to unit, with enlisted personnel, non-commissioned officers, and junior officers tending to take the admissions in stride, while senior officers seemed to be much more unpredictable. The older and more senior-ranking gay and lesbian veterans I spoke with were less likely to have come out to their comrades. But retirement or discharge from the service opened up the floodgates. Gay and lesbian veterans have been much more visible in the mainstream media, with interviews in the *New York Times* and appearances on television programs like the *Daily Show* and *Good Morning America*. Dozens of GLBT vets have been interviewed by volunteers for the Library of Congress Veterans History Project.[22] In other words, the official censure of gay military speech backfired. An exploration of the broader cultural context of the policy may help us to understand why.[23]

Outside the military, "Don't Ask, Don't Tell" had some strange consequences, beginning with speech surrounding sexuality but spinning out from that into silences throughout American politics and society. In much the same way that Watergate framed our understanding of many major political scandals from the 1970s to the 1990s, "Don't Ask, Don't Tell" ironically gave American politicians and pundits a language for talking about issues that society deemed should be kept quiet. This should come as no surprise, since "Don't Ask, Don't Tell" was a modern version of the old adage that same-sex attraction was "the love that dare not speak its name." Yet we should not make this comparison too lightly or remove "Don't Ask, Don't Tell" from the historical context in which it was created. The military policy was born at the height of the political correctness debates, and placing it in this historical context is instructive in assessing its broader ramifications.

In this context, "Don't Ask, Don't Tell"—and particularly the additional prohibition "Don't Harass"—theoretically did double duty: protecting the military from acknowledging that gays existed in the ranks while protecting gay troops from overt discrimination. This strange marriage of conservative thought (viewing people as individuals not as identities or groups) and liberal beliefs (protecting both individuals and groups from discrimination) contributed to the surprising longevity of "Don't Ask, Don't Tell." These bipartisan beginnings also made the policy quite adaptable to other political and social contexts with subtle, negative consequences for the images of gay troops and gay veterans.

Initially commentators used "Don't Ask, Don't Tell" as a metaphor for understanding the growing albeit gradual and grudging acceptance of homosexuality in mainstream American life. Unfortunately, but not unpredictably, the metaphor often conflated the military's policy regarding consenting, adult, homosexual relations outside of the ranks with silences about fraternization, pedophilia, workplace harassment, and other socially prohibited forms of sexuality. As sex and pedophilia scandals in the Catholic Church broke into the headlines during the 1990s, commentators were quick to point out similarities between the treatment of homosexuality in the church and the American military. A 1993 op-ed in the *New York Times* warned that passage of "Don't Ask, Don't Tell" would make the Pentagon "a cousin of the Catholic Church [where] homosexuals will be tolerated if they don't homosex." *Mother Jones* peered "inside the 'don't ask, don't tell' policy of the Catholic Church" in a 1997 exposé of priests breaking celibacy vows with consenting adults of the opposite sex. Such liberal critiques of church hypocrisy shared headlines with stories that suggested that the pedophilia scandal was a problem of homosexuality itself and not of the church policy on sexuality per se. In 2002, the *Washington Times* suggested that an informal "don't ask, don't tell" policy of recruiting homosexual priests had led directly to the church's pedophilia problems because gay priests were inherently morally lax. The conservative *Times* went on to suggest that political correctness in the media kept this aspect of the story a secret.[24]

Beyond the scandal in the Catholic Church, "Don't Ask, Don't Tell" was used to explain the sex scandals that ended the political careers of Florida Congressman Mark Foley and Idaho Senator Larry Craig. Representative Mark Foley, who had publicly opposed gay marriage and other rights, admitted that he was gay and resigned from the House after the publication of several salacious messages he sent to underage male pages working on Capitol Hill. In a *Boston Globe* op-ed piece arguing for the demolition of the Republican Party's gay closet, David Link called the Foley scandal "the revenge of don't ask, don't tell." "If this has a familiar ring," he quipped, "look in the Catholic Church for the bell." In another article on closeted gay Republicans, the *Los Angeles Times* noted that with the exception of the military, "perhaps no institution in America has as strong a 'don't ask, don't tell' approach" than the Republican Party. Liberals in the mainstream media delighted in hoisting the Republican Party on its own pink petard, but even as they critiqued the hypocrisy of the GOP closet, they unintentionally connected "Don't Ask, Don't Tell" with vice and deception, forging a double-edged sword.[25]

Some political commentators recognized the double-edged nature of these scandals and also found their origins in a culture of religious conservatism that had arisen simultaneously with the era of "Don't Ask, Don't Tell." When Senator Larry Craig was arrested and pled guilty to lewd public behavior for simply tapping the shoe of an undercover police officer in the next bathroom stall, the press hammered the conservative Idaho Republican for hypocrisy. It seemed clear to the police and most journalists that Craig was propositioning the undercover cop for sex, yet Craig had actually done very little to merit even the minor charge of disorderly conduct. In 1993, Craig voted in favor of the "don't ask, don't tell" policy, which made such overtures grounds for dismissal from the military. Even after his arrest but before it became a scandal, Craig explained to a constituent that he still supported the "don't ask, don't tell" policy, because "it is unacceptable to risk the lives of American soldiers and sailors merely to accommodate the sexual lifestyles of certain individuals." While it may be politically expedient to draw attention to the downfall of closeted conservative opponents of gay rights, thoughtful observers noted that it was not their actions or even their secrets that merited critique. It was the ideology that required such secrecy in the first place. Still, the lines blurred in the media as outing closeted conservative gays offered an overt critique of society's homophobia while subtly pandering to these same fears in the public mind. Society wanted to ask and the media wanted to tell, but was it for the right reasons?[26]

The broader cultural meaning of "Don't Ask, Don't Tell" linked gay and lesbian troops to a culture of duplicity, but it also inadvertently inspired more dialogue and discussion of gays in the military. The military prizes honesty, courage, and honor. While gay veterans did their duty and served their country with honor, they were not allowed to be completely honest about who they were when they served. The veterans I interviewed believed that this undermined unit cohesion, camaraderie, morale, and ultimately, fighting effectiveness. Oral history interviews provided a way for them to share in the long tradition of telling war stories and to come out against a policy they believed was bad both for them and for the armed forces. Beyond the military, popular usage of "Don't Ask, Don't Tell" conflated sexual and political duplicity in ways that subtly undermined the position and image of the gay and lesbian troops that the policy was initially intended to protect. The saving grace and final irony of "Don't Ask, Don't Tell" is that it unintentionally inspired journalists and oral historians to interview gay veterans to get the story "straight." In other words, the official censure of gays and lesbians in the military amplified the very speech it was intended to stifle. Once GLBT service personnel came out of the military closet and became openly gay veterans, they no longer said, "Don't ask." They said, "Ask and tell."

Notes

1. David Stolowitz transcribed the interview with Brian Hughes.
2. In 1999, nineteen-year-old Private Barry Winchell was stationed at Fort Campbell, Kentucky. When Winchell began to explore gay life in nearby Nashville, Tennessee, rumors spread

about his sexuality. "Pretty much everybody called him derogatory names," Sergeant Michael Kleifgen later told a reporter. "They called him a faggot, I would say, on a daily basis." Kleifgen, a friend of Winchell's, filed a formal complaint about the harassment, but nothing was done. When Winchell also complained, his captain simply told the other soldiers to "knock that shit off." On the fourth of July, Winchell got into a fight with another private, eighteen-year-old Calvin Glover, at a keg party outside of their barracks. On the surface, the fight had nothing to do with Winchell being gay, but when he knocked Glover down, the taunts began. Ashamed that he had been beaten by "a fucking faggot," Glover decided to get revenge. Later that night, he attacked Winchell with a baseball bat as he slept. Winchell died the next day. For more on this, see Thomas Hackett, "The Execution of Private Barry Winchell: The Real Story behind the 'Don't Ask, Don't Tell' Murder," *Rolling Stone*, March 2, 2002.

3. One of the leading stories to emerge from the initial U.S. invasion of Iraq was the ambush and capture of members of the army's 507th Maintenance Company, including a private from West Virginia named Jessica Lynch. Injured when her truck smashed into another vehicle during the ambush, Private Lynch was ultimately taken by her Iraqi captors to Saddam Hussein General Hospital in the town of Nasiriya. Though she was a prisoner of war, Private Lynch was treated well by the Saddam General doctors, few of whom were supporters of the hospital's namesake. When word leaked out that Lynch was being held at the hospital, American Special Forces were sent on a rescue mission. For more on Lynch, see Rick Bragg, *I Am a Soldier Too: The Jessica Lynch Story* (New York: Alfred A. Knopf, 2003).

4. Brian Hughes interview with Steve Estes (January 5, 2005): 1–15. Brian Hughes Collection (AFC/2001/001/43216), Veterans History Project, American Folklife Collection, Library of Congress, Washington, DC. Also deposited in the Oral History Collection, GLBT Historical Society, San Francisco, California.

5. For political and legal analysis of "Don't Ask, Don't Tell," see Aaron Belkin and Geoffrey Bateman, *Don't Ask, Don't Tell: Debating the Gay Ban in the Military* (Boulder, CO: Lynne Rienner, 2003); Janet E. Halley, *Don't: A Reader's Guide to the Military Anti-Gay Policy* (Durham, NC: Duke University Press, 1999); Gary L. Lehring, *Officially Gay: The Political Construction of Sexuality in the U.S. Military* (Philadelphia: Temple University Press, 2003); and Melissa Wells-Petry, *Exclusion: Homosexuals and the Right to Serve* (Washington, DC: Regnery Gateway, 1993).

6. "Don't Ask, Don't Tell" was a small part of the defense appropriations bill for fiscal year 1994. Pub.L 103–160 (10 U.S.C. § 654).

7. Allan Bérubé, *Coming Out under Fire* (New York: Free Press, 1990); Steve Estes, *Ask & Tell: Gay and Lesbian Veterans Speak Out* (Chapel Hill: University of North Carolina Press, 2007); and Randy Shilts, *Conduct Unbecoming: Lesbians and Gays in the U.S. Military, Vietnam to the Persian Gulf* (New York: St. Martin's, 1993).

8. For more on the regulation of speech and silence inherent in "Don't Ask, Don't Tell," see Judith Butler, *Excitable Speech: The Politics of the Performative* (London: Routledge, 1997), 103–26; Tobias Barrington Wolff, "Compelled Affirmations, Free Speech, and the U.S. Military's Don't Ask, Don't Tell Policy," *Brooklyn Law Review* 63 (1997), 1141–211; and Tobias Barrington Wolff, "Political Representation and Accountability under Don't Ask, Don't Tell," *Iowa Law Review* 89 (2003–04): 1633–716.

9. Alan Steinman interview with author (March 29, 2004). Full transcript of interview: Alan Steinman Collection, Veterans History Project, American Folklife Center, Library of Congress. For an edited version and analysis, see Steve Estes, *Ask & Tell*. Unless otherwise stated, all interviews included here are housed in individual collections at the Library of Congress and are also included in my book, *Ask &Tell*.

10. Patty Duwel interview with author (June 24, 2003).

11. Brian Hughes interview with author (January 25, 2005).

12. Lisa Michelle Fowler interview with author (September 20, 2004).

13. Steve Boeckels interview with author (September 24, 2004).

14. Robert Leeding Stout interview with author and Steve Gatwick (July 1, 2005).

15. Madeline Davis and Elizabeth Lapovsky Kennedy, "Oral History and the Study of Sexuality in the Lesbian Community: Buffalo, New York, 1940–1960," *Feminist Studies* 12 (Spring

1986): 7–26; Eric Marcus, *Making History: The Struggle for Gay and Lesbian Equal Rights, 1945–1990* (New York: Harper Perennial, 1992); Leslie Tutti, "The Voices of Older Lesbian Women: An Oral History" (Ph.D. diss., University of Calgary, 2001), 172–85, 217–18; Horacio Roque Ramírez, "My Community, My History, My Practice," *Oral History Review* 29 (Summer–Fall 2002): 87–91.

16. Allan Bérubé, *Coming Out under Fire*; Roger Horwitz, "Oral History and the Story of America and World War II," *Journal of American History* 82 (September 1995): 617–24.

17. William Winn interview with author (June 25, 2003).

18. Michael Job interview with author (October 3, 2003).

19. Melissa S. Herbert, *Camouflage Isn't Only for Combat: Gender, Sexuality, and Women in the Military* (New York: New York University Press, 1998).

20. Elizabeth Hillman interview with author (June 14, 2005).

21. Brian Hughes interview with author (January 25, 2005).

22. For more on this, see Steve Estes, "Ask and Tell: Gay Veterans, Identity, and Oral History on a Civil Rights Frontier," *Oral History Review* 32, no. 2 (Summer–Fall 2005): 21–47. In the article, I point out the irony that the government now asking for gay vets to tell their story is the same one that silenced them when they were actively serving their country in the military.

23. John Files, "Gay Ex-Officers Say 'Don't Ask, Don't Tell' Doesn't Work," *New York Times*, December 10, 2003; Bleu Copas appeared on the *Daily Show* (September 18, 2006); Brian Hughes appeared on *Good Morning America* (September 15, 2004).

24. Anna Quindlen "Another Kind of Closet," *New York Times*, June 27, 1993; Cheryl Jones, "Unfaithful," *Mother Jones*, November–December 1997; Daniel McGinn, "Keeping Different Kinds of Vows," *Newsweek*, April 22, 2002; and Liz Trotta, "Media Silent on Gays in Clergy, Catholics See 'Moral Laxity' at Root of Pedophile Scandal," *Washington Times*, March 25, 2002. For a more academic comparison of military and church policy, see Shannon Gilreath, "Sexually Speaking: 'Don't Ask, Don't Tell' and the First Amendment after *Lawrence v. Texas*," *Duke Journal of Gender Law and Policy* 14 (2007): 975.

25. David Link, "The Gay Problem in the GOP," *Boston Globe*, October 5, 2006; Maura Reynolds and Jennie Jarvie, "Path Is Risky for Gay GOP Politicians," *Los Angeles Times*, October 6, 2006; and Eugene Robinson, "'Values' Choice for GOP," *Washington Post*, October 10, 2006.

26. William Saletan, "Hypocritical? Don't Ask," *Washington Post*, September 2, 2007; and Aaron Belkin, "A Sting He Didn't Deserve," *Washington Post*, September 1, 2007. Beyond the realm of sexuality, "Don't Ask, Don't Tell" became a metaphor for understanding any political cover-up or silence. Within the military, cover-ups ranging from the torture of Iraqi prisoners held in Abu Ghraib to the poor treatment of wounded American soldiers at Walter Reed Medical Center have been linked to a "don't ask, don't tell" mind-set throughout the ranks. In politics more generally, stonewalling testimony from former Bush administration officials like Karl Rove, Alberto Gonzalez, and Harriet Miers was lampooned as a new definition of Executive Privilege known as "Don't Ask, Don't Tell." See M. Gregg Bloch, "Military Medicine's Toxic Silence: Walter Reed, Abu Ghraib, and Other Crises Are the Result of a Spreading Climate of Fear," *Los Angeles Times*, March 11, 2007; Monte Wolverton, "A New Definition of Executive Privilege," *caglecartoons.com*, 2007.

14

THANKS FOR THE MEMORIES

A Narrator Asks an Oral Historian for Validation

Eric C. Wat

Oral history by Eric Wat with Ernest Wada, Los Angeles, California, December 4, 1997

Japanese American, born and raised in Los Angeles, Ernest Wada (pseudonym) was sixty-two years old at the time of this interview. He was one of the twenty-five narrators I interviewed for my book, The Making of a Gay Asian Community: An Oral History of Pre-AIDS Los Angeles.[1] *Much of the book, especially its second half, addresses the founding of Asian/Pacific Lesbians and Gays (A/PLG), the first formal organization established by Asian American lesbians and gay men in Los Angeles, in 1980. The audio recording of the interview with Ernest Wada is archived at the Center for Oral and Public History at the California State University, Fullerton.*

ERNEST WADA: I am the youngest son after four sisters, no brothers. Like one of my sisters told me when I turned out gay, I had about the same chance as a snowball in hell of turning otherwise. Most men [in Terminal Island, where I was born] were fishermen, and they were out to sea a great deal of the time. So I was brought up with all these sisters and women. Up until then, my sisters were my role models. And I thought, I actually thought I grew up as the fifth sister. I had very feminine traits.

When we moved to East Los Angeles [in 1946, after being released from the Internment camp], there weren't too many Japanese in that particular area. Housing was very short during this period, so you had to take what was available. So we had to go out to the barrio. The grammar school that I went to was highly Latino. This area of Los Angeles had a preponderance of Latino Americans of the Mexican variety, along with whites and blacks. The thing is, these people were very sweet people to me. They just took me under their wings and never expressed any kind of bias. They accepted me right off the start.

I had a lot of good friends that were Mexican. We used to run around and do kid things. They were more sexually mature than I. Not only did they mature early in this respect but also knew what to do about it. Based on my experience, they just had a healthy appetite for sex and in many cases were not discriminating about engaging in sexual activities regardless of the partner's gender. Boy, did we engage in these activities. They taught me a lot, and I liked it. I began to discover my sexuality as far as preference for males only is concerned.

Being that I'm very, like, sissified—because I didn't know how else to be—they knew, they were aware. My Latino school buddies taught me how to masturbate and perform masturbation on them. When things became heated (even at this age), they'd enjoy penetrating me anally. Being so feminine, I thought all of this was natural. I recall an experience where I engaged in sex play with a special friend who was a couple of years older than I. Before he penetrated me, he kissed me in a manner that made me swoon. I really developed a big-time crush on him. Can you believe this behavior at age ten? Being as sissified as I was, the horny boys would always take advantage of me and single me out for their sexual release.

These boys were very protective of me. I mean, I had been picked on before. In those instances, it was a racial thing. There were just the bully types, the ignorant types, that made fun of other people anyway. For instance, the black boys used to terrify me by calling me a "slant-eyed Jap." The Latino boys always came to my rescue.

To me, I was always looking at the guys. Never a question. But girls also had crushes on me. Even when I went out with these girls, I liked their boyfriends and other friends in their circle. I like the guys.

ERIC C. WAT: Why would you date them if you knew for fairly certain that you were only attracted to guys?

WADA: See, you're asking this question from a very liberated point of view. In those days, you had to do that. Otherwise, immediately they'd think you were queer. I mean, you're as sissy as they come, but if you date girls, somehow it seems that maybe you're not. It's a guy thing. Even at that point, you were trying to do the right thing to be accepted. More for acceptance.

After high school, I tried to go into business college for a while, but I hated it. So I dropped out and went to work. And I hated that. At the time, everybody in our age group was subjected to the draft. It was mandatory that you had to meet your draft obligation when you turned eighteen. So rather than waiting for them to call us, a great number of us, right after high school, either volunteered or enlisted four years at a particular service branch. In my case, I volunteered for the draft to be called earlier to get my obligation out of the way.

We took basic infantry training. And then after that it was mandatory that you go on to advanced infantry training, which was all in Fort Ord in California. After the two eight-week cycles of both basic and advanced infantry training, they'd give you a short leave. I was then immediately stationed in Korea.

By then, I was aware that I was homosexual, but I was still closeted. Very much closeted because for one thing, it was not acceptable. If they had found out, they drummed you out. But I saw a lot of gay guys in the army. I didn't know what was going on, but these people were just blatantly gay.

A lot of them were in clerical capacities, medical capacities, and so forth. The line soldiers, the infantrymen, there might have been, but I couldn't tell. So I tried to butch it up because you were not going to survive if you acted like a sissy under those circumstances. That's what I did.

In the military, it was all about butching up. You have to. You're going on these bivouacs and sleeping in pup tents with these guys. In this one instance, there was this particular friend I had made. We were in bivouac; we had what you'd call shelter halves. It's on your backpack. It's your half of the tent that you're going to put up. So they call them shelter halves. You put your half and I put mine, and we push them in [to make the tent]. So we each had our half to keep us from the elements. I was in bivouac at one time, and I happened to set up tents with him. The local prostitutes were camp followers that knew when the men were going out in the field. That's their best chance to get out there and sell their work because they came out to the tents, and it was hard to keep track of them. Well, this particular friend brought one in, a very pretty girl. After he got through, he said, *Take some. I'll pay for it.* And no way. But that was one of the butch things that they'd do that I had to be subjected to. I didn't participate in that aspect, but all the other things I had to. Training itself was just a man thing. I don't see how these females survive in the military now.

But even though I was not out, I was having rendezvous. But not with gay guys. It was with straight guys. These were just guys who, I guess, knew what they were doing. They didn't view it as they were being queer. It was just release, sexual release. And I did it with them.

I mean, I was not entirely reckless about it. You know the process: You find somebody who's attractive to you, physically attractive, and then you get to know the person and they get to know you, and they find out you are decent and so forth, and then you wait for their vulnerable moments and see if they would submit to it. And 90 percent of the time, they would submit.

WAT: So you were pretty sure they wouldn't tell on you?

WADA: No, they came back for seconds. . . . I had turned twenty-one in the service. So by the time I got back here, I was old enough to go to the bars. I had bumped into this particular guy before then who was gay. He felt me out. He knew I was gay. In fact, he made a point of seducing me, which he did. He was very active in going to this bar. It was called the Red Raven. And through that seduction, he kind of educated me a lot about what was going on, as far as being gay is concerned.

WAT: What did you feel the first time you went to a bar?

WADA: I in particular feel that the whites set the standards of everything in this life. Whether we realize it or not, we tend to follow those standards and emulate them, which was no different in the gay circle then. But the selection process in the bar scene was just deadly because the whites were going for whites at the time, and Asian types were not a commodity.

The whites at the time, I feel, viewed us as more of the subservient type. They expected us to be submissive—this is an extreme analogy—a geisha type. We were supposed to wait on them hand and foot or something. They came off condescending or patronizing to you. But at that point, you took it, and then as soon as they talked to us, with what they were expecting out of us, we opened our mouths and started talking, and they discovered that we were just as Americanized as them. Then they felt intimidated. And after a while, it just became too ridiculous. This person was so stupid, so ignorant. And you let him have it. They didn't know what was going on because, well, *he's an Asian, how come he's behaving this way? He's just like the white queens, vicious, just as vicious.* Well, we learned.

I mean, what are their feelings on that, the white people that are attracted to the Asians? Is it a physical thing, or is it something they feel inside? I don't know.

WAT: I mean, I wouldn't generalize the whole white gay community, but there are certain people who believe in that.

WADA: It was very easy to generalize for me because that's all . . . that's the experience. You didn't have a chance if you were an Asian. That's the way I felt about it. Plus the fact that you had this preconceived idea that the white people were interested in other white people. They didn't know what to make of the Asians, and we were just a novelty they might try. Understand that we were in the bar environment or the gay scene with that type of prevailing feeling. That was the way I saw it.

It was compounded by the fact that, in the seventies, we had a tremendous influx of these immigrant types and refugee types that came over from Southeast Asia, Vietnam or Thailand. Well, we were in there having to compete with them as well. And they were the ones who were aggressive. Either that, or they didn't care. They were just going to all lengths to get a man. That's the part that used to piss me off. We [the American-born Asians] were not the aggressive types. I highly resented these foreign types. Especially in the bar scenes, thinking we were all Asians, at least we had that in common. But then, you started talking with them, and you discovered that's where it ended. As far as being people were concerned, they were worse than whites to me.

I'm not a troll or reject. I felt I was reasonably attractive in my younger days. You know, I could have suitors and so forth, but I never got that satisfaction. The ones that I was drawn to, they were interested in their counterparts, other Caucasians. You'd have to be really exceptionally beautiful for them to give you the time of day, to be seriously involved with you.

WAT: So what type of men were you looking for?

WADA: (Pause) You mean other than Caucasians? My physical attraction is whoever that turns me on. It's just not a specific type.

WAT: But not Asians?

WADA: No. No.

WAT: Why do you think that is? I mean, is it the white standards that you were talking about?

WADA: Well, for one thing . . . I never thought about it actually. At school, when I used to have these crushes and physical attraction, it was a mixture of Asians, Mexicans, whatever turned me on, you know. But once I became gay, I guess I was looking for . . . I don't want . . . I want someone that is masculine. I want someone that is masculine because I tended to be so effeminate myself. And you know, I'm glad this came up. Now that I think about it. I'm blaming all of this on the white standards and so forth. But I don't think that was so much it either. I think it was the fact that I was kind of too nelly, or too swishy or whatever. I didn't go out of my way to do it. I just adopted that nature. Then it became part of me. And so I supposed they saw that, and that's not particularly a turn-on to these guys that you get turned on to. And so that was me. I guess what it comes down to is who you are and how you carry on, whether you sell yourself or not. In my case, I guess I was a nelly faggot. That's not a turn-on. I never thought of it in those terms, but that's true.

WAT: So a lot of Asians that you would meet were sort of nelly types, too?

WADA: Yes, or they just weren't a turn-on to me. I'm not saying entirely. There were really nice, attractive guys, Asians. Do you know Roy? Well, Roy is a beauty. Now, in those days, I wouldn't have any qualms tricking with him because he's really good-looking. A lot of Asians . . . there were several that were very pretty and attractive. But they were just not my cup of tea because they had this particular demeanor about them that was not compatible with mine, regardless of how attractive. So in that regards, that's a turn-off.

In my earlier days when I was active in the social scene, that's part of how I felt. But not now. I see all these Asian American types that are just out there and doing things, and holding responsible positions, and really just integrated into the strata of things, as far as social acceptance and so forth. They hold good jobs. They are educated. See, I didn't see much of that when I was growing up. Maybe they [gay Asians] have something now. Maybe they have come into their own. What I'm saying is, there were no bars like Mugi's or Chopstix or Xanadu that you hear of now. There was no place that was exclusively Asian at the time. Most of us were the pioneers because our parents definitely weren't going on to universities. They came here and started working, and then they went into the [internment] camps. And we were always the down . . . I shouldn't say the downtrodden, but we were always like on poverty because we had to get started.

I don't want you to leave here thinking that I was just an Asian person trying to be white, but that's not it at all. I was just never comfortable with who I was. I supposed being Asian was a part of it, too, because I felt like an underdog in a lot of instances.

Commentary

At the onset of my research about the history of gay Asian men's organizing in Los Angeles, I was very clear that I did not want to explore Asian/Pacific Lesbians and Gays. When I came out in Los Angeles in the early 1990s, A/PLG had a reputation of being a cruising ground dominated by "rice queens," non-Asians (usually white and older) who have a particular and sometimes exclusive sexual interest in Asian men, often based on prevailing stereotypes of Asian men being boyish, submissive, and easily controlled. Only a few interviews into my project, however, I began to realize that A/PLG represented a breaking point in how gay Asian men viewed each other, and omitting the organization's story would leave their life histories incomplete.

Almost all of the twenty-five narrators in my book had occupied leadership positions in A/PLG and/or the Gay Asian Rap Group (GARP), another support group founded in Los Angeles four years after A/PLG. Twenty-three of them were Asian, and the remaining two were white. Seven of the narrators were immigrants. I was able to conduct all of the interviews in English, and, with one exception, the narrators were comfortable using English. Most narrators were Chinese and Japanese Americans, and there was a smaller representation of Filipino, Korean, Vietnamese, and South Asian Americans. The post-1965 influx of Asian immigrants and refugees into the United States had not percolated through the A/PLG leadership by the early 1980s, although they were a significant part of A/PLG membership. I interviewed only one woman, partly because A/PLG leadership had always been marked by a gender imbalance, and partly because I made a choice early on to focus my interviews on gay Asian men.

Wada was situated at the periphery of gay Asian organizing in Los Angeles. He was a few years older than the first A/PLG leaders, though he was good friends with some of them. Wada was also one of four narrators who chose not to use his real name. He also never went through the consciousness-raising experience that other narrators had in integrating their racial and sexual identities. Through their leadership roles, many narrators had contemplated how their racial and sexual identities contributed to their life decisions (including the organizations they led), but Wada never had to confront these contradictions in the same way. Michael Frisch has written that oral history can awaken the "beast of consciousness," the personal history and memories that guide the way the narrator has lived his life. Similarly, Ronald Grele argues that more than just a recording or a transcript, an oral history interview is a "cultural construct," a consciousness that is expressed in a complex merging of both the narrator's past and present and the different worldviews of the narrator and the interviewer.[2] In the act of our interview, conducted in the late 1990s, Wada verbally worked out the contradictions of his racial and sexual identities through recounting experiences and learned new truths (or at least new perspectives) about himself. As the researcher, I was unprepared for Wada's reinterpretation of his life history *on the spot* as a direct result of how I asked my questions.

I had conceived my research about the history of organizing among gay Asian men in Los Angeles as a political project. I had wanted to talk about the conscious act of community building among gay Asian men in Los Angeles that required vision, progressive ideology, and the hard work of organizing. My idea was a reaction to those who thought community is formed as a natural outcome of population growth. Before I had started this project, my friend Steven Shum and I facilitated a cross-generational roundtable discussion on the shape of gay Asian community in the 1990s, which was later published in the anthology *Q & A: Queer in Asian America*.[3] During the discussion, the elders challenged us to learn more about previous organizing efforts because many of the questions we wrestled with at the time were not new. To a political activist like me, one benefit of documenting this history was the ability to go back to a time when no formal organizations existed in Los Angeles for gay Asian men. From this vantage, I could see how early organizations worked collectively (even if by necessity) to create something out of nothing and, therefore, evidence how community formation is a political act.

Again, I had been deliberate in excluding Asian/Pacific Lesbians and Gays (A/PLG) from my research questions because of its reputation as a playground for rice queens. The stereotypes many of them held of Asian men—submissive, boyish, easily controlled, exotic—had been the kind of characteristics that Wada had felt imposed on him as he was becoming more active in the gay social scene of Los Angeles since the mid-twentieth century. These stereotypes, and the inferiority they engendered in Asian men, have persisted. In a personal narrative written in 1996, Sandip Roy talks about how racism in the gay community had often driven him to seek the approval of "curry queens" (the equivalent of rice queens who are sexually interested in South Asians in particular), even when he felt no attraction to them.[4] The story was all too familiar: the more our images were not celebrated in the gay community, the more desperate was our need to seek validation from the community that rejected us, and the more grateful we became for each morsel of attention.

The theme of seeking validation from white gay men was not unique to the gay Asian community. In his research on the gay Latino community in San Francisco, Horacio N. Roque Ramírez similarly found that the internalization of racism by gay Latino men presented a challenge to that community formation during the 1970s. One of his narrators, Jesús Barragán, observed, "What the problem here is everybody is after the white trophy. That's the problem here. And unless two people are *comadres*, you don't want to have nothing to do with each other. . . . And it's like, you tear each other down . . . viciousness, because you're *after the white trophy.* . . . I went around just saying these things to people and we need to organize."[5]

While these patterns of internalized racism were still at play for gay men of color a generation later, my peers and I had come out in an environment that resisted this sexual hierarchy and derided organizations like A/PLG (and any gay Asian man who was willing to associate with it) as unenlightened, even self-hating. Whenever I had thought about A/PLG at the time, I had this image of these rice queens leering or brushing against younger Asian men in the most inappropriate places. I had declined any opportunities to attend any A/PLG events since coming out, eschewing one of the very few places that had been developed exactly with gay Asian men like me in mind. So did I really want to spend a year of my time interviewing (and validating) a group of people who were willing to tolerate and include these rice queens in their milieu?

I had known it would be hard to tell the story of gay Asian men organizing in Los Angeles without mentioning A/PLG, precisely because it was the first formal organization for Asian gay men and lesbians in the city. Most of the narrators I had begun to recruit had at one point or another belonged to the organization, and many had assumed leadership roles in it. Several were even its founders. In what I thought was a clever move on my part, I had devised an interview guide that focused on the 1970s, asking these potential narrators to talk about life as gay Asian men before any formal organization existed. I wanted to capture the conditions under which community formation became necessary through organizing and establishing a formal organization—without mentioning anything about the organization itself.

Any researcher who begins with such a biased agenda would, sooner or later, meet his comeuppance. And thankfully, under the guidance of one of the faculty members on my thesis committee (who *is* an experienced oral historian), I learned early on that oral history, as a methodology, is a collaboration between the researcher and the subjects. In the words of another oral historian, Tamara Hareven, oral history is a "subjective process," and the interviewer is not like an academic expert but "like a medium, whose own presence, interests, and questions conjure corresponding memories."[6] The lack of distance between the two is what makes oral history feel like a bastard in the professional history discipline, that is, illegitimate in its scientific objectivity.[7] However, to those of us toiling in ethnic studies, feminist studies, and sexuality studies, this collaboration is central to our methodology. Gary Y. Okihiro writes, "Oral history is not only a tool or method for recovering history; it also is a theory of history which maintains that the common folk and the dispossessed have a history and that this history must be written. . . . Ethnic history is the first step toward ultimate emancipation; for by freeing ourselves from the bonds of a colonized history, they will be able to see their true condition, their own history."[8] To be in a true collaboration means that sometimes the researcher has to give up some control of the research process and let the

ed from narrators define for him what is important in the inquiry. After all, it is their lives that are being documented.

By the third life history interview, I had to throw out my interview guide, which contained no questions about A/PLG. I realized that to ignore A/PLG in the history of these gay Asian men would be like telling a story without the ending, for A/PLG was either the reference point to which the narrators compared the rest of their lives or the mark that had separated their lives from *before* and *after*. In one interview, a narrator interrupted his own answer about gay life in the 1970s and asked me if he could start talking about A/PLG. At that moment, I realized I had missed the story altogether.

Equally important in my transformation at this point was the fact that the men I had interviewed so far contradicted my own stereotypes of A/PLG and its founders. They all had a very strong sense of Asian identity, some having grown up in predominantly Asian communities or neighborhoods, and recalled those memories fondly and intimately. They continued to occupy leadership positions or were otherwise active in mainstream Asian American organizations. Frankly, a couple of them had displayed such strong and willful presence of mind that I had a hard time imagining them being pushed around by anyone, rice queens or not. The three men I had interviewed by then had dispelled my stereotypes. They were equally proud of being gay and Asian. That they had subscribed to a white beauty myth demanded a more complex analysis than that of a popular or conventional psychology that pathologizes them and their relationships as markers of self-hatred, helplessness, or low self-esteem. As much as I hated being wrong—because my own development as a gay Asian man had hinged on what type of gay Asian man I was to be, that is, not an A/PLG member—I had the good researcher's sense that A/PLG somehow was the Rosetta stone by which this complex interplay of race and sexuality could be decoded.

Around this time, I had also become more immersed in the early newsletters of A/PLG. At the end of the organization's first anniversary, A/PLG board members reviewed the challenges and accomplishments of the organization. One of them wrote about the part it had played in his identity development:

> I think I came to the first meeting of A/PLG because I was intrigued by the idea of an organization that was both gay and Asian. I was interested in knowing how to deal with both being gay and Asian. I wasn't sure it was possible to do this in a very compatible manner. I guess I also wanted to meet new people and possibly even to cruise. Through this, I got to meet many wonderful people I would not have been able to meet any other way—certainly not in the kind of lifestyle I had been leading. In many ways, it has been a tremendous growth experience for me.[9]

One can detect in this statement a transformation that the officer had not expected when he first joined the organization. At least for this officer, A/PLG had changed how he looked at his own racial and sexual identities and in turn how he related to other gay Asian men. His statement echoes the life histories of many narrators who credit A/PLG for their leadership development and self-esteem. Because of A/PLG's existence, the late 1970s and the early 1980s represent a disruption in the consciousness of gay Asian men in Los Angeles—from a lack of community to self-identification, one that integrates both gay and Asian in a "compatible manner." This disruption in their consciousness might not have eliminated the racist white standards that Wada and his generation had been subjected to, but it had provided an alternative where whiteness did not have to be the center of the gay Asian men's lives. By the end of this project, I realized that, ironically, it was precisely this disruption that allowed men in later generations like me to have other enlightened options in the community, to the point that we could deride A/PLG, fairly or not, as anachronistic in our own times.

My interview with Ernest Wada was my fourth, and it was the first with the new conceptual framework that included a satisfactory ending to the narrators' lives. Wada's narrative gave me one of the key insights into the kind of experience that shaped the identity and community formation for gay Asian men in Los Angeles at that time. Ironically, Wada was never active in A/PLG despite being a close friend of some of its early leaders. He was also one of few narrators who insisted on remaining anonymous. One of the main reasons he had stayed away from A/PLG is because Wada, who was born and raised in this country, was not entirely comfortable in associating with recent Asian immigrants in the organization. Some of his feelings toward immigrants were evident when he talked about the competition he felt from this group in the gay bar scenes before the formation of A/PLG. Regardless of what A/PLG had become to different people in the community when I came out, as I put his narrative into the context of other interviews for this larger history, I wonder how much of Wada's view of himself would have been different had he gone through the experience of A/PLG in its early years, as some of the other narrators had.

What I thought had complicated Wada's identity development was the naturalized conflation of gender and sexuality at the time of his coming of age, a time when queerness for boys and men was an epithet reserved only for those who did not outwardly conform to the gender expectations of masculinity. He talked about growing up in a fishing community, where men were often absent, and being raised in a family with four older sisters. He recalled thinking that he was the fifth sister. Later, after being released from the internment camps, his family moved to East Los Angeles, and Wada talked about his affairs with young Latino classmates there, presumably straight boys looking for "sexual release," targeting Wada because he was a "sissy." Gender and sexual identities were interchangeable to him, and he fulfilled the "feminine" role that made these sexual behaviors (such as masturbation and penetration) culturally acceptable for his friends.

Wada also had to contend with possible outright abuse or violence in less private arenas. He had to butch it up by dating girls (though he stopped short of sharing a prostitute with a fellow soldier). At a time before affirmative action, when many Asians were denied the opportunity to pursue higher education, Wada sought out the military. Within this homosocial environment, Wada found the cracks in American masculinist ideals, and he was able to find sexual expression with straight comrades. Yet these experiences enforced for him the proscription of both his gender and sexual identities.

What intrigued me most about this process for Wada—and for other gay Asian men I interviewed—was the additional racial layer. Because of the prevailing stereotypes of Asian men as effeminate and docile, the metonymy of sexual and gender identities found another expression in racist discourse for gay Asian men, which many internalized. For instance, as he explained why he was not sexually interested in other Asian men, he recognized he had "never thought about it actually. At school, when I used to have these crushes and physical attraction, it was a mixture of Asians, Mexicans, whatever turned me on, you know. But once I became gay, I guess I was looking for . . . I don't want . . . I want someone that is masculine. I want someone that is masculine because I tended to be so effeminate myself."

This passage stood out because it gave me an insight that contradicts the common notion that gay Asian desire toward white gay men is natural or changeless, a prevailing attitude in the community that I often had to contend with as someone who tried to resist this sexual hierarchy. Wada was describing a process of unlearning, where his childhood memories and multicultural desires were being replaced by a singular longing for white men as he became more active in the gay community, or "once I became gay." Not only did he forget that he had been attracted to Asians (and other people of color) when he was younger but he also rejected the possibility of having an Asian sexual partner because Asians—categorically—were not masculine, *yang* to his feminine *yin*.

This passage also stood out because it was expressed as a self-knowledge that Wada had not reflected on until our recording. There were pauses, false starts, and stuttering at this part of our interview. Initially, he genuinely thought he had not excluded anyone based on race when he said, "My physical attraction is whoever that turns me on. It's not a specific type." This statement might have been true before he became actively gay, and I believe it was also what he truly believed of himself at that point of our conversation, until I pressed him about how he, as a gay man, felt about other Asians. As soon as he stated that he "never thought about it actually," he immediately began to think out loud as he sorted out his memories and feelings, giving a litany of possible explanations for this newfound discrepancy. Sitting across from Wada, as he struggled to find these words to express his thoughts, I felt as if my probing had forced him to wrestle with a forgotten memory, the very idea of which contradicted his current self-identity.

In finding an answer to how such contradicting memories could exist in one person, I realized that this contradiction is essential to the naturalizing of the sexual hierarchy in the gay community. In his ethnographic study of Filipino gay men in New York in the 1990s, Martin Manalansan cites Martin P. Levine's study of the gay macho "clone" phenomenon, "a loose group of predominantly Caucasian men who dominated and set the tone for the post-Stonewall New York City gay scene in the 1970s and early 1980s."[10] The clone body manifested itself in gay bars, gyms, magazines, fashion, bathhouses and sex clubs, and personal ads, and it created a standard of masculinity that alienated and excluded people of color, including Manalansan's Filipino informants. While Manalansan documents the counterdiscursive spaces created by people of color to decenter white gay standards, he also found that "the ambivalent and mercurial quality of several queers of color spaces point to the abject and marginal status of these sites in relation to the mainstream gay topography." He concludes, "As participants in and observers of the various sites and places in the city, Filipino gay men are keenly aware of their location and acknowledge both the opportunities and barriers to staking a claim to any of these places."[11] Whether in New York or Los Angeles, post-Stonewall or post-AIDS, contradictions seem to be a common mark of experiences (and therefore identities) of queer Asian men across space and time, though it seems some are more aware of these contradictions than others.

I am also reminded here of Lisa Lowe's comments about Franz Fanon's *Black Skin, White Masks*. She writes,

> In alluding to the paradoxical fluency of the colonized subjects in the colonial language and culture, Fanon astutely names the twofold character of colonial formation. The imposition of the colonial language and its cultural institutions . . . demands the subject's internalization of the "superiority" of the colonizer and the "inferiority" of the colonized. . . . Yet the colonized subject produced within such an encounter does not merely bear the marks of the coercive encounter between the dominant language and culture. . . . Such encounters produced contradictory subjects, in whom the demands for fluency in imperial languages and empire's cultural institutions simultaneously provide the grounds for antagonism to those demands.[12]

Memories can be evacuated but not erased, and the process is never complete or irreversible. Lowe's concept of the replacement of memories became one of the main frameworks I used to analyze the experience of gay Asian men in the 1970s before and during the formation of A/PLG.

And this is the power of oral history: the power to unearth a memory and the potential to change the self-perception of a narrator in ways more immediate than any research method. Tamara Hareven believes that oral history "is not strictly a means of retrieval of information, but rather one involving the generation of knowledge."[13] I believe that the narrators I interviewed had expanded the conceptual framework of my study so that their stories could be told more fully. Yet, I know my power to ask questions tremendously shaped their stories. For me, nowhere was this more apparent and immediate than my interview with Ernest Wada. For other narrators in my research, they had begun to work out (even if they had not completed) the decentering of whiteness in the very public setting of A/PLG: by limiting the leadership to mostly Asian Pacific members, by setting up Asian-only rap groups, by exploring each other's cultures, or by defining what was appropriate or inappropriate behavior among members in the organization. Wada was never integral to these processes. At the age of sixty-two, while being interviewed by a graduate student not even half his age, he learned something new about himself.

But is self-knowledge always a good thing? At the time of our interview, Wada had a live-in partner he had met two years before, a man he described as the one he had been looking for. Wada was retired. He seemed happy. How useful was his new self-knowledge? Since oral history is a political project, I wondered how this knowledge would empower Wada.

The excerpt stimulated a series of reactions from Wada, ranging from innocuous uncertainties to mild anxieties. Wada looked to me to validate his feelings about white gay men who objectified Asians like him. He asked, "Is it a physical thing, or is it something they feel inside?" I thought it was a rhetorical question. When I realized it was not, the inexperienced interviewer in me, unaccustomed to having the table turned, answered the question and risked biasing Wada's subsequent narrative. His responses thereafter sometimes sounded like pleading for understanding or validation from me, the researcher. At the end of the interview, when I asked if he had anything else he would like to add, Wada told me, someone he had not met before the interview, "I don't want you to leave here thinking I was just an Asian person trying to be white." He said he always felt like an "underdog," never coming into his own, and pointed to his lack of opportunities growing up and the lack of gay Asian spaces like the bars and organizations we have today. Weeks later, when I asked him to review the transcript, he handwrote on the back of the transcript a long note in a similar tone. He reiterated that it might have made a difference if he had come out now, with gay Asian men more visibly in leadership positions and holding public responsibilities.

I had thought empathy and shared authority would prevent ethical dilemmas from arising during the oral history process. In some way, I believe it has made for a better and more empowering research product. Understanding the circumstances of the narrators' lives and being vigilant about my assumptions about them led me to insights that I would have otherwise missed. In return for the narrators' brave frankness and generosity of spirit, I knew I had offered most of them something valuable. For some who had lost touch with one another, I helped renew their friendships. Others gained a new perspective on their experience in very positive ways. I don't think any of them had thought of himself as a pioneer. When they began organizing in the early 1980s, they were just doing what they thought needed to be done. They did not do it because they wanted to be written about or honored decades later. I admire and learn from their humility, a mark of great leaders. For the readers, especially today's activists and organizers, I hope this history offers a continuity between what these narrators accomplished decades ago and the shape of our community now. They matter.

But with Wada, I am more ambivalent about my contributions, and my empathy and shared authority did not seem adequate. After all, the handwritten note attached to his transcript told me that he had continued to struggle with his recent self-revelation weeks after our interview. My empathy that day ended when the tape stopped rolling. While I tried to be empathetic during the writing and retelling of his stories, as well as those of his peers, Wada was left to deal with this new information about himself without me, the person who had a heavy hand in conjuring up that information. We oral historians do not want distance from our narrators, but how close should we get?

Gary Y. Okihiro discusses oral history as a method that involves two different worldviews: that of the narrator and that of the interviewer.[14] What if the two collide? Through my probing, I had unearthed something unpleasant for him (that "beast of consciousness"); even if not unpleasant, it was something he felt compelled to explain. It is clear to me now that my line of questioning had as much to do with my present anxiety about my own position as a gay Asian man, about my need to explain certain racial dynamics that are still present in my life (though perhaps not as dominant, thanks to the existence of organizations like A/PLG), as it had to do with a pure desire to document history. I came at this, as he aptly said, from "a liberated point of view." Likewise, the products of my research—the thesis, the book, and even this essay—reflect that worldview.

(I have not meant for this self-reflexive essay to be an apologia for my oral history approach, but perhaps it is inevitable. Owning a possible trespass is different from absolving a real one, but is it better than not considering the trespass at all? Or is thinking it merely academic, or can it preempt the next trespass? Whom does this essay help more, Wada or me?)

Because of the intimate nature of our research methods, we oral historians have endlessly debated the proper relationship between narrators and researchers. Daphne Patai writes, "When lengthy personal narratives, in particular, are gathered, an intimacy (or the appearance of intimacy) is generated that blurs any neat distinction between 'research' and 'personal relations.' We ask of people we interview the kind of revelation of their inner life that normally occurs in situations of great familiarity and within the private realm. Yet we invite these revelations to be made in the context of the public sphere."[15] However, I am not convinced that the solution is to dissolve our own authority as oral historians and avoid interpreting people's lives that are shared so intimately with us. In fact, some feminist oral historians believe that it would be a disservice to everyone. Katherine Borland writes, "To refrain from interpretation by letting the subjects speak for themselves seems to me an unsatisfactory if not illusory solution. . . . Feminist theory provides a powerful critique of our society, and as feminists, we presumably are dedicated to making that critique as forceful and direct as possible."[16] Yet, even Borland admits that the researcher's worldview cannot supersede that of the narrator. As oral historians, we walk a tightrope, balancing the intimacy of supposed equals and our responsibility as academics to produce a broader knowledge.

For what it's worth, I do not believe I am the right person to validate Wada's self-esteem (if any validation is needed at all). To do so would mean assuming an authority that I do not want for myself. How would this validation be different from the one he sought from white gay men when he was younger? I am no more a holder of truth for his life than those white gay men were standards of masculinity. In the end, I could only hope that I have kept the complexity of his life intact, which frankly has tempered my self-righteousness about being a proper gay Asian man. Furthermore, I hope he understands that in sharing his story he has expanded our understanding of race and sexuality.

Notes

1. Eric C . Wat, *The Making of a Gay Asian Community: An Oral History of Pre-AIDS Los Angeles* (Lanham, MD: Rowman & Littlefield, 2002).
2. Ronald J. Grele, "Directions of Oral History in the United States," in David K Dunaway and Willa K Baum, eds., *Oral History: An Interdisciplinary Anthology* (Lanham, MD: AltaMira, 1996), 67–68.
3. Eric C. Wat and Steven Shum, "Queer API Men in Los Angeles: A Roundtable on History and Political Organizing," in David L Eng and Alice Y. Hom, eds., *Q & A: Queer in Asian America* (Philadelphia: Temple University Press, 1996), 166–84.
4. Sandip Roy, "Curry Queens and Other Spices," in Eng and Hom, *Q & A*, 256–61.
5. Horacio N. Roque Ramírez, "'That's *My* Place!': Negotiating Racial, Sexual, and Gender Politics in San Francisco's Gay Latino Alliance, 1975–1983," *Journal of the History of Sexuality* 12, no. 2 (April 2003): 229.
6. Tamara Hareven, "The Search for Generational Memory," in Dunaway and Baum, *Oral History*, 247.
7. For a broader discussion on the evolution of oral history in this country and ongoing tension within the professional discipline of history, see Grele, "Directions of Oral History," 62–84.
8. Gary Y. Okihiro, "Oral History and the Writing of Ethnic History," in Dunaway and Baum, *Oral History*, 209.
9. *A/PLG Newsletter*, January 1982, Issue 1B.
10. Martin F. Manalansan, IV. *Global Divas: Filipino Gay Men in the Diaspora* (Durham, NC: Duke University Press, 2003), 64.
11. Ibid., 88.
12. See Lisa Lowe, "Decolonization, Displacement, Disidentification: Writing and the Question of History," in *Immigrant Acts* (Durham, NC: Duke University Press, 1996), 97–127.
13. Hareven, "The Search for Generational Memory," 247.
14. Okihiro, "Oral History and the Writing of Ethnic History," 205.
15. Daphne Patai, "U.S. Academics and Third World Women: Is Ethical Research Possible?" in Sherna Berger Gluck and Daphne Patai, eds., *Women's Words: The Feminist Practice of Oral History* (New York: Routledge, 1991), 142.
16. Katherine Borland, "'That's Not What I Said': Interpretive Conflict in Oral Narrative Research," in Gluck and Patai, *Women's Words*, 64.

AFTERWORD: "IF I KNEW THEN . . ."

John D'Emilio

The head spins. Or at least, my head spins, after reading the collection of essays and interview excerpts that Nan Alamilla Boyd and Horacio N. Roque Ramírez have assembled. The interviews themselves are compelling and revealing. They provide evidence to skeptics, converts, and advocates that oral history as a method has the power to enrich, deepen, and expand enormously the historical record. And the analyses that contributors have provided cover so much ground that it is difficult, even after more than one reading, to absorb it all.

When the editors asked if I would contribute an afterword to this book, I imagined that I would use it to wrap up neatly the disparate observations of the various authors. Instead, these pieces have moved me to reflect back on my own experience using oral histories and to comment on how this anthology helps me think about the process of producing as well as consuming oral histories.

Oral histories have played a part in my work since graduate school. Between 1976 and 1980, for what became *Sexual Politics, Sexual Communities*, I interviewed about forty men and women who had been active in the pre-Stonewall homophile movement. Then, in the 1990s, I conducted a comparable number for a biography of Bayard Rustin, a radical pacifist and civil rights activist who was also a gay man. Now, in my current work on the history of sexuality in Chicago, I am using oral histories done by others. In all these projects, I also pored through a large body of documentary evidence, some in archives and some in private hands.[1]

Oral histories functioned differently in these endeavors. In the case of the history of pre-Stonewall activism, I could not have produced a dissertation that was up to snuff without the interviews to which so many activists graciously consented. The archived materials at that point were slim; the private collections were hard to track down and unprocessed. For the Rustin biography, I faced the opposite situation. I could have spent a lifetime exploring every archive that touches upon Rustin's life and still have felt there was more to learn. But there were also absences in the written record, most obviously in relation to Rustin's sexuality, and the oral histories remedied some of that. In my current Chicago research, the oral histories of other researchers have functioned as an archival source.

In 1971, when I started graduate school at Columbia, the writing of U.S. history was in upheaval. The radicalism associated with the social movements of the 1960s was affecting the production of American history in at least two important ways. One set of historians was revising the past from the top down. A New Left school of researchers was reinterpreting foreign policy as a story of imperial expansion and writing studies of political economy under the rubric of corporate liberalism. Another set of historians was reshaping an understanding of the past from the bottom up. New social historians churned out books and articles on topics ranging from seventeenth-century New England towns to daily life within the antebellum slave community to worker militancy in early-twentieth-century industrial cities. Both groups shared a critical distance from heroic narratives of U.S. history, and both saw writing and disseminating these histories as transformative acts, capable of supporting progressive political change. Although not all of my peers approached their studies from this perspective, enough did to make graduate studies brim over with excitement. The sense of radical potential that some writers in this book attribute to oral history today was something that, a generation ago, I attached to historical research itself.

Oral history and the new social history might seem to be natural bedfellows, but, interestingly, oral history hardly figured in my graduate school reading. The new social history that appeared on my comprehensive exam lists covered eras too far in the past for there to be living interview subjects, though certainly students of slavery were mining the life histories collected in the 1930s as part of the Works Progress Administration. We did learn about the Columbia Oral History Project, started in the late 1940s by Allan Nevins and, as we were told, the first of its kind in the United States. But its purpose and focus were so far removed from the radical spirit of the new social history that oral history seemed less than compelling. The Oral History Project meant to remedy gaps in the written record created by the shift toward telephone conversation as a main mode of communication. Because presidents, cabinet secretaries, members of Congress, and other Important Men increasingly relied on the telephone instead of the memo or letter, interviewing had become a necessary form of research.

Still, the existence of the project at Columbia and the endorsement of the method by someone as respected as Nevins gave oral history legitimacy. In comparison with the novelty of a dissertation on a gay topic, the fact that I expected to do interviews created scarcely a ripple in the history department. And since this was before I or anyone I knew had ever heard of an institutional review board with the kind of power that Michael David Franklin references, a need to gain its approval affected me not at all.

In the fall of 1976, I set out on a research trip to California, where I conducted about three dozen interviews in four months. The interviews primarily covered events that had occurred ten to twenty-five years earlier. In reconstructing that experience now, I am acutely aware that I am drawing on memories of my own older than the ones I extracted from my informants. As virtually every contributor to this volume attests, memory is complicated. The issue is not merely how well or accurately we remember. Rather, we all have investments in our stories of the past. They are influenced by present-day agendas, some conscious and some not, that shape the telling. What investments do I have today in recounting my experience with oral history? Writing about it seems even trickier because, as will become apparent, I can't be the "good historian" and simply go back to the record—my transcripts—as a way of checking my recollections.

When I departed for California, I had already worked my way through runs of *ONE*, the *Ladder*, and the *Mattachine Review*, the main homophile publications of the 1950s and 1960s. I had pored through two file cabinets of records from the New York Mattachine Society and had read the small number of works that touched on pre-Stonewall activism. I intended during my stay in California to do both document research and interviews. But the boundary between the written and the oral was porous. For instance, I interviewed Jim Kepner in his apartment, the same space where he made available to me piles of clippings and folders of documents. Even when I worked in libraries, interview subjects like Dorr Legg and Don Slater were nearby, since they ran the libraries that housed the documents. To them, the history I was researching was still alive—and they lived with it. How did that influence their interviews and distinguish them from those who had left behind the experience of homophile activism?

My dissertation advisor had given me two bits of advice about doing oral histories. "Know as much as possible before going in to the interview," he told me. "And don't be too directive." The latter, which suited my personality, was rendered easier initially by how poorly I was able to comply with the former. Diligent as I had tried to be before approaching these activists for interviews, I still knew precious little about these organizations and their work.

With each successive interview, my ignorance diminished a bit, and this can serve as a reminder that doing oral history is itself a process that evolves in the course of a project. As I learned more, I could conduct my interviews differently. I was especially aware of this after I interviewed Jim Kepner. Kepner had made himself the unofficial historian of the homophile movement. He had accumulated massive documentary material; he stayed in touch with people; he remained engaged in activism. He also had an encyclopedic knowledge of the events, organizations, and people that constituted the movement.[2] Interviewing him was like opening an almanac and having the pages turn by themselves, with very little effort from me. After more than twelve hours of conversation with him, I was better equipped for future interviews. I continued to be nondirective and open-ended in my initial engagement with a narrator—"tell me about" rather than "did you"—but as the number of subjects I interviewed grew, I had a better sense of places that I hoped an interview would go, and I could intervene gently to steer the conversation in a direction.

A theme that courses through most of the essays in this collection is power. Power figures into every relationship, and it does not travel in only one direction. Power is also dynamic; it can shift over time. Heading into my interviews, I was a graduate student in my twenties, still uncertain as to whether I had a real dissertation topic. I was dependent on the power of my subjects to say yes or no to my request. I was also dependent on their power, given my initially paltry knowledge of the events under scrutiny, to tell me whatever version of their story they chose to construct. Put most bluntly, I desperately needed what they, and only they, knew. But once the interviews were over, my research done, and my book published, the tables would turn, and they would be dependent on me, the interviewer who had now morphed into author. I was interpreting their stories. I was selecting from their memories and arranging them in a way that made sense to me, without their continuing input. To become a historian, I needed them. But if I became one, their place in history would be constructed by me.

That is one way of describing the relationship between me and my subjects, and there is a certain truthfulness to it. But if I had to reconstruct where I think we actually were then, I'd describe the relationship with most of my subjects as one of mutual gratitude.

Why my gratitude? A key element of gay liberation rhetoric in the 1970s was its delineation of pre-Stonewall oppression. The queens of Stonewall rose up, and those who followed their lead burst out of the closet, rebels against the intolerable conditions of queer life. As I encountered men and women, all of whom belonged to the generation of my parents, aunts, and uncles and all of whom had lived under this earlier regime, it was hard not to be awed by their bravery. Regardless of how I measured the success of their work, they had set out on a path that, considering the objectively oppressive conditions in the 1950s and early 1960s, made the courage of my generation less impressive. These were pioneers.

Why their gratitude? In the last three decades, accounts of homophile-era activism have appeared in so many books that it is hard to appreciate today how thoroughly the Stonewall generation refused to acknowledge or validate this early activism.[3] A small number of the homophile generation—Frank Kameny, Barbara Gittings, Jim Kepner, Del Martin, and Phyllis Lyon come quickly to mind—had made the transition into the 1970s, and they continued to build their activist resumes. But most had not, and most felt thoroughly neglected and unappreciated. To have someone of the next generation affirm, as I was, that their work mattered and that it needed to be told as history, was gratifying.

In one sense, I could describe these interviews as an exercise in creating cross-generational ties, much as Daniel Marshall does in his essay on the Gay Teachers and Students Group in Melbourne, Australia. Certainly, for many years afterward, I carried with me a sense of those connections. I lived with those interviews and those subjects, metaphorically, for a long time. Through writing I did for a radical gay publication such as *The Body Politic* and through historical talks I gave to community groups in the late 1970s and early 1980s, I held out the left-wing origins of the Mattachine as a tradition from which my generation of queer leftists could draw. And my feelings for some of them were passionate. Reading Marcia Gallo's description of her connection to Stella Rush, I was reminded of something I wrote about Harry Hay and Chuck Rowland: "I could say that I fell in love, though that phrase barely touches the depth and variety of feeling that I have for them."[4]

At the same time, partly because I was writing a history of a national movement whose participants were dispersed rather than of a local community bound together by place, I was at most a momentary visitor in their lives. It would be interesting to test whether the appealing, almost utopian, hopes for oral history articulated by many of this book's authors materialize and are sustained. How would one need to conceptualize and implement an oral history project for it to realize such a vision? Did the oral histories, for instance, that Elizabeth Kennedy and Madeline Davis conducted for their community history of lesbians in Buffalo leave such a legacy behind in a way that, by contrast, my interviews of homophile activists did not?[5] Is the Twin Cities Project that Jason Ruiz helped found doing this in a sustained way?

I returned to the practice of oral history in the 1990s, when I began working on a biography of Bayard Rustin. There was a queer element to this work, of course. Rustin was gay, and he had to navigate the intense homophobia of the 1940s, 1950s, and 1960s as he pursued his fight for peace and social justice in the pacifist, civil rights, and labor movements. Yet oral history figured in this project very differently than in my earlier one. Rustin's life was not what one might call "queer-centric." His public career revolved around issues—nuclear weapons, racial justice, economic inequality—that were mainstays of twentieth-century U.S. history narratives. Thus, most of the individuals I interviewed were not in any way queer-identified. I was also conducting these interviews not to get the life histories of my subjects, but to have them elaborate on the life of Rustin. Finally, not only was there a rich documentary trail for the organizations and movements with which Rustin was involved but also the archives contained rich repositories of oral histories conducted by others, particularly of the civil rights movement. In working on Rustin's life, I not only did interviews of my own but also read transcripts of interviews in the Kennedy and Johnson presidential libraries (recall the model and motivation of the Columbia Oral History Project with regard to Important Men), as well as at Howard University, with its substantial collection of interviews with grassroots civil rights activists.

Early on, I made the decision not to interview the surviving civil rights leaders with whom Rustin had worked. In the oral histories that I was reading in libraries, I noticed a significant difference between the interviews that were done in the 1960s, close to the events, and those done in the 1980s. A revision of memory appeared to be going on, not so much in terms of the facts of history—what had happened—but in terms of the evaluation of people and their roles. I was not interested in conducting a third round of interviews in which participants, in the more gay-tolerant atmosphere of the mid- to late 1990s, revised their views of Rustin as an activist and a homosexual.

But the pacifist movement was another story. In certain ways, one could say its history paralleled that of the homophile movement. Pacifists in the United States of the 1940s and 1950s were beyond the boundary that separated normal from deviant. Like the homophile activists, they had been largely neglected, not only by historians but also by the antiwar activists who came after them. Most of them had not been interviewed endless times by journalists and historians; most of them did not have well-rehearsed versions of their history. As with homophile activists, one could make a claim for their bravery, since to be a pacifist during World War II and the height of the Cold War was to stand way outside the definition of a good American.

I also felt toward these pacifists a certain kinship. Just as the homophile movement broke ground that I later benefited from in the 1970s, male conscientious objectors in particular had, at mid-century, pioneered an opposition to war and militarism that, later, I struggled to express as a draft-eligible young man at the height of the Vietnam War. As I delved more deeply into the history of the Fellowship of Reconciliation and the War Resisters League, the organizations for which Rustin worked, I found myself wanting to give these pacifists their due. I hoped that my interviews with them would allow me to reconstruct in as rich and nuanced a way as possible Rustin's pacifist history.

I have to admit that I approached these interviews with a trepidation that I did not experience in my earlier project. While I carried respect, admiration, and, even, a bit of awe into both sets of encounters, my agenda, to the degree that I had one, was very much out there with the homophile activists. But with most of my pacifist subjects, I carried a worry that made me strategize how I would raise the issue of Rustin's sexuality. I did not want to make them defensive; I did not want the interview to shut down. After all, Rustin experienced in the peace movement a measure of censure and isolation because of his sexuality. Would my raising it, even half a century later, create a barrier between me and my subjects that would prove impossible to surmount?

I opted for an approach that seemed both sensible and ethical: waiting until we were well into the interview before I introduced the subject. It made sense to me because much of what I wanted from them was an understanding of pacifist activism and of Rustin's role in the peace movement. Talking about that had to lead eventually to a discussion of his sexuality because, at some point in the narrative, we inevitably came up against the scandals and controversies associated with Rustin's homosexuality. As it turned out, I need not have worried. To the best of my recollection, everyone was forthcoming about it. Some brought it up themselves, and others talked about it once I introduced the topic. Some said less than others, but not, I sensed, because of discomfort, hostility, or a conscious decision to withhold.

Interviewing heterosexuals about homosexuality is an interesting adventure. I suppose one could argue that these were not typical heterosexuals, if such a group even exists. As religious pacifists, these were good men and women committed to the dignity of every human life. They were devoted to building a world based on allegiance to a common humanity. I learned, or perhaps had confirmed, that homosexuality in that era was not something named among them, even as many also claimed to "know" about Rustin. And they knew about Rustin in part because of assumptions made about masculinity. Rustin's dress, his way of speaking, his carriage, and his interest in the arts and high culture all marked him as not traditionally male. I learned as well that there was a divide between private and public. Rustin's difference was of no consequence until there was a public naming that, almost inevitably given the era, caused scandal. And I learned that there was a difference between religious and secular pacifist circles. The latter could have cared less about Rustin's sexual desires. Indeed, the trouble he got into and the difficulty that religious pacifists had in dealing with it almost seemed to make Rustin more heroic in the view of these secular radicals.

Interestingly, work on the Rustin biography also pointed out to me how indissolubly linked are the practice of oral history and research in print materials. More revealing than any of the oral histories I conducted were two caches of documents that I never expected to find. One was a large set of records detailing Rustin's time in federal prison during World War II. It provided correspondence to and from Rustin, along with material from prison officials about Rustin's sexuality. It was a eureka moment unlike anything I've experienced in forty years of studying history. The other was the correspondence between Rustin and Davis Platt, his lover at the time. A generation older than me, Platt was someone who had been in my extended gay social circle in New York in the 1970s. He had been at parties at my home many times in that decade. I never knew about his relationship with Rustin, but when he learned that I was working on a biography, he contacted me and made available letters that Rustin had written while serving time in federal prison and that Platt had saved for half a century. He also consented to two interviews, which had a warmth and vitality that went beyond anything I experienced in interviewing Rustin's pacifist colleagues. In this case, the identity and the relationship of interviewer and subject deeply affected the experience. Oral history helped strengthen cross-generational connections, as well as friendship. With Platt, as it had been for me with Harry Hay two decades earlier, the experience of oral history was magical.

For the last three years, I have been doing research on Chicago. I hesitate to be more specific than that because, unlike my dissertation on pre-Stonewall activism or my biography of Rustin, this work has not yet coalesced into a clear and well-defined book project. Instead, I am allowing myself to roam around in materials about the history of sexuality in Chicago in the twentieth century. Queer topics, in the broadest sense, naturally figure in this, but I cannot claim yet that the project is queer centered.

For me, the most dramatic difference between this work that I have begun in the first decade of the twenty-first century and the research I started as a graduate student in the 1970s is that a huge mass of easily accessible material is available for me to examine without my having to search and search and search for it. The Gerber/Hart Library, a GLBT community-based library and archives, has lots of collections, as well as runs of newspapers and newsletters produced by GLBT community organizations. The Leather Archives and Museum, another community-based institution, does as well. But materials about sexuality, including things one could define as queer, are also to be found at such places as the Chicago History Museum, the University of Chicago, and the University of Illinois at Chicago. I know progress narratives are out of fashion these days, but to me this is progress.

So, unlike in the 1970s, when I had to track down informants to interview, I can now go to the Gerber/Hart Library and read transcripts of dozens upon dozens of oral histories of GLBT activists and community members done by researchers who came before me. It is a privilege and a thrill to be able to do this. And once again, it evokes in me feelings of immense gratitude. I know that because of this prior work, I will be much better prepared when I begin to do interviews of my own for this project. I am also grateful for another reason. Some of these interviews were conducted as long ago as the early 1980s. Since then, some narrators have died, and these oral histories are the best source of information we will ever have about their lives.

The transcripts can also serve as a curriculum for the practice of oral history, a curriculum that I never took before I learned interviewing by doing it. Some of these interviews are so rich, so overflowing with information and insight that I wish they went on forever. And some of them are, frankly, terrible. The difference between the valuable ones and the disasters is almost never about the narrator. Sure, sometimes one senses shyness or detachment in a narrator, a reluctance to speak, or an abrasiveness of style that almost any interviewer would have difficulty penetrating. But more of the time the failure is that of the interviewer. She or he goes in there with an agenda, and the agenda simply does not mesh with the life experience of the narrator. The interviewer poses too many questions of a factual kind: did you know so-and-so? Were you at such-and-such? Were you a member of this group? When the person says no, the conversation grinds to a halt.

Reading these weak interviews makes me cringe, and not only because of the wasted opportunity. Rather, I read them with the awareness that my interviews, too, are now accessible to others who can pass judgment on them. I wonder what they read like. I donated all my materials about Rustin to the Swarthmore College Peace Collection, the archive that has the largest number of collections that relate directly to his life. In the case of these interviews, I can just sit at home and reread the transcripts because, when I worked on this project, I had the privileges of a senior faculty member with a research assistant whose job it was to transcribe the tapes. But as a graduate student, taking forever, it seemed, to finish a dissertation, all I did was take notes on my interviews, as if I were listening to a lecture in class, and replay short segments to copy out what sounded like good quotes. Those tapes I donated to a community-based archive in New York City that later went under. Most of them made their way to the New York Public Library where I know they have been used by others. To me, it is amazing that they survive at all since, as a graduate student living at bare subsistence, I bought the cheapest possible cassette tapes for interviewing subjects. Writing this essay makes me want to go back there and listen to them.

Reading the interviews done by others and imagining listening once again to interviews I did a generation ago put into bold relief for me something I did not think much about when I made that trip to California in 1976. The living, breathing, face-to-face interview becomes, in time, another collection in the archives. For all the power and the magic of the experience, oral history requires of us critical skills of assessment and evaluation not unlike what all archival materials demand. Especially when our subjects are not the rich and the famous and the influential, for whom a well-cleared documentary trail already exists, oral history promises to make a place for them in accounts of the past—indeed, to make history read differently because of their presence. But interviews are not transparent. Like documents, they beg for analysis and interpretation. And once that work commences, the values and life experience of the interpreter—the historian—inevitably become part of the story.

Notes

1. *Sexual Politics, Sexual Communities: The Making of a Homosexual Minority in the United States, 1940–1970* (Chicago: University of Chicago Press, 1983; 2nd ed., 1998); and *Lost Prophet: The Life and Times of Bayard Rustin* (New York: Free Press, 2003).
2. See Jim Kepner, *Rough News, Daring Views: 1950's Pioneer Gay Press Journalism* (Binghamton, NY: Haworth, 1997).
3. See, for example, Nan Alamilla Boyd, *Wide Open Town: A History of Queer San Francisco to 1965* (Berkeley: University of California Press, 2003); Marcia M. Gallo, *Different Daughters: A History of the Daughters of Bilitis and the Rise of the Lesbian Rights Movement* (New York: Carroll and Graf, 2006); Martin Meeker, *Contacts Desired: Gay and Lesbian Communications and Community, 1940s–1970s* (Chicago: University of Chicago Press, 2006); and Marc Stein, *City of Brotherly and Sisterly Loves: Lesbian and Gay Philadelphia, 1945–1972* (Chicago: University of Chicago Press, 2000).
4. "Dreams Deferred: The Birth and Betrayal of America's First Gay Liberation Movement," in *Making Trouble: Essays on Gay History, Politics, and the University* (New York: Routledge, 1992), 55. The essay originally appeared in the *Body Politic*, February 1979.
5. Elizabeth Lapofsky Kennedy and Madeline Davis, *Boots of Leather, Slippers of Gold: The History of a Lesbian Community* (New York: Routledge, 1993).

Contributors

Kelly Anderson teaches women and gender studies at Smith College and is an oral historian at the Sophia Smith Collection. Her research interests include the history of feminisms, sexuality, and LGBT communities. She has been conducting oral history interviews for more than twenty years and is completing her dissertation about contemporary lesbian activists, titled "I Wanted It Like a Lover, I Wanted It Like Justice."

Nan Alamilla Boyd is a professor of women and gender studies at San Francisco State University. Her academic interests include the history of sexuality, historical methodology, and urban tourism. Her first book, *Wide Open Town: A History of Queer San Francisco to 1965* (University of California Press, 2003), charts the rise of gay and lesbian politics in San Francisco. Her current research explores the history of tourism in San Francisco.

John D'Emilio is a professor of gender and women's studies and history at the University of Illinois at Chicago. He is the author or editor of more than half a dozen books, including *Sexual Politics, Sexual Communities: The Making of a Homosexual Minority in the United States, 1940–1970*; *Intimate Matters: A History of Sexuality in America*; and *Lost Prophet: The Life and Times of Bayard Rustin*. His awards include Guggenheim, NEH, and ACLS fellowships; the Brudner Prize from Yale University for lifetime contributions to gay and lesbian studies; and the Stonewall Book Award of the American Library Association.

Steve Estes is a professor of history at Sonoma State University, where he specializes in modern American history. He is the author of *I Am a Man!: Race, Manhood, and the Civil Rights Movement* (University of North Carolina Press, 2005) and *Ask & Tell: Gay and Lesbian Veterans Speak Out* (University of North Carolina Press, 2007).

Michael David Franklin is a historian, writer, and educator who received his PhD in American studies from the University of Minnesota in 2011. His dissertation examines transgender cultural production on film and video over the last sixty years in order to theorize biopower at the intersection of medicine and mass visual culture. A member of the Twin Cities GLBT Oral History Project, he is the coeditor of *Queer Twin Cities* (University of Minnesota Press, 2010).

Jeff Friedman is associate professor of dance history and theory at Rutgers University. He researches theories, methods, and practices of dance documentation, focusing on oral history for dance and performance as research inquiry. He is a Fulbright Fellow and has received eight National Endowment for the Arts grants and the James V. Mink and Forrest C. Pogue awards for his oral history work. Friedman has published articles and book chapters in the United Kingdom, Spain, Germany, Korea, and New Zealand.

Marcia M. Gallo is assistant professor of history at the University of Nevada, Las Vegas. She received her PhD in 2004 from the City University of New York (CUNY) Graduate Center. Her 2006 book, *Different Daughters: A History of the Daughters of Bilitis and the Rise of the Lesbian Rights Movement*, won the Lambda Literary Award and was named a best book by the *San Francisco Chronicle*. Gallo also received the Passing the Torch Award from CUNY's Center for Lesbian and Gay Studies in 2007. Her next book is on the 1964 murder of Catherine "Kitty" Genovese.

Carrie Hamilton is reader in history at Roehampton University, London. Her research interests include oral history, cultural memory, histories of political activism, revolution and violence, feminism, and the history of sexuality, with particular focus on Spain and Latin America. Her book *Sexual Revolutions: Passion and Politics in Socialist Cuba* is forthcoming from the University of North Carolina Press (2012).

Karen Krahulik is associate dean of academic affairs in the College of Arts and Sciences at New York University. She specializes in LGBT history, oral history, and queer theory. She is the recipient of awards and fellowships from the Massachusetts Foundation for the Humanities, the Bay State Historical League, Harvard University, Princeton University, and New York University and is the author of *Provincetown: From Pilgrim Landing to Gay Resort* (New York University Press, 2005).

Daniel Marshall is a lecturer in the School of Education at Deakin University in Melbourne, Australia. His research interests include histories of sexuality and education in Australia, queer and sexuality studies, educational policy, sexualities education, and cultural studies and youth. He is vice president of the Australian Lesbian and Gay Archives and holds a PhD from the University of Melbourne.

Martin Meeker is an academic specialist with the Regional Oral History Office of the Bancroft Library at the University of California, Berkeley. He received his PhD in U.S. history from the University of Southern California and has published essays in the *Pacific Historical Review*, the *Journal of the History of Sexuality*, and the *Journal of Women's History*. His books include *The Oakland Army Base: An Oral History* (2010) and *Contacts Desired: Gay and Lesbian Communications and Community, 1940s–1970s* (2006), winner of the 2005–2006 John Boswell Prize.

Daniel Rivers is a visiting assistant professor at the James Weldon Johnson Institute for Advanced Interdisciplinary Studies at Emory University. His research interests include LGBT history, histories of the family and sexuality, radical social movements in the United States, and Native American history. He is currently finishing a book titled *Radical Relations: A History of Lesbian and Gay Parents and Their Children in the United States, 1945–2003.*

Horacio N. Roque Ramírez is associate professor of Chicana and Chicano studies at the University of California, Santa Barbara, where he is also affiliated with the Department of History, the Department of Feminist Studies, and the Latin American and Iberian Studies Program. His forthcoming book is titled *Memories from Queer Latino San Francisco: An Oral History, 1960s–1990s.* He specializes in queer/LGBT Latino history, oral history theories and methods, and Central American migration studies.

Jason Ruiz is assistant professor of American studies at the University of Notre Dame, where he is also a faculty fellow of the Institute for Latino Studies. He cofounded the Twin Cities GLBT Oral History Project with Kevin P. Murphy in 2003. The recipient of many fellowships and awards, Ruiz is the coeditor of *Queer Twin Cities* (University of Minnesota Press, 2010) and a special issue of the *Radical History Review* ("Queer Futures," Issue 100). He is currently completing his first book, which examines the politics of empire in representations of travel to Mexico during the late nineteenth and early twentieth centuries.

Eric C. Wat is the director of research and evaluation at Special Service for Groups, a nonprofit organization based in Los Angeles. He is the author of *The Making of a Gay Asian Community: An Oral History of Pre-AIDS Los Angeles* (Rowman & Littlefield, 2002). He has taught Asian American studies at various colleges in Southern California.

THE OXFORD ORAL HISTORY SERIES

J. TODD MOYE (University of North Texas),
KATHRYN NASSTROM (University of San Francisco),
ROBERT PERKS (The British Library), *Series Editors*
DONALD A. RITCHIE, *Senior Advisor*

Index